# Against the Map

## The Politics of Geography in Eighteenth-Century Britain

## Adam Sills

University of Virginia Press

Charlottesville and London

University of Virginia Press
© 2021 by the Rector and Visitors of the University of Virginia
All rights reserved
Printed in the United States of America on acid-free paper

*First published 2021*

1 3 5 7 9 8 6 4 2

Library of Congress Cataloging-in-Publication Data
Names: Sills, Adam, author.
Title: Against the map : the politics of geography in eighteenth-century Britain /
Adam Sills.
Description: Charlottesville : University of Virginia Press, 2021. |
Includes bibliographical references and index.
Identifiers: LCCN 2021010731 (print) | LCCN 2021010732 (ebook) |
ISBN 9780813945989 (hardcover ; acid-free paper) | ISBN 9780813945996 (paperback ;
acid-free paper) | ISBN 9780813946009 (ebook)
Subjects: LCSH: English literature—18th century—History and criticism. | Geography
in literature. | Cartography in literature. | Space in literature. | Neighborhoods in
literature. | National characteristics, English, in literature. | Cartography—Great
Britain—History—18th century.
Classification: LCC PR448.G47 S55 2021 (print) | LCC PR448.G47 (ebook) |
DDC 820.9/005—dc23
LC record available at https://lccn.loc.gov/2021010731
LC ebook record available at https://lccn.loc.gov/2021010732

*Cover art:* Top, *A New Map of the Cities of London, Westminster & ye Borough of
Southwarke,* W. Hollar, 1675, engraving (© British Library); bottom, *Gold London,*
Barbara Macfarlane, 2017, oil and ink on handmade Khadi paper (courtesy of Rebecca
Hossack Art Gallery)

For Jennifer and Izaak, Charles and Caryl
It's not the years; it's the miles.

Geographical diversity is a necessary condition for, rather than a barrier to, the reproduction of capital. If the geographical diversity does not already exist, then it has to be created.

—DAVID HARVEY, *The Limits to Capital* (1982)

# CONTENTS

# ILLUSTRATIONS

# ACKNOWLEDGMENTS

THIS BOOK began as a PhD dissertation at the University of Buffalo under the direction of Deidre Lynch, James Bunn, and Shaun Irlam, and I would like to thank them, first and foremost, for their support and encouragement during that process and for providing the necessary foundation for the project's continued growth and development after the completion of my degree. I would also like to extend that thanks to the entire English department at the University of Buffalo, especially those faculty members and colleagues who offered their input and guidance along the way. I am thinking, in particular, of William Beatty Warner, David Schmid, Barbara Bono, Jim Holstun, Tom Morgan, Stephen Meagher, Lee Kahan, Kyoko Takanashi, Abby Coykendall, and Ana de Freitas Boe. I also need to mention here the help and support of Tom Conley, whose seminar in mapping and French literature at the Folger Shakespeare Library was both informative and influential on my own work, and Catherine Gallagher, whose seminar on counterfactual history at the Cornell School of Criticism and Theory played a decisive role in shaping my ideas about alternative ways of conceiving both time and space. I also want to give a special thank you to Cynthia Wall, who gave me extensive and thoughtful feedback on early and later drafts of the book manuscript. Her work has been an inspiration to me and her contributions invaluable.

This book would not have been possible without the contributions of the English Department at Hofstra University and those colleagues who have supported my work during my time there, especially Lee Zimmerman, John Bryant, Scott Harshbarger, Erik Brogger, Robbie Sulcer, Iska Alter, Stephen Russell, Ethna Lay, Vimala Pasupathi, Paul Zimmerman, and Shari Zimmerman. I am grateful, as well, to my home institution, Hofstra University, which has provided numerous grants to aid my writing and research. I would also like to thank the faculty and staff at those libraries that assisted with my research and the acquisition of the map images in this book, including New York University, the New York Public Library, Yale University, Harvard University, the University of Chicago, the British Library, the National Archives, the National Library of Scotland, the National Library of Ireland, and Trinity College Dublin.

Lastly, I would like to thank the original publisher of this book, AMS Press, and its founder and editor-in-chief, Gabe Hornstein, for recognizing the potential of my work during its early stages and extending me a contract based upon that promise. Gabe, unfortunately, passed away in early 2017, and AMS Press filed for bankruptcy shortly thereafter, leaving my book in publishing limbo. The University of Virginia Press, however, came to my rescue the following year (with a timely assist by my *Digital Defoe* coeditor, Christopher Loar) and agreed to publish the book, with some judicious and much-needed editing of course. I would like to thank my editor, Angie Renee Hogan, who was willing to take on a book project that was, due to no fault of my own, a bit long in the tooth. She gave me hope that my work would eventually see the light of day, even in the midst of a global pandemic, and for that, I am truly grateful.

# AGAINST THE MAP

INTRODUCTION

# Against the Map

## Map and Nation

While the title of this book takes a decidedly oppositional tone, I want to begin by insisting on the map's centrality and importance to the formation of Great Britain during the early modern period, if only to offer a more qualified analysis of its role in that historical process. That is, I do not wish to challenge or discount the general premise that the history of the map and that of the modern nation-state are inextricably bound up with one another. Rather, my goal is, in part, to affirm and further expand on the existing wealth of scholarship detailing the various ways in which the map functions historically as a technology of nation and empire building.[1] As Benedict Anderson famously contends, the map serves as a normative, albeit reductive, representation of the nation that is easily recognized and widely disseminated in order to inculcate a sense of "imagined community" and national kinship among the general populace. Like the museum and the census, the map is a technology that "profoundly shaped the way in which the colonial state imagined its dominion—the nature of the human beings it ruled, the geography of its domain, and the legitimacy of its ancestry."[2] The map not only delimits the territory under the sovereign rule of the state; its very iconicity serves to reify and standardize an image of the nation that is then consumed and reproduced at every strata of society, the middle class perhaps most visibly: "Instantly recognizable, everywhere visible, the logo-map penetrated deep into the popular imagination, forming a powerful emblem for the anticolonial nationalisms being born."[3] While Anderson's main focus here is postcolonial Southeast Asia and its emergent forms of nationalism, his insights into the map, he rightfully suggests, should be read back into the history of European national and imperial expansion where cartographic technologies were first deployed and later perfected.

As many have demonstrated, the map became, over the course of the sixteenth and early seventeenth century, an indispensable technology in the military and economic expansion of the state as well as a consistent means of projecting a symbolic image of royalist power and monarchical authority to courtier and commoner alike. More than a mere footnote in the history of

Western-style bureaucracy, the increasing centrality of maps to the effective administration of the European nation-state is of interest to many map historians precisely because it speaks to these connections between the production of knowledge and the exercise of power. As David Buisseret argues, "It was one thing to 'know' the territory and another to exercise tight control over it.... But we can hardly doubt that the existence of accurate cartographic information eventually proved a powerful tool in the imposition of central authority on the recalcitrant periphery."[4] For Buisseret and others, the map engenders and promotes a particular politics of space that invariably serves the interests of a hegemonic national or imperial power against those who would challenge or upend its authority. The state's desire to impose a cartographic definition of space on the land is thus not only central to the functioning of the state and the formation of a coherent national identity; mapping, in this sense, also represents an attempt to pacify and control marginalized or dispossessed populations whose claims on the land are seen as antithetical to or critical of the national interest. The map becomes, in this sense, the reified image of state power and a means of disseminating that power to its subjects, whether at home or abroad. Lesley Cormack extends the general tenor of Buisseret's work to argue that "the study of geography was essential to the creation of an ideology of imperialism."[5] The two, in fact, cannot, and should not, be separated in her estimation. As Cormack shows, cartography, chorography, and other modes of geographic representation, both mathematical and descriptive, gain increasing popularity and legitimacy within many English universities, Oxford and Cambridge in particular, precisely because of the pragmatic and ideological demands created by England's imperial ambitions. She concludes that the scientific revolutions of the sixteenth and seventeenth centuries are anything but value neutral; rather, they are informed by an abiding politics of space in which the disciplines of geography and cartography are rightfully seen as crucial technologies of nation and empire building.

Building upon this central premise, Richard Helgerson argues that Renaissance cartography and chorography help to articulate and legitimate an emergent Whig political ideology that wished to replace the idea of kingdom with that of nation. In his *Forms of Nationhood: The Elizabethan Writing of England*, Helgerson applies a version of Benedict Anderson's thesis to his history of the British nation-state and the significant role that the map played within that history. Beginning with the early Renaissance, he contends that cartographic and chorographic representations of England embody the ostensibly organic ties between the monarch and the land such that no distinction could be drawn between the monarch as producer of the map and the monarch as the map's signified. Monarch and land signify one another in a seamless fashion, a relationship graphically reinforced through the mapmaker's use of detailed iconography, marginalia, and other ornamental touches that frame the national body as an extension of royal power and sovereignty. Christopher Saxton's *Survey of*

*England and Wales* (1579), for example, was sponsored and promoted, in part, by Queen Elizabeth, and the atlas is careful to underscore that these are not only the queen's maps but that this is also "the queen's land, her kingdom."[6] The appearance of royal and imperial arms on each map and the inclusion of a frontispiece depicting Elizabeth on the throne, surrounded on either side with figures representing cosmography and geography, proclaim the sovereignty of the queen over her lands.[7] The political allegory of Saxton's *Survey*, in this respect, is hard to miss. The map offers information and details about the physical geography of the nation, and more importantly, its elaborate machinery provides the proper context for viewing those details, a codicil of sorts for reading and interpreting the land as the expression of monarchical authority.

By the mid-seventeenth century, however, the dynastic claims of the map begin to recede with the Crown's inability to secure that set of meanings in any consistent fashion. As a result, the surveyor emerges as an authorial figure whose presence undermines these prior efforts to collapse the land into the body of the monarch and to make them one and the same. The surveyor had not previously been figured into the calculus of power that produced the map and that the map depicted in the form of royal iconography and marginalia; he did not willfully place himself between the monarch and the land itself. Nevertheless, with the continued proliferation of maps and improved methods of surveying, there emerged a "conceptual gap between the land and its ruler" that precipitated the increasing marginalization and eventual removal of dynastic insignia from the map in favor of depicting the land in accord with the more empirically oriented chorographies.[8] This turn in cartographic methods, for Helgerson, represents the "Elizabethan discovery of England" as a "confident source of identity and continuity."[9] It is a trend that would continue over the course of the seventeenth century with the further consolidation of both the land and the self as contemporaneous and interdependent units that, together, formed a bulwark against the forces of royal absolutism: "Land and self are semi-independent functions of one another. Neither has the absolute autonomy claimed by the king, but neither quite collapses into the other."[10] They are mutually sustaining fictions; the author of the map imbues the brute landscape with a sense of being while the land itself serves as the source of legitimacy and identity for mapmakers, such as John Norden, William Camden, John Speed, and Michael Drayton.[11] The land is ventriloquized to some extent, and it, in turn, conjures an authority rooted in nature itself, not the royal court. The conceptual gap between land and self is mediated by representations, such as the map and the chorography, that enable the subject to identify with the land, to feel for the land, yet remain apart from it.[12] Map and chorography thus come to play a central role in the consolidation of the nation-state as both a physical entity and as imagined community.[13]

However, while this logic perhaps gives the map its political and ideological raison d'etre during the sixteenth and early seventeenth centuries, I would suggest that Helgerson's argument must be amended to some extent when we turn to an examination of the role cartography assumed during the eighteenth century, a time when conflicts regarding national identity and imperial expansion became increasingly fraught and tendentious at every level of society. Unlike the period prior to 1650, the map's ability to foster a sense of national identification and inclusion runs up against some very real political, social, linguistic, and economic divisions, both in terms of the incorporation and assimilation of foreign territories into the national body, Scotland and Ireland most notably, as well as the production of a shared public sphere at home. Political and ideological contests regarding what exactly constitutes a normative image of the nation and its geography proliferated during the eighteenth century due to the dramatic increases in the size and diversity of Britain's population and the multiplicity of new, or novel, spaces that emerged in response to those demographic pressures.[14] This sense of fragmentation was further aided by significant changes in the production, distribution, and selling of maps, whether expressly political in nature or not. No longer a rarefied, expensive object available only to members of the nobility and landed gentry, as it was during the Renaissance, the map becomes a much more ubiquitous commodity throughout Britain during the eighteenth century, especially among the burgeoning merchant class.

As Mary Sponberg Pedley demonstrates, this democratization of the map, if you will, was largely contingent on the advent of print culture and the subsequent changes within the modes of production and distribution, such as the lower costs of making maps, the increased marketing and selling of maps to both general and specialized audiences, and the creation of copyright laws to protect the commercial interests of the printers and publishers of maps. The result of this market consolidation was that maps became increasingly available to citizens in a variety of formats: "The world of printed maps in the eighteenth century included everything from maps used as illustrations in books and periodicals to large-scale estate and town plans, military maps, regional maps, small-scale geographical maps, atlases, and globes."[15] The cost, quantity, and diversity of the printed map made it, according to Pedley, "the most accessible form of geographic information for the largest number of people throughout Western Europe."[16] In this transition from manuscript to print, the map first emerges as a tool of government, since it is the government that can, unlike many individuals or other institutions, afford to subsidize and oversee its production, but in its printed form, the map is able to insinuate itself into areas normally outside the purview of the state and state-sponsored institutions. Cartographic knowledge becomes, over the course of the century, an integral part of the intellectual, spiritual, and moral education of every British subject. Ecclesiastical maps, antiquarian maps, biblical maps, commercial maps, urban maps, fictional or literary maps, estate maps, cosmographic maps, geologic maps: the sheer diversity of kinds of maps available reflects the diversity and diversification of knowledge during the eighteenth century. As a form of knowledge no longer strictly tied to the interests of state power, the map is thus able to expand its duties beyond the study of the world's geography to become an accepted way of representing knowledge within a broad variety of academic and professional contexts. Cartographic knowledge finds itself increasingly liberated from the political, military, and economic imperatives of the nation-state. The "power of maps," to borrow Denis Wood's phrase, no longer resided solely with the administrative capacities of the state but rather was disseminated and diffused throughout society on both the public and private level.[17] That is, the map became routinized and integrated into everyday life in such a way that its power to influence and shape perceptions of space, whether on a local, regional, national, or global scale, now emanates from a greater variety of sites and for a far greater diversity of purposes, including, but not limited to, the exercise of state power.

This transition from manuscript to print culture, from the literal map to the map as metaphor, does not mean, however, that the imperatives of the nation-state fade from view or somehow become less relevant to an understanding of eighteenth-century cartographic practice. If anything, these bonds between cartography and nation were strengthened as the map began to move and circulate throughout eighteenth-century Britain and the world and, in the process, find greater acceptance as an authoritative and legitimate form of knowledge. The increased attention to geography and its representation was, in part, an extension of the fiscal-military state's broader agenda to quantify the national and imperial bodies in a way that promoted bureaucratic efficiency and administrative clarity. The abstraction of physical space into "calculable spaces" that could be manipulated and controlled with ever greater precision provided the necessary context for various state-sponsored enterprises.[18] The implementation and enforcement of the Excise, the construction of turnpikes, roads, and bridges, demographic surveys of Britain's burgeoning population, the improvement of the rural estate, and urban planning: all are dependent, to varying degrees, on cartography and its ability to make space legible and, ultimately, more responsive to the needs and demands of the modern nation-state. Like other information technologies of the period, such as double-entry bookkeeping, statistical accounts, indexes, almanacs, and dictionaries, maps were an extension of the political arithmetic of the state and its desire to standardize its operations, generate revenue, and increase its power at home and abroad. As John Brewer reminds us, the consolidation of the British state is predicated, first and foremost, on the acquisition, ordering, and dissemination of information relevant to its many administrative branches and their constituencies: "The power of governments has been and always will be in large part dependent on their capacity to order and manipulate different sorts of information. A growth in state power is usually accompanied—either as cause or effect—by changes in either the extent or the nature of a government's hold on social knowledge."[19] As one discursive mode within what John Brewer terms "the politics of information" that emerges during the latter half of the seventeenth century, maps helped to transform the national, if not global, landscape in dramatic and immediate ways that were scarcely conceivable a century earlier. While Brewer does not take up the subject of cartography explicitly, his general thesis that information does not simply reflect the activities of the fiscal-military state but rather shapes and mediates its course of action, I would argue, should be applied to our understanding of maps as well. By focusing on how knowledge is produced, distributed, and consumed, we move away from a definition of the map as the passive vehicle for various kinds of geographic information and toward a definition in which the map possesses a greater degree of agency. The map, in this sense, does not merely represent the space of the nation; it actively creates the very idea of the nation and, by extension, the empire.[20]

However, as I will contend in the chapters to follow, what is too often left out of this history, or viewed as something of an anomaly, are facts and details regarding specific acts of "cartographic resistance," meaning any activity that either directly or covertly challenges and opposes the cartographic imperatives of the nation-state, as outlined above. That is, a proper understanding of the relationship between map and nation should logically take into account the history of cartographic resistance, which would, in my estimation, force us to rethink and revise the work of those, such as Anderson and Helgerson, who place a great deal of weight on maps and their attendant descriptions as the bearers of national identification. In all fairness, there has been some work to date on cartographic resistance in both its colonial and postcolonial contexts, but none to my knowledge has read that history back into theories regarding the emergence of nationalism during the early modern period and the eighteenth century in particular.[21] Instances of resistance against surveyors and mapmakers, some violent, some more subdued (though no less subversive), are laced throughout the history of European colonial expansion from the late sixteenth century through the twentieth century, and numerous authors have documented, to what extent it is possible, the various forms of resistance encountered by those who surveyed and charted foreign territories and nations during this period. Such instances were neither isolated nor singular in nature, however. Rather, they are a recurring event, a conceit if you will, within the broader history of European colonialism. It is my primary contention that a fuller understanding of the emergence of an imperial Britain, a subject to which I return frequently throughout the book, reveals the extent to which maps, chorographies, and other modes of geographic, as well as demographic, representation helped shape and refine the ends of empire. However, as I hope to demonstrate, acts of cartographic resistance, whether ultimately successful or not, remain equally important and integral to writing a more complete, but perhaps quite different, history of British national and imperial development from the early modern period forward.

We see, in fact, throughout the colonial period, acts of cartographic resistance emerge within a variety of foreign settings and cultural contexts: Ireland, Scotland, India, North America, and Cyprus. As Samuel Johnson famously observes in *A Journey to the Western Islands of Scotland* (1775), the English military placed stones on roads throughout the Scottish Highlands for the purpose of measuring distances, but they were removed by local inhabitants who were "resolved . . . 'to have no new miles.'"[22] Johnson refers here to the military occupation of the Highlands following the battle of Culloden in 1745 and the construction of roads intended to establish British hegemony in what had been, up until recently, a recalcitrant corner of the empire. England's efforts to map Scotland, or Ireland for that matter, are integral to its pursuit of a unified Great Britain, but as Johnson's text suggests, the ultimate success of that project does not mean that we can or should overlook instances of cartographic resistance, to what extent they can be documented; they are as much a part of this history as the maps and mapmakers themselves. In his *Mapping an Empire: The Geographical Construction of British India, 1765–1843*, Matthew Edney demonstrates that British colonial forces "thought they might reduce India to a rigidly coherent, geometrically accurate, and uniformly precise imperial space, a rational space within which a systematic archive of knowledge about the Indian landscapes and people might be constructed."[23] This cartographic knowledge was constructed to serve British imperial interests in India as a pragmatic tool for controlling territory and local populations and as a symbolic image intended to project and promote European ideals of scientific rationality and enlightened progress. This project, however, was not without its detractors or its own forms of resistance: "Indians were not the passive and docile objects of the potent British vision which the British ontologically assumed them to be. They could and did object in various ways to the British conquest of the subcontinent and the reconstruction of an imperial space."[24] Edney notes, for example, an 1836 riot in Chittagong in which an assistant surveyor was beaten with his own instruments. In addition, survey parties in certain parts of the country were subject to capture by local groups who rightfully viewed such activity as hostile, merely prelude to the eventual appropriation and privatization of the land in question. Surveyors and mapmakers thus made convenient targets, as did the instruments of their trade. The flags that they would routinely use to mark territory came to symbolize British power and authority in such a way as to enflame local populations and force them to either remove the flags themselves or pressure their leaders to prevent their being planted there in the first place. Many of India's rajas, in fact, feared reprisal at the hands of their subjects if they should allow surveyors to plant the flag anywhere within their domain. This recalcitrant attitude also hampered British surveyors, who frequently relied on native guides and laborers to assist them in their efforts.

We again see a similar narrative played out in relationship to the North American colonies as territory in and around the Catskills was being settled and developed at a rapid pace. Alf Evers describes a series of "games" in which Native Americans routinely hampered the efforts of surveyors to properly chart and map land that they had either purchased or legally claimed, contrary to the interests and sympathies of the local population.[25] As Evers informs us, surveyors were seen by many Native Americans in the Catskills as evil omens, precursors to an inevitable wave of displacement and settlement, and so in response, they would remove any monuments demarcating the boundary lines of a contested property and toss them in the river. Surveyors were routinely held captive and their instruments destroyed as a means of forcing settlers to renounce their unwarranted claims on the land in question. In yet another corner of the empire, Michael Givens documents the application of similar practices and techniques in response to British colonial rule over Cyprus during the nineteenth century. Efforts to survey and delimit the range of forests, for example, were frequently undermined by either destroying boundary cairns, a familiar and frequently used tactic, or in more extreme cases, setting fire to portions of the forest itself.[26] "Resistance to [the demarcation of the forests of Cyprus] was expressed in a variety of conscious acts, systematic constraints, and creative transformations. . . . Hugely destructive arson attacks on the forest by [Michael Yiakoumi's] colleagues from villages to the west had made the issue notorious, emotive, and highly political."[27] These conscious acts of what Givens calls "deliberate disobedience" were applauded by fellow Cypriots, Greek and Turkish, who objected to the unjust policies and practices of British colonial forces. However, as Givens points out, the collective voices of dissent and resistance would not have existed were it not for these efforts to survey and map the forest, and so remove them from the public domain against the popular will. In short, Britain created a problem for which it had no real solution: "Because of its authoritarian and absolutist character, the colonial system contained the seeds of its own collapse. However proactive your resistance, you can only cross a line when that line has been laid down. Drawing a line between forest and pasture created the opportunity for goatherds to commit the offence of forest encroachment, where before they had merely taken their goats to pasture. The new experience of being prosecuted for crossing an imaginary line politicized the goatherds of colonial Cyprus, and taught them the powerful weapon of arson."[28] A cartographic history of the British empire, as Givens narrates it, must include an understanding of how the "authoritarian and absolutist character" of the map itself provoked these various forms of retaliation and, conversely, how acts of cartographic resistance helped shape the growth and development of the colonial system, as well as signal, if not effect, its ultimate demise. The writing of cartographic history, in this sense, must not only take into account the ways in which the map, as an instrument of national and imperial hegemony, has been resisted throughout its history but also how those acts qualify and place limits on the perceived power of maps during the early modern period.

As we see in each instance, surveying and mapping were clearly understood by those on the colonial margins as a threat to their land and way of life and as a harbinger of drastic and unwonted change; however, as I noted earlier, this imperial history is rarely, if ever, addressed by those, like Richard Helgerson and others, who remain invested in the notion that maps are an essential ingredient in the formation of British national identity.[29] The reason for this elision is quite clear. They tacitly assume that, unlike the aforementioned resistances to the map within its colonial and postcolonial contexts, the map failed to provoke such feelings of anxiety and animosity among those within the imperial center. The map was, from this perspective, accepted readily by English urban and rural populations for whom the practices of surveying and cartography were becoming, more and more, daily realities, weaving itself into the fabric of everyday life as a necessary and indispensable tool for demarcating property, settling territorial disputes, and at its most basic level, helping people negotiate the vernacular, as well as national, landscape. In contrast to the hostile attitudes toward surveys and maps in the colonial setting, they conclude (wrongly in my estimation) that the map was universally embraced by seventeenth- and eighteenth-century British audiences as a symbolic projection of the national body to which they belonged and with which they openly identified. Helgerson, as well as Benedict Anderson, advocates the idea that one cannot assent to the nation without first being able to see the nation, that the nation is somehow dependent on its visibility.[30] The map, then, is a mode of representation that makes the nation legible to the general public and projects a common space to which everyone, as subjects of the nation, belongs.[31] While this thesis is perhaps elegant in its simplicity, it fails to hold up when we read the history of imperial Britain, which is characterized by a much more conflicted and tendentious reception of surveys and maps. Theories regarding the rise of British nationalism tend to ignore this history and thus fail to address issues of cartographic ambivalence and resistance at home in the belief that such a thing either did not exist or was largely irrelevant. To recognize the possibility of cartographic resistance within England itself, however, would necessarily entail a more provisional, less decided understanding of the map's contribution to the formation of the nation-state, hence the reason for its omission. The fact is that ambivalent attitudes and feelings regarding maps, as well as outright acts of cartographic resistance, were not restricted to the colonial margins; they also manifested themselves within English society throughout the early modern period and in a variety of ways.

As I hope to show, critical attitudes and profound ambivalences regarding the social, cultural, and even moral value of maps can be found throughout seventeenth- and eighteenth-century Britain, suggesting that map and nation do not always signify one another in such a reliable or stable manner. The purpose of this book is, in part, to unearth those attitudes and ambivalences within Britain and then place them alongside the previously mentioned acts of cartographic resistance in Ireland, India, North America, and Cyprus in order to argue that this is, in some sense, a shared history. Like their colonial counterparts, many in England did not, in fact, view and understand maps as markers of national community, as Helgerson contends. Rather, maps were just as often seen, alternately, as signs of fraud, deception, worldliness, conquest, hubris, madness, artifice, greed, and excess, among others, thus licensing a general skepticism and wariness about the intentions behind the map's production and the ultimate effects of its application. The nation cannot, at least in the eyes of some, be reduced to a single mode of representation, such as the map, because they recognized that the map does not always serve their interests or those of their community. The cartographic representation of the nation is, as a result, subject to a countervailing skepticism intended to make us aware of the flaws and errors in thinking about the nation, and the world for that matter, in terms of a map. Rather than *the* sign and signature of the modern nation-state, maps can also carry a very different set of meanings and values for various audiences eager to challenge and even overturn some its most basic assumptions about the representation of terrestrial geography. In short, one must approach the map not as a monolithic symbol for national or imperial hegemony but rather as the formal embodiment of a host of conflicts and contradictions within the production of space in general.[32] This book thus posits a much more contingent, though no less valuable, understanding of the power of maps and, in the process, challenges the assumption that its assimilation into the material and cognitive life of the nation was anything but smooth and without its own forms of resistance. As Steve Pile states, "We occupy many places on many maps, with different scales, with different cartographies, and it is because we both occupy highly circumscribed places on maps drawn through power cartographies and also exceed these confinements, that it is possible to imagine new places, new histories—to dream that resistance is possible. Maybe resistance is already a place on the map."[33]

## The Heterotopic Conceit

Pile's somewhat ironic suggestion that resistance *to* the map may be thought of as a place *on* the map guides much of the thinking behind this book, as its chief aim is to identify, survey, and map those sites of resistance that have shaped and defined the landscape of eighteenth-century Britain. In the chapters that follow, I refer to such sites as heterotopias, or "other" spaces, because they articulate this idea of resistance to, if not outright conflict with, hegemonic modes of understanding and representing space, such as cartography. Heterotopias, in fact, are born of that very conflict. In a brief lecture entitled "Of Other Spaces: Utopias and Heterotopias," Michel Foucault offers the following definition:

> There also exist, and this is probably true for all cultures and all civilizations, real and effective spaces which are outlined in the very institution of society, but which constitute a sort of counter-arrangement, of effectively realized utopia, in which all the real arrangements, all the other real arrangements that can be found within society, are at one and the same time represented, challenged, and overturned: a sort of place that lies outside all places and yet is actually localizable. In contrast to the utopias, these places which are absolutely *other* with respect to all the arrangements that they reflect and of which they speak might be described as heterotopias.[34]

The essay goes on to outline some general characteristics of heterotopias and to provide some relevant examples in order to further illuminate these basic principles. Foucault mentions, for example, heterotopias of crisis and deviance, such as the honeymoon suite, the boarding school, the clinic, the rest home, where definitions of sexuality and gender are unstable and precarious and so must be placed "elsewhere." The tomb and the cemetery constitute heterotopias in their placement on the margins of many towns and cities, yet they are central in terms of helping define the ordinary cultural spaces that constitute life within those towns and cities. The colony may also be considered heterotopic in establishing a space that is other to the nation yet that the nation requires in order to define itself as normative in some sense. While structurally similar, heterotopias, Foucault concludes, may "assume a wide variety of forms" depending on the particular geography, culture, and history in which they appear.[35]

I do not address the specific instances Foucault raises in his essay; however, the following chapters do take up his basic premise in order to name and to delineate in greater detail the general features of various heterotopias operating in seventeenth- and eighteenth-century Britain.[36] I appropriate Foucault's concept of the heterotopia because it offers an alternative way of thinking about the construction of national space apart from Anderson's and Helgerson's cartographically informed "imagined communities." The British nation-state, I argue, must be defined both in conjunction with and against the map, and Foucault's concept of heterotopia helps articulate and contain both positions simultaneously. A heterotopia is not, in this sense, an unreal or unrepresentable space but can, in fact, have a recognizable identity and location. That is, the heterotopia resists being reduced to the cartographic projection yet, in that act of resistance, still internalizes the imperative to impose a sense of order and coherency on the spatial heterogeneity of early modern Britain. It is a form of mapping, but one at odds with the dominant modes and forms of cartographic representation. Rather than a totalizing space that levels all difference, the heterotopic conceit posits more localized, common sites of identification that do not necessarily cohere into a unified and organic national or imperial body, though their construction may very well service those projects.[37] These are not exotic spaces but instead more akin to what Franco Moretti terms the "intermediate space of the nation-state," or a space that is "large enough to survive and to sharpen its claws on its neighbors, but small enough to be organized from one center and to feel itself as an entity."[38] Not quite national, not quite local, this middle world constitutes an identity that is both and neither. A heterotopia would then be an intimate and familiar space that is simultaneously continuous and discontinuous with the nation-state. It resists any smooth incorporation into the national body yet still remains somehow an integral part of that body. I echo here Elizabeth Helsinger's critique of Benedict Anderson and his undue emphasis on "the means of consensus" as opposed to the "practice of dissent": "The nation approached as a partly divided, always uncompleted consciousness—rather than as the preexistent identity of its people or the political reach of the nation-state—will need to be studied through the contested forms through which it is imagined at a given moment, both by those who include themselves in it and by those who dissociate themselves from it."[39] The heterotopic conceit then articulates this more contingent view of the nation as the space of inclusion and exclusion, association and dissociation. The British nation-state, from this vantage point, cannot be defined strictly in terms of filiation, incorporation, and alliance but rather must take into account the ways in which those bonds are forged through the reciprocal practices of resistance, dissent, and disjunction. The heterotopic conceit accounts for this sense of conflict at the heart of national identity by projecting fragmented and partial spaces that internalize those conflicts and reproduce them on a variety of scales and in a variety of forms.

Literature from the period in question, as I will contend, can and does represent one such form or site of cartographic resistance that, in turn, serves to articulate a range of heterotopic spaces central to the formation of British national identity during the seventeenth and eighteenth centuries. Quite often, scholarship in this area, the novel in particular, has tended to argue for the congruence between the map and various literary works, suggesting that they mirror each other in many respects, both formally and thematically, so much so that "mapping" has become a pervasive, if not somewhat clichéd, metaphor to describe the ways in which a given piece of literature represents space. I draw on and address a number of these works in the chapters that follow, not to discredit them or argue that their conclusions are incorrect but rather to make the point that they present only half of the picture, as it were. That the techniques of describing and representing space found in many works of seventeenth- and eighteenth-century British literature have substantive connections to contemporaneous cartographic and chorographic practices and methods seems true enough; however, it is equally true that, in their appropriation of such practices and methods, many of these literary works are also commenting on and criticizing the map and its particular framing of Britain, exposing the limitations and gaps in its image of the nation, as well as the violence and brutality that lay just beneath the surface of that image. Like the map itself, literature does not just reflect the world around it; it actively refracts and distorts our understanding of the world in order to give the reader a different perspective, a different vantage point from which to see and know the world around them. In this sense, the literary work is not only able to reflect and reproduce an image of Britain that is, in many ways, akin to the map, but just as easily, it constructs the nation in ways that are also against the map, "against" here meaning both in opposition and adjacent to, antagonistic yet proximate. This I take to be the central point of Foucault's notion of heterotopia as a space that is Other. In their varied oppositions to and criticisms of the map, the literary works I discuss refract and distort our view of Britain to produce a different, more contingent understanding of the nation, one no longer rooted in the modalities of the cartographic projection but rather in the intermediate space of the heterotopia.

In the following chapters, I will offer a series of "heterotopologies" that describe and analyze a number of these spaces, such as neighborhood, scene, country, market, and home, all of which are critical to understanding the geography of Britain during a period of rapid and large-scale transformations within the political, social, and economic landscape. While the book proceeds chronologically, beginning with John Bunyan and concluding with Samuel Johnson, my method of argumentation here is not necessarily teleological. There is little if any cause and effect between one chapter and the next, and I have tried to deal with each chapter as a somewhat isolated instance in order to respect their differences. Chapter 1, "John Bunyan, Neighborhood, and the Geography of Dissent," recontextualizes Bunyan's construction of the neighborhood in *The Pilgrim's Progress* (1678) as the product of an allegorical geography that exposes the pitfalls of thinking religious community in terms of map and survey. The neighborhood emerges as both an extension of and a reaction to the state's attempts to quantify and locate Dissent as a means of containing its potentially seditious presence. The neighborhood gives "place" to Bunyan's particular brand of nonconformist thought at a time when the policies of Charles and James denied nonconformity any semblance of an organized structure that might pose a challenge to the Anglican parochial system. In chapter 2, "Aphra Behn and the Colonial Scene," I examine the relationship between Behn's use of the scenic stage and the geography of the British Empire as it is depicted in *Oroonoko, or The Royal Slave* (1688). Behn challenges representations of the triangular trade between England, Africa, and the Americas as an adequate spatial paradigm for understanding the colonial project. She translates the technologies of the scenic stage, such as shutters, wings, and drop curtains, into prose narrative in order to disrupt the continuity of the triangular model and to offer a much more fragmentary and divided sense of Britain's imperial geography. Rather than subjects within a particular space, both colonizer and colonized are subjected to the violent displacements of British conquest and settlement.

The following chapter, "Surveying Ireland and Swift's 'Country of the Mind,'" looks at Swift's satirical critique of the role and perspective of the surveyor, beginning with the production and use of plantation and estate maps in the settlement of Ireland during the seventeenth and eighteenth centuries. I contend that much of his writing, *Gulliver's Travels* (1726) perhaps first and foremost, evinces a strain of anticartographic thought that has its roots in the popular resistance to the mapping of Ireland, including numerous deliberate acts of violence directed at English surveyors and officials responsible for transforming their country into a colonial possession. Like those who resisted or thwarted such efforts, Swift understood the survey and map as technologies of confiscation and expropriation intended to dispossess Ireland's native population of their land; however, the profound impact of those technologies on the rural landscape was not, in his estimation, limited to Ireland but could be seen and felt in England as well, most notably in its fetishizing of the land itself, to borrow Helgerson's phrasing, as a source of national identity. In either instance, the survey and the map are revealed by Swift to be totems of worldliness and vanity that transform the very meaning of the word "country," upending and displacing its classical origins as the figurative ground of the republic and its citizenry in favor of its more modern definition as a literal place that can be located on a map and, more problematically for Swift, that is defined strictly in terms of private property. Swift's preference for the former, a "country of the mind" as it were, stands against the map in its placing of the public good over private interest, patriotic virtue over nationalist sentiment. Chapter 4, "Daniel Defoe and the Limits to the Market," situates Defoe's *Tour Thro' the Whole Island of Great Britain* (1724–27) within the context of prior efforts to consolidate and map England's market economy. The *Tour* incorporates and builds upon these earlier efforts to construct a geography of the marketplace in order to facilitate exchange and commerce and provide a sense of continuity between markets that may hold fast to their own individuated customs and practices. However, Defoe's market continually threatens to elude any such mapping. His attempt to construct a comprehensive and integrated picture of national space defined by trade and commercial activity is an implicit recognition that the marketplace may not, in fact, be a stable referent for economic prosperity and national wealth. Thus, the imperative to map and survey its terrain arises out of a need to both delimit and contain market activity while, at the same time, acknowledging that any such effort is, to an extent, difficult, if not impossible.

In chapter 5, "This Old House and Samuel Johnson's Scotland," I argue that conflicts and tensions within the formation of British national identity lead to a generic split between those geographies committed to a progressive vision of Scotland rooted in agrarian improvement and commercial development and those dedicated to unearthing Scotland's ancient past as a means of establishing a supposedly more local and more authentic form of Scottish national identity. The 1707 Act of Union, as well as the rebellions of 1715 and 1745, only further deepened the gulf separating these competing definitions of Scottish territory, thus driving a burgeoning market for both antiquarian and economic maps, surveys, atlases, travel narratives, and chorographies throughout the eighteenth century. Building on this cartographic history, I examine Johnson's critique of eighteenth-century commercial and antiquarian topographies of Scotland and argue that his *A Journey to the Western Islands of Scotland* (1775) posits a vision of a unified Great Britain that is not the product of conquest and dominion, military, commercial, or otherwise, but rather one that finds common ground in the minute details and particularities of domestic life. That is, the home, as both a material place and an abstract ideal, unifies and binds England and Scotland into a single nation, or homeland as it were, whose identity is rooted in the universal and universalizing experience of domestic labor and familial community. As the empirical traveler abroad, Johnson assiduously documents and comments on the virtues and failings of the various homes he encounters and constructs a history in which the Scottish home comes to mark the evolution and progress of civilization itself, from its primitive shelters and habitations to the solid and dignified forts and castles of the feudal period and, lastly, to the genteel, refined environs of the modern home. Johnson's secret history of domesticity enables us to witness and chart the gradual yet lengthy process by which a nation moves inexorably from barbarity to civility. The creation of a truly civil society, in Johnson's estimation, is something that cannot be imposed on Scotland through the exercise of force or sheer will; rather, it must and will emerge as a matter of course from within the modalities of domestic life.

I conclude with "The Neighborhood Revisited," which returns to Bunyan's conception of the neighborhood as a space of radical dissent in order to insist that, by the early nineteenth century, the neighborhood has instead become fundamental to the promotion of bourgeois values and national sentiment. Edmund Burke, for one, argues that the neighborhood is a critical mediating space in the translation of domestic feeling into a deep and abiding affection for and attachment to the national body. However, in *Mansfield Park*, Jane Austen challenges Burke's "affective geography" to suggest that the neighborhood, rather than a point of mediation between home and nation, is in fact the very place where these connections are either distorted or irrevocably broken, thus foreclosing any sense of reciprocity between both local and national identities.

Whatever virtues the neighborhood may represent, its effects are ultimately nullified by the fact that her characters remain forever trapped within a provincial worldview whose bearing on the moral condition of the nation is, at best, suspect and whose sense of shared feeling never circulates beyond the confines of the neighborhood.

# 1

# John Bunyan, Neighborhood, and the Geography of Dissent

What is an ideology without a space to which it refers, a space which it describes, whose vocabulary and links it makes use of, and whose code it embodies? What would remain of religious ideology—the Judeo-Christian one, say—if it were not based on places and their names: church, confessional, altar, sanctuary, tabernacle? What would remain of the Church if there were no churches?

—Henri Lefebvre, *The Production of Space* (1974)

## The Geographies of Dissent

Henri Lefebvre's series of questions offer some resonance with the life and work of John Bunyan and that of other seventeenth-century Dissenting ministers for whom itinerary was often a defining feature of their respective ministries, not by choice of course, but rather due to legal restrictions and prohibitions on their ability to preach from a physical church. Judeo-Christian ideology, or any ideology for that matter, Lefebvre suggests, is dependent on the places and spaces in which that ideology moves and operates, and so to separate the Church from the church, as it were, would threaten the very authority and legitimacy of Judeo-Christian ideology in all of its forms, including the radical Protestantism of Bunyan and others who, as a result of their dissent from the Anglican Church, were forced to rely on other means of communicating the word of God, itinerant preaching first and foremost. During the late seventeenth and early eighteenth century, theirs was indeed a Church with no church, an ideology without a well-defined and knowable place. That is not to suggest, however, that Dissent did not have its own geography, its own space to which it refers and describes, "whose vocabulary and links it makes use of, and whose code it embodies." As I will argue in the chapter to follow, Bunyan's conception of the "neighborhood," as a heterotopic locus of resistance, is intended to provide that sense of place, both metaphorical and actual, for his particular brand of nonconformist thought at a time when the policies of Charles II and James II denied him and others any organized, institutional presence that might challenge and upend the authority and legitimacy of the Anglican Church. Bunyan's neighborhood, as I hope to demonstrate, thus emerges as both an extension of and a reaction to the state's attempts to quantify and locate Dissent as a means of containing their potentially seditious presence, often through the use of demographic and geographic surveys conducted throughout the period in question.

Michael Watts, for example, in volume 1 of his *The Dissenters*, offers us a series of maps intended to illustrate what he terms "the geographic distribution of Dissent" from roughly 1715 to 1719.[1] Drawing upon a detailed survey of Dissenting congregations made shortly after the death of Queen Anne, the maps cover both England and Wales and depict the location and relative population, broken down to the county level, of the five Dissenting churches in question: Presbyterian, Independent, Particular and General Baptists, and Quakers. The survey that forms the basis for these maps was compiled by Dr. John Evans, a Presbyterian minister and secretary of the Committee of the Three Denominations, which had been set up in 1702 by various London ministers to "protect Dissenting interests from Tory designs upon the ascension of Queen Anne."[2] With the Hanoverian succession, the political motivations of the committee emerged more clearly when, in 1715, efforts to repeal the Schism Act demanded a fuller accounting of Dissent not only in terms of its sheer numbers but, just as importantly, in the geographic distribution of its population. To that end, every Presbyterian, Independent, and Baptist congregation in England and Wales was written to in order to obtain their location, the name of the minister, the number and quality of the adherents, and lastly, the number of votes they commanded. The survey was periodically updated through 1729, but by 1718, a comprehensive picture of Dissent had, for the most part, already taken shape, one that would not only help abolish the Schism Act but also impact state policy formation on a variety of levels over the course of the eighteenth century.

While the maps in Watts's text were not produced at that time, they nevertheless expose the geographic and cartographic logic behind the survey and the particular mode of "political arithmetic" that undergirds the production of space in general. The maps, like the survey, offer a somewhat reductive, though highly suggestive, representation of Dissent that spatializes many of the displacements and transformations in the nature and composition of religious community over the course of the previous century. Watts notes, for example, the "heavy concentration" of Presbyterians in the growing industrial centers of the North and West: Lancashire, Cheshire, Devon, Somerset, Dorset, and Northumberland, places not previously counted among the traditional centers of power south and east of London.[3] This is due, in part, to the emigration of Scots into those regions where manufacturing was dominant, thus providing a pool of cheap and accessible labor for burgeoning coal, textile, and shipbuilding industries, among others. Dissenting populations were urban on the whole, living primarily in cities, boroughs, or market towns, while numbers in rural areas tended to remain low, since many were dependent on the Anglican gentry for their economic livelihood. Urban infrastructure afforded more centralized populations that, in turn, tended to favor nonconformity, since adherents lived in close proximity to one another, their place of worship, and primary source of income.

In addition to economic factors, there is the tradition, dating back at least to the reign of Queen Elizabeth, of encouraging nonconformity in remote counties in order to offset the influence of Roman Catholicism. Dissenting congregations, like the Presbyterians, often emerged in the interstices of an Anglican parish system that could not adequately meet the demands of a rapidly expanding population: "The failure of the Church of England to adapt its parochial organization to the changing economic and demographic structure of the country provided Presbyterian ministers with fine opportunities for poaching on what Anglican clergymen regarded as their own preserves. . . . Such opportunities were exploited by ejected ministers of unusual zeal and energy."[4] Fears of Roman Catholicism, spurred by ever-widening gaps in the parish system, inevitably gave way to the further entrenchment of Dissent in these areas. Anglican chapels of ease were constructed, in addition to the more centralized parish churches, in order to accommodate these demographic shifts, but such efforts ultimately failed to provide a serious alternative to the more mobile and flexible structure of Dissenting churches. As a result, Presbyterian clergy, many of whom had been ejected from their congregations during the Restoration, maintained and preached in these chapels despite opposition by ecclesiastical authorities. The practice of itinerant preaching also aided Dissent's ability to cover more territory and reach more listeners than the parochial system afforded. Such a network allowed for the further entrenchment of nonconformity in those areas where the Church of England's control was weakest and most easily exploited.

Independents, such as the Congregationalists, however, tended to thrive in London proper and those counties just to the north of London where the established church maintained a much tighter control over the religious life of the nation: Essex, Hertfordshire, Northamptonshire, Bedfordshire, and Cambridgeshire, most notably.[5] This is due, in large part, to the legacy of Puritanism and its support for the parliamentary cause during the Civil War. Under the Protectorate, these congregations were able to flourish and develop a radical strain not easily subdued or contained by the Restoration governments of Charles and James. Particular and General Baptists, likewise, were found predominantly in those counties in and around London, though the Particular Baptists also had a strong presence, much like the Independents, in southern Wales. Quaker populations also tended to be higher in London and to the north, but unlike the aforementioned groups, they tended not to be as geographically restricted. The final map demonstrates that the Quakers were more evenly distributed over England and Wales even though their overall numbers were not nearly as large, a fact Watts attributes to their missionary zeal and superior organizational abilities in the absence of a unified parochial structure.

Much of this information is certainly nothing new or surprising, nor does it radically alter our picture of Dissent as it gains increasing legitimacy after 1688. However, I begin with Watts's maps and the survey from which they are drawn in order to examine more closely the implications of framing religious Dissent in explicitly cartographic and demographic terms. While, for Watts, the maps are primarily a heuristic device, a means of quantifying certain evidentiary material, they nevertheless raise a critical parallel to the nascent administrative and bureaucratic technologies of the state that were central not only to England's military and economic expansion of the late seventeenth century but also more effective rule at home, including the suppression of religious nonconformity.[6] The statistical approach to Dissent and its representability in the form of a "geography of Dissent" is part and parcel of larger trends in the formation of an English state increasingly reliant on current methods of accounting, calculation, and ordering. The Evans list offers an early, though by no means solitary, example of this new way of thinking about the role and function of the state. The survey provides a further means of legitimating Dissent and securing its place in the political life of the nation after the reign of Queen Anne, not through any charismatic appeal to Crown and Parliament, not by invoking moral and ethical dictums concerning religious tolerance. Rather, it is the quantification of Dissent, its sheer numbers and the distribution of those numbers within a given space, that will provide the most effective means of consolidating religious and political liberty.

Framing heterodoxy in a manner more readily associated with the technologies of the fiscal-military state may appear, on the surface, to be something of a contradiction, but by 1715, when the survey was undertaken, any such conflicts had, for the most part, been resolved or smoothed over, most significantly in the writings of Daniel Defoe, where nonconformity and the national interest were irrevocably joined.[7] The Glorious Revolution and the ascension of William and Mary to the English throne had forever altered the relationship between Dissent and the state, allowing for the formation of political entities such as the Committee of the Three Denominations. The geography of Dissent prior to 1688, however, was quite different, though no less the product of its historical moment. As we know, the often brutal policies of Charles II, the Clarendon Code most notably, specifically targeted Quakers, Puritans, Ranters, Presbyterians, Fifth-Monarchists, and other nonconformist congregations. They were routinely denied participation in local and state government, prohibited from meeting or congregating in public or private, and had their property seized for any infraction of these laws. As Richard Ashcraft notes, the original draft of the Conventicle Bill of 1670 equated conventicles with riots, "thus merging completely the notion of religious Dissent with political sedition and disorder."[8] The bill placed unprecedented powers in the hands of a single magistrate to prosecute and, if necessary, confiscate the property of those suspected of religious nonconformity. Laws against nonconformity during the Restoration, including the provisions in the Clarendon Code, were often enforced on the local level by the magistrate and his officers, transforming the once strictly ecclesiastical unit of the parish into an instrument of state power that wielded both civil and religious authority. Over the course of the seventeenth and early eighteenth centuries, Parliament was able to enforce religious conformity on the local level through the parish's expanding legal and political responsibilities, including the suppression of Dissent within its immediate jurisdiction.[9]

The desire on the part of Charles II and Parliament to regulate, confine, control, and manipulate the arguably seditious forces of nonconformity leads, in effect, to the implementation of legal and political measures intended to transform parish, county, town, and village into a well-ordered, administrative machine that could enforce the will of the state. It was not so much a matter of having to create local governance from the ground up, since many of these units were already in place, but rather the need to centralize and consolidate local authorities so that they might become a natural extension of parliamentary authority. Demographic information regarding Dissent again proves valuable in this regard, except that, in this instance, it is to consolidate the state's authority over nonconformist congregations rather than provide some means of reconciling their interests, as in the case of the Evans list. The differences in methodology, as I am suggesting, were small at best. The quantification and location of Dissent was certainly seen as necessary to the enforcement of such policies. For example, Gilbert Sheldon, Archbishop of Canterbury, ordered censuses of English and Welsh dioceses in 1665, 1669, and 1676 in order to determine the whereabouts of nonconformist clergy and their meetings, essentially mapping Dissent in a manner similar to the Evans list.[10] The gathering and analysis of demographic information thus offered a means of ordering and controlling Dissenting congregations prior to 1688. Such efforts to survey and map Dissent, however, were not always welcome, particularly on the local level, given the unstated, but no less apparent, purpose behind the survey. For this reason, the results of surveys, such as those conducted by Sheldon, were often flawed and incomplete, given the widespread resistance to the Stuart monarchy and its desire to locate nonconforming clergy and their adherents. A pervasive ambivalence regarding the collective policies of Charles and James hampered both the state's and the church's ability to obtain precise and objective data and, in turn, their ability to implement those policies in a consistent and effective manner. In fact, when we turn to many rural towns and villages during the Restoration, it becomes apparent that translating laws mandating religious conformity into purposeful action on the local level was neither smooth nor guaranteed.

As David Eastwood points out, the English Civil War did not so much dis-
turb or disrupt the consolidation of local government but rather precipitated
the extension of its powers and jurisdiction, often in ways that served to resist
unpopular or undesirable laws and policies, including those geared toward the
suppression of religious nonconformity. The relative weakness of the central
government in England during the seventeenth century, as compared to the
absolutism found on the continent, allowed for the development of a highly di-
versified and flexible system of local government.[11] As Joan Kent notes, English
local government in the later seventeenth century was still, for the most part,
unbureaucratic and run by "unpaid, unprofessional, part-time officers."[12] It was
informal and idiosyncratic; jurisdictions were not clear cut, nor was there uniformity in terms of the duties and responsibilities of local officials both within
a single administrative unit, such as the parish, or even from one parish to the
next.[13] Christopher Hill further demonstrates that, while Parliament and the
king were both able to fashion legislation intended to eradicate Dissent, there
was no guarantee of its success since the law was often circumvented or ignored altogether by local JPs (justices of the peace) or their subordinates: "But
even when they (JPs) wanted to enforce the laws against non-conformists, they
could not do so without the co-operation of lesser officials, themselves liable
to be influenced by local opinion. Where dissent was strong, blind eyes might
be turned to religious meetings, or *neighborly feelings* shield potential victims
of persecution [italics mine]."[14] The political valence of neighbors thus manifests itself within this discourse of allegiance and fidelity, who will and will not
support the cause of religious tolerance. Neighbors cannot always be trusted,
given the monetary incentives and political pressure to turn in their fellow man,
if they were not already so inclined. The Conventicle Bill of 1670, for example,
dispensed rewards (up to one-third of the fines levied) to any person willing to
inform on the activities of Dissenters, thus motivating the public to act against
itself in order to enforce state policy. While Charles believed such a network
of local informants to be a rather efficient and pragmatic method of quashing
Dissent, there were others who argued that the Conventicle Bill only deepened
the sense of distrust and suspicion that already pervaded the nation, especially
in regards to popish conspiracies and fears of despotic rule. The climate of
paranoia that surrounded the reign of Charles, as well as James, managed to
filter its way down to the local level, where public and private sympathies, including that of one's neighbor, were not always apparent or as readily parsed.

It is a dilemma that, in my estimation, informs Bunyan's thinking regarding
the virtues of "good neighborhood" as a response to the fracturing of religious
community during the Restoration period. Bunyan's image and conception of
the "neighborhood," as I will show, serves as a means of giving *place* to his particular brand of nonconformist thought at a time when the policies of Charles
and James attempted to deny nonconformity a legitimate place of worship and
any semblance of an organized structure that might pose a challenge to the

Anglican parochial system. Its suturing together of the public and the private offers a vision of local autonomy against a burgeoning English state bent on appropriating the local as simply the bureaucratic extension of royal and parliamentary authority. Bunyan's neighborhood, however, differs from Watts's maps, the Evans list, and the surveys of Archbishop Sheldon in that it registers a much more ambivalent attitude toward the routinization of Dissent through surveys, maps, and other forms of statistical or mathematical representation. Rather than embrace them wholesale, Bunyan's construction of the neighborhood in *The Pilgrim's Progress* stands as something of a satiric and ironic counterpart to these various projects, invoking them only to expose the flaws in thinking of religious community in terms of map and survey. That is to say, the neighborhood operates according to a principle of negation endemic to allegorical representation. The result is a twofold vision of the neighborhood that is, on the one hand, corrupt and corrupting, since neighbors are able to exercise undue influence over one another given their relative proximity. Neighbors represent the dangers of contiguity, of associative bonds based on physical distance, which will, in Bunyan's estimation, necessarily result in the dissolution and abdication of true community. Bunyan's wariness about neighbors, a theme he returns to repeatedly over the course of his career, may also be viewed as part of his overall critique of the logic of contiguity that informs the cartographic and demographic impulse, the spatial fix, behind the state's desire for uniformity and conformity. The homogenization of space is predicated on the production of both a spatial and temporal continuity that, as Benedict Anderson has argued, informs the consolidation of the nation-state.[15] Bunyan's representation of the neighborhood as a place of contagion is, in his estimation, the logical outcome of such a project.

On the other hand, the skeptical negation of contiguity that is the source of satire in Bunyan's text also opens up the possibility for a more affirmative definition of neighborhood that is predicated less on a geographic understanding of community and more on a theocentric one. That is not to say that Bunyan abandons the geographic altogether. Rather, the neighborhood, as an allegorical space, is an attempt to negotiate the geographic and the spiritual, or the concerns of this world and the next. The neighborhood then might also be viewed as an extension of these efforts to systematize and routinize Dissent through the production of a new kind of space that necessarily fails to fully inscribe itself in the landscape. There are no maps demarcating neighborhoods, urban or otherwise, or surveys that would delimit their size or location; it is neither a sanctioned legal entity like an estate or other forms of private property nor an instrument of ecclesiastical or governmental authority such as the parish or the county. The neighborhood thus eludes cartographic representation while simultaneously organizing a space against which the material practices of everyday life may unfold. This schema is neither aspatial nor apolitical but is, rather, a manifestation of a particular politics of space whose relevance can only be understood against the fragmenting of religious community during the latter half of the seventeenth century.

## Who Are the People in Your Neighborhood?

Neighborliness, or "good neighborhood," represents for John Bunyan a hierarchical system of valuation intended to promote the application of Christian virtues and moral absolutes to a set of localized relations, however loosely organized. It is an idealized conception of spiritual community in which the configuration of God's elect takes on a simultaneously spatialized and metaphorical cast; that is, the term "neighborhood" partakes in the nomenclature of contiguity and the discourse of the particular while leaving itself open to a mode of signification (allegory) that would exceed those boundaries to say something more general about the proper orientation of Christians, specifically Protestant Congregationalists, toward others. The mobility and the fluidity of Bunyan's conception of neighborhood, the oscillation it affords between geographic specificity and figurative abstraction, forces us to bracket the more current thinking about the neighborhood as a reified unit of space, good neighborhood then understood merely as an idealized set of practices found within those borders. Not that there aren't connections to be drawn, especially with regard to a certain nostalgia that informs the desire to resuture the always already fragmented community, but I wish to emphasize at the outset that there is a constitutive difference between the neighborhood's seventeenth-century inflection, including Bunyan's own particular articulation of "civil Neighborhood," and its modern and postmodern equivalents.

As a type of social space, the neighborhood of the seventeenth century retains very strong associations with religious thought, especially within the radical Protestant tradition of Dissenting churches, and is, as I will contend, an extension of a particular set of theological and ideological suppositions as well as a response to the political and economic forces that were drastically reshaping the landscape of Britain.[16] As an outgrowth of the humanistic strain within Calvinism, good neighborhood falls, for Bunyan, essentially under the category of works, defined as that which is a manifestation of grace but not a means to achieving grace. In his *Christian Behaviour; Being the Fruits of Christianity* (1663), the concept of good neighborhood appears primarily as a list of prescriptive behaviors: communicate about spiritual matters on a daily basis, assist the poor or those in need, be meek, turn your neighbor away from sin, do not provoke others with words, and avoid telling tales and gossiping. The section "Of Neighbors each to other" fleshes out these basic tenets with proper biblical citations and the proviso that one must be in "good & sound Conversation in thy own family, place, and station, shewing to all, the power that the Gospel and the things of another World hath in thy heart."[17] The practice of good neighborhood is dependent on first registering the divine within one's own heart; the Gospel must be felt in some sense in order that it be properly represented to others. Otherwise, to speak or act in a Christian manner without having the Word of God impressed on one's heart is to wantonly deceive others and to misrepresent the Word itself. As Bunyan states in *A Vindication of Some Gospel Truths Opened* (1657), "Now friend, this is fairly spoken: but by words in general we may be deceived, because a man may speak one thing with his mouth, and mean another things in his heart; especially it is so with those that use to utter themselves doubtfully."[18] Meaning here is tied to the heart, while words potentially distort that meaning. The divine must be felt or experienced as something that lies outside of us yet must be internalized in a fashion that can elide the ambiguities and instabilities of both written and spoken language.

This individualized conception of personal salvation and redemption, or "heart-religion," presents a thoroughly Christianized model of civil society that would be the logical extension of private virtue, a progress from the home outward: "As persons must be of good behaviour at home, that will be good Neighbors, so they must be full of courtesie and charity to them that have need about them."[19] The establishment of "civil Neighborhood" spatializes this continuity, or progress, from the heart of the Christian who possesses grace to the manifestation of grace in the performance of one's domestic responsibilities and, finally, to its extension beyond the home to the fulfilling of neighborly duties. In *Christian Behaviour*, as well as numerous other works, Bunyan specifically addresses his reader in the language of a progress, asking at the outset "if thou wouldst walk to the edification of thy neighbor, and so to God's honor."[20] Such a movement signals the translation of grace into works and, in turn, gives that movement its own geography, specifically that of the neighborhood. Good neighborhood represents an attempt to theorize the proper relationship between grace and works in expressly spatial terms, since it concerns not only spiritual matters but practical and worldly ones as well. It is a way of mapping the community of the godly whose sense of identity is dependent, in part, on its own locatability and the legibility of that locale.

However, as Bunyan is well aware, there are many impediments to realizing this continuum of grace and works that informs the production of good neighborhood, including, paradoxically, neighbors themselves. Grace must always be the source of neighborly acts, yet Bunyan recognizes that one can engage in the practice of good neighborhood without necessarily possessing faith in God, a problem he will return to on a variety of occasions. In *Saved By Grace* (1676), Bunyan makes clear his theological position on the proper relationship between grace and works through the example of the bad, or false, neighbor:

And now observe him, he is a great stickler for legal performance; now he will be a good Neighbor, he will pay every Man his own, will leave off his Swearing, the Alehouse, his Sports, and Carnal Delights; he will read, pray, talk of Scripture, and be a very busie one in Religion (such as it is). . . . But all this while he is as ignorant of Christ, as the stool he sits on, and no nearer Heaven then was the blind *Pharisee*, only he has got in a cleaner way to Hell then the rest of his Neighbors are.[21]

The observance of Mosaic law (i.e., love thy neighbor as thyself) is an empty gesture without faith and so constitutes a sin.[22] The false neighbor appears to participate in the protocols of good neighborhood when, in fact, he or she merely fulfills the letter of the law rather than the spirit of the law. How then can one discern the false from the true neighbor and what are the consequences for good neighborhood given the potential presence of the "blind Pharisee," a figure not of manifest evil and malevolence but one who adheres strictly to notions of juridical rigor and accountability? The specter of the false neighbor will raise a theological as well a practical problem Bunyan must negotiate as he seeks to define good neighborhood against that other definition of the neighborhood that emerges in Paul's letter to the Galatians.

In a telling gloss on that particular passage (love thy neighbor as thyself), Bunyan reminds us that its invocation was intended to heal divisions within Galatia between those who professed the keeping of Mosaic law and those who adhered to the doctrine of justification by faith. Having established the church at Galatia on a previous mission, Paul discovers that, in the interim, certain Jewish factions there had contravened his prior teaching that faith in Christ alone, and not works, was sufficient for redemption and salvation. The ensuing rift in the church precipitates Paul's letter to the Galatians so that he may re-state his position in a clearer, more forceful manner. However, his exhortative appeal to "love your neighbor as yourself," as Bunyan notes, is itself a point of law whose necessity only emerges fully in light of the verse that follows: "But if ye bite and devour one another, take heed that ye be not consumed one of another."[23] Neighbors, in this sense, appear as preternaturally antagonistic toward one another, existing in an almost Hobbesian state of nature where neighbor is inclined to "devour" neighbor if not for the adherence to moral law rooted in the Christian faith. Paul's recourse to the law attempts to finesse the political and religious tensions in Galatia and serves to placate those who believe that justification by faith alone means the wholesale abandonment of Mosaic law and the need for works. However, he also recognizes that the need for the law can only be understood against a vision of a community divided against itself, of neighbor pitted against neighbor, and so the neighborhood remains, at its most fundamental level, base and corrupt.

Bunyan recognizes this paradox within his own attempts to theorize the concept of neighborhood. His attempts to establish the parameters of "good neighborhood" are always haunted by the figure of the false neighbor who fails to understand the workings of grace. The neighborhood, rather than an ideal vision of religious community, reveals itself to be quite the opposite, more akin to Vanity Fair than the Celestial City. Bunyan's conception of religious community, in fact, has no place for neighbors. In *Grace Abounding to the Chief of Sinners* (1666), his spiritual autobiography, Bunyan describes his own congregation at Bedford: "And methought they spake as if joy did make them speak; they spake with such pleasantness of Scripture language, and with such appearance of grace in all they said, that they were to me as if they had found a new world, as if they were people that dwelt alone, and were not to be reckoned among their neighbors (Num. 23:9)."[24] The reference here to the book of Numbers sets up a parallel, in typological fashion, between the Bedford congregation and the nation of Israel, underscoring that they are people with a destiny apart from that of their neighbors and that the congregation is perhaps a nation unto itself. The gesture to this "new world," then, suggests a deep affinity between religious community and the formation of national bodies; both are constituted through both a temporal displacement of the past in favor of newness, of novelty, and a spatial exclusion of anyone or anything "neighboring" that body so that the "world" may appear as a neatly circumscribed, self-sufficient unit. Neighbors, then, always represent a threat that is alien to the nation of the elect and, consequently, must be marked in some fashion so that they may be vigilantly resisted at all times.

Living in close proximity to one another perhaps leads the Christian subject to abandon the quest for salvation in deference to neighborly pressures, which are usually of a sinful nature. Consequently, neighbors precipitate the spreading of such behaviors in contagious fashion: "For where the ungodly do live, and die, and descend into the pit together, the one is rather a vexation to the other, than anything else. . . . If there live one in the town that is very expert and cunning for the world, why now the rest of his neighbors that are of the same mind with him, they will labour to imitate him and follow his steps: this is commonly seen."[25] The entropic logic of exemplarity here transforms the neighborhood from a community of grace to one of iniquity. The neighborhood, in this instance, is not only the site of sinful activity; it is the very idea of neighboring, its organizational principle, that will further spread profligacy in all its forms, hence completing the transformation. Bunyan reinforces this connection between neighbors and sin by equating the two metaphorically: "Departing from iniquity, with many, is but like the falling out of two neighbors, they hate one another for a while, and then renew their old friendship again."[26] The difficulty in resisting sin resembles the difficulty in resisting a neighbor, but we are inevitably drawn to each. To extend the metaphor even further, the rejection of one's neighbor is tantamount to the rejection of sin, a formula that seemingly contradicts Bunyan's earlier statements on the value of good neighborhood. How then to reconcile both perspectives on neighbors and the value of neighborhood? It is a paradox that, as I have demonstrated, runs throughout the corpus of Bunyan's writings and one that continues to inform *The Pilgrim's Progress* and its attempt to construct a geography of Dissent that will redefine neighbors and the concept of neighboring in critical ways.

As Bunyan explains in his opening apology of *The Pilgrim's Progress*, he did not write to "please his neighbor" but only "mine own self to gratify," as if neighbors would only appreciate the pleasure of reading his text, its entertainment value as it were, and not its moral import. One immediately receives the impression that the addressee of the apology is, in fact, a neighbor. Who else would require that point of clarification? The apology is essentially an extended defense of the text aimed not at a generalized reader but, rather, the reader who will most likely misunderstand or misconstrue his designs. Bunyan narrates the origins of *The Pilgrim's Progress* in order to dramatize the conflict between himself and detractors who question his desire to write and publish. And like Christian, who ignores the warnings of his neighbors to become a pilgrim, Bunyan, in analogous fashion, disregards those who would cast doubt on his intentions. Even when the text has been completed, an unidentified voice questions the use value of such a work: "Well, yet I am not fully satisfied / That this your Book will stand, when soundly / try'd," prompting Bunyan to launch into a defense of "my dark and cloudy words."[27] While Bunyan does not explicitly address this voice as neighbor, his pronouncement that "this book will make a traveler of thee" can only rightfully be intended for someone who remains within the City of Destruction and refuses to travel beyond its borders. The figure of the neighbor then is properly a denizen of the City of Destruction. Rather than sympathetic well-wishers, neighbors in *The Pilgrim's Progress* are often a source of confusion, gossip, and misinformation for the would-be pilgrim, markers of the domestic, carnal world that must be left behind in favor of the way and its panoply of strangers. When Christian resolves to leave his home, he leaves against not only the cries and protests of his wife and children but those of his neighbors as well. "The Neighbors also came out to see him run, and as he ran, some mocked, others threatened; and some cried after him to return."[28] Obstinate and Pliable, two of Christian's neighbors, succeed in overtaking him and try to persuade him to return, but only Pliable, as the allegorical import of his name would suggest, goes with Christian after he expounds briefly on the virtues of the way. Pliable quickly concludes, "My heart inclines to go with my Neighbour."[29]

Rather than a valorization of neighborliness, Pliable's sentiment becomes a point of satire in Bunyan's text. The fixation of one's heart on a neighbor is a false sentiment that leads to sin. In fact, the very association of affect and emotion with a neighbor is an epistemological error that subverts the call to pilgrimage. Pliable does not take up the journey of his own accord but rather chooses to follow Christian simply because they live adjacent or in close proximity to one another within the City of Destruction. He hastily invests his faith in a neighbor, even one as worthy as Christian, thus mistaking physical contiguity, the appearance of things near or next to, for spiritual calling. Pliable, subsequently, does not make it past the Slough of Despond, since, when mired in the bog, he cannot locate Christian, who is rapidly sinking. "*Then said Pliable, Ah, Neighbour Christian, where are you now? Truly, said Christian, I do not know.*"[30] The repetition of Christian's status as neighbor reinforces the false and tenuous nature of their relationship, which ends shortly thereafter when Pliable escapes the Slough of Despond only to return to the City of Destruction. However, it would be incorrect to lay the blame on Christian for somehow misleading or enticing Pliable, an accusation Pliable himself levels at Christian while in the bog. Pliable's sin here is not listening to Christian or even being moved to action by his words. The heart may be "pliable," yet Pliable's real sin exists not in feeling but rather in attaching his feelings to his neighbor, which results ultimately from his failure to read the allegorical significance of "neighbor."

We see this formulation repeated at the outset of Christiana's journey; however, there it is dramatized as a corrective to the earlier episode with Pliable, which functions more as a negative example. Christiana is visited by two neighbors, Mrs. Timourous and Mercie, who have come to dissuade her from following in her husband's footsteps. Mrs. Timorous, the elder of the two, questions her desire to leave the City of Destruction and chides her resolve: "*Prithee what new knowledge hast thou got that so worketh off thy mind from thy Friends, and that tempteth thee to go no body knows where?*"[31] Christiana, in response, tells of her dream the previous evening in which she sees Christian residing in the Celestial City and of the visit the following day by Secret, who delivers a letter inviting her and her children to come and live there "in the presence of the King of the Country." Mrs. Timorous dismisses her story as madness and quickly reminds her of the many difficulties Christian faced in his pilgrimage (everyone being familiar in Quixotic fashion with part 1 of *The Pilgrim's Progress*), to which Christiana quickly replies, "'Tempt me not, my Neighbour . . . for that you tell me of all these Troubles that I am like to meet with in the way, they are so far off from being to me a discouragement, that they shew I am in the right."[32] Christiana correctly reads her detractor's name as designating one who is fearful of leaving her home for the vicissitudes of the way, but she is also quite aware of the allegory of the neighbor and the temptations that they present to the would-be pilgrim. Names only partially indicate character, if at all, as in the case of Mr. Shame; one must also be wary of more general social designations such as neighbor. Mrs. Timorous, as her name suggests, is afraid to place her faith in God and go on the pilgrimage to the Celestial City and, as a neighbor, would seek to prevent others from doing the same.

Not that someone who is a neighbor is patently evil and incapable of conversion. Mercie, the younger woman who accompanies Mrs. Timorous, is swayed by Christiana's narration and the force of her convictions. She occupies, to some degree, the same role as Pliable in part 1 in that she is deeply moved by

Christiana's words, to the point that she questions her own adherence to the beliefs and values of Mrs. Timorous, driving a decisive wedge between the two. However, Mercy, unlike Pliable, is not simply abandoning one authoritarian figure for another. Christiana provokes her to perhaps contemplate her own faith, but the decision to leave with her does not rest solely on charisma:

> But *Mercie* was at a stand, and could not so readily comply with her Neighbour, and that for a twofold reason. First, her Bowels yearned over *Christiana:* so she said with in her self, If my Neighbour will needs be gon, I will go a little way with her, and help her. Secondly, her Bowels yearned over her own Soul, (for what *Christiana* had said, had taken some hold upon her mind.) Wherefore she said within her self again, I will yet have more talk with this *Christiana*, and if I find Truth and Life in what she shall say, my self with my Heart shall also go with her.[33]

Bunyan makes a crucial distinction in this repetition with a difference. While affect has its function within the conversion process, the invocation of Mercy's heart does not preclude the need for rational discourse in helping her make a decision. Her "yearning" for Christiana is only precursor to the yearning over her own soul, which must be approached with a careful balance of reason and emotion. Pliable, as we have seen, stops short of this second critical realization, desiring only to go with Christian out of sympathy and fellow feeling. Consequently, his journey ends at the Slough of Despond while Mercy proceeds with Christiana and her sons to the Celestial City.

The scene involves a complex negotiation of proper names and broader social categories, such as neighbor, in order to suggest the instabilities inherent in a purely nominal conception of the Christian self and its community. The necessary distrust of one's neighbor, and all things proximate for that matter, requires at once a thorough skepticism about appearances, of surfaces, and names, proper or otherwise, are simply external signifiers that are arbitrarily related to their signified. Names, then, are perhaps unreliable signs for the pilgrim, who must be conscious of that arbitrary relation at all times. Proper names are mutable, as is the case with Christian and Christiana, both of whom adopt their names only once they decide to lead the pilgrim's life; their prior names are cast off like the rags that they wear. And, as we see in the case of Mercy, one can be a neighbor yet transcend that label to become a pilgrim.

The difference between the narratives of Pliable and Mercy hinges on the correct reading of the term "neighbor." As Thomas Luxon reminds us, much of the dramatic grist of *The Pilgrim's Progress* is derived primarily from its characters', Christian's in particular, continual and repeated inability to properly distinguish between the literal and the allegorical: "Virtually the entire plot of Bunyan's allegory is generated by a string of occasions in which the pilgrim characters temporarily forget the allegorical status of their experiences in this world. Mistaking this-worldly experience for reality, they fall, as it were, back into the allegory and take it for the real thing."[34] As an allegory of reading, *The Pilgrim's Progress* is structured around a series of misreadings in which the allegorical is taken for the literal, a process that is then allegorized in Bunyan's text as the difference between the Christian and the profligate reader. Representing the latter category, Pliable's failings as an interpreter are a manifestation of false grace. His belief in his neighbor ("My heart inclines to go with my Neighbour") is not belief at all but rather a gross overdetermination of spatiality as the sole determinant of one's relationship to others and to the Godhead. Luxon here echoes Stanley Fish in his chapter on Bunyan in *Self-Consuming Artifacts*, which argues that the idea of progress in *The Pilgrim's Progress* is illusory, since "progress" would connote an investment in the physical world that Bunyan's text continually denies despite the fact that it continually encourages the "correlation of physical and spiritual place."[35] We are "invited" to understand progress as a progression in space when, in fact, to do so would be to fall prey to temptation, the temptation of spatial reasoning or spatial logic. Allegorical figures are to be rightly seen, in this sense, as "self-consuming artifacts" because they make us aware of the inadequacy of form to disclose the truth of the gospel.[36] It is Pliable's misrecognition, or misreading, of the allegory that is ultimately his undoing.

Three pilgrims can be walking together, Fish continues, yet each of them may travel a different road; the physical proximity of the pilgrims is not indicative of any spiritual and moral affinity, and their contiguity may rightfully be construed as a sign that there is some form of disparity. Such is the case when Christian happens on Formalist and Hypocrisy, two would-be pilgrims who climb over the wall protecting the way, circumventing the Gate which is, as Christian reminds them, the only proper entrance. Formalist and Hypocrisy make no such distinction and reason that "if we are in, we are in," regardless of how they happen to have gotten there. The three travel together, yet "they went on every man in his way, without much conference one with another."[37] They appear to be a group of pilgrims when in fact each remains a single, isolated unit. Formalist and Hypocrisy's transgression is not just that they have violated the rules by taking a shortcut but rather that they read the way literally, as an actual, physical location. However, the way should not be viewed as a worldly place, and to accept it as such is perhaps the surest sign that one is not truly in the way. The apparent conclusion here is that spatiality represents a kind of false consciousness that may lead to a potential misapplication of values. Time and space, as products and producers of this world, will burn away with the eschaton, since they are no longer required as the bearers of meaning. It is incumbent on the pilgrim to remember this and vigilantly view the world allegorically, always bracketing time and space and situating them properly within the spiritual order of things. Fish concludes: "What this suggests is that the form of *The Pilgrim's Progress*, because it spatializes and trivializes the way, is as great a danger as any the pilgrims meet within its confines; so that if we are to read the work correctly, we must actively resist the pressure of its temporal-spatial lines of cause and effect."[38] Fish's ideal reader appears to embrace a more modern conception of the hermeneutics of suspicion whereby resistance is an a priori condition of any act of reading or interpretation. Pressure, from this vantage point, can be seen as another word, thinly disguised, for ideology, here construed as the wanton manipulation and reconfiguration of time and space for the purposes of establishing a causal chain. In Fish's brief but evocative allegory of reading, Pressure and Resistance function dialectically to produce a correct and faithful reading of the text.

However, while there is a good bit of time and energy spent on the subject of reading and interpretation as resistance in Fish's analysis, he never fully investigates the source and nature of this pressure, which must be countered at all costs, even if that requires the text to finally "consume" itself in an act of complete negation. The culprit, if I may use that term, is not really cause and effect relationships, since within a Providential worldview, such as Bunyan's, causation is always a known, though epistemologically unavailable, quantity. Any effect, provided that it is read and understood properly as an effect, can always be traced back to its origin in God as the prime mover. Much of *Robinson Crusoe* devotes itself to this very problem, whereby Crusoe must learn to reconcile causes and effects, to attach a footprint to a foot as it were, through an awareness of God's Providence. The difficulty only arises when we fail to recognize the workings of Providence and remain trapped within the fallen world in which cause and effect are reasoned strictly along "temporal-spatial lines." Hence, time and space are potentially coercive forces intended to allure and tempt the unwary pilgrim who either refuses or is unable to view these categories allegorically. Interpreter makes this point explicitly earlier in Christian's journey: "*For the things that are seen, are* Temporal; *but the things that are not seen, are* Eternal: But though this be so, yet since things present, and our fleshly appetite, *are such near Neighbours one to another,* and again, because things to come, and carnal sense, are such strangers one to another, therefore it is, that the first of these so suddenly fall into *amity,* and that *distance* is so continued between the second."[39] The lesson here is twofold. Things present are given readily to the senses, "our fleshly appetite," because of their spatial and temporal proximity, while things to come, understood as the promise of "the glory of the next world," are empirically unavailable and so divorced from the wants and desires of the physical body. The second lesson alludes to the incident with Pliable and Bunyan's conception of the proper orientation toward neighbors.

As before, neighbors signal danger and so must be vigilantly resisted, to return to Fish's phraseology. Their nearness appeals to the senses and to the body. Neighbors take on a kind of literal quality when, in fact, they are to be understood allegorically as a totem of worldly bonds, an attachment to the here and now. The very notion of touching, being near or next to, the haptic logic of neighboring, is anathema to a Puritan hermeneutics that wishes to ground itself within the modalities of allegory, as opposed to the symbolic. Interpreter fleshes out this reading for us by turning away from neighbor as a social category or designation and instead focusing on neighbor as a strictly spatial concept or relationship independent of that which is being related. Bunyan does this in order to underscore that it is not the moral fiber of one's neighbor that needs to be assessed. Nor is he suggesting that one should not act in a Christian fashion toward those that live near us. Rather, what is subject to critique here is a sociology of Christian community that conflates a certain kind of spatial reasoning with spiritual matters. While neighbors function primarily as a spatial marker in Interpreter's homily as opposed to a social category, as was the case with Christian and Pliable, I wish to suggest that the term "neighbor" serves both purposes in *The Pilgrim's Progress*. It allows Bunyan and his reader to move allegorically between the spatial and the social in order arrive at a notion of Christian community that does not merely resist the pressures of temporal-spatial thinking but, in some sense, gains a control and mastery over how time and space are ordered, divided up, and meted out, a remapping as opposed to an outright rejection of or resistance to spatiality. The denigration, or trivialization, of time and space, while certainly a predominant theme in Christian thought broadly speaking, does not seem to resonate when viewed in the light of Bunyan's preference for and extended defense of allegory.[40]

My central claim here is that we must not view Bunyan's use of allegory as a way of getting us out of spatial matters, as Fish would have it, but rather as a mode of signification that will order and redistribute space in particular ways that perhaps contradict or resist a hegemonic Cartesian logic and its role in the consolidation of the English state.[41] James Turner has argued that Bunyan's use of the allegorical dreamscape represents a direct challenge to the homogenizing effects of Newtonian and Cartesian conceptions of space, whose advent is often linked to the neoclassical preference for realism.[42] This understanding of Bunyan and his work has perhaps been occluded or ignored to some extent as a result of the critical devaluation of allegory throughout the eighteenth and nineteenth centuries, the legacy of which unfortunately still remains with us today.[43] However, to examine Bunyan from a more historicized vantage point reveals a figure actively engaged in the organization of Dissent and the realization of grace within its godly community. As an allegory of space, *The Pilgrim's Progress* does not require its reader either to dismiss or to transcend a certain spatial logic that is ostensibly secular in nature. Rather, a proper understanding of the cosmos and humanity's place within it cannot be achieved apart from a discourse about lived space, the language of roads and ways, hedges, and walls. What allegory makes possible, then, is a spatialization of the divine, a theography if you will, and, conversely, the transformation of the space of everyday life into the constitutive grounds for God's elect on earth. This is critical to Bunyan's project of addressing both the matters of the soul and the more immediate challenges to religious community in the face of intolerance and political repression.

## A Map of Salvation and Damnation

To suggest that Bunyan was not concerned with the politics and economy of space simply fails to take into account the history and the geography of Dissent during the Restoration. If the parish system can be said to constitute a spatialization of civil and ecclesiastical power, the means by which state and church integrated the local and managed the polity, then Dissent might be seen not as a mere theological or political challenge to hegemony but rather as an effective counterspace, a "geography of resistance" to borrow Steve Pile's terminology.[44] While it is true that Puritans, Methodists, Presbyterians, Ranters, and Quakers presented anything but a unified front during Bunyan's lifetime, Charles II and Parliament's attempts to locate and pacify radicalized congregations, as well as restrict the mobility of itinerant preachers, point to a general concern with both physical and ideological transgressions of the parish borders. In response, Bunyan became an active proponent of organizing Dissenting congregations and communities in a manner that he hoped could weather the vicissitudes of religious intolerance that mark late seventeenth-century England. As Richard Greaves notes, Bunyan and his fellow clergy were quite cognizant of the need to organize given the geographic constraints placed on their activities, including Bunyan's own imprisonment from roughly 1660 to 1672.[45] Greaves documents this systematic response to repression and intolerance in Bedfordshire, Bunyan's home county, despite the fact that, ironically, the bulk of this activity occurred while Bunyan himself was in jail. He had been arrested in 1660 while preaching in an open-air meeting and prosecuted under the act of 1593, For Retaining the Queen's Subjects in their due Obedience, which had been extended to include preaching without a license.[46] While the plan to create "a network of preachers and teachers in the local villages" throughout Bedfordshire was essentially worked out during these years of imprisonment, it was not actually implemented until 1672 when Bunyan was freed by a royal pardon.

The overall intention was basically to organize Dissent in the hopes of not only strengthening and consolidating religious community but also guaranteeing in some sense that they would be able to survive well into the future, irrespective of the political ups and downs that future may bring. Its lasting impact would be a framework in which the ministerial work of nonconformist preachers could be carried out, allowing them to move freely between congregations, often crossing parish and county boundaries to do so. Such mobility was instrumental in terms of their ability to service communities that were either remote or had relatively small populations. It also provided preachers to areas where perhaps the local minister had been imprisoned for whatever infraction of the law. Most importantly, Greaves suggests, the organizational imperative that drove Bunyan helped prepare the way for gains made after 1688: "The repressive policies of Archbishop Sheldon and his Tory-Anglican supporters had only served to provoke imprisoned Nonconformists to respond with a more effective organizational plan that strengthened the roots of the movement at the local level. The toleration that finally came on a permanent basis in 1689 was in part an implicit recognition that this organizational re-sponse had been successful."[47] Greaves admits that Bedfordshire, while not alone, was perhaps a shining example of this organizational response because it is the "best documented." Still, his assertion that the systematization and routinization of Dissent on the local level played a decisive role, or was at least a critical factor, in the Glorious Revolution remains valid.

Like Greaves, Christopher Hill sees the activities of Bunyan and other Dis-senters during the Restoration as formative in terms of the changes that would follow after 1688. The real legacy of Dissent, in Hill's estimation, is the local and communitarian ethos that informed the ways in which these congrega-tions distributed authority and deliberative power internally and redefined their relationship to the nation through various organizational efforts, such as Bunyan's own projects in Bedfordshire. A probable influence on Bunyan in this regard was Paul Hobson's *A Garden Inclosed: and Wisdom Justified only of her Children* (1647), which advanced a vision of religious community as autonomous and self-sufficient. As Christopher Hill describes it, "Such a church can only be a small group: The Church of England with its parishes, by contrast, was no garden but a 'confused wilderness.' More special fruit grew in the enclosed garden, more care was taken of it by special watching; it gave 'sweet refreshings,' and Christ took satisfaction and content in it."[48] While Hobson was more antinomian and ecumenical in his own religious practice, Bunyan was, nevertheless, sympathetic to many of his ideas and incorporated into many of his own sermons the image of the congregation as garden. Such an image, however, was to be construed as neither pastoral nor utopian but rather a highly politicized way of demarcating the space of the congregation, the necessary borders circumscribing the community of grace. The garden was not an idyllic place but, given the changing nature of property relations during the seventeenth century, more like a forceful, if not violent, act of enclosure; it is the garden appropriated as opposed to the garden deferred, or the millen-nial landscape.

The garden provided an image of a small and intimate community guided by the experience of grace and made visible through good works and neigh-borly acts. As Bunyan states in the opening epistle of his *Christian Behaviour*, "When Christians stand every one in their places, and do the work of their Relations, then they are like flowers in the Garden, that stand and grow where the Gardner hath planted them, and then they shall both honour the Garden

in which they are planted, and the Gardner that hath so disposed of them."[49]
Bunyan deploys the garden imagery to make the connection between Christian community and the need for good works: "Christians are like flowers in
the garden. . . . They have upon each of them the dew of heaven, which being
shaken with the wind, let fall their dew at each other's roots, whereby they are
jointly nourished, and become nourishers of one another."[50] Dew, flowers, and
soil commingle as a single organic unit. The orderliness of the garden is predicated on this naturalized depiction of the ideal relationship between grace and
works; in marking off a space for Christian community, the garden suggests a
certain equipoise whereby grace and works are as much a function of natural
law as they are God's law, as if there were no difference. This looking within constituted a form of political resistance that engendered other ways of imagining
and representing space in response. The democratic spirit that emerged from
these "voluntary communities of the godly," Hill maintains, should be viewed in
the light of the revolutionary movements of the following century, which were
perhaps the logical extension of this egalitarian vision: "The appeal of Bunyan's
dream to the second-class citizens who were English dissenters, American colonists French Huguenots, Welsh peasants under English-speaking landlords,
Polish peasants in Germany, and to colonial peoples, suggests a common factor: the divisions between the rich and powerful on the one hand, subject poor
and native people's on the other. *The Pilgrim's Progress* is the epic of dissent
which grew out of and discarded the revolutionary radicalism of the 1640s and
1650s but retained much of its popular ideology."[51] The geography of Dissent
emerges as a response to both the repressive policies of the state and the forces
of capital that dispossessed entire rural communities as the land itself was
converted into private property.[52] Bunyan's garden evokes an Edenic setting
in which the establishment of true religious community may unfold, yet the
image also provides a critique of the often brutal nature of the Enclosure Acts,
or the Garden privatized, as it were.

Bunyan's notion of Christian community was composed primarily of those
who benefited least from the tide of capitalist accumulation in the form of
private property. The demise of the traditional village community was precipitated by these varying and often conflicting socioeconomic forces, demanding, for Bunyan in particular, a reconceptualization of just what community
might mean in a world where privatization was increasingly the rule. Bunyan's
emphasis on charity, the rights of the poor, and "good neighborhood," then,
are rightly construed as attempts to accommodate capitalism; they are reac-
tions that point to Bunyan's awareness of class and the deep divisions that the
agrarian revolution of the seventeenth century produced. In his biography of
Bunyan, *A Tinker and a Poor Man*, Christopher Hill argues that Bunyan was
cognizant of the burden the advent of private property placed on the poor
and dispossessed, many of whom were active members of his congregation
in Bedford:

The abolition of feudal tenures in 1645 (confirmed 1656 and 1660) had established absolute property rights for the gentry in their lands, but no such security of tenure for copyholders, lesser landholders. So the agricultural revolution of the later seventeenth century was made at the expense of tenants who could now be more easily evicted when this was convenient for their landlord. Traditional customary rights beneficial to the peasantry were being eroded. All these developments imposed new stresses on relations between rich and poor, those whose property rights were protected by law and those whose customary rights were ceasing to be legally enforceable. Of these strains Bunyan was very much aware: and his sympathies were wholeheartedly with the poor.[53]

Bunyan himself had born witness to many of these depredations firsthand. During the Interregnum, the selling-off of crown lands placed a substantial amount of property in private hands, mostly that of London's merchant class, in order to mobilize capital that was otherwise tied up in what was perceived to be uncultivated and undeveloped land. Estates owned by Royalists and the church were targeted through a number of techniques such as racking of rents, sequestration, raising of fines, enclosure, and outright confiscation, all of which succeeded in transferring large amounts of wealth from the landed aristocracy to a nascent gentry who were much more interested in immediate capital that could readily be invested in other projects. The destruction of the older lord-tenant relationship gave way to a new and very different relationship to the land, one in which private property increasingly became both a fundamental generator of wealth and capital for the individual owner as well as the nation as a whole and the founding principle of legitimate political authority, most notably in the writings of John Locke.[54] In short, the emergence of private property was coeval with the notion of government whose primary responsibility was to protect that property, or as Hill puts it, "England was made safe for commercialism."[55]

The narrative Hill presents here is valid for the most part as is his assertion that Bunyan consistently displays a certain degree of "class awareness" in many works, especially in *The Pilgrim's Progress*, where evil and malicious characters often take on the guise of the new gentry and the poor and downtrodden are portrayed as good and righteous. However, I would extend this thesis to suggest that surveying and mapping were also targets of Bunyan's opposition to the institutionalization of private property. Given his underclass status, he was perhaps sensitive to the elisions and expulsions required to construct this uniform, homogeneous space. As someone who was not a property holder and whose career as a mechanic preacher required him to travel extensively (when he was not in prison), it is easy to conclude, as Fish does, that Bunyan was critical of place to the point of utterly rejecting it, and spatiality in general, as the mere product of carnal rationality. Theologically speaking, mapping and surveying appear not only as technologies of exclusion; they also represent the desire to master the world and should rightly be construed as a temptation that can only lead to damnation. However, as I have suggested earlier, Bunyan is not presenting an antiprogress or a picaresque undoing of time and space. Rather, his vision of the neighborhood represents a "fresh space" engendered by an increasing sense of alienation from the land and the subsequent need to *produce* spaces that reconceptualize and reconfigure the subject's relation to that land; it is a place that, in contrast to the cosmopolitan or "worldly" ethos of the new merchant class, offers an alternative understanding and construction of time and space that is perhaps critical of hegemonic modes of representation (cartography for one) that wish to carve up and order space in ways that will service the nation yet fail to account for moral and religious truths. Thus, it is not space qua space that is the object of Bunyan's critique. Rather, it is rather a particular technology of space, albeit a dominant one, which does not recognize or allow for the community of the godly.

Bunyan's clearest articulation of this position appears in his *Mapp Shewing the Order & Causes of Salvation & Damnation* (1663), which is less a map than it is a lesson about the provisional nature of maps (fig. 1).[56] The diagram is split down the middle by "The passage into and out the world" with the world on the bottom and the Holy Trinity at the top. On either side of the divide, we find two separate paths, one for those who are saved, or "the line of Grace," and the other for those who are damned, or "the line of Justice." Each path or line is depicted as a series of connected circles and boxes that contain some bit of scripture relevant to that particular progression, and in the areas outside of those bounded spaces are free-floating scraps of text which gloss and comment on the scriptural passage. The *Mapp* thus invokes cartographic space yet stands against the map by emphasizing its textual dimension and the need for reading and interpretation; rather than present the viewer with an image to be passively consumed, Bunyan requires his reader to confront this allegorical space through words that are Janus-faced in that they are simultaneously both image and text. The goal, however, is the ability to distinguish the one function from the other, to recognize the image as useful but ultimately subservient to the written word. The image is only purposeful insofar as one is an attentive reader.

We see this problematic restaged in *The Pilgrim's Progress* where Bunyan literalizes the cartographic toponym by affixing the name "Difficulty" to a hill Christian must contend with: "but the narrow way lay right up the Hill, (and the name of the going up the side of the Hill, is called *Difficulty*.)"[57] The "difficult" path, of course, is the correct path, but what is interesting here is Bunyan's decision to inscribe the name of the place on the landscape itself. Christian encounters a variety of locations, all of which bear some allegorical designation: the Slough of Despond, the country of Coveting, the Mountain of Error. While the name reveals the nature of the evils to be found there, Bunyan resists

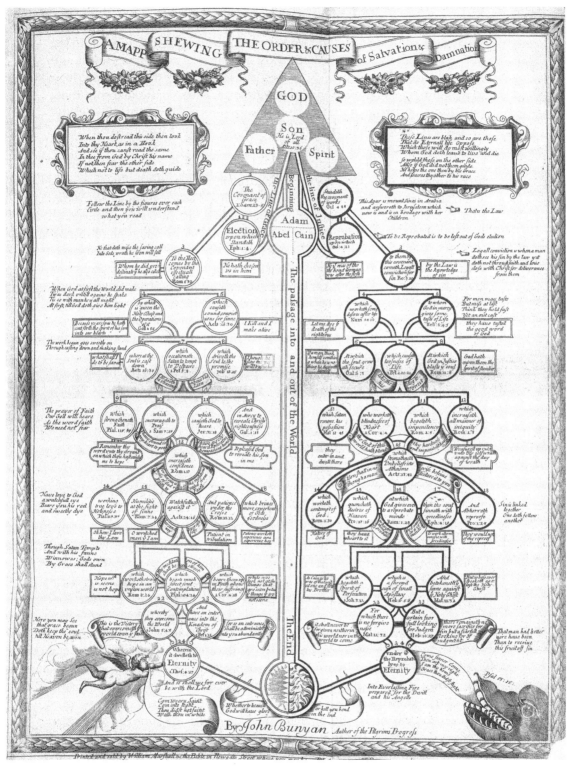

FIGURE 1. *Mapp Shewing the Order & Causes of Salvation & Damnation*, John Bunyan, 1663. (© The British Library Board, shelfmark General Reference Collection 697.m.17)

making the name manifest and legible within the progress; however, with the Hill of Difficulty, we encounter the name as a physical element of the hill, as if one could actually walk over the letters. Bunyan satirizes the toponymic logic of the cartographic projection in that Christian, when confronted with those very letters, understands that this is the way to proceed because his knowledge of scripture informs him that the "difficult" way is the path to righteousness. The false pilgrim places too much stock in the literal value of the toponym, but Christian is neither persuaded nor dissuaded by this encounter. Rather, his motivations are located elsewhere. The toponym rides the line between text and image, a potential problem for Bunyan in that it fails to distinguish the one from the other. In short, the map threatens to extinguish its own textuality and, consequently, to offer a representation of the world and a definition of spatiality that is wholly consumed by the pictorial. Bunyan underscores the dangers and the limitations of the toponym in *The Pilgrim's Progress* by emphasizing its graphic quality. At the same time, he insists on an allegorical understanding of space that would perhaps offer a different relationship between text and image, one that insisted on their interdependence rather than their simultaneity.

Bunyan's *Mapp* deploys this hermeneutic frame by, once again, courting the pictorial logic inherent in any text yet subverting that logic as essentially inadequate for deciphering the Word of God.[58] He warns at the top of the page, "These Lines are blak and so are those / That do Eternall Life Oppose / Which those will do most wittingly / Whom God doth leave to live and die." Not coincidentally, this warning appears above the side that depicts the "line of Justice," reinforcing the connection between the blackness of the inscription on the page and the dark, malignant nature of those without grace. The move from the graphic quality of the words to the profligate reader is further reinforced by outlining the circles on that side of the map with a solid black line, while those on the other side, the line of Grace, are merely inscribed with two concentric circles, the space between which remains blank. The difference suggests a degree of permeability, that these borders are properly not borders at all. Rather, the Christian reader understands that the iconography of Bunyan's *Mapp* must be read in light of the scriptural content found within each circle while the map itself always remains bracketed in some sense. However, it is critical to remember that Bunyan is not advocating that the map or the diagram be done away with altogether. Recall that Bunyan's reliance on allegory represents neither a wholesale embracing of the spatial nor a desire to get out of the spatial. Rather, allegory is a particular mode of representation that offers its own way of organizing space that must come to terms with the image, despite the problems it raises. Bunyan recognizes the imagistic properties that inhere in any given text, and, given that realization, he sets out to theorize their proper relationship. The problem to be addressed is neatly summarized in a small note on the right margin of the *Mapp*: "Sin is linked together / One doth follow another." The idea here is not simply that sin breeds sin or that sin can always be traced back through some causal chain. Rather, linking together, in and of itself, is a sinful act; to invest oneself in the idea that links are something real and tangible is to sin. The literalization of these links within the *Mapp* is formally expressed as a heavy, dark line while the provisional and allegorical sense of linking is represented with the hollowed-out line. The lesson here is much the same as the one we encountered in the stories of Pliable and Mercy, where Pliable places undue weight on the physical proximity of neighbors. He assumes a link between himself and Christian, his neighbor, to be manifest, yet his reasoning is faulty, a marker of false grace. Therefore, it is reasonable to conclude that Pliable's logic is also part and parcel of a cartographic logic that emphasizes continuity and contiguity at the expense of differential or relational theories of space, among which I would include the notion of allegorical space and Bunyan's neighborhood in particular.

The many spatial inconsistencies and contradictions that inhere in a text such as *The Pilgrim's Progress* are then more than just the outward manifestation of the dreamer's interior states. They are the embodiment and product of the very contradictions between the space of the New Science, including the Cartesian grid and Newton's absolute space, and an older, Christian model of space as a rigid and fixed hierarchy of formal correspondences between heaven and earth, or what I am calling allegorical space. It would be incorrect, however, to view this conflict as a displacement of one mode of representation with another or that Bunyan is narrating their possible synthesis. Rather, I would argue that *The Pilgrim's Progress* is invested in allegory as a way of organizing space that stands in sharp contrast to the cartographic projection. A text such as *The Pilgrim's Progress* not only takes this conflict as its content, it also dramatizes the limitations of the former by adopting the modalities of allegory so that this thematic is then recapitulated at the formal level. Allegory thus opens up the possibility of discontinuity and difference within a system that seeks to paper over the disparities and uneven developments engendered by capitalism and becomes something like a formal analog of uneven development between the literal and the figurative, between physical and abstract space. Allegory simultaneously produces and is a means of articulating a vision of the local that is bounded and separate from the national body and a conception of neighbors and neighborhoods that is not predicated on the notion of contiguity, an essential feature of this tendency toward homogenization. Rather, proximity, the rhetoric of contiguity, is conceptualized as a nearness not reducible to a map or any other two-dimensional representation; these neighboring bodies cannot be located in any formal sense of the word, yet they are neighboring nevertheless. The neighborhood in seventeenth-century England opens up the possibility of a new kind of space, one that is relational and fiercely local yet necessarily fails to fully inscribe itself in the landscape. It eludes becoming a thing in and of itself while simultaneously organizing a space against which the material practices of everyday life may unfold. This schema is neither aspatial nor apolitical but is a manifestation of a particular politics of space whose relevance is to be found not only within the Dissenting churches of the Restoration but also, to varying degrees, within the political and social movements of the following century.

# 2

# Aphra Behn and the Colonial Scene

Wouldst thou the map of slavery survey,
And the dire circuit of trade display,
Dart thy astonish'd eye o'er distant land,
From Senegal to Gambia's burning sands,
Pursue the blushing lines to Congo's shore,
Then traverse many a league, Benguela o'er,
Career immense! o'er which the merchant reigns,
And drags reluctant MILLIONS in chains!

—SAMUEL JACKSON PRATT,
*Humanity; or, The Rights of Nature* (1788)

## SURVEYING THE MAP OF SLAVERY

As we saw in the previous chapter, Bunyan's neighborhood constitutes a heterotopic site within the landscape of seventeenth-century Britain precisely because it exists in tension with more hegemonic forms of geographic and demographic representation that further the interests and power of the state. It is this tension that defines the neighborhood as a simultaneously real and imagined space whose identity is forged against the map and, by extension, an overweening state apparatus bent on denying Dissent a place within that national landscape. The neighborhood, however, represents only one such instance, among many, in the production of heterotopic spaces that resist or are, in some way, antagonistic toward the map. I would like to examine then, in the following chapter, the ways in which the British stage, and specifically, the mechanics and architecture of the scenic stage, informs Aphra Behn's representation of the Atlantic world and the British slave trade in her 1688 novel, *Oroonoko, or The Royal Slave* (1688). Behn's conception of the "scene," as both theatrical device and as an actual place in the world, offers yet another heterotopic site of resistance to the mapping of Britain's colonial possessions and the various routes that connect them to one another, otherwise known as the triangular trade between England, Africa, and the Americas. The map as an instrument of state power plays an equal role here with respect to its function in the previous chapter; it is a means of subjugating marginalized or recalcitrant populations to the totalizing standard of the cartographic projection and so bring them to heel. This power, as we will see, was exercised not only at home within the imperial center but also on its colonial margins with respect to Britain's expanding slave trade throughout the so-called Atlantic world. As I will argue, Behn challenges the map as an adequate spatial paradigm for understanding and representing the colonial project given its alignment with the interests of the state and those engaged in the slave trade itself. Against the map, she offers in its stead the technologies and modalities of the scenic stage, such as shutters, wings, drop curtains, and discovery areas, as a way of framing her narrative of Oroonoko's enslavement and transportation to a plantation in Surinam and his tragic demise while in captivity there. The colonial scene, in this sense, offers a more fragmented and divided sense of Britain's imperial geography than the map can otherwise afford.

As Samuel Jackson Pratt recognizes in his poem of 1788, with which I began this chapter, the map is intimately bound up with the institution of slavery as a technology that enables the domination and exploitation of the African continent by merchants, agents, and seamen of various national origins. He well understood that the history of cartography and that of the slave trade cannot rightfully be separated from one another given that maps play such a pivotal role in opening up the Atlantic world to commerce and trade throughout the seventeenth and eighteenth centuries and, by extension, the traffic in African bodies across that geography. To read or survey the "map of slavery," in this regard, is to make visible the horrors of the slave trade in a way that perhaps no other medium quite could. Rather than an objective or neutral representation of the territory in question, Pratt's map is suffused with emotion and affect as the reader's "astonish'd" eye observes the "burning" sands of Gambia and the "blushing" lines of the Congo and then follows this "dire circuit of trade" that connects Africa's so-called "slave" and "gold" coasts to Europe and the Americas, or as it came to be known during the eighteenth century, the triangular trade. Most importantly perhaps, we see something frequently absent from maps of Africa and the Atlantic world during this period: actual slaves in chains, a detail that Pratt includes for obvious reasons given the abolitionist intent of his poem. By placing the figure of the slave within the frame of his map, as well as the merchant who "reigns" over this territory, Pratt exposes the unstated purpose behind maps that made the slave trade possible in the first place; his metaphorical "map of slavery" is thus a satirical gesture to the very real and historical associations between cartography and slavery that, as I will argue, date back to at least the mid-seventeenth century when Europeans first began to transform Africa and the Americas into objects of colonial appropriation and possession.

Pratt's desire to reintroduce the figure of the slave into his particular map of slavery represents something of a parodic inversion of many seventeenth-century maps that included slaves and native inhabitants as a regular feature of the imperial landscape. A substantial number of these maps were produced and distributed by Dutch cartographers, whose work was seen as vital to Holland's increasing involvement in the slave trade and colonial exploration around mid-century. For example, Frans Post and Georg Marggraf's 1640 map "Praefecturae Paranambucae pars Borealis" offers an image of one of Holland's most productive colonies at that time, Pernambuco, which is situated on the northeastern coast of Brazil (fig. 2). The map generally limits its scope to the coastline and the many rivers that extend from the interior toward the ocean, to which are affixed toponyms demarcating the numerous settlements, plantations, and factories associated with Pernambuco's thriving sugar industry and, of course, the slaves that made their success possible. In order to further underscore that link, the map pictorially represents one of the Dutch sugar plantations in the

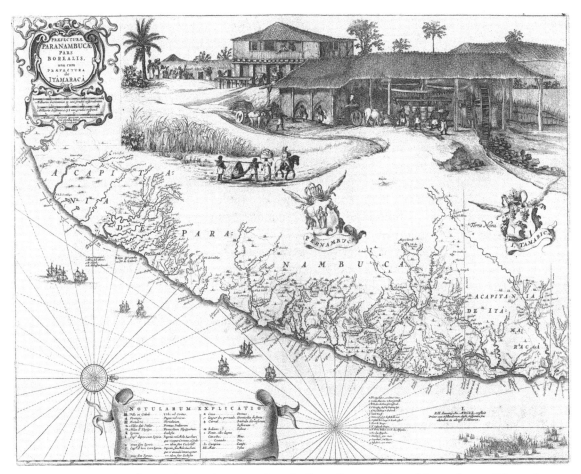

FIGURE 2. *Praefecturae Paranambucae pars Borealis*, Frans Post and Georg Marggraf, 1640. (Harvard Map Collection, Harvard Library)

upper left-hand corner where the Brazilian interior would otherwise be depicted. Rather than provide that detail, most likely because such information
was either unavailable or nonexistent at the time, the mapmakers chose instead
to fill the space (which is quite large indeed) with a colorful and no doubt idealized portrait of life on a typical Dutch sugar plantation, including slaves working the mill, transporting the planter's wife in a hammock, and what appears
to be celebratory or ritualistic dancing of some sort in front of the great house.
Unlike the cartographically rendered image of Pernambuco's coast and rivers,
the pastoral scene provides no discernible pragmatic function but appears to
be mostly ornamental in nature, typical for maps at this time. Nevertheless, its
inclusion does reveal an imperial ideology in which slaves are viewed as a natural part of the landscape, working peacefully and in harmony with one another,
their masters, and the land itself. Post and Marggraf's map thus legitimates the
use of slaves by placing the cartographic projection of Pernambuco alongside
an idyllic picture of plantation life, as if the two were somehow commensurate
with one another.

These accompanying images of a productive and well-heeled slave economy,
as I am suggesting, are more than ornamental flourish. Rather, they are keys
to guide our reading of the map as the expression of national sovereignty over
foreign peoples and their land. The deployment of native bodies in maps associated with the Atlantic slave trade can likewise be found in Joan Blaeu's prodigious *Atlas Major, sive Cosmographia Blaviana* (1662–65), an eleven-volume
work encompassing Africa, the Americas, the Arctic, Europe, and Asia. Blaeu
had served as the official cartographer for the Dutch East India Company,
taking the position from his father Willem Janszoon Blaeu following his death
in 1638, and many of the 596 maps included in the atlas were based on surveys
made either by himself or his father while in its service. Volume 9 of the atlas, for example, contains a map of Guinea that had originally been engraved
and published by Willem Blaeu in 1635 and afterward appeared in a variety
of incarnations and formats throughout the century, including John Ogilby's
*Africa* (1670) and Olfert Dapper's *Description de l'Afrique* (1686).[1] Like the
map depicting Pernambuco, Blaeu's map delineates places, rivers, and other
geographic features along the coast where trade and commerce were largely
conducted, while the interior remains empty for the most part, save for the
occasional image of an elephant, lion, and mountain range (fig. 3). Blaeu does
manage to incorporate colored boundary markers to highlight the surrounding
African nations, but as before, the emphasis here is on Guinea as a site of commercial activity, a fact underscored by the inclusion of ships just off the coast
as well as rhumb lines and a compass rose for the purposes of navigation. At
the bottom of the map, Blaeu provides the title for his map, simply "Guinea,"
embedded in an ornate cartouche and surrounded by a pair of half-naked African males on either side and a trio of monkeys. In a telling detail, the mon-
key sitting atop the cartouche possesses a strangely human face, suggesting a

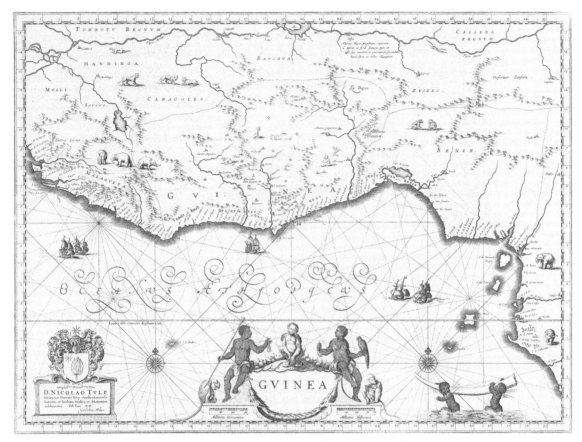

FIGURE 3. "Guinea," Joan Blaeu, 1662. (Harvard Map Collection, Harvard Library)

degree of affinity between the savage Africans and the animals inhabiting that continent. To the right of the cartouche are two African children holding up a large ivory tusk, a valuable commodity sought by many traders. The inclusion of such figures in the margins of seventeenth-century Dutch maps, however, was not limited to the work of Willem and Joan Blaeu but can be found in any number of maps from the period, including, among others, Olfert Dapper's "Nigritarum Regio" (1668), Frederik de Wit's "Totius Africae Accuratissima Tabula" (1680), and John Overton and Philip Lea's "A New Mapp of Africa divided into Kingdom and Provinces" (1687), all of which depict not only natives and animals, as in Blaeu's map, but European traders, merchants, and explorers as well.[2]

While atlases, such as those of Blaeu, were expensive productions available to a limited number of people, their work was often copied, plagiarized, and liberally borrowed from in order to create maps affordable to more pedestrian audiences, including merchants and traders who valued the information they contained above their artistic merits or ideological function. On a utilitar-

ian level, these maps helped to facilitate trade and commercial activity across
the Atlantic world, including the movement of slaves between Africa and the
Americas. In turn, topographic and hydrological information obtained by those
directly involved in the slave trade served as the basis for maps of Africa and
the Americas throughout the seventeenth and eighteenth centuries. Many of
the most prominent mapmakers of the period, in fact, never even set foot in the
territory in question but instead relied on either preexisting maps or the re-
ports and surveys of someone who had direct firsthand knowledge of a given
place, or some combination thereof. John Ogilby's *America: Being the Latest,
and Most Accurate Description of the New World* (1671), for instance, is little
more than an English translation of a Dutch work published that same year,
Arnoldus Montanus's *De nieuwe en onbekende Weereld* (1671), yet while much
of Ogilby's atlas remains faithful to Montanus's original, he does manage to include newer material culled from recent surveys of English colonies, including
maps of the Carolinas, Maryland, Jamaica, and Barbados. Despite never having
visited these places, Ogilby nevertheless produced maps based on information
provided by unidentified sources who were more likely than not implicated in,
if not at least cognizant of, the slave trade.[3] For example, Ogilby prefaces the
section on the islands of North America with a map entitled "Insulae Americanae in Oceano Septentrionale, cum terris adiacentibus," which offers numerous images of slaves working in both the upper-left- and lower-right-hand
corners of the map (fig. 4).[4] Similarly, his map of Barbados, which is included
in this section, not only depicts an outline of the coast, some basic topographical features, and the names of settlements and rivers but also provides images
of slaves laboring on a plantation in order to fill the otherwise empty space of
the island's interior (fig. 5).[5] The description accompanying the map is likewise
brief, but Ogilby does mention, in critical fashion, that English plantations on
Barbados are routinely "molested by the Caribbeeans of Dominico."[6]

A more comprehensive survey of Barbados and its relationship to the slave
trade can be found in Richard Ligon's *A True and Exact History of the Island
of Barbados* (1657), which incorporates a wealth of information regarding the
geography and natural history of Barbados along with a map of the island, illustrations of local plants and vegetation, numerical tables detailing the expenses
of a sugar plantation, and plans of the mills and other structures necessary
to the processing of sugarcane.[7] Ligon's map, "A topographicall Description
and Admeasurement of the Yland of Barbados in the West Indyaes with mrs.
names of the seuerall platacons," is rendered simply in black and white with no
particular royal or national icons and symbols (fig. 6). However, in the center
of the map, he does overlay a bit of text on a parcel of land in order to identify
its proper owners: "The tenn Thousande Acres of Lande which Belongeth to
the Merchants of London." Along the coast, ports are indicated along with the
requisite image of ships to signify robust commercial activity, and toponyms
mark the locations of the many plantations and settlements on Barbados. In

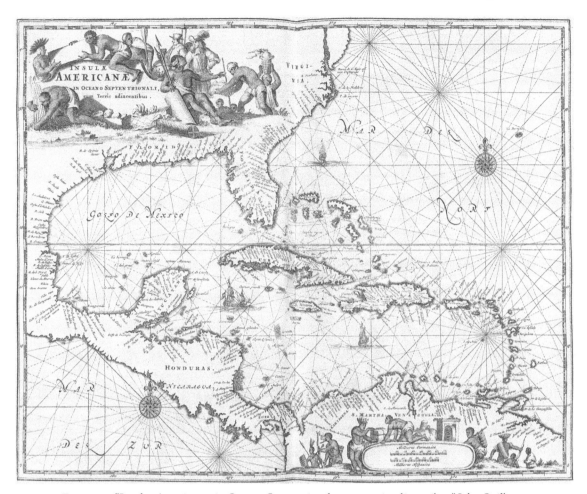

FIGURE 4. "Insulae Americanae in Oceano Septentrionale, cum terris adiacentibus," John Ogilby, 1671. (Lawrence H. Slaughter Collection, The Lionel Pincus and Princess Firyal Map Division, New York Public Library, Astor, Lenox and Tilden Foundations)

addition, we see images scattered across the island depicting rivers and mountains, various kinds of livestock, animals transporting goods and materials, landowners on horseback, and like Ogilby's map, slaves working the land. In a telling image in the upper left corner of the map, Ligon reveals a man on horseback with what appears to be a whip of some sort in his hand, chasing down two slaves who are running away from him for obvious reasons. The detail is suggestive of Pratt's mapping in its depiction of the realities of slavery, though of course, in this instance, Ligon is more concerned with providing a degree of empirical accuracy rather than an abolitionist polemic, slavery illustrated as opposed to slavery decried. Nevertheless, I juxtapose Pratt's poem against the maps of Post and Marggraf, Blaeu, Ogilby, and Ligon in order to highlight the fact that such images of the slave trade all but disappear from maps during the eighteenth century when the slave trade was at its peak, hence Pratt's need to reinsert the figure of the slave back into his poetic mapping of the Atlantic world. Pratt strategically puts back what had been removed in order to remind his reader of the historical connection between cartography and slavery.

Of course, not all seventeenth-century maps depicting the geography of the Atlantic world necessarily included images of slaves. Robert Morden's map of Barbados in his *Geography Rectified: or, A Description of the World* (1688) presents a much more complete accounting of the island, including the interior, than either Ogilby or Ligon and is entirely devoid of extraneous or marginal images of any kind. Similarly, Moses Pitt's map of the Atlantic in his *Nova*

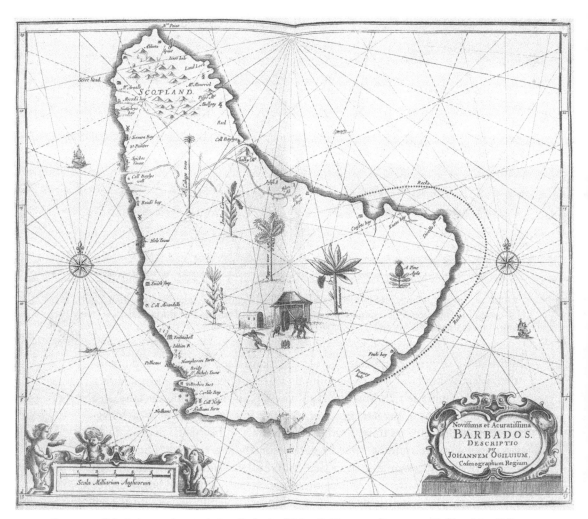

FIGURE 5. "Novissima et Accuratissima Barbados," John Ogilby, 1671. (Lawrence H. Slaughter Collection, Lionel Pincus and Princess Firyal Map Division, New York Public Library, Astor, Lenox, and Tilden Foundations)

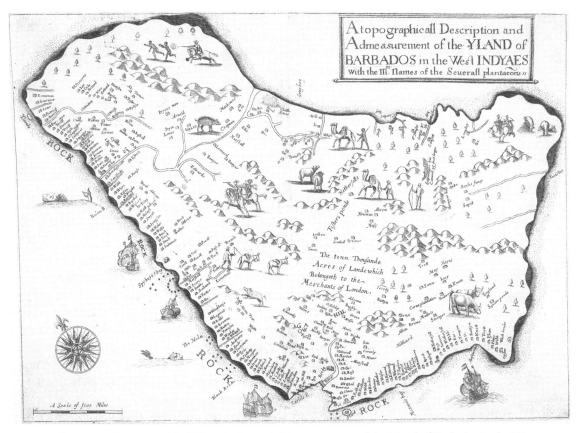

FIGURE 6. "A topographicall Description and Admeasurement of the Yland of Barbados in the West Indyaes with mrs. names of the seuerall platacons," Richard Ligon, 1657. (© The British Library Board, shelfmark K.Top.123)

*Totius Terrarum Orbis Geographica* (1680) hews to standards of cartographic objectivity and accuracy more in keeping with the eighteenth century when maps of this variety were increasingly the norm. Conversely, some eighteenth-century maps of Africa and the Americas contain images and details more in keeping with cartographic practices of the previous century, such as Captain John Leach's "A Map of the River Gambra from its Mouth to Eropina" (1732), which focuses on trade along the river and includes the standard cartouche with a native and an elephant.[8] However, despite the lack of a precise or neat divide separating seventeenth- and eighteenth-century mappings of the slave trade, we can still discern a general turn from a pictorial approach that directly represents figures associated with slavery and colonial trade in general to a more abstract, geometrically based mode of cartographic representation that largely eschews such ornamentation. This removal of the signs and symbols of empire, however, does not signal a lack of interest in mapping the slave trade; rather, it marks, somewhat paradoxically, Britain's expanding investment in surveying and knowing its geography in an increasingly rigorous and objective fashion.

We can see this transformation quite starkly in the hydrological charts of the popular sea atlas *The English Pilot* (1671–1701), which manifests elements of both cartographic traditions over the course of its lengthy publication history.[9] The first three books of *The English Pilot*, which cover Britain and northern Europe (1671), the Mediterranean (1672), and the Orient (1675) respectively, were published by John Seller, who, as official hydrographer to His Majesty, was also responsible for a number of sea atlases, including *The Coasting Pilot* (1673), *Atlas Maritimus* (1675), and *Hydrographia Universalis* (1690), each of which were critical to the expansion of Britain's naval power and its control over trade and commerce across the Atlantic during the latter half of the seventeenth century. However, due to Seller's financial difficulties and declining health, the fourth book of *The English Pilot* detailing the Americas was completed and published by John Thornton and William Fisher in 1689. A fifth book bearing the same title and containing maps of Africa's coasts was subsequently issued in 1701 by Charles Price and Jeremiah Seller, the son of John Seller, who had died in 1697. As a result of these changes in ownership, numerous emendations and revisions to the maps, some small and others more significant, were made to reflect the expanding base of geographic and hydrological knowledge available to mapmakers as well as improvements in methods and technologies of surveying. These changes resulted not only in more accurate maps but also, it is important note, the erasure of the native, or indigenous, peoples from the map, thus reflecting a cartographic sensibility quite different from Seller's original efforts. For example, the fourth book of *The English Pilot*, which covers the seas, coasts, rivers, and harbors of North America and the Caribbean, includes at the outset a map, "A General Chart of the West India's," that depicts the entire Atlantic and its adjacent land masses (fig. 7). The title of the map is embossed on a tapestry that hangs over one side of a large, intimidating elephant whose likeness covers most of northern Africa, and riding atop the elephant in an equally enormous saddle, there are a group of bow-and-arrow-wielding "savages" to signify that continent's inhabitants. However, in a subsequent edition of that same text published in 1706, the map has been replaced by another projection, "A Generall Chart for the West Indies," which bears many similarities to the former save for the minor change in the title and the now absent cartouche depicting the elephant and the natives; the map, in fact, contains no extraneous or marginal images whatsoever (fig. 8).

This latter version is most likely based on a map published a few years prior, Jeremiah Seller and Charles Price's "A New Generall Chart for the West Indies" (1703), which was engraved by the prominent and influential eighteenth-century mapmaker Herman Moll. Perhaps more than any other cartographer of his day, Moll was responsible for deepening the already existing ties between mapping and trade, and the slave trade in particular. However, despite the fact

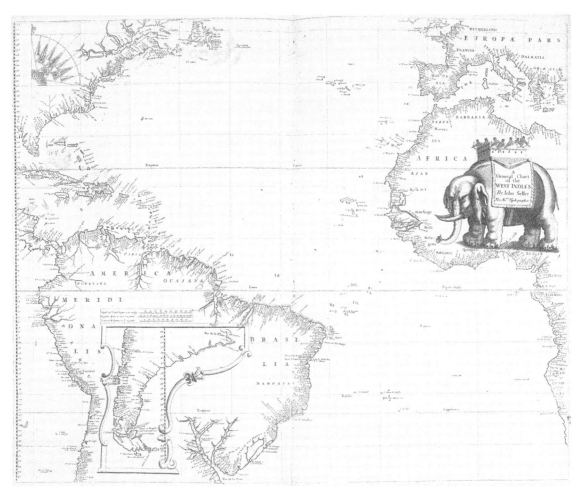

FIGURE 7. "A General Chart of the West India's," John Thornton, 1698. (Lawrence H. Slaughter Collection, Lionel Pincus and Princess Firyal Map Division, New York Public Library, Astor, Lenox, and Tilden Foundations)

that his maps of the Atlantic and its various trade routes facilitated and helped to legitimate the slave trade, they nevertheless remained entirely divested of any images or marginalia denoting either slaves themselves or the indigenous peoples of Africa and the Americas. Moll's "A New and Exact Map of Guinea Divided into Slave, Gold and Ivory Coast," for example, prefaces the second edition of William Bosman's *A New and Accurate Description of the Coast of Guinea* (1721), which not only documents the geographical, political, and natural history of the place but also offers, as the title page states, "Just Measures for Improving the several Branches of the *Guinea* Trade," including the slave trade (fig. 9).[10] Bosman was an agent of the Dutch West India Company and chief factor for their fort at Elmina on the Guinea coast during the late seventeenth

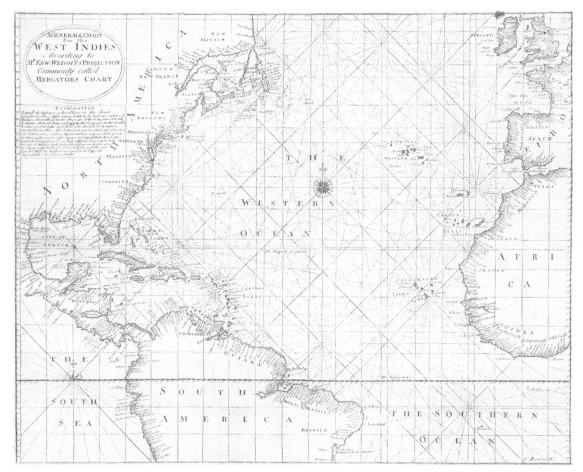

FIGURE 8. "A Generall Chart for the West Indies," John Thornton, 1706. (Lawrence H. Slaughter Collection, Lionel Pincus and Princess Firyal Map Division, New York Public Library, Astor, Lenox, and Tilden Foundations)

and early eighteenth century, and his text provides one of the earliest and most descriptive accounts of the African slave trade. Moll also produced maps that aided British efforts to consolidate its hold over the Atlantic slave trade following the War of the Spanish Succession and the Treaty of Utrecht, which gave them a monopoly over the slave trade in the West Indies and South America. His "A New and Exact Map of Coast, Countries and Islands Within the Limits of the South-Sea-Company" (1711) reflects this new reality in that it takes into its purview the holdings of the South Sea Company, which possessed the exclusive rights to Britain's slave trade after 1713.[11] Given the fact that this was still contested territory, maps such as those produced by Moll and others enabled Britain to literally and figuratively lay claim to the geography of the slave trade in ways that differed from official treaties and compacts.

Maps were, in fact, routinely appended to chorographical works that made the slave trade their primary focus, more often than not, with the intention of improving the buying, selling, and transportation of slaves throughout the Atlantic world. Like Bosman's text, Captain William Snelgrave's *A New Account of Some Parts of Guinea, and the Slave Trade* appends "A New Map of that part of Africa called the Coast of Guinea" to his extensive description of the region's geography, history, and culture, including the practice of slavery by both Africans and European traders. Snelgrave was intimately familiar with the Guinea coast since he himself was a slave trader from roughly 1704 to 1730, and he offers his account as a way of justifying the "lawfulness of that trade" to those who found slavery to be morally objectionable. However, as George Boulukos demonstrates, Snelgrave's arguments for the slave trade did not rest entirely on essential ideas of racial difference, as did many defenses of slavery during the period in question; rather, he believed that slavery was a form of rescue for many captives who faced death, and allegedly cannibalism, at the hands of their often brutal kings.[12] This sentimentalized narrative of slavers, including Snelgrave, rescuing native Africans from certain death is then paired with the cartographic text in order to substantiate his claims to a readership whose views on slavery might differ from his own. The map, as a rhetorical device,

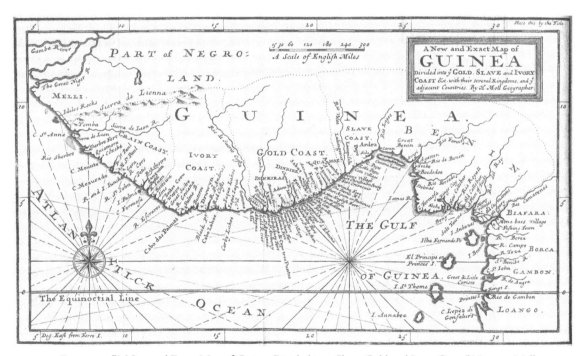

FIGURE 9. "A New and Exact Map of Guinea Divided into Slave, Gold and Ivory Coast," Herman Moll, 1721. (Manuscripts, Archives and Rare Books Division, Schomburg Center for Research in Black Culture, New York Public Library, Astor, Lenox and Tilden Foundations)

thus lends his account an authenticity and sense of credibility that Snelgrave sees as necessary to his defense of the slave trade.

We find a similar tactic in Malachy Postlethwayt's *The National and Private Advantages of the African Trade Considered* (1746), which also provides a map of the territory under discussion in order to "ground" his arguments for Britain's involvement in the slave trade. Like Snelgrave, Postlethwayt believed that slave traders were, in effect, rescuing Africans from otherwise barbarous conditions in their native countries; however, Postlethwayt's account is much less sentimental and sympathetic in tone, as he makes explicit the case for the economic and political advantages of slavery, not only here but also in numerous other works, including *The Africa Trade the great Pillar and Supporter of the British Plantation Trade in America* (1745), *Britain's Commercial Interests Explained and Improv'd* (1757), and *Great Britain's True System* (1757).[13] In addition, his translation of Jacques Savary des Brûlons's *Dictionanaire Universel de Commerce* contains a handful of maps that highlight various regions of the African continent, as well as China, India, Turkey, Persia, Japan, Malaysia, and the Philippines.[14] As a forceful proponent of the mercantile system and an agent of the Royal African Company, Postlethwayt well understood the value of geographic and cartographic knowledge of the African coast and the West Indies to Britain's continued investments in the slave trade, as did those merchants, plantation owners, seamen, and colonial officers who directly participated in it. The map can, in this regard, facilitate the slave trade in a pragmatic fashion, providing the necessary information to make travel and trade possible in the first place, or as we see in the case of Snelgrave and Postlethwayt, it can serve as a symbolic or rhetorical gesture on the part of an author eager to promote the virtues and benefits of slavery to the nation as a whole. More often than not, maps of the slave trade served both purposes simultaneously throughout the course of the seventeenth and eighteenth centuries.

As I have tried to demonstrate in this somewhat cursory overview, the economic and ideological imperatives of slave trade drove, in part, the production and distribution of maps, surveys, hydrological charts, and chorographies, which collectively brought into focus the geography of slavery in ever greater detail and clarity. While this fact is perhaps most visible in the seventeenth-century maps that represent the slave trade in a direct and forthright manner, such as those of Blaeu, Post and Marggraf, and Ligon, it is no less evident in eighteenth-century maps of the slave trade, despite the removal of such obvious signifiers. These supposedly more objective forms of cartographic representation facilitate Britain's commitments to and participation in the slave trade while simultaneously erasing any traces of their true purpose, which obfuscates to some extent the connection between mapping and slavery but by no means eliminates it entirely. Certainly, Samuel Jackson Pratt recognized the extent of the relationship of cartography to the enslavement of foreign subjects; his poem, with which I began this chapter, returns us, in a sense, to those maps of the slave trade from the previous century in order to make visible that which had been subsequently buried and covered over. However, I would contend that the satirical gesture behind Pratt's own "map of slavery" is neither singular nor the first of its kind but, rather, is part of a longer tradition that extends back to the Restoration period and, more specifically, to Aphra Behn's *Oroonoko* (1688), which is a text that also displays an anticartographic approach to the geography of the slave trade. Her novel, as I will argue, implicates the map as an integral part of her critique of British colonialism and exposes the carto-graphic imperative underlying its participation in the slave trade, a fact which is often lost on modern scholars who assume Behn's complicity with the map rather than the ways in which her novel posits an alternative to its rationalized perspective of the world.[15]

## Triangulating Oroonoko

In her edition of Aphra Behn's *Oroonoko; or, The Royal Slave*, Catherine Gal-lagher offers the reader two different, albeit related, maps for understanding Behn's text and its attendant geography. The first mapping, as outlined in the introduction, is intended to provide a comprehensive picture of the Atlantic world defined by an emergent colonial system of trade and commerce, includ-ing the various routes, rivers, ports, and plantations integral to its continued growth and overall success. During the latter half of the seventeenth century, Britain, West Africa, and the Caribbean were yoked together into an "unprec-edented integral structure" that would later be termed "the triangular trade," understood here as that system of trade founded on the movement of slaves from Africa to the Americas and the subsequent transportation of goods, sug-arcane and tobacco mostly, back to England.[16] Behn's novel, according to Gal-lagher, "traces the outlines of a new, interlocking, transcontinental order" by narrating the ways in which each location is, to varying degrees, dependent on the other points within the triangle: European slave traders abduct Oroo-noko from Coramantien in Africa and transport him to Surinam, where he is sold and forced to work on an English plantation; the plantation owner and his various functionaries exploit the labor power of Oroonoko and his fellow slaves in order to increase the production of sugarcane; the sugarcane is in turn distributed and sold to consumers in England and the rest of Europe, and a portion of the profits is reinvested in developing the infrastructure of the slave trade in hopes of building upon the already existing labor force. The physical geography of the triangular trade thus emerges as the necessary backdrop for Behn's tragic tale of colonial violence and brutality.

Gallagher's mapping of Behn's *Oroonoko* is predicated on the fundamental assumption that literary representations of space and geographic models, such as the Atlantic world or the triangular trade, are essentially coterminous, if not identical. However, we must ask whether or not *Oroonoko* represents its various settings with any degree of fidelity to the geography that Gallagher uses to ground her explication of the text. Are the mapping of the novel and the geography of the slave trade in fact the same? Do they perhaps differ, and if so, in what respect? To begin to answer these questions, it is, first, important to consider that the very existence and viability of the triangular trade during the Restoration remains in doubt. It may have applicability as the slave trade and the plantation system became increasingly consolidated and regimented by the early eighteenth century, yet its instantiation as a general feature of English overseas trade during the Restoration appears to be more of an anachronistic imposition than a documentable fact. Scholarship on the subject is conflicted at best. Eric Williams is perhaps the most notable and forceful proponent of the triangular trade model, and his work has continued to influence others in the field.[17] While I do not mean to question the overall validity or significance of this body of research, questions still linger as to *when* we can begin to speak of the existence of such a model and, more specifically, whether or not Behn's audience and Behn herself would have viewed *Oroonoko* with that geography in mind. K. G. Davies, for one, notes that the first known triangular voyage did not occur until 1689, a year after the novel's publication.[18] He goes on to highlight a variety of routes that existed prior to the formalization of the triangular trade, many of which were either polyangular in nature or, more commonly, specialized bilateral shuttles in which ships traveled between, for example, England and Africa or Africa and the West Indies without making the full circuit.[19] Phillip Curtin concurs for the most part with Davies, arguing that, because patterns of the slave trade were prone to flux, our ability to quantify its geography and demography prior to the eighteenth century is compromised by the rather scanty nature of the historical record. "As with most economic processes . . . the slave trade was a pattern of changing sources of supply, changing destinations, and changing rates of flow."[20] Patterns do indeed emerge, but they are varied and do not necessarily adhere to a single model, especially during the latter half of the seventeenth century when the slave trade was a loose amalgam of state-sponsored entities, such as the Royal African Company, or private (often illegitimate) business interests.

Davies and Curtin are certainly not alone in suggesting that the triangular model has little applicability to England's forays into the slave trade during the seventeenth century.[21] Why then the desire to read Behn's text through that particular geographic and economic lens? I would suggest that the answer lay with the general turn toward transatlantic studies within the academy and our subsequent desire to view the seventeenth- and eighteenth-century Atlantic world as always already transnational, if not postnational, in its effects. As current borders and boundaries are transgressed and older territorial designations give way to an increasingly globalized and homogenized world economy, the tendency has been to renarrate the history of the slave trade and colonialism with an eye toward a geography amenable to our contemporary sense of "fluid" space. The Atlantic Ocean and its contiguous landmasses serve as that geography because they articulate and embody quasi-Foucauldian notions of power and cultural transmission that speak not only to the early modern period but also to our current preoccupations with the global. Hence, England and Europe are rightly no longer separate from those nations and peoples who have, either willingly or unwillingly, been subjected to its force and its influence. Rather, they are part of a web of interdependent relationships in which power does not merely flow one way but instead, like the image of the triangular trade itself, moves and circulates, distributing its benefits and depredations with an uneven and often unjust hand. Hybridity supplants hegemony as the cultural logic of imperial relations. The Atlantic, broadly defined, thus comes to represent more than a body of water that connects these disparate places; it serves as the central metaphor for the ways in which power works within both colonial and postcolonial contexts. In Benedict Anderson's terms, it is the use of geography as logo that serves to promote and to legitimate a particular ideology, whether national, transcontinental, or merely local in its outlook.[22]

Nowhere is this conflation of geography and ideology more apparent than in Paul Gilroy's *The Black Atlantic: Modernity and Double Consciousness*, in which he suggests that "cultural historians . . . take the Atlantic as one single, complex unit of analysis in their discussion of the modern world and use it to produce an explicitly transnational and intercultural perspective."[23] The history of slavery is shot through this more holistic perspective in order to put forth a theory of black subjectivity that exists in concert with and, at the same time, counter to Western definitions of modernity. However, while Gilroy is willing to acknowledge that any such subjectivity exists simultaneously within and against the "grand narrative of Enlightenment and its operational principles," he does not extend his notion of modernity's double consciousness to the very geography that is the grounds for his argument.[24] That is, the Atlantic serves as both the literal place in which black and Western subjectivities come into contact with one another *and* the figure for the racial and ethnic hybridity that is at the heart of the modern, yet any sense of slippage between the literal and figurative is effaced as the Atlantic is transformed into the reified image of modernity itself. This applies as well, I would argue, to Gallagher's deployment of the triangular trade as a mode of explicating and analyzing *Oroonoko*. The geography that the novel inscribes is placed in the service of a transatlantic, transnational definition of modernity that, while valid in some respects, fails to acknowledge its own status as a figure that is politically and ideologically loaded. The result, as I noted earlier, is essentially the collapsing of any difference between the literary representation of space and the historical geography to which the text refers, a typical strategy in most realist fiction. To be sure, *Oroonoko* does, in part, represent the Atlantic world of the late seventeenth century in the ways that Gallagher suggests. However, rather than merely depict that world in a realistic or accurate fashion, Behn's novel, I would suggest, appropriates the geography of the triangular trade in a manner that questions the political and economic motivations that undergird its production. If *Oroonoko* can be said to function as a critique of slavery and colonialism, at least of the Whiggish variety, then it stands to reason that the geography of the triangular trade and its antecedents must also be included as part of that critique.[25]

We can see this critique operative at the narrative level in the novel's many references to the various geographic discourses that directly engender and facilitate the slave trade and colonial expansion more generally. For example, early in the novel, Oroonoko is introduced to the science and practice of navigation by the commander of an English slave ship who has recently arrived in Coramantien. Oroonoko readily sells many of his own slaves to the captain, unaware that he will soon fall victim to the very same person. This fatal myopia regarding the captain's true intentions, as well as the fate of his fellow countrymen, is, as our narrator suggests, an extension of Oroonoko's partiality "to the European mode" and his preference for "men of parts and wit," which prompts him to invite the captain to reside at court for an extended period of time. Oroonoko's apparent "delight in the white nations" is, in turn, reciprocated by the captain, who entertains "the prince every day with globes and maps, and mathematical discourses and instruments."[26] Oroonoko learns, in effect, the rudiments of navigation and cartography at the hands of an English slaver, thus reinforcing the connection between a specific mode of geographic understanding and representation and the consolidation of the slave trade. Behn emphasizes that these scientific discourses are anything but value-neutral, but rather signify a way of thinking about the so-called Atlantic world that is saturated with the values and interests of England's mercantile class. Oroonoko, of course, fails to read the map and the globe in their proper political and ideological contexts. For him, they are merely a source of entertainment and delight that enable the captain to gain his respect, admiration, and even love. While the captain certainly plays on Oroonoko's sympathies in order to lure him on the boat and, ultimately, to enslave him and his compatriots, Oroonoko's fateful decision to board the ship, Behn appears to suggest, is driven largely by his desire for the kind of power, wealth, and knowledge that the captain seems to promise, if only tacitly.

It is often assumed that the wine is Oroonoko's principal undoing here; he is left weak and defenseless after having drunk too much and, with his judgment so impaired, he becomes easy prey, as do his men. However, many fail to note that it is not the wine only that is directly responsible for Oroonoko's demise but also his deep fascination with the ship itself: "The prince having drunk hard of the punch, and several sorts of wine . . . was very merry, and in great admiration for the ship, for he had never been in one before; so that he was curious of beholding every place, where he decently might descend."[27] His attraction to the ship recalls his earlier interest in the science and technology of navigation, as well as with the potential uses for such knowledge. Behn intentionally pairs Oroonoko's naïve interest in the captain's profession with the scene of his own inebriation in order to suggest that each is informed by a shared set of desires. Wealth and power, like liquor, can be intoxicating when unmoored from traditional patriarchal and royalist values and hierarchies and so, in Behn's estimation, represent a potential problem in need of examination and dissection. She effects such a critique not only through the figure of the duplicitous and untrustworthy captain but also by showing her reader the extent to which Oroonoko, even as a royal figure, aspires to, or is seduced by, the kinds of knowledge that the captain possesses. Rather than rejecting him and his ship as the bearers of this knowledge, or viewing them cautiously and with some degree of suspicion, Oroonoko feels a sympathetic pull toward them because of their obvious novelty, as well as because he understands, to some extent, the value and importance of trade and shipping to a small nation, like England or his own Coramantien, that borders on the Atlantic. There is profit and benefit in what the captain knows, and Oroonoko is keenly aware of that fact, so much so that it leads him into error and enslavement.

The scene not only associates the map and the globe with the captain of the slave ship but also connects these various cartographic discourses with colonial trade, and slavery in particular, in such a way that the map and globe become symbolic of a whole way of *seeing* the world, one that is deeply suspect in Behn's estimation. They are, as I am suggesting, figures that Oroonoko fails to read properly. He does not see that the kinds of knowledge the captain has to offer are profoundly imbricated within the Atlantic slave trade, or assuming for a moment he is aware of the connection, he simply fails to understand how that may affect him personally or others around him. Either way, Oroonoko's gross misreading is, I would argue, meant to be seen as more than an error specific to himself or slaves in general. Rather, his error serves as an allegory for an English readership that is also unable to perceive the ways in which cartography both facilitates and glosses over the realities of colonial violence and subjugation. Behn recognizes the reader's propensity to place trust in the cartographic image, such as those depicting the Atlantic world, yet is also aware of readers' failure to understand the motives and ideologies of those who require such images for the purposes of military conquest and commercial domination. Behn evinces here a form of "anti-cartographic" discourse intended to call the reader's attention to the ways in which the map and the globe can distort and pervert one's understanding of the world, which can in turn lead, as in the case of Oroonoko, to tragic consequences. Her text brings some pressure to bear on this particular economy of representation in order to expose its limits and enable us to see beyond its horizons. We see this not only in the previous examples, but also later in the novel when we shift from Coramantien to Surinam, where Behn, in stark contrast to the cartographic projection, offers us fantastic and quasi-utopian images of "Nature . . . joined with Art," constructions that are irreducible to any map. In one of her first descriptions of the colony, the narrator offers the following detail: "'Tis a continent whose vast extent was never yet known, and may contain more noble earth than all the universe be-sides; for they say, it reaches from east to west, one way as far as China, and an-other to Peru."[28] The indefinable, mysterious nature of Surinam and the South American continent is reinforced by the inability of modern surveyors and cartographers to accurately assess its size and shape. Behn leaves the "they" in "they say" intentionally ambiguous in order to assert the primacy of rumor and conjecture when more realistic and precise representations of space are want-ing. Rather than a critique of this kind of speculative knowledge, Behn instead amplifies it, transforming Surinam from a "real" place that can be located on a map to a more spectacular and romantic setting that, at least in the eyes of the narrator, cannot adequately be conveyed to a reader. Concluding her descrip-tion of a beautiful and serene grove located on St. John's Hill, reportedly the site of John Harley's original plantation, the narrator notes that "the whole globe of the world cannot show so delightful a place as this grove was."[29] Again, Behn juxtaposes the native landscape of Surinam against the cartographic image, albeit in the form of a globe, in order to differentiate this place from the known world and so prevent it from being reduced to mere territory or property.

The inability of the map to properly represent and contextualize the world beyond the confines of Parham, the plantation where Oroonoko is enslaved, proffers in its absence the pastoral and romantic landscape of the grove, as well as other sites detailed in the novel. That is, the gaps and elisions in the map provide ample opportunity for Behn to convey and color them as she sees fit. However, I would argue that Behn's idealization of the "blank spaces" of the South American interior is neither naïve nor uninformed but rather is meant to serve as an effective counterpoint to the violent and brutal activities that unfold there. Behn understands that this is contested territory, literally and figuratively, and that competing visions of the Atlantic world often require competing modes of representing space, whether they are a novel or a map. Her novelistic treatment of the geography of the slave trade is both response to and critique of cartographic abstraction and Cartesian certainty. The map, in its rationalized projection of what Henri Lefebvre refers to as "homogenous space," offers a democratizing picture of the Atlantic world, one that belies the very real ways in which space is divided, carved up, and organized by cer-tain economic, political, and social hierarchies. Such hierarchies are, for Behn, not simply ideological in nature, or merely categories of perception, but rather manifest themselves within the built environment; they have a material and substantial life in their shaping of one's immediate environment and the world writ large. Behn would argue that this is true with regard to her preference for royalist politics and patriarchal values, both of which require their own spatial vocabulary and syntax, yet it is also applicable to competing social and political systems, such as those of the Whigs, who will certainly leave their signature on the space of the nation and the empire. However, while the need to master space, to designate property, seize territory, and demarcate social borders and hierarchies, is common to virtually all political economies, Behn suggests that the map is a mode of representation that facilitates these activities, yet does so in a way that seeks to cover over its purpose and intent. Unlike the visibility and centrality of the monarch to earlier conceptions of national space, the modern map's homogenous depiction of space, its rationalization of the world, serves the ends of English imperialism and makes possible the political and economic ascendancy of England's merchant class, even as it erases the material consequences of that ascendancy. However, in the same gesture, the map fails to register the heterogeneity of space, its unequal and uneven distribution, and the realities of colonial violence and subjugation that inevitably result from these profound inequities. Behn thus places her novel simultaneously within and against the map in order to parody and expose those who would promote such a view of the world for personal benefit and social gain.

Rather than simply participate within the cartographic and chorographic discourses associated with the slave trade and England's imperial expansion in general, Behn chooses instead to present her reader with a much more differentiated and heterogeneous conception of the Atlantic world, one that explicitly dramatizes the ways in which power inscribes itself spatially and, in the process, calls into question the putative neutrality of those discourses. In order to achieve this, Behn eschews the modalities of seventeenth-century Whig topography, including the map and chorography, whose associations with the slave trade and conquest were all too apparent, in favor of the spatial vocabulary of the scenic stage, with which Behn and Restoration audiences were already quite familiar. Behn translates the order and operations of the scenic stage, including the use of the discovery, into prose form in order to depict a world that, unlike the map, is uneven and fragmented and whose varied spaces are anything but equal in terms of their value and importance. If the map reduces the Atlantic world to a relatively uniform and cohesive image, then, for Behn, the scenic stage's ability to carve up and segment a given performance in interesting and often disjunctive ways enables her to defamiliarize that image to some extent. *Oroonoko's* scenic "mapping" of the slave trade thus counters the idea of a stable and objectively knowable space and instead presents us a world in which borders and boundaries continually move and shift in ways that her characters, Oroonoko and Imoinda most notably, can neither control nor comprehend. Rather than subjects able to move and operate of their own accord, both colonizer and colonized are subjected to the scenic logic that guides Behn's representation of the Atlantic world and her critical examination of the British colonial project.

## The Scene Changes

While a number of recent critics have plumbed the depths of *Oroonoko's* many references and allusions to the Restoration stage, few have examined the text and its relationship to the scenic stage in their accountings.[30] Behn embraced the technological innovations associated with the scenic stage from the beginning of her career as a playwright and integrated its operations not only into many of her plays but also, as I will show, into her prose work, and *Oroonoko* in particular.[31] According to Peter Holland, Behn was "positively obsessive" in her use of the scenic stage and the use of the discovery in particular. By his count, she uses no fewer than thirty-one discoveries in ten of her comedies.[32] Behn deploys discoveries to make use of the upstage area for comedic effect in works such as *The City Heiress* (1682), in which a man is discovered tied up, and *The Rover* (1677), where the discovery of Belvile upstage, alone and in the dark, marks the passage from day to night. *The Amorous Prince, or, The Curious Husband* (1671) deploys scenic convention to break a street scene up into many different locations, while act 2 of *The Dutch Lover* (1673) contains no less than three consecutive discovery scenes, which were considered a few too many by some standards.[33] The discovery area is loosely defined as the space revealed by either the opening or closing of the shutters on the stage. To provide a brief sketch, the scenic stage employs a frontispiece that functions, more or less, like a proscenium arch; it frames the scene as well as covers up the mechanisms, such as the windlass and pulley system, by which the scenic stage operates. Behind it, there are six wings (three to a side) which decrease in size as they move upstage toward the back shutters. While the number of wings deployed varied according to the size of the theater and the requirements of the production, they functioned, with the addition of a border that spanned the wings, as smaller versions of the basic proscenium structure. They were either fixed set pieces that were painted to suggest a particular setting, or they were mobile, tracked by grooves on the floor and suspended from flies above so that they could match the scene depicted on the shutters. The shutters served as the terminus of the stage picture and constituted a background of sorts. Rather than a single, uniform piece, the shutters were halved and tracked in grooves on the stage floor so that they could be pulled open to reveal a scene behind it, which was also backed by a shutter, usually inscribed with a different location. A single production would often include several of these shutters, allowing for the possibility of multiple discovery areas.[34]

The net effect was an unprecedented flexibility of control over scene changes and a more active and mobile conception of the scene. As Richard Southern reminds us, the changing of scenes became as much a part of the spectacle as the words and actions of the players on the stage: "The changing of scenes was intended to be visible; it was part of the show; it came into existence purely to be watched."[35] More than just background setting intended to establish a sense of place in which the dramatic action could unfold, the scene itself was a part of that action; it served as a device to propel the action forward in a way that enabled the exposition of plot and even commentary on the plot through a sort of counterpoint. William Davenant's revival of *The Siege of Rhodes* (1661), the first play to fully exploit the possibilities of the scenic stage, would often change scenes while the actors remained on stage, occurring, if needed, during an exchange of dialogue. The scene could also remain in place while actors exited the stage and new actors entered to suggest some degree of temporal continuity or to stage a kind of simultaneity without having both scenes literally depicted one atop the other. Scenes could change contra breaks in dramatic action, or they could be used to signal the commencement of a new action. Frequently, a scene emerged from the splitting of a prior scene to reveal something entirely new and perhaps shocking: "The shutters opened to reveal scenes of horror, death and torture: Victims were shown being broken on the wheel, roasted over fires, or thrown down on the ganches. Prisons were revealed in which the captives were allowed sufficient length of chain to wander beyond the restricted discovery space. Hells or Heavens were shown, and tombs and vaults."[36] Discoveries were not all necessarily gruesome in nature, though the increased popularity of tragedy during the Restoration certainly made these kinds of displays more desirable and feasible. The discovery could be as simple as converting an exterior setting into an interior one, or vice versa, suggesting perhaps a heightened permeability between the interior and exterior spaces for either dramatic or comedic effect. The revealing of the discovery space also extended to the representation of divine revelation. Another set of shutters located above those attached to the stage floor could be opened independently to reveal a heavenly scene.[37]

The scenic stage thus appears, on the surface, to be a more rationalized, more ordered space in that it can be manipulated and controlled with ever-increasing precision; however, its deployment often satirizes that possibility to reveal to a more chaotic vision of theatrical space, one in which walls move unannounced, outsides become insides, and faraway places are revealed with a change of the shutter. Perhaps more than any other playwright of the day, Aphra Behn seized upon this fragmented, chameleonlike quality of the scenic stage and was quick to take full advantage of the various scenic technologies offered at Lincoln Inn Fields and, later, Dorset Garden. As Dawn Lewcock argues, Behn was able to exploit the visual potential of the discovery in ways that supplemented the text yet just as often provided an ironic commentary on the dialogue and the action. She stresses this point for critics who would marginalize or dismiss a dramaturgical analysis of Behn's work: "What is unique to Behn is not only her appreciation of the visual effects of a performance but also the way that she uses this to affect the perceptions of the audience and change their conception and comprehension of her plots and/or her underlying theme as she wishes by integrating the theatrical possibilities into her dramatic structure."[38] The scene and dramatic action worked together in a way that was not only visually engaging for the audience but also served Behn's own thematic predilections. According to Lewcock, her use of the discovery often served to embody a world of deceit and deception, one in which the concealment and

revelation of the truth, whether for good or ill, was rendered all the more spectacular. The scenic space was crucial to the production of misunderstandings
and general confusion, allowing Behn to then lead the audience through the
web of deceit to arrive at the not always quite satisfying resolution, or final
disclosure. We see an example of this in Behn's early "tragicomedy" *The Forc'd
Marriage, Or the Jealous Bridegroom* (1670), where, as Janet Todd, argues, "Behn
used the shutters to open on tableaux which, freezing gazed and postures in
great set pieces of wedding and funeral, provoke audience emotion and help
to clarify an over-complicated plot."[39] While Behn's use of the scenic stage in
*The Forc'd Marriage* does fulfill these respective functions, I would suggest the
discovery, in this instance, is more than a device to "clarify" the plot or to merely
elicit a visceral reaction from her audience, as Todd would have it. Rather, Behn
deploys the scenic tableaux in order to underscore the vexed nature of romantic
desire and the ways in which duty to the sovereign complicates that desire, a
theme which is prevalent not only in many of her plays but in *Oroonoko* as well.

The play opens with the king wishing to show gratitude to his two greatest
warriors: Phillander, the king's son and heir to the throne, and Alcippus, the
king's favorite, but he leaves it to them to choose their proper reward. Phillander, unwilling to claim any glory beyond that of the battlefield and their
service to the king, surrenders the title of general to Alcippus. The selfless act
seems to please everyone save Alcippus, who confesses that his true desire is
to marry Erminia, the daughter of Orgulius, the king's aging general whom
he has just replaced. Orgulius gladly assents to Alcippus as his successor and
to the marriage unaware that Phillander and Erminia are secretly in love with
one another. Phillander, realizing the dire consequences of his generosity, can
only reply in a brief aside, "Oh Gods! What have I done? . . . I'm ruin'd."[40] We
then see Erminia lament her and Phillander's fate as she must resign herself
to the "forc'd wedding" between herself and Alcippus so that she may obey the
dictates of her father and the king. Act 2 then opens with a discovery of the
wedding scene, as detailed in the following stage directions:

> The REPRESENTATION of a WEDDING: The Curtain must be let down; and
> soft Musick must play: the Curtain being drawn up, discovers a Scene of a
> Temple: The King sitting on a Throne, bowing down to joyn the Hands of
> Alcippus and Erminia who kneel on the steps of the Throne; the Officers of
> the Court and the Clergy standing in order by, with Orgulius. This within
> the Scene—Without on the stage, Phillander with his sword half-drawn,
> held by Galatea, who looks ever on Alcippus; Erminia still fixing her eyes
> on Phillander; Pisaro passionately gazing on Galatea: Aminta on Falatius,
> and he on her; Alcander, Isilia, Cleontius, in other several postures, with
> the rest; all remaining without motion, whilst the Musick softly plays; this
> continues a while till the Curtain falls; and then the Musick plays aloud till
> the Act begins.[41]

The wedding in the temple takes place within the scene, occupying the upstage area and framed by the smaller proscenium arch and shutters, which are open when the curtain is drawn. Outside the scene, on the forestage, we have the spectators of the wedding, all of whom can see one other and those within the scene yet are frozen, resigned only to look but not to act. Action is implied in the kneeling of Alcippus and Erminia or Phillander's hand on his sword, but the real movement of the scene is in the revealing and concealing of the wedding, which is, to refer back to the play's title, forced not only in the sense of being imposed on Erminia but also in its forcing of Phillander outside the immediate scene of its unfolding.

In terms of a structure of power and desire, there is a constitutive differ-ence between the space in which the wedding takes place and the space of the wedding's spectators, most notably, Phillander. The order of things has been inverted so that the royal authority vested in the body of the monarch appears to act against itself by excluding the prince and perhaps jeopardizing the line of succession by giving Erminia away to another. In turn, the heir to the throne is unable to act against Alcippus and thus restore himself to his proper place alongside Erminia without violating the duty to both king and father, which would constitute an abdication of his role as prince. The gaze of the two lovers represents an attempt to resolve this paradox and unify these two disparate spaces, yet it also marks their perhaps fatal separation. The discovery thus presents the scene of the wedding to the audience as tragic spectacle; it is a revelation intended to, in one sense, arouse our sympathies for the prince, plac-ing us in the position of powerlessness that the prince occupies. However, the revelation also enables us to see something exemplary in Phillander's behavior in that he desires to act, signified by his half-drawn sword, but doesn't when confronted by the very thing that has aroused his anger and sense of vengeance. In the subsequent scene, we see Galatea continue to entreat Phillander, asking him to defer revenge until she can enact a plan that will reunite the lovers and make Alcippus hers alone. With the wedding concealed and removed from sight, Phillander assents to her wishes and bloodshed is averted. Phillander desires to consummate the act of revenge but cannot; he is relegated to a mo-ment of stasis, or inaction, in response to the discovery of the wedding, and the possibility of tragic action is thus deferred into comedic resolution (everyone ends up with his or her proper partner by play's end) in a manner typical of the "tragicomic" plays that were so popular during the Restoration. As I am arguing, the discovery scene is critical to the genre in its provocation of violent responses to the play's many revelations and the ensuing comic deferral of that violence by play's end; however, in a text such as *Oroonoko*, Behn forgoes the comedic qualities of the discovery, choosing instead to emphasize its tragic possibilities. Of course, we are dealing with prose narrative rather than the stage; nevertheless, Behn transposes the partitioning of scenic space from the theaters of London to the colonial margins, where those conflicts and tensions visible in the aforementioned discovery of the wedding fail to find resolution or closure.

The deployment of scenic space in *Oroonoko* echoes Behn's *The Forc'd Marriage*, as Oroonoko, like Phillander, must somehow try to reconcile his desire for Imoinda with his sense of duty to the king, who is also his grandfather. As in the play, this conflict is not simply ideological in nature but is also manifest in the novel's use of setting, which dramatizes the often violent ways in which colonial space gets divided, arranged, and hierarchized by those in power, whether a king, plantation owner, or a slave. For example, while in Coramantien, Oroonoko attempts to conceal his feelings for Imoinda from the "old king" because he knows intuitively that he is obligated to conduct himself in a manner befitting the grandson and subject of the king. However, a crack in his statuesque facade emerges with the discovery of the king's bed:

> But when he saw another door opened by Onahal, a former old wife of the king's who now had charge of Imoinda, and saw the prospect of a bed of state made ready with sweets and flowers for the dalliance of the king, who immediately led the trembling victim from his sight, into that prepared repose. What rage! What wild frenzies seized his heart! Which forcing to keep within bounds, and to suffer without noise, it became the more insupportable and rent his soul with ten thousand pains. He was forced to retire to vent his groans, where he fell down on a carpet, and lay struggling a long time, and only breathing now and then, "O Imoinda!" When Onahal had finished her necessary affair within, shutting the door, she came forth to wait, till the king called.[42]

The revelation and concealment of the bed occurs in much the same fashion as the discovery scene in *The Forc'd Marriage* and for the same purpose: to dramatize the conflict between romantic desire and allegiance to the sovereign. However, unlike the earlier play, this conflict has no resolution. The affirmation of Oroonoko and Imoinda's love that precedes the discovery is abruptly ended with the "prospect" of the "bed of state" where the king and Imoinda are to consummate their union. The noble mien of Oroonoko crumbles at the sight as his inability to change their situation only precipitates frustration and anger. This is not the first time we will witness such a transformation, since Oroonoko continually modulates between the positions of royalty and slave, noble and savage, without ever occupying any one fully. Interestingly, the emotional turn occurs in tandem with the discovery scene, suggesting that his moods are subject to change with the change of scene. The opening and closing of the doors by Onahal, like the shutters on the stage, mark this turn in Oroonoko. While the discovery of the king's bed chamber deeply affects him, even after the door is closed and the bed removed from sight, Behn here underscores Oroonoko's ability to keep it together and to not expose his feelings for Imoinda to the king. Oroonoko's frustration is the direct product of the imperative to "keep within bounds," to police the margins of his own conduct even as the boundaries of the space that he occupies are depicted as fluid and mobile. The fluidity of scenic space is counterpoised with the self-discipline of the noble prince who must still adhere to the rules and dictates of the court and the otan. He is able to vent his feelings but only afterward and "in the other room" where Onahal and Aboan try to console him.

The fragmentary nature of social space in Coramantien announces a problematic that will haunt Oroonoko throughout much of the text, specifically, his inability to control or manipulate how space gets meted out, how it moves and shifts in ways that he cannot control or predict. The spatial syntax of Coramantien, in fact, resembles any number of Behn's plays in which the participants in the intrigue must negotiate various strictures on entering certain rooms, buildings, or public spaces, even if that negotiation means violating one's duty to the father and the sovereign. Oroonoko's continued desire to see Imoinda, despite the king's suspicions, requires that he breach the otan and her apartment at night, but he is unable to do so alone. Aboan, his friend and loyal servant, seduces Onahal, Imoinda's keeper, in order that Oroonoko may gain entrance. However, the king's spies discover their plans and later arrive at the threshold of Imoinda's apartment to expose the tryst:

> But while they were thus fondly employed, forgetting how time ran on, and that the dawn must conduct him far away from his only happiness, they heard a great noise in the otan, and unusual voices of men; at which the prince, starting from the arms of the frighted Imoinda, ran to a little battle-axe he used to wear by his side; and having not so much leisure as to put on his habit, he opposed himself against some who were already opening the door; which they did with so much violence, that Oroonoko was not able to defend it.[43]

The door, once again, serves as the scenic device that divides the space of the lovers from that of the king's authority, yet unlike the previous discovery of the bed, Oroonoko strives, in this instance, to keep the doors closed, to conceal their love from any spectators. Despite Oroonoko's stature and strength, he cannot keep out the king's men, who threaten to overwhelm the door and Oroonoko. Realizing the dire nature of the situation, Oroonoko addresses them through the closed door in a bid for privacy: "'Who ever ye are that have the boldness to attempt to approach this apartment thus rudely, know that I, the Prince Oroonoko, will revenge it with the certain death of him that first enters. Therefore stand back, and know this place is sacred to love, and me this night; tomorrow 'tis the king's.'"[44] Where his physical strength falters, discourse prevails. His commanding tone and the force of his request succeed in getting them to desist in their efforts.[45]

More importantly, the division between inside and outside is starkly dramatized here in order to underscore the divisibility of space that is both the solution to Oroonoko's problems and the very crux of the problem itself. Oroonoko's opposition to the king's men represents his desire for a utopian space separate from the authority of the king where Oroonoko and Imoinda can be together without fear of reprisals, yet the production of such a space is always beyond his control because the otan is properly under the authority of the king, and it is he who determines its rites of passage. Oroonoko is left only with the choice to either respect or rebel against the wishes and commands of his grandfather. This powerlessness, as I am contending, is rooted in a scenic conception of space whereby a character is not in charge of the physical space he is occupying. Oroonoko is robbed of any sense of agency in that the spaces that comprise Coramantien move and shift not by divine or providential action but according to the wishes and desires of the sovereign. Oroonoko registers this truth most visibly after he is told that Imoinda was put to death for her actions (when, in fact, she was sold into slavery by the king). While the men of Coramantien prepare for battle against a neighboring tribe, Oroonoko, in a state of grief, "shut himself into his pavilion all that day," resigned not to fight or ever take up arms again. His men beg and implore him to join them, but "he made no other reply to all their supplications but this, that he had now no more business for glory; and for the world, it was a trifle not worth his care. 'Go,' continued he, sighing, 'and divide it amongst you; and reap with joy what you so vainly prize, and leave me to my more welcome destiny.'"[46] Without Imoinda, he no longer desires to conquer his foes and claim his share; even if the so-called world were at stake, he could not be moved to action. Oroonoko's passivity here marks a paradoxical agency whereby his decision *not* to participate in the campaign becomes an expression of his nobility. Oroonoko cannot usurp the authority of the king and attain some measure of control over Coramantien, nor can he carve out a protective space for himself and Imoinda while still maintaining his allegiances to family, king, and country.

Oroonoko clearly recognizes the ways in which power inscribes itself in the built environment, but rather than an impetus to action, to seize control, that recognition leads Oroonoko to reject the world, or more specifically, a world valued for its ability to be carved up and commodified as the spoils of war. Rather than resolve the impasse one way or the other, Oroonoko and Imoinda are quickly subjected to the fetters and chains of slavery and transported to a plantation in the Americas; however, the contradictions and conflicts inherent in the spatial economy of Coramantien do not disappear by any means. If anything, they are amplified on the much larger "stage" of the Atlantic slave trade and the emerging geography of British colonialism. Surinam initially holds forth the promise of reconciliation in its projection of an idyllic setting, one in which Oroonoko and Imoinda can live together in a state of blissful domesticity. Rather than conquer the world, Oroonoko's love for Imoinda leads him to reject such an action, just as he had in Coramantien: "Caesar [Oroonoko] swore he disdained the empire of the world, while he could behold his Imoinda, and she despised grandeur and pomp, those vanities of her sex, when she could gaze upon Oroonoko. He adored the very cottage where she resided, and said, that little inch of the world would give him more happiness than all the universe could do, and she vowed, it was a palace, while adorned with the presence of Oroonoko."[47] Oroonoko trades the auspices of imperial design for a more intimate sphere. Oroonoko's emotional investment in "that little inch of the world" represents a vision of a space apart from the machinations of slave traders and colonial officers, a domesticated enclave of sorts in which the depredations of slavery are held at bay; it is a site of resistance to the overwhelming forces of colonization and the slave trade that have subjected Oroonoko and Imoinda to their respective fates. Oroonoko marks off this romantic space in yet another attempt to gain control over the constantly shifting landscape of his world, including his forced transportation from Coramantien to Surinam, yet as we have seen previously, Oroonoko's attempts to realize such a space prove futile, his hopes continually deferred and, ultimately, left unfulfilled.

Oroonoko and Imoinda's liberty is repeatedly denied despite the promises of their captors, and as a result, the threat of slave revolt emerges, the fear of which grips Parham and the neighboring plantations for the remainder of the narrative. Whereas Oroonoko resisted outright violence against the king, his grandfather, out of a respect for his authority and an intuitive sense of order, including the spatial order of things in Coramantien, the dissociative logic of scenic space there extends to Surinam, where violent recapitulation against plantation owners and colonial officials becomes a very real possibility. Even though Oroonoko's revolt proves ineffectual and the slave colony never officially materializes, it nevertheless hovers on the margins of the text in a way that organizes much of the action, especially the numerous efforts taken to prevent its occurring. The narrator notes the practice of separating slaves during the auction and selling them off to different owners, "not daring to trust them together, lest rage and courage should put them upon contriving some great action, to the ruin of the colony."[48] The narrator is later called in to divert and entertain Caesar, Oroonoko's slave name, from realizing that fact: "I was obliged, by some persons, who feared a mutiny (which is very fatal sometimes in these colonies that abound so with slaves that they exceed the whites in vast numbers), to discourse with Caesar, and to give him all the satisfaction that I could."[49] Despite her sympathy for and defense of Oroonoko, the narrator too fears revolt, so much so that she feels she must either prevent its occurring or, as she does later in the novel, absent herself from critical moments when Oroonoko is subjected to punishment for his misdeeds.

We see this as well when Trefry, a friend and ally of Oroonoko, declares the property of his lord, Parham, a "sanctuary" from the governor's council and the tyranny of Byam: "Trefry . . . told Byam his command did not extend to his

lord's plantation, and that Parham was as much exempt from the law as White-
hall; and that they ought no more to touch the servants of the lord—(who
there represented the king's person) than they could those about the king himself; and that Parham was a sanctuary, and though his lord were absent in person, his power was still in being there, which he had entrusted with him, as far
as the dominions of his particular plantations reached, and all that belonged
to it."[50] Byam and his council are then turned "out of doors" while Oroonoko
resides safely, at least for the moment, within Parham. The very possibility of
sanctuary, however, must be viewed as provisional and, given previous attempts
to establish consistent and firm boundaries anywhere in the text, with a good
measure of irony. The idea of sanctuary, even one legally and politically sanctioned, can offer no possible solution for Oroonoko, as it represents yet a further fragmenting of colonial space, divided in this instance not between slave
and slave owner but rather between competing interests represented by the
well-intentioned Trefry and the tyrannical Byam. That is, Oroonoko's safety is,
in the end, relegated to a minor consideration within the larger power struggle
between the various factions in Surinam, a struggle that will manifest itself
spatially in the cordoning off of Parham as a "sanctuary" for Oroonoko, and,
more importantly, a refuge from the perceived excesses of the current political
order. Either way, it is a space whose integrity is quickly violated when Oroonoko, realizing that this too cannot hold, leaves Parham to take his own life and
that of Imoinda, opting instead for "the next world."

The surreptitious and often chaotic nature of scenic space that Oroonoko
encountered in Coramantien returns, once again, in Surinam but recast as an
economy of space that is the product of colonial violence rather than courtly
intrigue. The threat, however, is not simply one of violence at the hands of
rogue slaves, the destruction of Parham, or the possible usurpation of colonial
authority by Oroonoko; rather, it is the potential creation of a slave colony, a
space that effectively cuts itself off from intercourse and commerce with the
English colonists that drives much of Behn's text. It is this notion of a space
apart that fuels Oroonoko's drive toward redrawing the boundaries within
Surinam so as to reflect the divisions between the noble ethos of the slave
community and the amoral and strictly financial motivations of their captors.
As Catherine Gallagher reminds us, the history of Surinam attests to the reality of slave revolts and their culmination in independent slave colonies: "As
early as the 1660s, a group of self-emancipated former slaves, led by Coroman-
tines like Oroonoko, were raiding plantations there. . . . Africans continued
to rebel successfully against their European masters, migrating into the rain
forests of Suriname, and establishing independent and populous communities there. Despite numerous efforts to destroy them, those communities won
their autonomy and, according to anthropologists, became preserves of West
African civilization transplanted to South America."[51] While the formation
of slave colonies is more of an eighteenth-century phenomenon, Behn is not

completely unaware of their existence given her knowledge of the numerous revolts in and around Surinam during the period, fleshed out, of course, with a good deal of speculation in her narrative. More importantly, the cycle of violence engendered by the slave trade is dramatized through her recourse to the modalities of the scenic stage. The production of an autonomous slave colony marks the logical culmination of a spatial practice that, like her use of the scene, fosters division and segmentation as much as it does integration and homogenization. It is the undiscovered scene, the concluding scene that is gestured to yet never revealed.

In his pursuit of that utopian space, Oroonoko actively participates in a form of violence that is at the heart of Behn's critique of British colonial practice. As Richard Frohock argues, Behn was clearly a proponent of British colonialism, yet she objected to the violence that resulted from the establishment of trade and territorial expansion, preferring what Mary Louise Pratt describes as the "desire to subject without violence."[52] More often than not, she displaces the origin of this violence onto Whig colonial officers and mercantilists, who are either the product of a lower-class upbringing or convicts who have been transported to the Americas.[53] Behn's narrator comments at one point that the governor's council in Surinam "consisted of such notorious villains as Newgate never transported, and possibly were originally such, who understood neither the laws of God or man, and had no sort of principles to make them worthy the name of men."[54] *Oroonoko*, Frohock contends, seeks to retheorize colonial authority as somehow rooted in the natural privilege of nobility, ostensibly represented in the figure of Oroonoko himself. However, the territorial impulse asserts itself not simply in the form of a wayward and misguided attempt on the part of slave traders and plantation owners to establish British hegemony in foreign lands; it is also manifest in Oroonoko's actions as he tries to gain his liberty and establish an independent slave colony. Behn makes this clear when, in their journey through the woods and mountains of Surinam, Oroonoko rallies his fellow slaves by comparing himself and his mission to that of another great military leader: "He told them that he had heard of one Hannibal a great captain, had cut his way through mountains of solid rocks, and should a few shrubs oppose them, which they could fire before them? No. 'Twas a trifling excuse to men resolved to die, or overcome."[55] The analogy to Hannibal, like his given name of Caesar, neatly places Oroonoko into a genealogy of Western imperialism in order to suggest that the pursuit of liberty easily degenerates into territorial violence.

Oroonoko's potential reterritorialization of Surinam, and subsequent failure, again points to the ways in which power inscribes itself spatially, both literally and figuratively. The creation of the slave colony would represent an alternative geography to that of the plantation system and serve as a bulwark against colonial definitions of the Atlantic world, such as the map, that cannot accommodate or allow for "other" spaces, spaces that would contest or challenge in some fashion the legitimacy of British rule. Oroonoko's desire to create such a space is legitimate in Behn's eyes because it is an attempt to reassert the heterogeneity that characterizes the Atlantic world, whether we are in South America, Africa, or England itself. The failure to give place to the noble ethos the slave community and its heady blend of stoic virtue, patriarchal authority, and romantic desire is, for Behn, tragic to be sure, but from that tragedy emerges a sense that their demise is the result of a Whig ideology that cannot permit the existence of marooned societies and the spaces that they occupy. In this sense, the struggle for control between Whig proponents of colonial trade and the royalist-inflected slave community serves as an allegory for various political conflicts back home in England. However, as I am arguing, these conflicts involve, in part, competing definitions and articulations of space. There are no politics without a politics of space according to Behn, and this truth extends to representations of the Atlantic world that, like the map, seek to promote a Whig ideology of commerce, wealth, property, and military supremacy. To return to my earlier point regarding Gallagher's edition of *Oroonoko*, the conflation of cartographic renderings of the Atlantic world with Behn's own imagined geography of the slave trade would suggest an affinity between map and novel that, in essence, is simply not justified by a closer consideration of Behn's text. Rather than offering us a geographic setting complicit with the map, her novel proposes to counter the "map of slavery" by presenting a much more differentiated and contested sense of colonial space, one that complicates and undermines the kind of homogeneity that the map seeks to disseminate to unwary readers. Behn's novelization of the geography of the slave trade enables her to reject, or at least question, the geographic truths on which Gallagher and Gilroy appear to rely. Rather than simply transcribe the geography of the slave trade in a realistic and plausible manner, *Oroonoko* leaves the reader with a picture of the Atlantic world that owes as much to the Restoration stage as it does the various kinds of writing from which eighteenth-century realism takes its cue, such as the map, chorography, natural history, diary, or travel journal. Her incorporation of the discovery scene and the modalities of the scenic stage into her prose narrative give Behn a means of addressing the very limits of these methods of putatively realistic representation and, in the process, dramatize the politics of space that is at the heart of Great Britain's colonial ambitions.

# 3

# Surveying Ireland and Swift's "Country of the Mind"

Great, Good and Just, was once apply'd
To *One* who for his Country died,
To *One* who lives in its Defence,
We speak it in a Happier Sense.
O may the *Fates* thy Life prolong!
Our Country then can dread no Wrong.

— Jonathan Swift, "To His Grace the
Archbishop of Dublin, A Poem" (1724)

## Surveying Ireland

Aphra Behn places her geography of the slave trade against those maps and surveys of the Atlantic, Africa, and the Americas, which I discussed at the outset of the previous chapter, in order to tell a story about the colonial margins that the map is either unable or unwilling to convey. Her fictional account of Oroonoko and Imoinda's demise in Surinam blends the modalities of realism with the theatrical conventions of the scenic stage in order to offer a critique of Britain's imperial designs and the cartographic and chorographic traditions on which those designs rely. That critique, as I have argued, must be qualified to some extent given the fact that Behn's objections are highly partisan in nature, aimed principally at those opponents of Toryism whose conception of a greater Britain differed sharply from her own. When viewed in the context of political conflicts in England over matters of colonial trade and commerce, Behn's romantic and sentimentalized portrayal of Oroonoko may be viewed as strategic rather than as the expression of genuine sympathy for the indigenous peoples of Africa or the Americas. Behn's critique of empire is thus less a defense of those subjected to slavery than it is an attack against the mercantilist policies that mandated Britain's further investment in the slave trade. This particular vision of empire is predicated largely on commercial values and the logic of the market rather than the ideals of honor, stoic virtue, and courtly love associated with Behn's own brand of royalist politics. The map, when viewed in this light, becomes symbolic of a Whig mercantile ideology dedicated to the production and development of markets around the globe in order to generate wealth and capital at home. The military expropriation of land, the movement of labor, raw materials, and finished goods, and the creation of a colonial marketplace in which those items may be traded and exchanged, including the buying and selling of slaves: all are dependent, to some extent, on the map's ability to make vast amounts of territory legible and intelligible in a convenient, transportable format. The map is thus central to the promotion of colonial trade and commerce, the dispossession of native peoples, and the subsequent transformation of their lands into colonial possessions. As David Buisseret reminds us, "It was one thing to 'know' the territory and another to exercise tight control over it. . . . But we can hardly doubt that the existence of accurate cartographic information eventually proved a powerful tool in the imposition of central authority on the recalcitrant periphery."[1]

A similar dynamic also runs through the work of Behn's fellow Tory and critic of Britain's imperial ambitions Jonathan Swift, who viewed the map as an instrument and symbol of Whig power that was antithetical to republican virtue and a right understanding of the duties and responsibilities each citizen owes his or her country, including dying for it, as he notes in his 1724 poem to the Archbishop of Dublin. In much of his writing, *Gulliver's Travels* (1726) perhaps first and foremost, Swift routinely evinces a strain of anticartographic thought that, as I will demonstrate, has its origins in the popular resistance to the mapping of Ireland during the sixteenth and seventeenth centuries. Like those who engaged in numerous, deliberate acts of violence directed at English surveyors and officials responsible for transforming their country into a colonial possession, Swift well understood that the survey and map were technologies of expropriation intended to dispossess Ireland's native population of their land. The profound impact of those technologies on the rural landscape was not, however, limited to Ireland in his estimation but equally impacted England as well, most notably in the fetishizing of "the land itself," to borrow Helgerson's phrasing, as a source of national identity. Rather than an image of the nation with which subject and citizen might identify, maps are revealed by Swift to be totems of worldliness and vanity that transform and upend the very meaning of the word "country," displacing its classical origins as the figurative ground of the republic and its citizenry in favor of its more modern definition as a literal place that can be located on a map and, more problematically for Swift, that is defined strictly in terms of private property. Swift's preference for the former, a "country of the mind" as it were, thus constitutes a heterotopic space that stands against the map in its placing of the public good and patriotic virtue over and above private interest and nationalist sentiment, both of which are identified, in Swift's estimation, with England's colonial ambitions in Ireland dating back to at least the mid-sixteenth century, well before the establishment of the so-called first British Empire as depicted in Behn's novel.

In fact, the British plantation system, at least as Behn would have understood it, had its origins in the surveying and mapping of Ireland beginning in roughly 1580, when every English settlement in Ireland would require some form of survey and map.[2] Ireland does make an appearance in the world maps of Ptolemy's *Geographica* (1477) and its various reproductions by Gerard Mercator, Abraham Ortelius, John Goghe, and Lawrence Nowell over the course of the sixteenth and seventeenth centuries (fig. 10).[3] There is also the first known English map of Ireland, the "Cotton" map of the 1520s; however, while these maps were riddled with numerous inaccuracies and distortions, reflective of the "geographical ignorance" of the early Tudor period, they did represent, in some way, "England's dream of ruling all of Ireland."[4] The increased production of field surveys, chorographies, commentaries, and maps was critical to this

FIGURE 10. *Hibernia: Insula non procul ab Anglia vulgare Hirlandia vocata*, John Goghe, 1567. (© The British Library Board, shelfmark Cartographic Items 2081.d.)

process as the true extent and nature of Ireland's geography remained largely unknown, strange even, at least to the English, prior to the sixteenth century. The mapping of Ireland during this period was not so much a systematic effort to construct a complete and integrated picture of the nation and its geography, like the Ordnance Survey of the eighteenth and nineteenth centuries.[5] Rather, the cartographic history of Ireland reveals a much more chaotic, fragmented, and violent process by which the land was physically and graphically divorced from the people living on it, predominantly Catholic, and transformed into a source of revenue and capital for a Protestant English landowning class who firmly understood that maps and surveys were both a means to and a potent symbol of their wealth and power.[6] The cartographic appropriation of Irish lands relied largely on cadastral and field surveys of Irish estates and plantations that served to determine the boundaries and extent of a given parcel of land, as well as its "legal" title, condition, and market value.[7] I place the word "legal" in quotes here in order to underscore the fact that the land in question was confiscated, or rather, expropriated by the English, either through direct military or governmental action; usually, it was some combination of the two. Regardless of the methods employed, the geography of that land, whether held in private or in common, needed to be determined with some degree of precision so that it could then be properly divvied up and parceled out to soldiers, settlers, merchant adventurers, and those members of the English aristocracy who supported, either directly or indirectly, the colonization of Ireland and the pursuit of the Protestant cause there.[8] Robert Lythe's *A Single Draught of Mounster* (1571) is widely considered "the first detailed and comprehensive survey of any major region in Ireland" (fig. 11).[9] Under the guidance and supervision of Sir Henry Sidney, the Lord Deputy of Ireland, Lythe's map provided an unprecedented level of geographical detail and knowledge of the province in order to exert greater administrative control over the lords residing there and so bring them under English rule. Ironically, Lythe's map was ignored entirely when the Munster plantation was being planned only fifteen years later. However, despite this curious elision, later efforts to survey and map the Munster plantation nevertheless shared a common political and ideological goal with Lythe's map, specifically, to identify and displace the ancient Irish feudal lordships and to transform Munster into English property for the purposes of economic development and profit.[10] The promise of Lythe's map would, in fact, be fully realized some twenty years later by Lord Burghley, who oversaw the planning of the Munster plantation, including the creation of surveys and maps that offered an even more refined and precise image of the proposed settlement (fig. 12). His 1589 maps of Munster, based on surveys conducted by Arthur Robins and Francis Jobson, were the first to cartographically inscribe the seigniorial boundaries of the newly formed plantation estates onto the "blank canvas" of Ireland, at once emptying out and erasing what had existed prior and, in its place, inserting a view of the land that had been at once

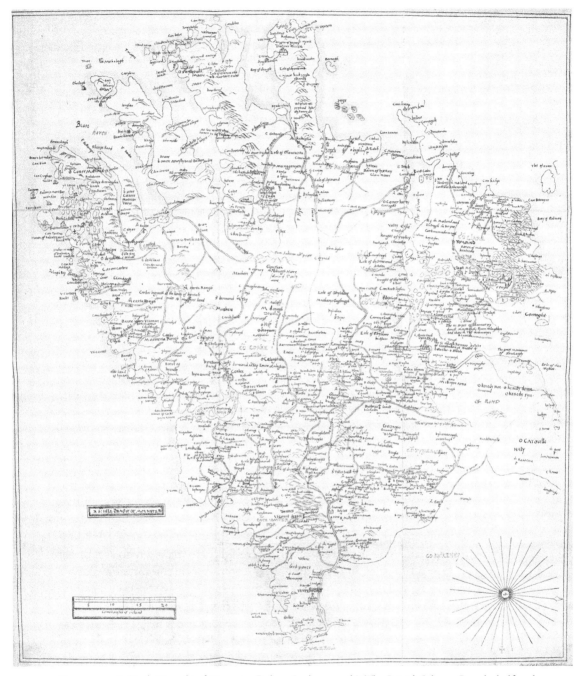

FIGURE 11. *A Single Draught of Mounster*, Robert Lythe, 1571. (© The British Library Board, shelfmark Cartographic Items 2080.f )

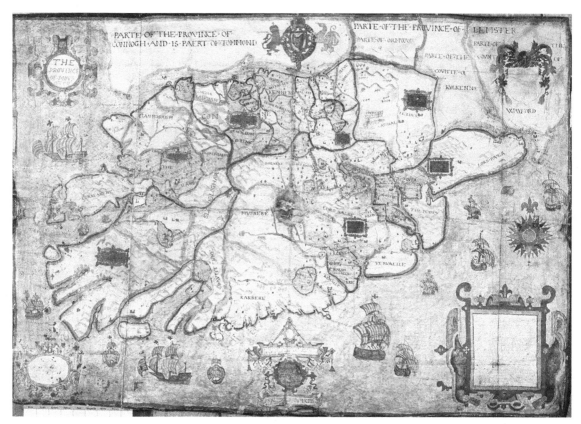

FIGURE 12. *The Province of Mounster,* Francis Jobson, 1595. (Courtesy National Library of Ireland)

dissected and carved up yet utterly naturalized through the inclusion of salient topographical details, "a new framing (as it were) in the forge," to borrow Edmund Spenser's phrase.[11] This "new framing," however, was not without its complications or impediments.

Partly in response to Sir Warham St. Leger, then provost-marshal of Munster, and his lament that "there is no man here skilful to make a map as it ought to be,"[12] Lord Burghley, in 1584, appointed Robins to the commission charged with surveying and mapping Munster for the purposes of establishing a plantation there. Somewhat of an outsider with respect to the workings of the Tudor court and the geography of Ireland, Robins represented, in J. H. Andrews's words, "a surveyor of a new breed, new to Ireland that is, who actually measured the land instead of just looking at it and who then expressed his measurements in graphic form."[13] Perhaps because of his lack of familiarity with Ireland and relative inexperience with court politics, Robins, along with his fellow commissioners, including most notably Francis Jobson, chose to abandon past practice and instead adopt a more objective and rational standard in their plans for the proposed Munster seigniories, one that would carefully detail the layout and distribution of farms, settlements, and roads in clear, diagrammatic form.[14] The principle difficulty, however, for Robins and his team of surveyors lay in reconciling their geometric, linear approach to planning the Munster plantation, which was favored by many at court for political rather than technical reasons, with the varied, difficult, and often impenetrable nature of the Irish landscape and "the stiffer realities of deeply rooted boundaries, peoples and ecologies," including native systems and methods of mensuration that were, at times, radically incompatible with English standards.[15] William J. Smyth aptly describes this conflict between English and Irish understandings of and approaches to the land as an "uneven battle between the power to shape and flatten worlds which are defined more by accounting, geometry, mathematics and perspective mapping" and "a gaelicized/Gaelic world . . . where territories and peoples were ruled and administered mainly by the words and the living images associated with manuscripts, memory, local lore and myth."[16] The cartographic expropriation of Irish lands in Munster, as conceived by the likes of Burghley, Robins, and Jobson, inevitably runs up against indigenous hierarchies of space and forms of geographic knowledge that had developed and accrued over time, and so are neither easily dismissed nor overcome.

While not always successful in their efforts, Robins and Jobson sought to apply their more modern, scientific approach to actual conditions on the ground and to accommodate, wherever possible, the numerous challenges presented by Munster's recalcitrant geography, including dense wastelands, unpredictable weather, ancient land divisions, and quite often, a population resistant to the English surveyors and their work, even to the point of violence. On this last issue, Robins wrote in 1587 that he would need to increase pay in order to attract quality surveyors to Ireland because the people were "for the most part discontented with the course to be observed" and so made their work "dangerous . . . by reason of the stratagems that may be laid by the evil disposed."[17] Robins then goes on to cite the story of a surveyor who was "bombarded with rocks from an upper-storey window when approaching an Irish castle to ask for topographical guidance."[18] Such stories are, in fact, commonplace in the history of the surveying and mapping of Munster and Ireland in general. Philip Bysse, the archdeacon of Cloyne, was appointed in 1642 to head a special commission charged with taking depositions from Protestant landowners in Munster following the Catholic uprising the preceding year. The purpose of the depositions was, in part, to determine the nature and extent of the property losses incurred as a result of the rebellion and then, using the depositions as evidence, however questionable, to seek remuneration from England, often in the form of confiscated Catholic lands. The 1641 Depositions, as they are commonly referred to, were thus used, much as the surveys and maps themselves, as "documents of conquest" throughout the seventeenth and eighteenth centuries.[19] For his troubles, Philip Bysse, like some of those earlier surveyors responsible for the mapping of the Munster plantation, was murdered in the summer of 1643 while gathering so-called evidence of Catholic atrocities committed against the Protestant settlers.

Even in the absence of outright violence and hostility, the efforts of the English surveyors in Munster were routinely frustrated by local informants who, as James Delle notes, would often insist on speaking only Gaelic in order to intentionally confuse and mislead the would-be cartographers, compromising the accuracy and integrity of their maps in the process. "When informants described the landscape literally in Gaelic terms, or in vague, obfuscating ways, they were in fact frustrating the efforts of the surveyors to scientifically interpret and render the landscape."[20] The Munster commission also faced numerous internal threats to the legitimacy of their work, in particular, accusations that Robins and other surveyors intentionally skewed the numbers in order to reap personal financial gain or to curry favor with the new estate owners, who invariably complained when their total acreage appeared to fall below their allotted amount.[21] While mistakes and errors are to be expected, the willful manipulation and distortion of a survey for profit was a common charge leveled at surveyors; it is one we will see frequently made against Sir William Petty and his Down Survey of Ireland later in the century, even though he was never officially found guilty of bias or favoritism one way or another. Further, the enormity of the undertaking, the size and varied topography of the area, the pressure to meet certain deadlines, and the general lack of material support and necessary personnel made surveying and mapping the entirety of Munster difficult, if not impossible. In order to continue their work in the face of such obstacles, surveyors often submitted estimates and projections based on the work they had done, with the intention of returning to check and, if necessary, amend those estimates with a proper field survey. However, even when they were able to dedicate themselves to a thorough plotting and measuring of the confiscated lands, differences and irregularities in surveying methods and technologies emerged between Robins, Jobson, and the other members of their company, often diverging to the point that they could neither corroborate their findings for the very same bit of ground nor stitch together their respective surveys into a single, complete picture of the Munster plantation, thus leaving us with a more fragmented and contingent view of the Irish landscape than is suggested by the map.

The resulting surveys and maps produced by Burghley and his commission were, for many of these reasons, deeply flawed and, by some accounts, a complete failure.[22] While certainly a failure by modern standards, or even those of the eighteenth century, the surveying and mapping of the Munster plantation, nevertheless, represents a decided turn in England's desire and ability to make Ireland visible in ways that had not been possible before the work of Lythe, Burghley, Robins, and Jobson. Collectively, they helped to transform surveying from an informal process rooted in local, customary modes of geographic inquiry and representation to a skilled profession dedicated to formal measurement, geometric order, and mathematical certainty.[23] Bernhard Klein, among others, notes that, traditionally, the surveyor was viewed as an overseer, or "steward," of the land, less concerned with "the shape of the land and its cartographic representation" and more with "the complex network of duties and responsibilities that defined the relationship between soil and subject, between tenant and lord."[24] That older, more expansive understanding of the surveyor as a mediating figure within the social space of feudal England and Ireland, however, gives way to its more modern definition as a person principally concerned with the measurement and representation of the land for the purposes of establishing legal title and determining its monetary or commercial value.[25] Surveyors were increasingly employed solely to survey and map the physical terrain in question, whether on behalf of the state or a private individual, and to assess the relative value of the land so that it could be divided up and apportioned in a putatively equitable and lawful manner. The surveyor was, in this sense, less a figure of socialization and mediation and more an "independent specialist" with "a newly legalistic appreciation of tenurial relationships and newly rationalistic standards of land measurement and estate planning."[26] By the seventeenth and eighteenth centuries, the surveyor would become a critical figure in shaping the spatial economy of agrarian capitalism and the colonial plantation system as it emerged first in Ireland and later the Americas.

As noted earlier, this revolution within the science and practice of surveying was not without its detractors, both at home and on the colonial margins. The surveyor frequently appears as a target of intense criticism and hatred throughout the early modern period, in part because surveyors were associated, rightly, with "the new spatial rationalism in land quantification" that principally served the interests of the landowner over those of the tenant, especially in terms of the enclosure and privatization of common lands.[27] Andrew McCrae observes that surveyors, whether in England or Ireland, were viewed with deep suspicion and "frequently faced the threat of popular action against their attempts to measure the land."[28] In sixteenth- and seventeenth-century England, the work of surveying and mapping was often resisted for political, economic, and religious reasons stemming from their intimate connection with the overturning and transformation of the traditional agrarian order, prompting many authors to decry such activity as a form of sin and a general sign of a growing moral decay. As John Norden notes in *Surveyor's Dialogue* (1607), surveyors were routinely seen as the "cordes whereby poore men are drawne into seruitude and slauery."[29] In Ireland during this same period, the resistance to surveying and surveyors was, to be sure, a bit more palpable and immediate, as many surveyors faced openly hostile and violent conditions on a routine basis, the nature and purpose of their work well known and well understood in advance by the local population. For many native inhabitants, "surveying was considered a form of territorial invasion, designed to dispossess people of their land," and so "called for rigorous resistance."[30] As William J. Smyth argues, any historical

assessment of the surveying and mapping of Ireland during the early modern
period must take into account the many acts of resistance to England's efforts
to impose its own modes of geographic calculation and representation on the
Irish: "Colonized people are not passive, even if—as in colonial mapping—
they lose control of the representation and narration of stories about their
own lands and lose their own voice as the language of the map translates Irish
landscapes, localities and placenames into English language forms."[31] Rather
than capitulate or accede to those surveyors and mapmakers working on behalf
of England's colonial interests, the Irish actively sought to defend and protect
their land by preserving the geography of Ireland's precolonial past as it appears in their myths, annals, genealogies, and topographical poems, as well as
directly impeding and stymieing the work of surveyors tasked with mapping
Ireland in one form or another.[32]

    We see, for example, many such acts of open resistance in response to the
planning and settlement of the Ulster plantation during the late sixteenth and
early seventeenth century. As Mark Netzloff points out, the Ulster plantation
was not included in John Speed's 1610 map of Ireland, which appeared in his
*The Theatre of the Empire of Great Britain* the following year, precisely because of Ulster's affiliations with the Gaelic Irish resistance to English rule.[33]
Netzloff concludes that, "among English colonial holdings in the seventeenth
century, the Ulster plantation's status is exceptional as a space whose identity
is produced out of its resistance to and absence from cartographical representation."[34] And as in Munster, violent reprisals by hostile locals remained a very
real possibility, prompting many surveyors to request the assistance of armed
escorts in order to protect them while in the field. Robert Lythe, an early surveyor of Ulster whom I discussed earlier, required military escorts wherever he
went, and even then, there were regions, particularly in the north and northwest
part of the country, that he was entirely unable to survey.[35] In his first attempt
to map Ulster in 1567, Lythe was "obliged for security reasons to withdraw
southwards to the more peaceful lands of Munster and Leinster," and some
years later, after a second attempt, he declared the territory "unfit" and "unsafe"
for surveying.[36] Likewise, in 1590, Francis Jobson, who had worked previously
with Arthur Robins in Munster, declared the inhabitants of Ulster "a most savage and rebellious people from whose cruelty ... God only by his divine power
delivered me being every hour in danger to lose my head."[37] While this never, in
fact, came to pass in the case of Jobson, other surveyors were not as fortunate.

    John Browne, a cartographer and sheriff who produced a highly regarded
map of Mayo in 1584, was killed while surveying Connacht at the outbreak of
a rebellion there in 1589.[38] In a letter to the Earl of Salisbury, dated August 29,
1609, Sir John Davies, the Irish attorney general, offers this brief tribute to
Richard Bartlett, a prominent surveyor and cartographer who was beheaded,
circa 1603, while working in Donegal: "For though the country be now quiet
and the heads of greatness gone, yet our geographers do not forget what enter-

tainment the Irish of Tyrconnell gave to a map-maker about the end of the late
great rebellion: for one Barkeley [Bartlett] being appointed by the late Earl of
Devonshire to draw a true and perfect map of the north parts of Ulster (the old
maps being false and defective), when he came into Tyrconnell the inhabitants
took off his head, because they would not have their country discovered."[39]
Richard Bartlett had served as a cartographer under the command of Lord
Mountjoy and was largely responsible for producing maps of Ulster that aided
the conquest of and subsequent military campaigns against the province and its
inhabitants, including most notably *A Generalle Description of Ulster* (1602–3)
(fig. 13). And like Lythe, Burghley, Robins, and Jobson, rather than copy from
older, outdated maps or engage in wild speculation, Bartlett relied principally
on direct measurements and firsthand knowledge of heretofore unseen and
unknown parts of Gaelic Ireland. As a result of this more empirical approach,
his surveys and maps brought an unprecedented level of clarity and legibility

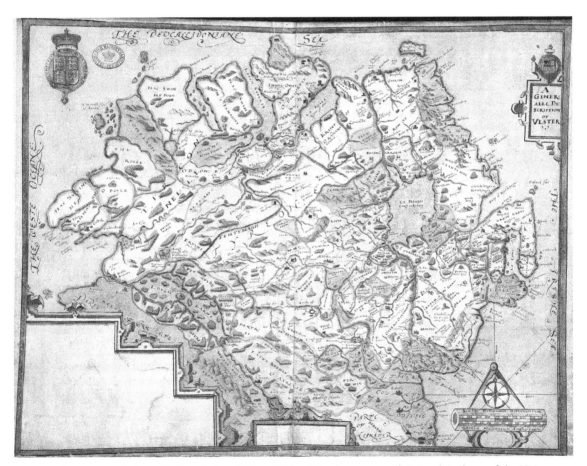

FIGURE 13. *A Generalle Description of Ulster,* Richard Bartlett, 1602–3. (National Archives of the UK,
ref. MPF1/37)

to their subject and ultimately helped place Ulster under the rule and control
of the English, both physically and symbolically. While there still remained a
good deal of conjecture and outright speculation in the mapping of Ireland,
Bartlett sought to invest himself in direct observation and the kinds of surveying methods and technologies necessary to a faithful and "intimate" portrait of
Ulster and to its further conquest and exploitation as a model English plantation. For these reasons, Bartlett's efforts were often resisted by those Gaelic
Irish who did not wish their country to be "discovered," as Davies characterizes
the inhabitants of Tyrconnell, and he ultimately lost his life at the hands of
a local population who grasped the dire consequences of Bartlett's work and
who, quite understandably, opposed it at every turn, even if that meant behead-
ing a surveyor or two in the process.

Despite his untimely death, the colonization of Ulster would not, in fact,
have been possible without Bartlett's highly detailed surveys and maps: "No
other cartographer in Ireland mapped, painted and narrated the story of a con-
quered and subjected landscape and people as eloquently as Bartlett did."[40] He
possessed a unique ability to incorporate local knowledge regarding the people
and the land into his surveys and maps of Ulster, if only for the purpose of
usurping their claims to that land and declaring sovereignty over it: "Bartlett's
brilliance as an artist and cartographer is further confirmed by his ability to
move from the intimate and deeply symbolic bird's-eye sketches to panoramic
map-views depicting with the whole of, or major regions within, Ulster. The
English military conquest of Ulster is now matched by his precise portrait of
the topography of one Old World going down and a New World in embryo."[41]
The precision of Bartlett's maps, which were largely produced for the English
military, is the product not only of an increased attention to direct observation
and measurement but also a greater reliance on local informants and documents to provide guidance and critical information regarding the geography
of Ulster and the "Gaelic ordering of the landscape," including the location of
ancient families, land divisions, and town sites.[42] He and his fellow surveyors'
use of local knowledge, often hearsay of varying quality, was due in part to Ireland's lack of a professional class of native surveyors and mapmakers, as well
as patrons to support and encourage their work.[43] The English surveyor was
thus, quite often, at the mercy (or lack thereof in the case of Bartlett) of local
inhabitants whose geographical knowledge was central to the production of a
fuller, more complete map of Ireland. At the same time, Ireland's indigenous
population, not wishing to be dispossessed of their lands and their country,
proved a constant impediment to the realization of such a map through their
various acts of resistance and subversion, both individual and collective. It is
a tension that will continue to play itself out over the course of the following
centuries as plantation and estate maps bring the geography of Ireland into
increasingly sharper view, while simultaneously erasing the very source and
cause of their production.

The Bodley Survey of Ulster (1609–10), for example, favored an approach similar to Bartlett's in that it also incorporated a significant amount of local geographical and topographical knowledge into its findings, along with sketches of the landscape and, when possible, actual measurements carried out with surveying instruments. As with Munster, a commission, organized and led by Sir Josias Bodley, was appointed in May 1609 to survey and map the proposed Ulster plantation. However, given the size of the area, the variety of terrain, and the relatively short amount of time allotted to conduct the survey, Bodley and his fellow commissioners, including the cartographer Thomas Raven, decided instead to rely on the expertise of local informants to help them complete their work. Bodley himself writes: "We thought it our readiest course that . . . we should call unto us out of every barony, such persons as by their experience in the country could give us the name and quality of every ballibo, quarter, tate or other common measure in any of the precincts of the same; with special notice how they butted or merged interchangeably the one on the other. By which means and other necessary helps, we contrived those maps."[44] Those "contrived" maps were not always precise field surveys, which were time consuming and costly. Quite often, they were little more than "transcriptions" of verbal information and descriptions offered by local inhabitants, who would also routinely walk, or perambulate, the boundary of the property or area in question. As a result of this assistance on the local level, whether volunteered or coerced, the maps produced by the Bodley Survey reveal an unprecedented degree of accuracy and detail with respect to the estates, townlands, and parishes of Ulster, capturing in particular the contours and nuances of the Irish landscape just prior to its formalization as part of the future English settlement: "[The Ulster Irish] had a most intimate knowledge of their own dynamic landscapes and could translate this oral knowledge into a language that the English cartographers could turn into map form."[45] The Bodley Survey participates in this "intimate knowledge" but with the sole purpose of mapping and carving out new baronial estates for the future landlords of the Ulster plantation. The commission's embracing of modern surveying methods and technologies, as well as its investment in local knowledge of the Irish landscape, lent the resulting maps a degree of clarity and precision that was no doubt instrumental to the conquest and settlement of Ulster.

To be sure, Bodley's maps were still a far cry from those produced by other, more comprehensive surveys conducted later that century, such as the Strafford Survey of Connaught (1635–37) and William Petty's Down Survey (1654–59), as well as the Trustees' Survey (1705–6) early the following century.[46] The maps remain deeply compromised due the inherent difficulties and numerous resistances that surveyors faced in their pursuit of a more refined and detailed image of Ulster, including, among others, the dubious quality of geographic information offered by native informants, without whom, ironically, the surveyors could not complete their work. Nevertheless, the Bodley Survey served

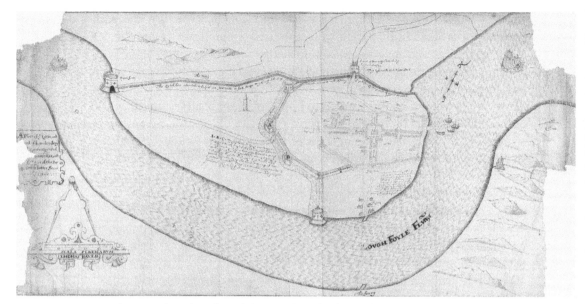

FIGURE 14. *The River of Lough Foyle, with the citty of Londonderry,* Thomas Raven, 1625. (The Board of Trinity College Dublin)

as a model for and an important precursor to these later efforts to map Ireland, its decided focus on matters of property and tenurial rights in particular.[47] Thomas Raven, a professional cartographer whose work was instrumental to the success of the Bodley Survey, was later employed by Sir Thomas Phillips to survey and map Londonderry as part of the Irish Commission of 1622 (fig. 14). As Bernhard Klein notes, Raven applied "the specific mode of conceptualizing space in a plantation context" to the entire county by emphasizing the "political and economic inscriptions on the landscape generated by the forceful change of ownership" rather than the natural features of the landscape.[48] Raven's principle interest in the "new proprietary boundaries imposed on the regional topography," Klein continues, was the logical extension of his background and training in plantation and estate mapping, both of which were becoming, over the course of the seventeenth and eighteenth centuries, increasingly aligned in terms of their respective methods and practitioners. By the eighteenth century, in fact, there is little distinction to be drawn between plantation and estate mapping in Ireland other than that the former was commissioned and conducted by the state and the latter by private citizens, many of whom had originally acquired their respective properties through conquest and settlement.

J. H. Andrews argues that both the Strafford Survey, under Charles I, and later the Down Survey, conducted by Sir William Petty during Cromwell's rule, informed and spurred the burgeoning practice of estate mapping, while many surveyors, like Raven, who were employed by both the English government and private landowners, utilized techniques and methods developed "for small-scale geographical purposes" in their plantation maps: "Not only did the official surveyors have something to teach their brethren in the private sector, but much of their influence could be interpreted as 'feedback.' In many ways, after all, the Down and Strafford Surveys and the rest were not so very different from estate surveys. . . . To this extent the term 'plantation survey' is a misnomer, at least in a professional and technological context; and the same may be true of the term 'plantation surveyor.'"[49] Many surveyors who were employed by the state to map the Munster and Ulster plantations, including, among others, Francis Jobson, also availed their services to the new landlords, who were eager for accurate surveys in order to further subdivide their estates for the purpose of leasing them out, thus establishing Andrews's feedback loop between the two cartographic genres.[50] Further, both the Strafford and Down Surveys were routinely cited in legal cases involving the transfer of private property and the settlement of disputes regarding rents, acreage, and boundaries throughout the eighteenth and nineteenth centuries.[51] Their respective maps also frequently appeared, in one form or another, as part of advertisements for the sale or lease of estate lands and, at least in the case of the Down Survey, were included in one seventeenth-century estate atlas.[52] This intimate relationship between plantation and estate surveys and surveyors, I would contend, underscores the map's increasing association with England's expropriation of Irish lands and the subsequent transformation of those lands into private property. The transformation of the Irish landscape into a colonial possession is perhaps nowhere more evident than in the work of Sir William Petty during the latter half of the seventeenth century. Petty's efforts to map Ireland during this period, as David Buisseret observes, "formed the foundation of the British occupation of a large part of Ireland; it is a fine example of what Karl Marx might have called the map as the instrument of the possessing classes."[53]

The Down Survey, conducted by Sir William Petty and his chief cartographer, Thomas Taylor, from roughly 1654 to 1659 as part of the Cromwellian conquest and settlement, represents the first systematic, parish by parish field survey of Ireland. Much like its predecessors, Petty's Down Survey involved the gathering and collection of geographic information on the local level in the form of direct observation and measurements, "bird's eye" sketches, and extensive interviews with native inhabitants. An amateur surveyor, Petty also borrowed heavily from the methods and technologies used to conduct the Strafford Survey and, in some instances, reproduced its measurements and maps, much to the chagrin of those professional surveyors who viewed Petty as little more than a clever plagiarist.[54] Regardless, his efforts, however suspect, were far more comprehensive and expansive than any of England's previous attempts to map Ireland. The Commonwealth Act of 1653, which officially designated Cromwell as England's Lord Protector, stipulated "the exact and perfect survey and admeasurement of all and every the honors, baronies, castles, manors, lands, tenements, and hereditaments, forfeited by force or virtue of all

or any of the said Acts."[55] In response, a Gross Survey was immediately commissioned by Ireland's then surveyor general, Benjamin Worsley, to determine
how the so-called forfeited or confiscated lands, largely occupied by Catholics
but also Protestant royalists, were to be allocated to the respective officers, soldiers, and adventurers under Cromwell's command.[56] Worsley's survey, however, was widely viewed as inadequate to the task, especially by Petty, because
it relied too heavily on overly broad estimations as to the amount and value of
the confiscated lands, estimations that were proved incorrect in subsequent
surveys, such as the Civil Survey (1654–56) and Petty's own Down Survey.
Petty's chief objection to Worsley's methods and general approach to surveying
was that he focused exclusively on "the [civil] boundaries of the forfeited lands,"
baronies, parishes, townlands, and so forth, rather than the "permanent record
of physical and territorial boundaries," such as rivers, mountains, ridges, bogs,
loughs, and other natural features of the Irish landscape.[57] Petty's interest in
this more comprehensive approach, which Worsley believed would take far
too long for the intended purpose, stemmed from his desire to not only survey
and subdivide the forfeited lands but also to precisely map out the shape and
boundaries of the estates to be allocated and to determine, as accurately as
possible, the proportion and distribution of arable to nonarable land within a
given estate, something Worsley's Gross Survey failed, or rather refused, to do.

Petty's style and approach to cartography in the Down Survey was perhaps not unique or particularly original when viewed in the context of other
seventeenth-century plantation surveys of Ireland, the Bodley and Strafford
Surveys in particular; his rigorous and nearly single-minded interest in assess-
ing the value and productivity of the land would have a profound influence on
the mapping of Ireland well into the eighteenth century.[58] A primary benefi-
ciary of this approach was, not surprisingly, Petty himself. In a relatively short
period of time, he had amassed a considerable fortune from his Irish lands,
which led to charges from merchant adventurers, soldiers, and officers, all of
whom had a vested interest in the equitable distribution of the confiscated
lands, that his findings were less than objective and only furthered Petty's am-
bitious financial and political goals.[59] As I noted earlier, it is an accusation
commonly leveled at surveyors, who, at times, put their own interests above
that of the landholder and his tenants. While Petty made frequent claims to
scientific and mathematical certainty in defense of his Down Survey against
the accusations of his detractors, Worsley and Sir Jerome Sankey most notably,
the reality was that his attempt not only to map Ireland but also to render judgments as to the productivity and profitability of the land was highly subjective
and riddled with both personal and political interests, interests that the map
was constructed to obscure and render impervious to criticism. Mary Poovey
raises this issue in her assessment of Petty and the application of his dubious brand of "political arithmetic" to the surveying and mapping of Ireland:
"By representing expert interpretation as superior to personal interests, Petty

helped forge the relationship between numbers and impartiality that has made the modern fact such a crucial instrument for policy-making. In the complex amalgam he created from experimental philosophy and Hobbesian deduction, expertise linked particulars that seemed to be (but were not) observed to theories that seemed not to be (but were) interested, for his representation of expertise made interpretation (and interest) seem incidental to method and instruments."[60] Surveying and cartography are, in this sense, less a scientific discipline or methodology intended to produce objective, verifiable truths and more a kind of discourse, a rhetorical mode, that serves to legitimate private and state interests by displacing and, ultimately, effacing the political, religious, and economic impact of those interests on Ireland and its native population. Petty's appeal to the survey and the map as a putatively impartial authority is an extension of what Poovey refers to as the "gentrification of mathematics," or the incorporation of certain mathematical processes and skills, including, among others, surveying, astronomy, navigation, architecture, and bookkeeping, into the private sector as a legitimate way of knowing and representing the world.[61] Surveying and cartography offered Petty, as a gentleman scientist, a means of reducing the Irish landscape to a set of calculable numbers, facts, and figures that no longer reflected its history and its people but rather England's vision of an Ireland divorced from its past, subsumed and fully assimilated into the imperial map.

Poovey concludes, "In theory, substituting economic categories for religion, political affiliation, and language would encourage the Irish . . . to realize that their true interest lay not in clinging to their Irishness but in embracing habits that would make them like the English."[62] Surveying and cartography are two such modes, or technologies, of substitution, translation, and exchange that served Petty's and, by extension, England's imperial ambitions in Ireland. While the effects of Petty's Down Survey were immediate and profound, the maps themselves were not widely available to the general public until 1685 and the publication of *Hiberniae delineatio*, an atlas of national, provincial, and county maps based upon he and Taylor's original plantation maps (figs. 15 and 16). Despite its shortcomings, including a number of scribal errors, unverifiable or misattributed place-names and geographic features, and an overall lack of production values, Petty's atlas was, nevertheless, quite popular, due in part to its relatively modest cost, especially when compared to previous atlases that contained maps of Ireland, such as John Speed's *The Theatre of the Empire of Great Britaine* (1610–11).[63] The atlas was even reprinted, unedited and unrevised, in 1735 by Petty's son, the Earl of Shelburne, and the Dublin bookseller George Grierson, testament to either its enduring appeal to English and Irish audiences or, as J. H. Andrews suggests, the "low state of Irish cartography in the post-Petty era."[64] His comment is not without some truth. Given the general lack of original, comprehensive plantation surveys and maps in the years following the Down Survey, save for the Trustees' Survey (1705–6), which had

FIGURE 15. "A General Mapp of Ireland," Sir William Petty, 1685. (© The British Library Board, shelfmark Cartographic Items Maps * 10805.(7))

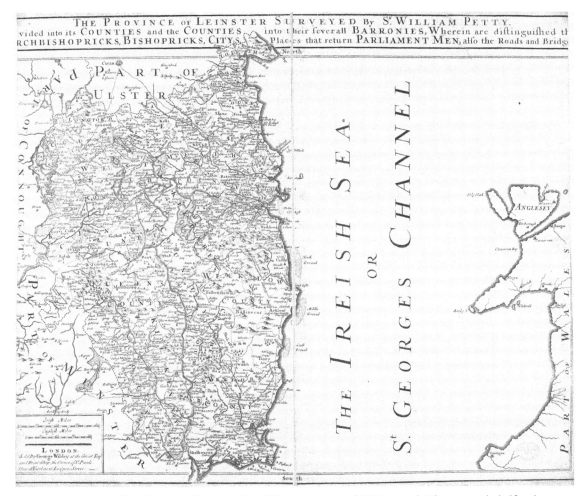

FIGURE 16. "The Province of Leinster," Sir William Petty, 1685. (© The British Library Board, shelfmark Cartographic Items Maps * 10945.(5))

been ordered by William III, Petty's atlas would become a mandatory reference point and important touchstone for many contemporary and future cartographers of Ireland, quite a number of whom openly and liberally appropriated, revised, and reproduced its maps for both English and Continental audiences, including, among others, Robert Greene, Charles Molyneux, William Berry, Thomas Moland, Edwin Sandys, Robert Morden, Henry Pratt, Francis Lamb, Philip Lea, Herman Moll, and Robert Molesworth. Their collective articulations of and improvements upon Petty's original maps, including the creation of less weighty and expensive volumes, as well as detailed single-sheet maps, help make his particular version of Ireland a definitive one for nearly a century and a half following the atlas's publication. As Johann Georg Kohl, a German map historian, said in 1844, "It is scarcely credible, yet it is not the less true, that all the maps of Ireland which were made during the last century, were based on an old one, drawn towards the close [sic] of the seventeenth century."[65] Kohl was referring, of course, to Petty and his *Hiberniae delineatio*.

Petty's influence on the surveying and mapping of Ireland, however, extended well beyond his atlas and the subsequent production of regional and national maps that both imitated and improved upon his original; his contributions to cadastral and field surveying, I would argue, played an equally formative role in the development and production of estate maps during the eighteenth century.[66] Robert Southwell, who would later become secretary of state to Ireland under William III, asked Petty for copies of the Down Survey maps that included his estate so that he might know not only the true extent of his property but also the larger context of Ireland's administrative and territorial units by which that property is bounded and, in some sense, defined. Pleased by this "reassuring image, in map form, of a country parcelled into successively smaller units each in the care of an appropriate authority," Southwell recommended to his friend and fellow landlord Viscount John Perceval that he also commission an estate map in order to see just how his property was geographically bounded to the county, the province, and the kingdom of Ireland.[67] Further, Sir Richard Cox, echoing Southwell's advice, believed that "the best view of an estate is a pattent or settlement and the next is a rent roll, yet it must be allowed me that the map and topography of it is neither unpleasant nor unprofitable."[68] Many agreed with Cox's sentiment and soon were also having their estates surveyed and mapped. In 1659, Thomas Taylor, Petty's chief cartographer himself, produced maps of Edward Robert's estate based on the Down Survey. Josias Bateman, an Anglo-Irish professional surveyor whose work first appeared in the 1690s, not long after Taylor's and Petty's, delivered an estate atlas to the Earls of Burlington and Cork (fig. 17). The atlas, dated 1717, was modeled expressly on Southwell and Perceval's more "progressive" estate maps, meaning that it eschewed rough estimates and figures, a common practice for which Bateman had great contempt, in deference to a more refined and detailed image of the land.[69] Estate maps, of varying quality and accuracy, were privately commissioned by prominent members of the English and Anglo-Irish gentry from the late seventeenth to the eighteenth century, including, among others, the Irish estates of the Earl of Cork, the Earl of Kerry, the Earl of Antrim, Viscount Kenmare, and the Marquess of Downshire. As I noted earlier, the estate map served a variety of financial, legal, and political functions with respect to the settlement of Ireland throughout the sixteenth and seventeenth centuries, but they were also increasingly seen as aesthetic objects to be contemplated, admired, and treasured by the landowner and his family, as well as other members of their social circle. For this reason, the estate maps were highly baroque affairs, with many decorative flourishes, ornate illustrations, and allegorical marginalia, often boldly colored, in order not only to announce the beauty and grandeur of the property depicted but also to legitimate the

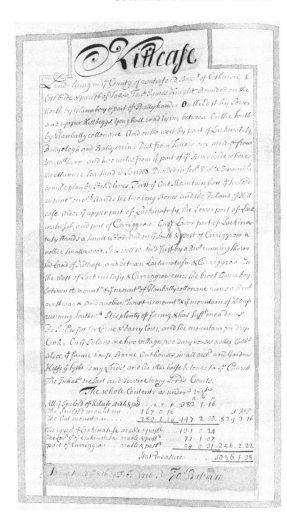
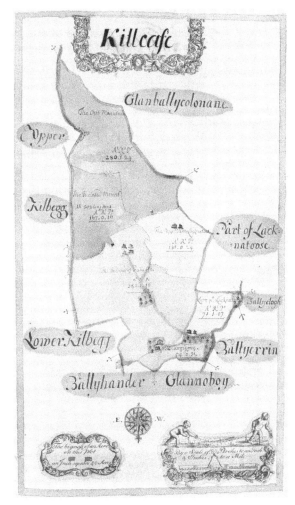

FIGURE 17. *Killcalfe*, Josias Bateman, 1717. (Courtesy National Library of Ireland)

power and authority of its dignified and tasteful owner. By the eighteenth century, the estate map had become something of a vogue among Ireland's nobility and landed gentry, with more and more of the Protestant landowning class there wishing to see the expanse of their respective properties laid out before their eyes all at once, to possess symbolically and graphically what they already possessed by law and by repeated acts of war and aggression.[70]

This turn toward the estate map is thus the logical extension of the seventeenth-century plantation surveys and maps, which were principally concerned with expropriating Irish lands for the purposes of settlement. The two genres of cartography are in fact intimately associated with one another throughout Ireland's colonial history, and they share similar methods and technologies of surveying, as well as cartographers who worked in both contexts.

J. H. Andrews observes that plantation maps routinely informed estate surveys and maps, such as those of the Egmont, Southwell, and Herbert estates in Ireland, all of which "owed much in style as well as scale to the kind of barony maps drawn by the plantation surveyors."[71] He later concludes that "the typical early eighteenth-century estate map showed little advance on run-of-the-mill lease maps of the same period, or for that matter on the kind of plantation map from which they both have the air of being derived," with both the Down and Trustees' Surveys being a common source for many subsequent estate maps.[72] Henry Pratt's estate maps for the Earl of Kerry, for one, were particularly derivative of Petty, "more like the Down Survey than the Down Survey itself," at least in Andrews's estimation (fig. 18).[73] Pratt was chiefly known for his work as an estate surveyor and cartographer, having availed his services not only to the Kerry estate but also to that of Sir William Robinson. Recognizing his

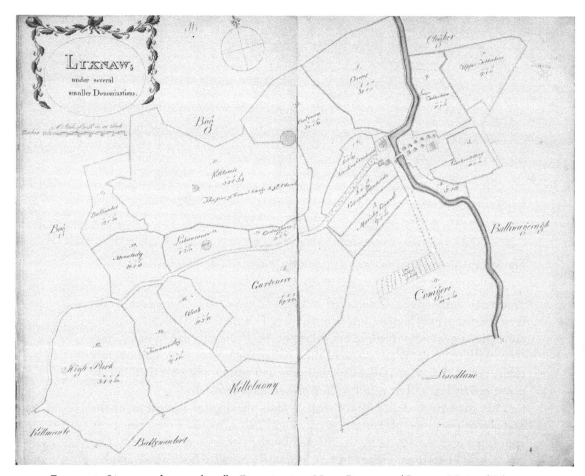

FIGURE 18. *Lixnaw, under several smaller Denominations,* Henry Pratt, 1697. (Courtesy National Library of Ireland)

talents at the estate level, Robinson hired Pratt to assist with his mapping of a proposed system of English barracks throughout Ireland, a position that Pratt eventually assumed in full, among other private and government-sponsored jobs, shortly following the turn of the eighteenth century. Pratt was also responsible for a 1708 single-sheet map of Ireland, *Tabula Hiberniae novissima et emendatissima*, which draws on a wide variety of sources, including, among others, Petty's Down Survey, as a "base on which to plot his own design" (fig. 19).[74] Pratt looked not only to plantation surveys and maps in the making of his national map but also his own 1697 survey of the Kerry estate, which enabled him to correct and revise Petty's original measurements. For Pratt and many of his contemporaries, there is a clear feedback loop between plantation, estate, military, and national maps in terms of their respective methods, technologies, practitioners, and even consumers; one cartographic genre informs and determines the shape of the other, further blurring the distinction between the private and public market for maps that would facilitate the conquest and settlement of Ireland.

Perhaps this fact gets lost as we move into the eighteenth century and the geography of Ireland comes into ever sharper focus, but it need not, and should not, if we take into consideration the idea of cartographic resistance as an ongoing and integral part of Ireland's colonial history. While there is decidedly less research and scholarship devoted to this history after the plantation period of the sixteenth and seventeenth centuries, that absence does not necessarily mean that surveying and mapping were no longer viewed as technologies of empire or that they were openly and warmly embraced by all segments of Irish society. William Smyth, one of the few cartographic historians who has explored this issue in some depth, asks: "How many local and regional expressions of resistance in the seventeenth and early eighteenth centuries to this process of enclosure, social engineering and marginalization have gone unnoticed and unacknowledged in the written record?"[75] Certainly, we know that the imposition of a new agrarian order on the Irish landscape during the eighteenth century, facilitated by the work of both English and Irish surveyors and cartographers, was met by various resistance movements, large and small, to that process of enclosure and privatization throughout the period. The paucity of direct evidence of anticartographic sentiment, if not direct action taken against surveyors and mapmakers, should not, in short, be taken as a sign of acceptance or capitulation. While the historical record may be filled with silences and gaps that are, to some extent, irrecoverable, we do find ample evidence of an anticartographic strain running through the works of Jonathan Swift, whose numerous and trenchant criticisms of the map place him, alongside Bunyan and Behn, within a much longer tradition of anticartographic thought that emerges during the Renaissance and only continues to gain legitimacy as the map becomes, over the course of the seventeenth and eighteenth centuries, increasingly necessary to the expropriation and privatization of common

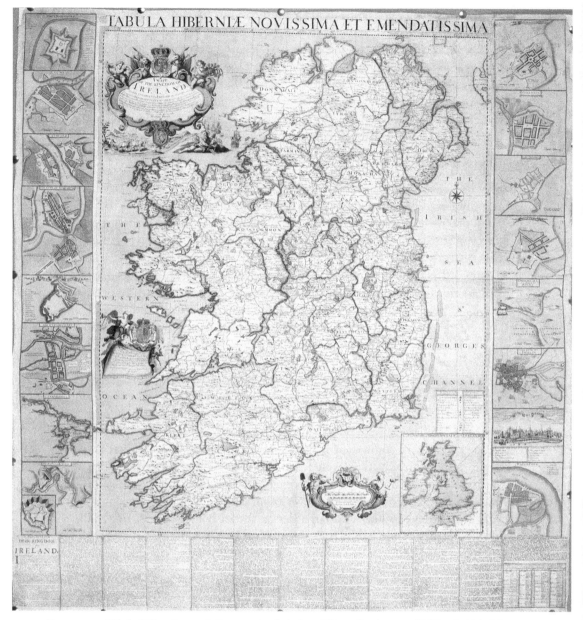

FIGURE 19. *Tabula Hiberniae novissima et emendatissima*, Henry Pratt, 1705. (© The British Library Board, shelfmark Cartographic Items Maps K.Top.51.18.11)

lands, as well as the subjugation of indigenous peoples, under the aegis of improvement and the capitalist imperative to turn the land to better account. His writings represent a critical turning point between the sixteenth and early seventeenth centuries, when the map was almost exclusively an instrument of the monarch, necessary for the purposes of waging war and establishing dominion over his or her subjects, and the eighteenth and nineteenth centuries, when the map became more and more a technology of everyday life, one that served not only royal or state interests but also those of a growing merchant class eager to develop and expand markets at home and abroad. As I will argue, it is this context, and Ireland more specifically, that is uppermost in Swift's mind when he takes up the map as the object of his satire and ridicule, exposing not only its faults and outright fallacies but also the very real limits of the cartographic imagination. His familiarity with the mapping of Ireland, his deep understanding of its history and its impact on the land and its people, the condition of its estates in particular, deeply inform Swift's reservations and outright skepticism regarding maps and surveys.

## Swift and the Cartographic Impulse

In the early eighteenth century, Swift emerges as a staunch critic and satirist of the map as the result of his experiences in Ireland and his knowledge of the history of its colonization, including the roles cartography and demography played in that history. As many scholars have noted, Swift was intimately familiar with the mercantilist writings of Sir William Petty, as well as John Graunt, Charles Davenant, and Josiah Child, and he understood all too well their impact on the Irish landscape of the eighteenth century.[76] His satirical appropriation of their collective works, and their shared discourse of political arithmetic in particular, are evidenced in a number of Swift's works, *A Modest Proposal* perhaps most famously.[77] As George Wittkowsky notes, "Swift's technique in the *Modest Proposal* . . . can be traced to the influence of contemporary economic literature. It is the technique of the political arithmetician."[78] Swift's narrator imitates the likes of Petty and Graunt in order to expose their true interests and to underscore the immediate, as well as potential, dangers of applying statistics and demographic forms of analysis to human populations, in Ireland or anywhere for that matter. While many today remember Petty chiefly for his economic and political writings rather than for his work as a surveyor and cartographer, it is an association that would certainly not be lost on Swift, who was surely aware of the Down Survey and the resulting atlas, *Hiberniae delineatio*. Petty's work as a cartographer was, to his mind, the logical extension of his demographic approach to political and economic matters. Swift's criticisms of the map are thus echoed in his equally contemptuous view of census taking and demographic thinking in general, which was just another form, another iteration, of surveying and quantifying, a "mapping" of the people as it were. Swift understood the ways in which England deployed census taking and demographic analysis as tools to further its control over Ireland and its native population and so were, in this regard, no less suspect than the map and its hyperrationalized, dehumanizing worldview. As Charlotte Sussman argues, demographic surveys were implemented in Ireland, as well as Scotland and

Jamaica, as a means of accounting for and mobilizing subaltern populations in order to maximize their productivity and so generate greater wealth for England.[79] The colonial margins served as the laboratory, if you will, for this kind of demographic analysis rather than the imperial center of London, where it was openly resisted and summarily rejected, at times in a hostile manner. The English, on the whole, remained wary of the taking of censuses because they understood that such forms of enumeration and calculation were not benign but rather an integral part of the power of the state over dispossessed and mobile populations. It was one thing to subject Ireland to a census for just this purpose, but the English, Swift included, did not see such political arithmetic as necessary or warranted at home. Many believed, in fact, that it was a sin or a blasphemy since, according to scripture, 2 Samuel 24 to be precise, David is punished with plagues for taking a census of his troops in the mistaken belief that his own powers of reason and understanding, rather than his faith in God's will, would bring him victory on the battlefield. Demography is, in this sense, a form of hubris because it presupposes the knowledge of God and offers our own limited and corrupt understanding of the world in its place.

The historical relationship between demography and empire, I would argue, also informs Swift's representation of cartography not only as an instrument of imperial conquest and control but also as an expression of and symbol for pride and self-interest. The map, like the census, is a form of political arithmetic and, as such, a totem of worldliness. As Swift asks rhetorically in "A Tale of a Tub," "For, what Man in the natural State, or Course of Thinking, did ever conceive it in his Power, to reduce the Notions of all Mankind, exactly to the same Length, and Breadth, and Heighth of his own?"[80] It is a question that pervades and informs many of Swift's satirical writings, those that take direct aim at the subjects of geography and cartography in particular. In his "On Poetry: A Rhapsody," for example, Swift displays a critical attitude toward maps through the satiric comparison of a Grub Street hack and a "geographer" who perhaps takes a few too many creative liberties in his various mappings of the world. Having already cataloged the would-be poet's numerous failures and shortcomings, Swift facetiously encourages him to continue writing and to ignore his detractors' claims that he indulges in "similes that nothing fit" and deploys epithets "like a heel-piece to support / A cripple with one foot too short."[81] The poet's inability to grasp the fundamental nature of poetic similitude is then likened to the failings of the geographer, who cannot adequately represent the territory to be mapped:

> So geographers in Afric maps
> With savage pictures fill their gaps;
> And oe'r uninhabitable downs
> Place elephants for want of towns.[82]

Rather than provide any accurate sense of Africa and its geography, the poet and the cartographer both choose to resolve the gaps in their knowledge by introducing a figure that distorts our perceptions and, in the process, forecloses the possibility of a better, more fully realized understanding of their respective subjects. The cartographer's mapping of the "uninhabitable" interior of Africa proves difficult if not impossible to render in any reliable manner given the scant amount of existing information regarding the geography of the African interior. However, rather than abandon the project altogether, he chooses instead to supplement his map with topographic markers, such as the elephants, which are intended to fill in the blank spaces as a substitute of sorts for the perceived lack of town sites. As the poem makes clear, the substitution of the figure of the elephant for that of the town represents the creation of a figure predicated on ignorance and folly, which Swift contends is endemic to both the methodology of the cartographer and the dubious practices of the hack poet. That is to say, the production of equivalences and similarities with no rational or coherent basis is the mark of bad poetry and, likewise, bad maps.

While the vagaries of poetic creation remain the primary subject of Swift's poem, his analogy here reveals a more fundamental problem of signification that plagues both poem and map alike. The map's demand for legibility and comprehension leads to the particularly egregious similitude of the elephant and the town; however, their association, Swift is eager to point out, serves to cover over England and Europe's profound lack of knowledge of the continent's geography, promoting instead an image of Africa as a wild, savage place rather than civilized or enlightened.[83] Swift's poem, in this sense, constitutes a plea for greater accuracy in mapping Africa's geography. His satirical comments regarding the mapmaker represent, in effect, his own desire for an improved map, one that faithfully depicts the world as it is rather than as the mapmaker imagines or wishes it to be.[84] Swift thus places himself against the map in his opposition to its lack of empirical rigor and willingness to substitute deceptive figures and skewed perspectives for a more detailed, more authentic rendering of the earth's geography. I would, however, like to take issue with that reading of Swift's poem and to refute the notion that his critique of the map is a call for a more substantive investment in the modalities of empiricism as a meaningful remedy to the problem.[85] That is, an empirically responsible map divested of bogus ornamentation and allegorical marginalia does not resolve Swift's difficulties with cartographic representation; simply replacing the icon of an elephant with another icon whose relationship to the physical landscape is more assured or verifiable will not, in short, do the trick.

While Swift's critique of the map may suggest an appeal for more exacting methods of transcription and a greater fidelity to actual conditions on the ground, that appeal should, in fact, be viewed as a satiric rejection of any empirical solution to the limits of cartographic representation. As is clear from the remainder of the poem, the real target of Swift's satire here is the pride and vanity of the hack poet, his overinflated sense of himself and his talents, which leads to the creation of bad poetry. Likewise, the integrity of the map is also deeply compromised by the character, values, and intentions of its creator, whose pride and vanity may infect and distort the imagination and, hence, a proper understanding of the world. To continue Swift's analogy, mapmaking, like the writing of poetry, is a profession of hacks who conjure pleasing deceptions and outright lies in the hopes of making a profit off unsuspecting audiences or pleasing a wealthy and powerful benefactor. Regardless of their avowals of empirical rigor and mathematical certainty, mapmakers deform and distort our perceptions of the world by offering the illusion of mastery and order that, for Swift, as well as Bunyan, represents a form of *vanitas*, or worldliness. The map promotes and represents an undue investment in this world and, in the process, obscures spiritual truths and a true understanding of God. The map, in this sense, is an emblem of worldliness and carnality that, properly understood, should serve as a reminder to approach God's creation with humility and devotion rather than pride and avarice. It is an interpretation surely familiar to a high Tory churchman like Swift.[86]

In his essay "The Folly of Maps and Modernity," Richard Helgerson points to the enduring association of the map with a Christian understanding of vanity and the unnatural desire for the pleasures of this world, or worldliness, as it is commonly known during the period. The map's blasphemous appropriation of the deity's perspective was understood by many during the Renaissance to signify the pride and vanity of the mapmaker, as well as the reader of maps, both of whom appear to ignore spiritual concerns for more worldly matters, like the acquisition of land, power, and wealth: "Maps were regularly inserted into interpretive contexts that radically altered their meaning, contexts that turned their worldly uses against themselves, revealing the folly of both maps and the modernity to which they were so actively contributing."[87] In something of an addendum to his earlier work on the role of cartography in the formation of British nationalism, Helgerson reveals here an anticartographic strain extending back to the late sixteenth and early seventeenth centuries, a time when the map was still a relatively unfamiliar commodity for most commoners but, as we have seen, one routinely in circulation at court. This critical posture toward the producers and consumers of maps, I would suggest, does not fade with the subsequent growth in the market for maps throughout Britain and its colonies during the eighteenth century. To the contrary, such critiques will only continue to proliferate as the map becomes an increasingly indispensable part of everyday life, Swift being a notable example of this anticartographic strain, or tradition, within early modern British literature. The figure of the map in "On Poetry: A Rhapsody" functions in much the same fashion Helgerson describes; it is a symbolic gesture intended to signify the worldly and prideful nature of the poet and, by extension, the mapmaker. Hence an empirical approach to surveying and representing space, no matter how thorough, merely places emphasis on the subjective impressions of the observer while ignoring the hand of God that created and shaped the land. Not only is the map incapable of registering this spiritual truth, but its remediation via a more thorough commitment to empirical methodologies only exacerbates the problem because it does not address the fundamental problems of pride and vanity that are the signature of all forms of cartographic representation. The solution, then, is not a more formally or ethically sound brand of mapmaking (it doesn't exist) but rather a more thorough investigation of the motivations and intentions of its practitioners who have, according to Swift, usurped the authority of God in some sense in their desire for private gain.

Swift's criticism appears to be directed not at the map so much as those who would exploit the map and its particular manner of framing the world to further their own political, religious, and economic goals. The anticartographic strain in Swift's writings thus reveals a real antipathy toward the map as an instrument of imperial violence and aggression that emerges in conjunction with England's early forays into colonial trade, the conquest and settlement of Ireland in particular.[88] Swift illustrates this idea perhaps most famously in his treatment of Captain Lemuel Gulliver, a figure who makes man the measure of all things in his use of cartography and chorography to document his travels through Lilliput, Brobdingnag, Laputa, and the country of the Houyhnhnms. As Peter Wagner argues, *Gulliver's Travels* engages intertextually with the illustrations commonly found in travel literature, including maps, in order to satirize their claims to truth and legitimacy. Textual and graphic elements in the text work in conjunction with one another to simulate the trappings of an authentic travel narrative, including prefatory letters and advertisements, an engraved frontispiece containing a portrait of Captain Lemuel Gulliver, a title page announcing the book's subject matter, various Latin epigraphs and mottoes, and of course, maps illustrating each voyage. All contribute to the illusion of authenticity, asking the reader to buy in and to beware in the same gesture: "Appropriating the tradition of 'comely' frontispieces and engraved title-pages, the *Travels* explodes a technique of graphic representation (including cartography and portraying) by carrying it to the point where the careful observer begins to notice both the traditions and the problematics of signifying as such."[89] Swift marshals together much of the same graphic information one would normally find in an "authentic" travel narrative only to mock those generic expectations. The most obvious example is the novel's inclusion of maps created by Herman Moll, who was also responsible for producing *A Set of Twenty New and Correct Maps of Ireland* (1728). Found at the beginning of each book, the maps are intended to guide the reader through Gulliver's journeys while, at the same time, forcing us to contend with their pointed blending of fact and fiction. Lilliput and Blefescu, for example, lie off the coast of Sumatra, while Laputa is located due east of Japan and the Korean peninsula. In the map that precedes part 2, Brobdingnag is depicted as a peninsula attached to what is identifiably the northwest coast of America, which is signified through the inclusion of real topographical information, such as place-names and coastal features. Brobdingnag, along with the other places Gulliver encounters, does not exist somewhere else or in some other world; rather, it rests, uncomfortably perhaps, within the confines of this world. Swift juxtaposes known maps with his own fictive embellishments to produce a text that simultaneously participates in the cartographic rationality of the traveling subject while at the same time exposing the semiotic instability of all maps and the folly of our reliance on them. By giving us maps that intentionally blur the line between fact and fiction, Swift would appear to commit the very same error he accuses the mapmaker of making in the aforementioned poem, yet in this instance, his indulgence in cartographic fiction is intended as a satirical comment on the graphic logic of the map and as a warning of sorts to his reader about the dangers inherent to the form.[90]

Rather than give us a straightforward polemic on the deceptive nature of maps, Gulliver's text mimics a kind of cartographic rationality in its endless referencing of prior travel literature, its claims to scientific rigor and methodological objectivity, and its inclusion of graphic material and other supplementary information that contribute to its "reality effect." An ironic understanding of the ways in which maps can lie and distort our perceptions of the world cannot be achieved without some degree of familiarity with the form, and Swift relies on that sense of familiarity in order to trap and, hopefully, enlighten his reader. Swift's critique of cartography in *Gulliver's Travels* is thus explicitly linked to the burgeoning genre of travel narratives and other firsthand accounts of discovery and conquest that often incorporate maps into that narrative as a visual supplement. Swift affirms this connection when he has Gulliver, at the conclusion of his survey of Lilliput, tell his reader that he intends to publish "a greater work . . . containing a general description of this Empire."[91] Gulliver reveals himself to be much like those who profited, in one way or another, from the public's zeal for all things foreign and the exotic, whether it is the author of a travel narrative or someone engaged in colonial commerce and trade who is reliant on maps to achieve his or her financial and political goals. Likewise, in his description of Brobdingnag, Gulliver chooses to include a brief "Proposal for correcting modern Maps" in which he concludes that "our Geographers of *Europe* are in a great Error, by supposing nothing but Sea between *Japan* and *California*."[92] Given the relative dearth of information regarding the Pacific and its contiguous landmasses, most maps erroneously depict the presence of water where, as Gulliver has just discovered, there rightfully should be land. "For it was ever my Opinion, that there must be a Balance of Earth to counterpoise the great Continent of *Tartary*; and therefore they ought to correct their Maps and Charts, by joining this vast Tract of Land to the North-west Parts of *America*, wherein I shall be ready to lend them my Assistance."[93] Gulliver's discovery of Brobdingnag confirms his general theory about the earth's geography, an idea which had been fixed in his mind prior to his ever setting out from England. Landing upon Brobdingnag is, in this sense, less of a discovery than a corroboration of what Gulliver already knew to be true based on the geographic methods and principles he had learned while in England and put to use in the course of his travels.

While the presence of Brobdingnag is fortuitous in that it does manage to affirm Gulliver's hypothesis, this is not always the case. As the rationalist geographer, Gulliver's attempts to bring a sense of cohesion and order to a rather bewildering array of details and circumstances do not always conform to his preconceived ideas about the world and its geography. More often than not, Gulliver's cartographic gaze runs up against its own internal limits, as when, for example, he offers his reader a brief chorography of the city of Mildendo, the metropolis of Lilliput, as he moves through and over the city. Gulliver seems quite impressed (as he is so often) with the order and regularity of the buildings and structures and their proportionality in relation to the Lilliputians' diminutive size and ability. We get a picture of an enclosed, fortified city that is "an exact Square" with "two great Streets, which run cross and divide it into four Quarters."[94] In the center of the city, where the two streets meet, is the emperor's palace, which is also enclosed by a wall. Gulliver is able to take in all of this at once from his lofty vantage point, noting the many lanes and alleys that verge from the main thoroughfares, the size and spacing of the houses, and the distribution and quality of the shops and markets. His perspective is that of the surveyor who views the city much as one would a map, a fact reinforced by the symmetrical geometry of the city, which approximates the often grid-like facade of the cartographic projection. For Gulliver, Lilliput resembles a map due to the large disparity in size with his hosts, which affords him a semidetached position that is at once inside and outside of that world. Gulliver's cartographic perspective is the inevitable product of that spatial difference. As Michael McKeon observes, "Gulliver's facility for assimilative comparison depends on his ability to abstract himself from the fact of difference onto a plane of similarity, to manipulate a kind of epistemological exchange value that accommodates qualitatively dissimilar objects to a more general and equalizing standard."[95] That standard, however, fails to hold since neither he nor the Lilliputians can ignore the intrusive nature of Gulliver's massive frame, a situation that continually threatens to devolve into outright violence.

Recognizing the threat that Gulliver poses for his nation and its people, the emperor grants him a license to enter the city on the condition that he does not hurt the inhabitants of Mildendo or their homes: "I stept over the great *Western* Gate, and passed very gently, and sideling through the two principal Streets, only in my short Waistcoat, for fear of damaging the Roofs and Eves of the Houses with the Skirts of my Coat. I walked with the utmost Circumspection, to avoid treading on any Stragglers, who might remain in the

Streets, although the Orders were very strict, that all People should keep in their Houses, at their own Peril."[96] Gulliver's narration reveals the tensions that exist between the desire to see and to observe the city and the potential risk of destroying it at the same time. His omniscient viewpoint is achieved only at the expense of the city, as his body cannot successfully negotiate the space he would otherwise try to describe. Gulliver cannot even see the whole of the palace without causing a degree of collateral damage to its structure. In response, Gulliver is prompted to build a set of wooden stools in order to elevate him above the inner courts, and so enable him to see the emperor's palace in greater detail without destroying it. His ability to see clearly and accurately is dependent on the recognition that his body is a problem and that it must be removed in some fashion. However, that recognition, in effect, collapses the cartographic fantasy of a neutral and objective perspective and replaces it with an acute awareness of the violence that can result from the embodiment of that perspective. Gulliver cannot successfully achieve a detached position in relation to the subject of his investigation without inserting himself into that space and causing potential harm. Nor can he ever fully integrate himself into the landscape without compromising his status as a rational and neutral observer since he is now the thing being scrutinized, something that Gulliver would rather avoid. In Swift's allegory of the scientific principle known familiarly as "the observer effect," the violence latent in the cartographic projection, or the impact the observer has on the thing being observed, is made explicit as the bodies of Gulliver and his captors come into physical contact with one another, a situation that proves to be untenable in the long run.[97]

Swift thus satirizes the "cartographic impulse" of the scientific traveler, in this case, Gulliver, whose various rationalizations of space cannot, by their very nature, accommodate or acknowledge the place of the observer without doing some violence to the illusion of order and uniformity. I borrow the concept of the "cartographic impulse" from Tom Conley, who defines it as the subject's drive or desire toward the production of a space that both confirms and acknowledges that subject's being in the world. The preconscious gesture of the cartographic impulse gives rise, in Conley's terms, to the "graphic construction of the self" whereby the identity of self and world are forged as an inseparable totality. However, as he notes, the self must also be able to remain detached in some respect from the world that she or he inhabits: "The self's emergence is evinced where discourse and geography are coordinated, and the self becomes autonomous only (1) when it is fixed to an illusion of a geographic truth (often of its own making) and (2) when it can be detached from the coordinates that mark its point of view, its history, its formation, and the aesthetics and politics of its signature."[98] It is this contradiction, I would suggest, that Swift exploits in *Gulliver's Travels*, a novel that places considerable pressure on the idea of a cartographic subjectivity in order to reveal the discursive and diagrammatic limits of such a project. The cartographic fiction, as it were, enables the author of the map to stand outside of that space when, as Swift is careful to point out, that is not really possible given the body's potentially violent resistance to such an exclusion. The Cartesian space of the map is a pure fiction, a homogenizing gesture that flattens out difference into a smooth order of equivalences, yet such an idealized projection depends on the exclusion of the observer from representing him- or herself within the space of the cartographic gaze.

Gulliver's mapping of the urban landscape in Mildendo is one example among many in which Swift exposes the double bind of the cartographic impulse, or how the embodied perspective of the observing subject, whether scientist, merchant, soldier, or casual traveler, can never fully divorce itself from the object of its inquiry. The map offers a surface on which to record and translate space into an ordered and rational system; however, the space of the observer must always remain other to the map. The rationalization of space is dependent on the abstraction of a neutral observer whose existence is, by definition, antagonistic to the space being observed. Ostensibly no longer tied to the physical location of the body in which it is contained, the mind may contemplate and observe space as one would an object from afar, yet the space from which that gaze emanates remains undisclosed, shut off, and utterly private. The production of a continuous, homogeneous space, such as the map, requires the necessary exclusion of the embodied perspective of its author, the mapmaker, in order to legitimate its claims to an authentic and objective means of looking at the world. For Swift, Gulliver's cartographic agenda precipitates his need to place himself at once inside and outside the urban space of Mildendo in order to render himself both producer of the map and the object of that mapping. The map, however, does not and cannot acknowledge the spatial disjunction between both positions and so presents its findings as a uniform and complete space, one utterly divorced from the motives and ideologies of its author. The map gives us continuities that seemingly ignore this underlying difference. Rather than construct a space that will allow for both positions to cohere in some fashion, the map works on the basis of exclusion and radical separation. However, in bringing these disparate positions into contact with one another, Swift reveals the subjective nature of the cartographic projection, in essence reattaching the map to the occasion of its production and so exposing the lie. The space of the mapmaker thus constitutes a critical difference that can never be fully assimilated into the well-ordered map without fundamentally disrupting that order. The spatial discontinuity that informs the production of the map then becomes the basis for Swift's critique of the map as the extension of efforts to rationalize space while failing to disclose the subjective nature of its findings. Again, the map lies and deceives but only because it betrays a deeper problem within the epistemology and ideology that informs the map's production.

My argument here regarding Swift and his relationship to the practices of surveying and cartography is, in many respects, similar to the one Carole

Fabricant makes in *Swift's Landscape* with respect to his critique of pastoral and neoclassical forms of representation, which Swift viewed in much the same fashion as maps, that is, as gross abstractions and highly subjective idealizations of the landscape divorced from any semblance of material or lived reality. Fabricant articulates my central contention that Swift's landscape is "inescapably and pervasively political"[99] in its recognition of the ways in which certain aesthetic codes and norms may blind us to the actual material and economic conditions under which many people live, those in Ireland especially. As Fabricant rightly argues, Swift often rejected and decried neoclassical notions of beauty, harmony, and order, which were the fashion among many of his contemporaries and fellow Tories, Pope most famously.[100] The very idea of a disinterested aesthetic contemplation of the landscape in which these virtues are properly consumed, however, seemed a kind of absurd fiction to Swift given his knowledge of the realities of everyday life in Ireland, hence his desire to mock such forms of pastoral representation and to expose the ways in which they blind its viewer to those realities: "Swift's realization that 'official' contemporary art forms, such as neoclassical landscape painting and pastoral poetry, were inadequate for conveying (for example) the facts of Irish life as he knew and observed them on a daily basis reinforced his preference for literary forms such as burlesque and travesty, his reliance on a popular satiric tradition represented in broadsides and ballads, and his consistent use of *mock*-pastoral throughout his verse."[101] Swift well understood the imperialist ideology at work behind the Anglo-Irish gentry's preference for neoclassical principles in the construction and improvement of their various estates, in essence, transforming the Irish landscape into an English one. His writings, more often than not, sought to expose and dissect their "suburban or dormitory dream" of "the cool country," which Raymond Williams defines as a landscape devoid of labor, class, poverty, violence, excrement, or any other sign of actual rural existence.[102] Swift certainly wished to improve the economic fortunes of the Irish countryside, but with the intention of ameliorating the general welfare and not merely satisfying the aesthetic imperatives of a small group of Anglo-Irish landholders.[103] Pastoral landscape gardening, painting, and poetry, for Swift, all betray and perpetuate a colonialist fantasy that had devastating effects on Ireland politically and economically, while also helping to obfuscate the imperial ambitions of its producers, as well as its consumers. As Fabricant concludes, Swift "insists on the inextricable links between aesthetic and economic matters, refusing to contemplate the beauties and elegancies of the landscape in a vacuum, apart from the money begged, borrowed, or stolen to put them on display for the acquisitive, carefully conditioned Augustan eye."[104] The map, I would suggest, was equally "inadequate," in Fabricant's terms, and so routinely satirized by Swift in order to make those "links between aesthetic and economic matters" visible to his readers as they found themselves increasingly confronted with maps of all different genres and varieties.

Fabricant's analysis of Swift's landscape and his contentious relationship with neoclassical aesthetics thus needs to be extended to his understanding of cartographic representation, given that the map, like those overly romantic and idyllic images of nature, also embodies and promotes the fiction of a disinterested, detached observer who imposes a sense of order, balance, and harmony on the putatively barbarous colonial landscape. The map gives us what Fabricant refers to as the prospective "long view" of the aristocratic figure who commands a privileged and elevated position with respect to the landscape he surveys and over which he exerts his power; it is a perspective that represents and embodies the exalted social, political, and economic status of its viewer while, conversely, blotting out and erasing those on the "lower rungs of the social hierarchy" whose perception and understanding of the land was contrary or antagonistic to that of its owners and landlords.[105] The viewer is then invited to identify with that loftier perspective as he or she surveys, for example, a map of Ireland, which offers an image of the land that, while perhaps not beautiful in the Augustan sense, is nevertheless an idealization, a sanitized abstraction that seeks to transform Ireland, literally and figuratively, into a version of England and, hence, part of a greater Britain. The map is, in this sense, less an objective and rational depiction of Ireland's geography and more the object of a certain kind of aesthetic contemplation that refuses to acknowledge its own status as a fiction or the political and economic agendas that undergird its production. As Fabricant notes, Swift could not look upon a beautiful landscape without considering the economic and material conditions that went into its making, preferring the "short view" over the imperious "long view" because it uncovers and starkly reveals the "intractable realities" and often grotesque horrors of the Irish landscape.[106] The same, I would suggest, is also true for Swift's relationship to the map, which I believe needs to be more fully considered in any analysis of his "excremental vision" of the landscape, with its savage Yahoos living, much like the Irish, in a state of filth, poverty, and privation.[107] While Swift's preference for the scatological and the grotesque is, as Fabricant contends, evidence of the "the yawning epistemological, ideological, and literary gap separating Swift from the idealized, manureless environs of the affluent Augustans' sumptuously re-created and elegantly versified Edens," it also marks the distance between Swift's landscape and those surveys, chorographies, and maps of England and Ireland that, not coincidentally, played a critical role in the settlement, construction, and improvement of such "Edens."[108]

From establishing the legal title to a given parcel of land to determining the boundaries and borders separating one property from another to computing the extent of an estate's tillable acreage or the value of its pasturage, the map, plantation and estate maps in particular, is, for Swift, not unlike the pastoral image or poem; both are symbols of the ways in which certain monied interests, whose wealth was often derived from colonial trade and commerce in one form or another rather than the land itself, usurped and displaced the rural values and virtues associated with the traditional English estate and its Anglo-Irish equivalent. As a member of the Tory or country party, Swift ascribed to the general notion that land and property, embodied and symbolized by the country estate, were the true source of national power and prosperity, not the sea with its decidedly mercantile, commercial interests, and he often espoused in his writings the country house ideals of hospitality, friendship, paternal care, and agrarian community, virtues that were, for Swift and other Tories, intrinsic to the kind of "neighborhood" that constituted itself in and around the ancient landed estate.[109] Just as often, however, Swift was quick to point out the ways in which the actual conditions of the English and Anglo-Irish estate failed to comport with these ideals as the landed gentry, over time, succumbed to capitalist interest. Underscoring this discrepancy between a professed set of moral principles governing country life and the actual material conditions Swift observed in many rural estates often meant openly breaking ranks with his fellow Tories and the country house ideology to which they subscribed but apparently failed to apply.[110] Swift lamented, for example, the increasing prevalence of absentee landlordism in Ireland and the ways in which these absent stewards of the land overworked and abused the soil in order to wrest every drop of potential wealth.[111] Perhaps more importantly, absentee landlordism was, as Fabricant reminds us, helping to destroy the country house ideal because it severed the "intimate bond between the estate owner and the soil" and, in its place, substituted a mediated relationship to the land, one characterized by "a bureaucratic remoteness and impersonality inimical to the country house code of hospitality and direct participation in all aspects of the domestic economy."[112] The map, as well as the surveyor, is an integral part of that mediated relationship between the land and its owner, and so a potent symbol for Swift of the ways in which money, especially money acquired through trade and commerce, was influencing and corrupting the once pristine and virtuous environs of the traditional English estate.

Ultimately, the influence of money, in Swift's estimation, served to erode any meaningful distinction between the country and the city, between landed gentry and urban capitalist, a problem perhaps most visible in Ireland, as both settings were equally devastated by colonial rule and commercial interests.[113] As Fabricant observes, "Finally one cannot distinguish between city and country, because they have become basically interchangeable embodiments of Ireland's wretchedness and general deterioration."[114] Country life, and Tory ideology more broadly, no longer offers a compelling alternative to or bulwark against the tyranny of the imperial center, London, and its more urbane concerns; the traditional forms of culture associated with the ancient landed estate are thus hollowed out and robbed of their customary meanings and replaced by "an essentially private and solitary vision, devoid of both familial or communal harmony."[115] Unable to fully inhabit and embrace the ideology of the country party and the landed gentry in his criticisms of England's colonization of

Ireland, Swift finds himself in the position of the reluctant Tory, an itinerant, liminal figure who simultaneously affirms the virtues and values of country life while also lamenting what it has become, both in England and Ireland. This ambivalence is perhaps best articulated in Swift's various writings about Thomas Sheridan's Cavan estate, Quilca, which was the "absolute negation" of the country house ideal in its primitive, rustic landscape and lifestyle.[116]

Unlike those pastoral images that celebrate and romanticize the landed estate, such as Jonson's Penhurst or Marvell's Appleton House, Quilca was viewed by Swift as a place of disintegration and dissolution, marked by a harsh and unforgiving landscape, endless labor and toil just to provide for the basic necessities, and a fractured, contentious society devoid of hospitality and comity. However, despite these barbarous conditions, Swift also found himself inexplicably attracted to Quilca and saw something of value, if not beauty, in its grotesque inversion of traditional country life. As Fabricant concludes, "Swift seems to have had a love-hate relationship with Quilca; he was simultaneously attracted to and repelled by its unadulterated rusticity and primitive conditions, its severe climate, and its harsh, angular beauty. . . . Perhaps more than any other place, Cavan became for Swift *a country of the mind* as well as a physical terrain, which reflected his profoundly ambivalent feelings toward Ireland and his basic insight into the irrelevance of pastoral and country house conceptions of the Irish landscape [italics mine]."[117] Fabricant's passing reference here to Quilca as a "country of the mind" suggests that, like Bunyan's "neighborhood," country was as much an abstraction for Swift as it was a referent to an actual physical place, however abject. As a kind of cognitive mapping, to borrow Fredric Jameson's terminology, Swift's so-called country of the mind is, in fact, the result of a cognitive dissonance that is unable to reconcile his prospective vision of the landed estate with the harsh, material realities of rural life, realities that were, to his mind, precipitated by those estate owners whose political and financial interests were dependent on the surveying and mapping of Ireland. Swift's response to Quilca is perhaps best summed up in a marginal comment he makes regarding Joseph Addison's *The Freeholder,* "No. 8 Jan. 16, 1716." In the piece, Addison argues that women need to play a more substantial role in public life and that they should "use their Charms," or their beauty, in service to their country, stating, "I will only desire her to think of her Countrey every Time she looks in her Glass." To which Swift responds, "By no means, for if she loves her Country, she will not be pleased with the Sight."[118] For Swift, love of country is not predicated on its beauty or our identification with the beautiful place but rather on the sense of alienation and dissonance one feels when looking into the mirror and, like Gulliver, recoiling at what we see reflected back.

As I will argue in the remainder of the chapter, it is this tension, if not outright conflict, between material and abstract meanings of the word "country," between the land itself and a set of values and ideals embodied by that geography, that places Swift against the map and its ability to project a false sense of closure and reconciliation to the dilemma presented by a place like Quilca, even as it exacerbates and further exploits those differences. "Country" denotes a geographic unit that is, for Swift, implicitly "against the map" because it resists such forms of quantification, rationalization, and representation that seek to reduce the land to little more than private property and a source of revenue and capital. As we have seen, Swift rightly viewed the map as a technology of conquest and possession that undermines and effaces the land as the locus of social and collective identity and, in the process, supplants those traditional meanings and values with the individualistic and subjective desires of the landlord or property holder eager to improve his stock, regardless of the consequences to his tenants or those dispossessed entirely of their land, as was often the case in Ireland. The map subjects the land to the homogenizing tendencies of the capitalist marketplace and its pervasive logic of equivalence and exchange renders it an abstraction that, like currency itself, becomes infinitely fungible and thus no longer a stable or fixed form of value. Against the map, Swift offers the term "country" as an alternative way of understanding the land, a geography of difference that is at once more material and physical in conception, often to the point of sublimity and grotesquery, as Fabricant argues, but also ideological, partisan, and deeply political in its overt opposition to Whig power and influence, particularly over the question of Ireland. As suggested by its etymological root, *contra*, "country," by definition, already contains within it notions of difference and alterity that Swift readily expands and builds upon in his desire to correct the inevitable distortions and manipulations presented by cartographic representation.

## Coming into the Country

Swift often deploys the term "country" as a heterotopic site whose identity is not determined by either the map or survey but rather one's fidelity to the republic and the ideals of patriotic virtue, understood properly as love of country rather than love of nation or state or kingdom for that matter.[119] It is, for Swift, a term of nostalgia denoting an ancient and more virtuous form of connection, one that stands in sharp contrast to the relatively modern constructs of nation and state, both of which fail to sufficiently animate the public spirit and so move it to perform acts of true and authentic patriotism. While we tend to think of "country" strictly in terms of an identifiable and knowable place on the map, whether as a referent for a rural area or an entire nation, it is also, in both its classical and neoclassical forms, a metaphorical geography that lends a sense of place to the republic, its citizens, and most importantly, its constitution.[120] Country is, in short, the figurative ground of the republic and, as such, the proper object of our love and our care; it represents, within the context of classical republican ideology, a form of association that supersedes party and private interest in its appeal to the public, or the commonwealth, and the need for its continued care and love, otherwise known as patriotism. As Simon During notes, this understanding of patriotic virtue is not specific to Swift's writings but rather a common strain throughout much of the Tory and Whig opposition to the Walpole administration during the early half of the eighteenth century. Lord Bolingbroke's *Idea of a Patriot King* (1749), for one, borrows considerably from both Greek and Roman political models, both of which define a patriot "by his love of country rather than personal ambition," a charge commonly leveled at a ruling Whig party whose interests remained, according to Bolingbroke and his fellow Tories, focused largely on matters of trade and commerce.[121] In an essay from the *Craftsman*, Bolingbroke explicitly aligns the "Genius" of the English people with "those Fathers of Mankind, who, being actuated by the noble Principles of universal and unconfin'd Benevolence, have made the welfare of their Country, their great and only Care."[122] Bolingbroke champions "those Fathers of Mankind" whose understanding of patriotism emphasized "universal" benevolence and care for the welfare of the country over and above more parochial or private concerns. The former is, to borrow Hazlitt's words, "the creature of reason and reflection," while the latter is "the offspring of physical or local attachment" and so incompatible with authentic patriotism as practiced by the ancients and valorized by the Tory opposition.[123] The map and survey, as I am suggesting, are also "the offspring of physical or local attachment," those previously discussed Irish plantation and estate maps in particular; they embody and fetishize the land itself, contrary to Swift's conception of the country, a "country of the mind" as it were, as a heterotopic site that resists the cartographic logic of the map and its appeal to private interest over and against the public good.

Swift's sermons, those addressing conditions in Ireland in particular, frequently extol the merits of loving one's country in this fashion, while, at the same time, informing his readers, in suitably graphic detail, of the dire consequences for the nation should their love falter. In "Doing Good: A Sermon, on the Occasion of Wood's Project" (1724), Swift identifies "this love of the public, or of the commonwealth, or love of country" as the "greatest of all virtues" in the ancient world and praises those men who routinely sacrificed their lives "for the good of the country, although they had neither hope or belief of future rewards."[124] Swift observes, with all due sense of irony, that patriotism once flourished in a society absent of Christ and the scriptural call to self-sacrifice in service of the public good, yet oddly, in his own day and age and, moreover, in a Christian and Protestant nation, such selfless acts of patriotic virtuosity are rare and in serious decline. Swift underscores this paradox in a later sermon, "On the Testimony of Conscience" (1744): "Those Heathens did in a particular manner instill the Principle into their Children, of loving their Country; which is so far otherwise now-a-days, that, of the several Parties among us, there is none of them that seem to have so much as heard, whether there be such a Virtue in the World."[125] In yet another iteration of the battle between the ancients and the moderns, Swift criticizes his contemporaries, and their respective political parties, for seeking to advance their own cause rather than serving the interests of the country, all the while demonstrating his great veneration for the ancient Roman model of the *res publica* and its promotion of patriotic and civic virtue as a means of tempering such factionalism in political life.[126] Swift, naturally, views himself as just such a patriot, the so-called wise man whose voice can barely be heard above the din of faction and interest. Despite these obstacles, or perhaps because of them, Swift advises his reader in the poem "On the Irish-Club" (1723) to place him- or herself above such partisan rancor: "Be sometimes to your country true, / Have once the public good in view."[127]

Swift notes, for example, in "A Project for the Advancement of Religion and the Reformation of Manners" (1709), "I am fully convinced, that the unbiased Thoughts of an honest and wise Man, employed on the Good of his Country, may be better digested, than the Results of a Multitude, where Faction and Interest too often prevail."[128] Deploying a familiar Swiftian metaphor, the country is likened to a body whose health is, in large measure, dependent on the selfless individual whose "unbiased Thoughts" feed and nourish public life rather than glut it with the unbridled and unchecked appetites of the "Multitude." It is, in fact, the duty and responsibility of "any man who wishes well to his Country, to offer his Thoughts, when he can have no other End in View but the Publick Good," especially when the highest stations of power have been infected with the "Disease" of vice and corruption, which are the inevitable product of partisan governance.[129] Recognizing the extent to which this disease has taken hold within England's own government and its ruling class, Whig and Tory alike, Swift observes in "The Sentiments of a Church-of-England Man, With Respect to Religion and Government" (1708), that "to sacrifice the Innocency of a Friend, the Good of our Country, or our own Conscience to the Humour, or Passion, or Interest of a Party . . . shews that either our Heads or our Hearts are not as they should be."[130] The solution, or cure as it were, for such factionalism, however, may be found in the writings of Cato, whom Swift refers to as "the wisest and best of all the Romans."

Echoing the patriotic philosophy of his classical forebearer, Swift instructs us that, when the "parties that divide the whole commonwealth come once to a rupture" and "the public is embroiled" as a result, "the truest Service a private man may hope to do his Country, is by unbiassing his Mind as much as possible, and then endeavouring to moderate between the Rival Powers."[131] Swift acknowledges, here and elsewhere, the difficulties of freeing oneself from bias given that it is a "principle in human nature to incline more in one way than another," yet patriotic service to country requires an engagement with public affairs that denies the tendency to consider only the desires and wishes of the individual or the party to which he or she belongs. Rather, it is the unbiased mind of the patriot who places the welfare and interests of the country over and above self and party when engaged in matters of public concern. Not that acting upon such a principle is, by any means, easy or without conflict. In "A Letter to the Right Honourable the Lord Viscount Molesworth" (1724), Swift acknowledges just how difficult a proposition this can be, particularly in matters related to Ireland: "I cannot but observe to your Lordship, how nice and dangerous a Point it is grown, for a private Person to inform the People; even in an Affair, where the publick Interest and Safety are so highly concerned, as that of Mr. Wood; and this in a Country, where Loyalty is woven into the very Hearts of the People, seems a little extraordinary."[132] Swift clearly views his own writings in defense of the "publick Interest" as heroic given the opposition he faced over the issue of Wood's coin, yet he remains incredulous that he should face such resistance in a country where "the very Hearts of the People" are predisposed to patriotic feeling and sentiment.

Swift often reinforces this correlation between love of country and care for the public interest to such an extent that they are often rendered virtually indistinguishable from one another. Later, in the aforementioned sermon "Doing Good," he states: "From hence, it clearly follows, how necessary the love of our country, or a public spirit, is in every particular man, since the wicked have so many opportunities of doing public mischief."[133] Swift invokes the language of sin in order to contrast the "wicked," or those who exclusively pursue their own ends irrespective of their country and their nation, with the virtuous, whose love of country is "necessary" to the health and overall integrity of the public sphere. He then roundly chastises "the farmer and tradesman" who complain of hard times when, in fact, their condition is, according to Swift, due to "the want of that love of their country, and public spirit and firm union among themselves, which are so necessary to the prosperity of every nation."[134] We see a similar formulation in "A Letter to the Lord Chancellor Middleton" (1724): "Now, I should be heartily glad if some able Lawyers would prescribe Limits, how far a private Man may venture in delivering his Thoughts upon publick Matters: Because a true Lover of his Country, may think it hard to be a quiet Stander-by, and an indolent Looker-on, while a publick Error prevails; by which a whole Nation may be ruined. Every Man who enjoys Property, hath some Share in the Publick; and therefore, the Care of the Publick is, in some Degree, every such Man's Concern."[135] Swift, in the guise of the Drapier, defends his critique of Wood's coin on the grounds that he is, despite the claims of his detractors, a true patriot whose love for his native Ireland demands that he speak up when "publick Error prevails."[136] Later, in the same letter, he refers to the "Love of our Country" as "the best Publick Principle . . . than, perhaps, hath been known in any other Nation, and in so short a Time," again revealing the extent to which love of country and care for the public are intimately bound together in Swift's understanding of patriotic virtue, the absence of which, he warns, may tend toward the ruin of the nation.[137]

Swift is careful to note here that, while the fortunes of the nation are tied to our respective love of country, the two are, by no means, identical or equivalent, a point often lost on modern readers of Swift and eighteenth-century literature more broadly. Today, we tend to use country and nation interchangeably, as if my country and my nation were, indeed, one and the same. For Swift, however, love of country meant fidelity to a set of laws and principles (including patriotism itself) that should rightly govern public life as opposed to a sentimental and affective allegiance to one's physical homeland or native soil, which is more typical of nationalism. Republican patriotism emphasizes "the intentional political identity of citizens within a free rational polity" and is more inclusive and universal in its outlook, while nationalism "implies unwitting ethnic and cultural identity" that is exclusionary and particular, often to the point of aggression against those who remain outside that specific ethnic or cultural grouping.[138] Swift thus distinguishes between country, whose origins are properly located within the republican discourse of patriotism, and nation, which signifies a much narrower form of cultural, linguistic, racial, and ethnic identity rooted in one's nativity rather than fidelity to the republic and its constitution.

In "The Advantages Proposed by Repealing the Sacramental Test" (1732), for example, Swift offers a distinction between country and nation and their relationship to one another that is quite similar to the one in the letter to Middleton: "If there be any maxim in politics, not to be controlled, it must be the following: That those whose private interest is united with the interest of their country . . . will heartily wish, that the nation should thrive."[139] Swift separates not only country and nation from one another here but also private from public interest, or as he terms it, the interest of the country. Swift makes it clear that the mutual interest of both the private and public spheres should be to see the nation, as a whole, thrive and prosper, yet his maxim's separation of the public interest from private also suggests an underlying tension, at least in Swift's mind, between his country and his nation, as well as an understanding of their dependence on one another. At times, they speak univocally, as in his "Letter to the Whole People of Ireland" (1724) where he declares to the Irish people that "by the Laws of GOD, of NATURE, of NATIONS, and of your Country, you ARE, and OUGHT to be as FREE a People as your Brethren in England."[140] Swift again distinguishes between the laws of nations and those of the country, even though both reach the same conclusion with respect to the inherent freedom and liberty of the Irish people. This unanimity, however, is quickly undermined by the economic and political realities surrounding England's relationship to Ireland during this time, hence Swift's conditional "ought." In another letter addressing the conflicts between Ireland and England, Wood's coin most prominently, Swift refers to English weavers and merchants as "a Race of *Traytors,* and *Enemies* to God and their Country" for producing woolen and silk cloth of dubious quality and then charging an exorbitant fee for their shoddy wares.[141] Such practices, Swift insists, have effectively damaged England's prominence within the larger European market for woolen and silk cloth. More importantly, Swift suggests that these manufacturers and merchants, in their avarice, "do not only ruin themselves, (for that alone would be an *Example* to the rest, and a *Blessing* to the Nation) but sell their Souls to Hell, and their Country to Destruction."[142]

In making this distinction between country and nation, I do not mean to suggest that Swift's brand of patriotism eschews particularity entirely in deference to universal and abstract legal values, such as individual liberty and freedom, balanced government, civic duty, allegiance to the republic, and political support for its constitution. In fact, many scholars acknowledge the extent to which seventeenth- and eighteenth-century expressions of patriotism were often a thinly veiled defense of England as a distinctly Protestant, Anglo-Saxon nation whose rights and liberties are guaranteed by the Ancient Constitution, which had been abandoned following the Norman conquest in 1066.[143] Such calls to restore England to its ancient purity were intended as a check on the power of the state and the king as well as a means of protecting the nation against Catholicism and other foreign influences, which were, to the mind of the patriot, undermining England's cultural, religious, ethnic, and racial integrity, a fear that only continued to grow following the 1707 Act of Union and the formation of Great Britain. Furthermore, the rights and liberties enshrined in the Ancient Constitution only extended to those citizens who were white, property owning, and male, again suggesting the ways in which the patriotic imperative to love one's country remains, despite its pretentions to a more universalist and humanitarian vision of political community, profoundly narrow and insular in nature, if not in effect.

This contradiction is certainly true of Swift. While his particular understanding of patriotism enabled him to balance and reconcile, to what extent he could, his conflicting loyalties to both England and Ireland, that unique sense of accommodation did not necessarily extend to Catholics or Dissenters on either side of the Irish Sea, many of whom Swift derided and lampooned, explicitly and implicitly, in his writings. Swift's designation as the "Hibernian Patriot"[144] (a label that Swift, himself, did not care for) was not one readily embraced by Irish Catholics, who viewed him with contempt for his often bigoted statements against the church and its adherents, including charges of savagery and even cannibalism.[145] Swift was not unique in this regard. Eighteenth-century patriotic discourse, as Jacqueline Hill argues, has its origins in the Exclusion Crisis and the Whig opposition's fears regarding popery among the Stuarts and their supporters. This anti-Catholic strain within the late seventeenth-century Whig patriot movement does not necessarily disappear after 1688; rather, it is appropriated by many Tory patriots who, like Swift, viewed the Catholic Church as a continuing threat to the health and welfare of the nation.[146]

Tory definitions of "country" also routinely excluded Dissenters and Presbyterians, whose various religious orientations placed them in direct opposition not only to the Anglican faith but also to the kind of public spirit and sense of civic duty Swift championed elsewhere.[147] While Dissenting congregations in England were, by and large, not viewed as a threat to Whig patriots and their interests, for many High Church Tories, particularly those residing in Ireland, love of country precluded acceptance of any faith that did not swear fealty to the Church of England.[148] Swift was typical in this regard. In *The History of the Four Last Years of the Queen* (1758), he openly mocks and scolds Quakers for holding it "an unlawful Action to take an Oath to a Magistrate" because it violates the biblical doctrine that commands us never to swear under any circumstances, an overly literal reading to Swift's mind and one likely attributable to a religious enthusiasm perhaps common to all Dissenting sects. Even more galling, Swift continues, are the Quakers' complaints of unfair treatment under the law when they refuse to take such an oath and their subsequent efforts, after 1688, to change the law in order to accommodate their doctrinal beliefs. Commenting on the passage of a 1696 act that allowed Quakers to offer "their Solemn Affirmation and Declaration . . . instead of an Oath in the usual Form," Swift takes particular issue with this period in English history because Dissenters were, regrettably, being given entrée to public life irrespective of their sect or denomination: "The great Endeavour in those Times was to lay all Religion upon a Level; in order to which, this Maxim was advanced, That no man ought to be denied the Liberty of Serving his Country, upon account of a different Belief in Speculative Opinions; Under which Term some People were apt to include every Doctrine of Christianity."[149] It was a maxim, in Swift's words, "formed upon the Inconsistent Principles of Faction" rather than "the Standard of Truth and Reason," which are central to his conception of country ideology.[150] Swift proudly notes that the act proved to be only temporary, and once it had expired, the House of Commons refused to even debate its possible renewal. However, he continues, the House of Lords, despite the objections of those in the lower chamber, did promptly pass the bill in response to the Quakers' petition for a continuance of the act, leaving Swift to wonder how "the Legislature of so great a Kingdom could descend so low as to be ministerial and subservient to the Caprices of the most absurd Heresy that ever appeared in the World."[151] Certainly, as is evident from this brief example, Swift did not believe that one should be denied the right to serve his or her country just because he or she holds opinions, speculative or otherwise, different from those in power. Church doctrine, on the other hand, is, for him, not a matter of opinion and should not be treated as such. To do so is to create a false equivalency between an Anglican faith that genuinely moves us toward a public spirit and acts of patriotism and the heretical beliefs of those sects, like the Quakers, who seek only to promote faction and division, even as they cloak themselves in the guise of the patriot.[152]

This kind of false patriotism remains a pernicious problem for Swift as he attempts to sort out the true lover of his or her country from those who only seek to further their own private interests or that of their party. As he notes in the *Examiner* no. 14, from November 9, 1710, "It [political lying] gives and resumes Employments; can sink a Mountain to a Mole-hill, and raise a Mole-hill to a Mountain . . . can wash a *Black-a-moor* white; make a saint of an Atheist, and a Patriot of a Profligate."[153] Not only does Swift use the language of race here to distinguish between the authentic and false patriot, but he also suggests that even an authentic, or white, patriot can, over time, degenerate into becoming the false patriot, who is black and a profligate. In the *Examiner*, no. 13, from November 2, 1710, he observes that, at the time of the Glorious Revolution, "most of the Nobility and Gentry who invited over the Prince of *Orange*, or attended him in his Expedition, were true Lovers of their Country and its Constitution, in Church and State."[154] However, shortly after, "an under Sett of Men, who had nothing to lose . . . found means to whisper in the King's Ear, that the Principles of Loyalty in the Church of *England*, were wholly inconsistent with the *Revolution*."[155] This "under Sett of Men" were, of course, those who promoted the interests of Dissenters against that of the established church and, by extension, the country itself, despite their seemingly authentic claims to patriotic duty. Swift echoes these concerns and fears regarding those Dissenting sects demanding the right to provide service to their country in "The Sentiments of a Church-of-England Man, With Respect to Religion and Government" (1708): "If the Church wants Members of its own, to employ in the Service of the Publick; or be so unhappily contrived, as to exclude from its Communion, such Persons who are likeliest to have great Abilities; it is time it should be altered, and reduced into some more perfect, or, at least, more popular Form: But, in the mean while, it is not altogether improbable, that when those, who dislike the Constitution, are so very zealous in their Offers for the Service of their Country, they are not wholly unmindful of their Party, or of themselves."[156] Swift warns his reader that even those who seem most earnest in their patriotic desire to provide some form of public service are, in fact, motivated solely by personal and partisan interests rather than a genuine love of country. These "supple Patriots of the Modern sort," as Swift describes them in his paraphrase of Horace's "Ode XIV," change their "course with every sudden gust" and "turn with ev'ry Gale that blows from Court."[157] It is thus increasingly difficult to distinguish, in Swift's words, between "a *patriot* and a *plunderer* of his country."[158] For Swift, such professions of patriotic fervor should rightly be met with skepticism, if not outright mockery and ridicule. In a marginal comment on Gilbert Burnet's *History of His Own Times* (1724–34), Swift chides Burnet's desire to "enlarge . . . on the affairs of Scotland," in part, "out of the inbred love that all men have for their native country," asking pointedly, "Could not he keep his inbred love to himself?"[159] Swift later responds to Burnet's statement that "my love to my country, and my private friendships carried me perhaps too far" with a brief, declarative, "Right."[160] Swift suggests here that there is a form of patriotism that is, in fact, inbred and extreme to the point that it may blind a person as to the true nature and condition of their nation, an irrational and even dangerous love of country that, I would argue, is consonant with nationalism and its more nativist perspective, as opposed to Swift's Tory brand of patriotic virtue.

We see yet another critical example of this "inbred" love of country in *A Modest Proposal*, whose narrator, as noted previously, offers a satirical doubling of Sir William Petty and his demographic and cartographic appropriation of Ireland. Not only does Swift's narrator engage in such forms of political arithmetic in order to "remedy" the dire poverty and destitution he observes there, but he also, quite tellingly, has "no other Motive than the *publick Good of my Country, by advancing our Trade, providing for Infants, relieving the Poor, and giving some Pleasure to the Rich.*"[161] Further, the narrator discusses his gruesome proposal to cook and eat Ireland's children with a "very worthy Person, *a True Lover of his Country,*" whom he later describes as "so deserving a Patriot," even though he ultimately rejects his further "Refinement upon my Scheme" that young boys and girls, "not exceeding fourteen year of age, nor under twelve," also be consumed as a replacement for venison.[162] Swift deploys the discourse of patriotism here in a satirical fashion in order to criticize those who profess love for their country but whose actions are wholly antithetical to any genuine expression of patriotic virtue, at least as Swift defines it. More importantly, like the map itself, this corrupt version of patriotism is the result of a distorted perspective and vision of the country that sees the physical landscape and its residents as little more than commodities to be exchanged and exploited for the purpose of private gain. *A Modest Proposal* thus brings together Swift's critique of the surveying and mapping of Ireland and the bogus claims that these attempts to rationalize and quantify its geography and its people are somehow in the best interest of the country. To underscore this point, Swift counters the narrator's pretense to patriotism by having him summarily dismiss any expedients other than the one proposed, including "*learning to love our Country, wherein we differ even from Laplanders, and the Inhabitants of Topinamboo*" and "*being a little cautious not to sell our Country and Consciences for nothing.*"[163] Swift ironically juxtaposes the narrator's false notions of patriotism, which are once again racially coded, and the political and economic calculus on which they rest, against Swift's own more authentic understanding of what it means to truly love one's country, which is expressly anticartographic and antidemographic in nature.

This association between the cartographic impulse and false patriotism is also manifest in Lemuel Gulliver's naïve and solipsistic love for his native England, which Swift reveals, over the course of the novel, to be a form of nationalist sentiment rooted in an irrational and uncritical attachment to a particular place rather than fidelity to a set of moral principles and ideals that should rightly govern the nation. As we have seen, for Swift, patriotic duty entails the responsibility to criticize the state when it fails to live up to those principles and ideals; however, love of country, for Gulliver, often translates into a passive acceptance of its laws and its government and a need to defend them to his strange and exotic hosts, who, despite his best efforts, remain incredulous at Gulliver's otherwise upbeat descriptions of life at home in England. Early in his voyages, we hear Gulliver frequently invoke his love for his native country, especially as he becomes increasingly familiar with the laws and customs of his hosts. For example, Gulliver notes that some of the Lilliputians' laws and customs are "so directly contrary to those of my own dear Country, I should be tempted to say little in their Justification."[164] His love and veneration for his native country also prompts Gulliver, while a guest in Lilliput, to "eat more than usual, in Honour to my dear Country, as well as to fill the Court with admiration," even though Flimnap, the lord high treasurer, looks upon Gulliver with a "sour Countenance," no doubt in response to his prodigious appetite.[165] Swift expressly links Gulliver's so-called patriotism to a monstrous form of consumption that will, in effect, threaten the very existence of Lilliput itself, hence Flimnap's perhaps justified recoiling at the sight of Gulliver eating. It is a relationship that is, no doubt, meant to invoke England's relationship to Ireland as a destructive and wanton consumer of its land, its resources, and its people, both literally and figuratively. By contrast, for the Lilliputians, the practice of moral virtues, such as "Truth, Justice, Temperance, and the like . . . assisted by Experience and good Intention," are sufficient to "qualify any Man for the Service of his Country."[166] Also, the male children of nobles are "bred up in the Principles of Honour, Justice, Courage, Modesty, Clemency, Religion, and Love of their Country."[167] The Lilliputians' understanding of what it means to love one's country, I would argue, is decidedly closer to that of Swift than Gulliver, who, despite his encounter with this very different model of patriotic virtue, nevertheless exclaims toward the end of his travels there, "It is not easy to express the joy I was in upon the unexpected Hope of once more seeing my beloved Country, and the dear Pledges I had left in it."[168]

This tension between Gulliver's misguided and myopic love for his native country and his host's inability to comprehend how and why he would feel that way, especially given his relation of the otiose state of affairs plaguing both England and Europe, only escalates during his subsequent journey to Brobdingnag. While conversing with the prince, Gulliver says: "But, I confess, that after I had been a little too copious in talking of my own beloved Country; of our Trade, and Wars by Sea and Land, of our Schisms in Religion, and Parties in State; the Prejudices of his Education prevailed so far, that he could not forbear taking me up in his right Hand, and stroaking me gently with the other; after an hearty Fit of laughing, asked me whether I were a *Whig* or *Tory*."[169] Once again, Gulliver's patriotism is marked by a kind of excess, however, not of appetite, as in the previous example, but rather of patriotism itself, which prompts him talk at great length about subjects that his host can only find simultaneously sad and humorous. Afterward, Gulliver is filled "with Indignation to hear our noble Country, the Mistress of Arts and Arms, the Scourge of *France*, the Arbitress of *Europe*, the Seat of Virtue, Piety, Honour and Truth, the Pride and Envy of the World, so contemptuously treated." Incapable of accepting the intent and import of the prince's laughter, Gulliver falls back on his sense of patriotic righteousness, however unjustified and unwarranted by the facts he relates regarding his native country. He is neither able to reflect critically on the faults and shortcomings of England, its system of governance and its laws in particular, nor does he, by his own admission, possess the rhetorical skills necessary "to celebrate the Praise of my own dear native Country in a Style equal to its Merits and Felicity," as Gulliver later tells the king of Brobdingnag when he is again pressed to educate his host about life at home in England.[170] Rather than take seriously the king's subsequent criticisms of his native country, including its preference for an "odd Kind of Arithmetick . . . in reckoning the Numbers of our People by a Computation," Gulliver instead places the blame on himself and his inability to adequately translate his patriotic love of country into a proper description of what he believes are England's true virtues, despite all evidence to the contrary.[171]

Gulliver's less than satisfying attempts to educate and enlighten both the prince and king of Brobdingnag never lead to any direct confrontation with his hosts, as he demurs from explicitly refuting their pointed responses to his narration out of a sense of decorum and propriety, which Gulliver lauds as yet another intrinsic national virtue. In the following chapter, however, Gulliver does vent to his reader about being "forced to rest with Patience, while my noble and most beloved Country was so injuriously treated."[172] His patience having run out, Gulliver thus proceeds to offer his understanding of true patriotism, which demands that he "artfully" elude the questions put to him and give "every Point a more favourable turn . . . than the Strictness of Truth would allow": "For, I have always born that laudable Partiality to my own Country, which Dionysius Halicarnassensis with so much Justice recommends to an Historian. I would hide the Frailties and Deformities of my Political Mother, and place her Virtues and Beauties in the most advantageous Light."[173] To be sure, Gulliver's definition of patriotism is directly at odds with the one Swift outlines in many of his sermons and writings on the subject. His inclination toward "partiality" in his patriotic discourse, as well as an aesthetics of the beautiful rather than the sublime or the grotesque, runs counter to Swift's belief that private and partial views, such as the map or the picturesque landscape, are antithetical to the interests of the public and the country. More importantly, it is Gulliver's deference to his "Political Mother" that leads him to prefer such partial and beautiful views of his native country, regardless of the horrible truths lurking just beneath the surface of that facade. The real problem here, for Swift, are the "grounds" on which Gulliver bases his patriotic feelings, which are familial and territorial in orientation and so more typical of a nativist, if not nationalist, understanding of the country. While nationalism would, by the nineteenth century, come to appropriate and subsume the term "country" as a signifier for the physical geography of the nation, the land or territory with which the patriot should rightly identify him or herself, for an eighteenth-century author like Swift, this emergent form of national identity, satirically embodied by the figure of Gulliver, conflicts with and contradicts that more ancient definition of country as the republic and its citizenry, which are the proper objects of our patriotic love and care.

In the subsequent Laputa section of *Gulliver's Travels*, Swift articulates this very distinction during Gulliver's visit to Glubbdubdrib, an island of sorcerers and magicians who are able to conjure the spirits of the dead, including notably those of Caesar, Pompey, and Brutus. Gulliver is immediately struck with a "profound Veneration" for Brutus in particular, as he displays "the most consummate Virtue, the greatest Intrepidity, and Firmness of Mind, the truest Love of his Country, and general Benevolence for Mankind in every Lineament of his Countenance."[174] Here, Brutus symbolizes, as he frequently does in Tory ideology, republican virtue, including a true and abiding love of country, while Caesar, by contrast, is identified with tyranny, corruption, and imperial aggression, despite the apparent contrition he expresses to Gulliver for such acts in the spiritual afterlife. Gulliver has little regard for the figures from modern history he encounters and shows great contempt for the kings, princes, and royal families who have ruled Europe's courts for the past one hundred years. He notes that many have earned their "high Titles of Honour" and "prodigious Estates" by "betraying their Country or their Prince," although he does clarify that "I do not intend my Country in what I say upon this Occasion" in a desire not to offend any potential readers.[175] Gulliver's clarification, of course, is meant to be taken ironically, as it enables Swift to critique the acquisition of ever larger estates, and the subsequent generation of wealth from those estates, as an antipatriotic betrayal of one's country that elevates of the value of the land itself over the needs of the republic. This truth, however, has been obscured, as Gulliver observes, by those modern "prostitute Writers" and historians who "ascribe the greatest Exploits in War to Cowards, the wisest Counsel to Fools, Sincerity to Flatterers, *Roman* Virtue to Betrayers of their Country, Piety to Atheists, Chastity to Sodomites, Truth to Informers."[176] Once again, the problem of the false patriot asserts itself; however, perhaps for the first time, Gulliver appears to be aware of the discrepancy between the claim to patriotism and actually serving the interests of one's country.

Gulliver's other-worldly experience conversing with kings, emperors, potentates, and philosophers from both the ancient and modern worlds leads him to conclude that degeneration is a fact of all political systems. He observes that vice and corruption, "by the Force of Luxury," had grown beyond control not only in Glubbdubdrib, but also "in other Countries, where Vices of all Kinds have reigned so much longer" and "where the whole Praise as well as Pillage hath been engrossed by the chief Commander, who perhaps had the least Title to either."[177] These "melancholy Reflections" extend as well to his native England, as Gulliver acknowledges for the first time the extent to which this sort of corruption has tended toward the degeneration of his own country and its people. In response, Gulliver wishes that "some *English* Yeomen of the old Stamp, might be summoned to appear" because, unlike their modern counterparts, they were regarded for "the Simplicity of their Manners, Dyet and Dress," "their true Spirit of Liberty," and "their Valour and Love of their Country."[178] Gulliver's idealization of the yeoman here is telling, as he embodies, for Swift, the simple virtues of rural life as well as the need for service and duty to one's country, both of which are central to his definition of patriotism. Yeomen were typically private landowners who farmed and cultivated their own land; however, they were not titled members of the landed gentry or nobility, from whom they earned their land as payment. Rather, the role of the yeoman historically was to dutifully serve the manorial lord or the king in a variety of capacities during times of war and peace, hence Gulliver's nostalgic characterization of the yeoman as an authentic and genuine patriot whose relationship to the land and his native country differed greatly from the modern estate owner, who often placed his personal interests above those of the public. Swift's valorization of the yeoman suggests that country is neither coterminous with nor equivalent to the physical geography of the nation, a mistake Gulliver makes throughout his travels up to this point; rather, country is an imagined and conceptual geography that mediates and determines the relationship between the private citizen and the land, the cultivation and improvement of which should rightly serve the public interest and not only that of the individual landholder. Gulliver's redemption, I would argue, is dependent on this understanding of patriotism.

Interestingly, this last section of *Gulliver's Travels*, "A Voyage to the Country of the Houyhnhnms," is the only one expressly defined by the indigenous inhabitants of the country rather than by place. That is, all of the previous voyages have been to *somewhere*: Lilliput, Brobdingnag, Laputa, Glubbdubdrib, and so on. The people who reside in those places take their names from the place, as in Lilliputians, Brobdingnagians, etc. In this last voyage, however, he arrives in a "country" occupied by Houyhnhnms, and not some other, more official name to designate this previously undiscovered land. While Gulliver does make, on occasion, a passing reference to "Houyhnhnmland," in both its hyphenated and non-hyphenated forms, we get the sense that this is a construction of his own devising rather than an actual place-name. He also refers, just as often, to the "Houyhnhnm Country," suggesting that its name resists the same kind of toponymic fixity as the other countries Gulliver visits.[179] This is, I think, an important distinction to note. Why name the place the "country" of the Houyhnhnms if not to emphasize the centrality of country, in its positive and affirmative sense, to the society and culture of the Houynhnhnms, who, in many ways, embrace and embody the patriotic ideals and rural virtues Swift professed? It is, in fact, Gulliver's identification with the "country" of the Houyhnhnms that will precipitate his further alienation from his native England, suggesting a transformation in Gulliver's very understanding of the meaning of "country." As Gulliver admits to his reader, "I must freely confess, that the many Virtues of those excellent *Quadrupeds* placed in opposite View to human Corruptions, had so far opened my Eyes, and enlarged my Understanding, that I began to view the Actions and Passions of Man in a very different light; and to think the Honour of my own Kind not worth managing."[180] The phrase "my own Kind," here may be read in the context of "human Corruptions," meaning that Gulliver is ashamed of his barbarous humanity in light of his experiences among the virtuous and patriotic Houyhnhnms, whose "Prudence, Unanimity, Unacquaintedness with Fear, and their Love of their Country would amply supply all Defects in their military Art."[181] However, I would suggest that Gulliver's understanding of his "own Kind" may be, as well, a reference to his own nation of England and, more broadly, the kind of nativism that, contrary to true patriotism, tends to govern the individual's relationship to his or her respective country.

Toward the end of his voyages, having returned to England, Gulliver gives voice to this transformed understanding of his country when he proclaims that his "sole Intention" in writing down an account of his journey was the "PUBLICK GOOD," which, as we have seen, is a critical component of Swift's definition of country and patriotism.[182] Gulliver's statement of intention is not meant to be ironic or satirical on Swift's part but rather a demonstration of the profound change within Gulliver and, more importantly, his turn toward a more authentic and proper understanding of patriotic virtue, one that places the public good over and above private interest. In addition, Gulliver expresses, yet again, his contempt for his "own Kind," but in this instance, with an important qualifier: "For, who can read of the Virtues I have mentioned in the glorious *Houyhnhnms*, without being ashamed of his own Vices, when he considers himself as the reasoning, governing Animal of his Country?"[183] He includes here not only himself but also "those remote Nations where *Yahoos* preside," excluding, of course, the Brobdingnagians, "whose wise Maxims in Morality and Government, it would be our Happiness to observe." The context here is not simply a general corrupt and sinful humanity but rather the ways in which that corrosive nature perverts and distorts humanity's understanding of what it means to govern properly and its relationship to the territory upon which those institutions are erected. I do not mean to suggest that the Houyhnhnms are, in Swift's eyes, an ideal or utopian society to which we should all aspire. As the long history of scholarship on *Gulliver's Travels* shows, the image of the Houyhnhnms is, at best, conflicted and somewhat ambivalent, not only noting the ways in which Swift holds up the rational society of the Houyhnhnms as a model of virtue and moral perfection but also pointing out its numerous flaws and shortcomings, its treatment of the Yahoos in particular.

That being said, I would insist that the Houyhnhnm section of *Gulliver's Travels* does provide Swift an opportunity to articulate his own understanding of what a "country of the mind" can and should mean for a truly patriotic citizen and, more importantly, to force Gulliver into reflecting critically on the limits of his own more narrow definition of country as the land and place where he was born and from which he derives his sense of self as a national subject. Gulliver is thus left at the end of the novel suspended somewhere between these two competing yet mutually constitutive senses of country: between the land itself and the polity that, for Swift, gives that land purpose and meaning. The map is capable of representing the former, while the latter remains against the map in its resistance to that reified and reifying image of the nation and the empire. Gulliver ultimately cannot reconcile this fundamental antinomy by the end of the novel, leaving him with an understanding of his country as a heterotopic space that is not reducible to the map and the cartographic discourses on which he, and other so-called patriots, formerly relied.

# 4

# Daniel Defoe and the
# Limits to the Market

Consider common usage of the word that lies at the very heart of capitalism: "market." Almost every definition of *market* in the dictionary
connotes an *opportunity:* as concrete locale or institution, a market is
a place where opportunities exist to buy and sell; as an abstraction,
a market is the possibility of sale. Goods "find a market," and we say
there is a market for a service or commodity when there is a demand
for it, which means it can and will be sold. Markets are "opened" to
those who want to sell. The market represents "conditions as regards,
opportunity for, buying and selling," The *market* implies offering and
choice. What then are market *forces?* Doesn't force imply coercion?

— Ellen Meiksins Wood, *The Origin of Capitalism* (1999)

## The Visible Hand

The surveying and mapping of Ireland, as I suggested at the outset of the previous chapter, was an important precursor to England's later forays into the
colonization of Africa and the Americas, a subject which Behn addresses and
redresses in her novel, *Oroonoko.* Swift's critique of the cartographic impulse
and its role in the colonization of Ireland represents yet another example of the
ways in which many authors during the seventeenth and eighteenth centuries
placed themselves and their respective works "against the map" in an attempt
to resist and counter the emerging forces of imperialism and capitalism, both
of which were dependent, to some extent, on the map and its attendant technologies. However, as we see in the history of the English settlement of Ireland, it is not only Swift who articulates this anticartographic sentiment in his
various satirical treatments of the subject or in his defense of "country" as an
alternative mode of conceptualizing the nation and its geography. It is also the
native inhabitants of Ireland themselves who, first and foremost, recognized
the destructive and exploitive nature of England's efforts to survey and map

the Irish landscape and who, in response, engaged in open and covert forms of resistance to the expropriation of their land, both physically and symbolically. While much of this history of resistance remains somewhat murky and uneven in its outcomes, there is enough evidence and documentation to confirm that it did, in fact, occur, leaving us only to speculate about the inevitable and perhaps irretrievable gaps in the historical record. What is clear, however, upon further examination and analysis is that the history of cartography is also, by definition, a history of indigenous forms of resistance to the surveying and mapping of colonized lands, not just in Ireland, Africa, or the Americas but notably, the Indian subcontinent as well.

In his book *Empire of Free Trade: The East India Company and the Making of the Colonial Marketplace*, Sudipta Sen identifies the market and its attendant infrastructure as a primary site of conflict between the expansionist aims of the English East India Company and indigenous forms of commerce and exchange specific to premodern India throughout the seventeenth and eighteenth centuries. His text documents how local rights of exchange predicated on religious and feudal notions of tribute, gift, reciprocity, and dynastic prerogative inevitably run up against the administrative imperatives of the fiscal-military state and merchant companies to generate profits, minimize losses, and secure a stable source of revenue for shareholders at home. This conflict, however, is not simply one of competing social and cultural definitions of what it means to engage in exchange with others, nor does this conflict necessarily result in the violent subjugation and displacement of one system of exchange for another that is ostensibly more modern in its practices.[1] As Sen argues, the politics of the colonial marketplace involve an examination of how different conceptions of exchange are mediated by the spaces in which exchange occurs, such as the marketplace, and through which the identities of both colonizer and colonized are produced. Much as in Ireland, the East India Company's attempts to wrest control of the rights, duties, and privileges of domestic trade from provincial rulers and local aristocrats required an understanding of the physical topography of trade and commerce, including the geographic distribution of sites of exchange, the architecture of the marketplace itself, and the system of roads and transportation necessary for the movement of raw materials and commodities. The basic framework of markets, fairs, and bazaars found in India was not altogether that different from England, which had a functioning market economy since the Middle Ages, yet the organization and regulation of that framework differed in critical ways, posing real challenges to English attempts to gain access to and control over the colonial marketplace. "Colonial India provides an early historical instance where the East India Company's demands for commerce and markets came face to face with a *different* organization of trade, market exchange, and authority."[2] Sen characterizes the juxtaposition of these antithetical patterns of market activity within the colonial setting as the brutal imposition of a neutral, homogeneous economic space on an already existing geography of markets defined by overlapping domains of power that were not coextensive with one another.[3]

The production of such a homogeneous space is here aligned with the various technologies of order, such as cartography, that force a degree of uniformity and standardization on the colonial marketplace in the hopes of eliminating barriers to trade and, consequently, facilitating the flow of revenue into the coffers of the East India Company:

> In colonial gazetteers, statistical accounts, and guidebooks that begin to flourish by the first half of the nineteenth century, this invasive agenda of the late eighteenth century is rendered routine, as a neutral or neutralizing public political realm, a territory marked by uniform rules of law and revenue. Here a colonial officer can figure out with ease exactly how long it would take him to travel from one station to another, the quality of water, the situation of transportation and supplies, the length of rivers, the size and time of market gatherings and fairs, and the size and population of villages and towns.[4]

This empirical approach to the geography of Bengal required extensive surveys and expeditions whose primary objective was to gather information relevant to the administration of the colonial marketplace.[5] The production of a market geography was, according to Sen, an extension of efforts to codify and reform market activity, a move justified by the company's view of the Indian political economy as a loose amalgamation of territorial interests that lacked a cohesive set of regulations and laws governing trade within and between markets. As he demonstrates, the mantra of reform helped displace a differentiated, heterotopic understanding of territorial relations that had existed, in one form or another, since the late medieval period. Market activity, in this sense, is defined less by financial motivations than it is by the production and maintenance of discrete social orderings rooted in notions of patronage, religious obligation, and lineage. Precolonial marketplaces in northern India were thus "the physical extension of a certain vision of patrimony" that was ultimately inconsistent with the English imperial project.[6]

This difference in conceptions of market relations, however, is not restricted to a kind of anthropological accounting of the ways in which disparate sociocultural practices ultimately come into conflict with one another in the colonial setting, though that is the primary focus of Sen's text. The central problem lay within shifting definitions of the market precipitated by the nation-state's forays into what we would now recognize as the early stages of capitalism, and as I will argue, this problem is not specific to colonial interventions in places such as India, Africa, or the West Indies but rather is endemic to economic relations within both core and periphery. As Sen correctly points out, any investigation of England's political economy during the early modern period must contend with the often antithetical invocations of the market as signifier for a more open-ended understanding of commercial relations, a process if you will, and the market as an identifiable assembly of places with their own individuated practices and history. His attention to the latter is, when viewed in this context, strategic: "My goal here is to *name* and *place* the market, its patrons, claimants, and clientele, and, above all, to *mark* its site and genealogy. In the study of the market as an epicenter in the battle for colonial conquest, and the attempts at a colonial account of that victory, which is part and parcel of the surviving documentation, only the particularities of place and person in the market may provide the clues to the rich and many valences of the encounters between (at least two) widely differing political and material conceptions."[7] The contention implicit in this statement is that English imperial forces wished to efface the marketplace as a physical location since that set of identifications offered a measure of resistance to a more generalized system of production, distribution, and consumption. Hence, Sen "locates" the market as a means of resisting historical critiques of capitalism that unwittingly assume an imperialist conception of the market.[8] He does, at times, suggest that "the idea of a market as a notional space charted on the axes of production and consumption, distinct from the actual physical place of exchange" is part and parcel of larger trends within the consolidation of the English nation-state during the seventeenth and eighteenth centuries.[9] However, he fails to consider the fate of marketplaces in England during this period, assuming that their trajectory will inevitably be subsumed by Smithian notions of free and unfettered market activity that mark the telos of this particular history, which as I intend to show is only partly true.

The mapping of Britain's various marketplaces during the eighteenth century, much like their colonial counterparts, large and small, metropolitan and rural, was geared toward facilitating, consolidating, and regulating trade and commercial activity on a national scale. Maps, surveys, and chorographies were increasingly produced and deployed for just this purpose, providing a useful resource for would-be merchants, tradespeople, and consumers eager to do business in and between those respective marketplaces. However, the construction of a geography of the marketplace was not without its critics and detractors who resisted such efforts to efface local customs and practices with respect to market activity and, in the process, subsume and integrate those local and regional markets into a more comprehensive, integrated system of national trade and commerce. As I will argue in the following chapter, Daniel Defoe was one proponent, among others, of this approach to the construction of a geography of the marketplace and for many of the same reasons as the East India Company. An early advocate and practitioner of what would later be termed economic geography, Defoe saw great value in the production of maps and chorographies that could make trade and commerce visible in a way that allowed for its direction and management toward national ends, which inevitably lead him to create his own map of Britain's diverse marketplaces in his *Tour Thro' the Whole Island of Great Britain* (1724–27). However, as I will demonstrate, Defoe's marketplace, as a heterotopic locus, continually threatens to elude any such mapping. His attempt to construct a comprehensive and integrated picture of national space, defined largely by trade and commercial activity, is an implicit recognition that the marketplace, in its resistance to being mapped in any formal sense, may not be a stable referent for economic prosperity and national wealth. For Defoe, the imperative to map and survey the market arises out of a need to both delimit and contain commercial activity while at the same time acknowledging that any such effort is, to an extent, difficult, if not impossible, given the very fluidity and dynamic nature of market forces. The market thus remains against the map in that it is a site of contestation and conflict between that more abstract concept of the market as process, the invisible hand in Smith's terms, and the market as a physical, knowable place shaped and determined by the material practices of exchange, or the "visible hand" in my terms.

Like Sen, I also desire to name and place the market, albeit in Britain rather than India, in order to echo and underscore the idea that this, too, is contested ground, not between colonizer and colonized of course but rather between competing definitions of the market. While many classical political economists would seize on the concept of an abstract and placeless "market economy" during the eighteenth century, including not only Adam Smith but also Richard Cantillon, David Ricardo, and Francois Quesnay, the end result is neither a movement away from the physical sites of exchange nor a wholesale abandonment of that older but by no means antiquated system of local marketplaces.[10] As Jean-Christophe Agnew acknowledges, the transvaluation of the market during this period does not mean that its existence as a physical and material place is no longer relevant or necessary: "The historical shift in the market's meaning—from a place to a process to a principle to a power—suggests a gradual displacement of concreteness in the governing concept of commodity exchange. . . . It remains a matter of some debate, of course, whether the market's concreteness was displaced by events or misplaced by theory, but it is nonetheless useful to bear this shift in mind when traversing the seemingly unbridgeable divide between the colorful mythologies of antiquity and the relatively pallid folklore of capitalism."[11] The temporalization of this split within the signified promotes a teleological view of capitalist development that hypostatizes one view of the market over another; however, as Agnew suggests, this narrative is perhaps incorrect in its relegating the "market's concreteness" to a distant past: "Like the commodity, the word 'market' comes to live a dual existence in language. Within the word, a reference to marketability appears alongside a reference to the marketplace, subordinating the particular place to the abstract process that has ranged itself around it."[12] The etymological transformation of the "market" represents a doubling of the signified in which the market as a physical place now coexists, perhaps uneasily, with the market as exchange value divorced from its material instantiation, yet the movement toward an idea of the invisible hand of the market is historically accompanied by the increasing need for regulation, order, and control within the material sites of production and exchange. That is, the allegorical status of the marketplace, its redeployment as a signifier for a progressive sense of national health and prosperity, does not imply a movement away from a concern with the physical sites of commercial activity. Rather, the rapid pace of market consolidation and specialization from the Renaissance through the eighteenth century demonstrates a substantive reinvestment in the marketplace as a regulatory and regulated agent of the nation-state and its desire to generate revenue for military and economic expansion abroad.[13]

We must then consider not only Adam Smith's "invisible hand" of the market here but, just as importantly, the visible hand of the nation-state and local authorities in constructing an ordered, well-managed marketplace that serves the interests of legitimate trade and commerce while at the same time mitigating the more pernicious and corrupting effects of illegitimate trade on the social body. As Alan Everitt demonstrates, the history of the marketplace and the market town does not suggest an overall movement toward unregulated forms of exchange but instead attests to the increasing demand for order and standardization in matters of intranational trade. The sanctioning of trade through market charters, or grants, represents one of the earliest attempts at codifying and documenting what I am calling the geography of the marketplace. In fact, the term "market" only emerges in conjunction with the official recording of "statutory efforts to set aside public places and times for the purchase and sale of provisions and livestock."[14] Marketplaces were also required to have a "market cross" as a sign denoting its legal status, thus delimiting the space of the market in a public and overt manner. The medieval market was a clearly demarcated, physical locale whose continued growth and influence was dependent on its visibility within the social nexus of trade and commerce and its accountability in terms of the need to represent the necessary limits to exchange. The identification of functioning centers of trade, usually agricultural villages, rural fairs, and primary towns located at the intersection of established roads, becomes a first crucial step in generating revenue for the local manorial and episcopal estates through the collection of tolls and other forms of taxation on market activity. The granting of a market charter serves to differentiate between the strictly agricultural function of these settlements and a newer urban sensibility in which trade assumes a larger role within the economic and social development of the English town. While there was certainly overlap between agricultural and commercial life in these burgeoning urban centers, market status represented an attempt to foster the "growth of a permanent body of resident craftsmen, food processors and providers of various services" independent of more traditional patterns of subsistence.[15] The market charter thus provides the earliest means of establishing a geography of legitimized trade by consolidating all commercial activity into public sites of exchange that were then subject to royal scrutiny. This, of course, did not preclude the presence of illegitimate forms of trade that escaped the purview of lord and Crown. Many markets continued to operate without charters, circumventing the imperatives of visibility and accountability, while others remained strictly nominal in character, their existence relegated entirely to paper for either legal or political reasons. Privatized trade, often within the extended family, also represented a real challenge to these efforts to body forth the mechanisms of exchange in a manner that was regular and predictable.

These clandestine marketplaces escaped the strictures and legal requirements of Britain's existing marketplaces and, in so doing, the demand for visibility and legibility in matters of exchange. Buying and selling could occur outside socially proscribed limits and in a multiplicity of sites that may or may not be accessible to the general populace. In order to circumvent legal and economic control over matters of trade, merchants, artificers, and consumers alike began to occupy "a new extraterritorial zone of production and exchange" outside of traditional public marketplaces and its regulatory strictures.[16] In short, trade became privatized in ways that displaced the older conception of the marketplace for a more abstract, less bounded notion of exchange that was difficult to account for or make visible in any sense. This change was, of course, not without a great deal of social anxiety about the dubious effects of unregulated and unrestrained commerce within both the national body and the emerging colonial markets. The perceived threat of private marketing legitimated the further imposition of state-sanctioned forms of control within the marketplace. Under the Elizabethan and Stuart monarchies, the jurisdiction of the clerk of the market was substantially widened by statute to include matters of trade within both the marketplace proper and the areas immediately adjacent where the risk of illegal activity was highest.[17] The policy of the Crown, in this instance, bears the implicit recognition of the fact that private forms of trade needed to be brought under control and that the marketplace could serve as a regulatory agent of the state. Such efforts were often not welcome by townsfolk and local officials, who resented the interference of both Parliament and Crown, despite their claims to protect the interests of the consumer and the poor in particular. The desire to control the marketplace, of course, is not quite so altruistic since the state had a vested financial interest in reaping some of the profits of market activity, and capital generated outside the confines of the open market flowed, undeniably, in the other direction. Despite the success of private marketing and its ability to circumvent the strictures of the public marketplace, the mantra of reform and regulation would continue into the eighteenth century as trade became increasingly integrated and markets exerted an ever-greater influence over one another.

According to John Chartres, regulated markets would be the focus of local and central government at least up until 1750.[18] As trade proliferates in the expansive and expanding British marketplace of the seventeenth and eighteenth centuries, the legal, political, and bureaucratic infrastructure must adapt and change in order to secure the various forms of revenue generated by market activity, such as market tolls, market grants, transportation fees and tolls, and excise taxes. In its earliest phases, regulation took the form of administrative bodies and local officials whose duty was to oversee the marketplace and police its margins: "Everywhere marketing was subject to more or less strict regulation. . . . Virtually every town had its tollgatherers, sweepers, and bellmen, and many appointed a couple of 'market lookers' for the general inspection of the market. Aleconners and bread-testers enforced regulations and statutes governing the price and quality of bread and beer; leather searchers carried a hammer with a die or seal in its head and stamped skins and hides; 'aulnagers' performed similar functions for various types of cloth; and 'appraisers' were appointed to settle the value of goods in the event of a dispute."[19] A marketplace could contain anywhere between five and fifty such officials, who either were elected to the position by the manorial court or assumed those duties through a legal inheritance. Their overall function was to provide a safe and regulated space in which merchants and consumers could engage in trade without fear of reprisals or other forms of civil disturbance. This included enforcing strict laws concerning the days and times in which trade could occur, the specifics of which were codified in the original market charter. Their other primary function was the gathering and recording of tolls and levies for the estate that oversaw and managed that particular marketplace. The revenue generated by the marketplace was meticulously recorded in toll books that were then audited on an annual basis. The proceeds were often reinvested in improving the physical infrastructure of the marketplace and thus represented an important source of wealth for the manorial estate, one that would continue to grow and, in some cases, would come to displace agriculture as the sole means of subsistence and economic livelihood.

The more prominent role of the marketplace after the Elizabethan period precipitates an even greater need for regulation and control as various factions—urban freemen, local officials, manorial lords, and the church—began to assert their right of access to the marketplace and its spoils, leading inevitably to disputes and contests over everything from the imposition of tolls and fines to the time and place market activity could transpire. Legal battles proliferated in the courts over who, for example, controlled the passage tolls over local bridges and roads leading to and from the marketplace or how to establish fair and just use of the common balance beam when there were often multiple beams operated by private citizens within a single marketplace.[20] A major source of contention in many of these political and legal disputes concerned just *where* market activity should and should not take place since the growth of privatized trade was breaking down the traditional boundaries of the marketplace. The emergence of private marketing outside the public marketplace, or as it was termed, the "open market," fostered anxieties about the lack of visibility in matters of exchange that precipitated the very strictures

governing the creation of the marketplace itself. Animosity toward private traders and itinerant merchants, most of whom were based in the larger urban centers and London especially, entails a revaluation of the marketplace as a public
space that can vitiate the more negative effects of "free" trade. If trade can occur
anywhere and at any time, how can it be regulated and, more importantly, how
can it be made visible to the public eye in a way that assuaged general fears of
moral decay and licentiousness that accompany the pursuit of private gain and
profit? Private marketing certainly fulfills a need in terms of its ability to provide an unprecedented volume of goods and services to the average consumer
in a less constrained fashion, yet it also produces a reciprocal movement in
which the need to define and contain market activity becomes even more acute.

On occasion, these conflicts between older notions of a regulated market
economy and more open patterns of buying and selling played themselves out
within the eighteenth-century marketplace in dramatic and violent ways. Riots
were, in fact, a common occurrence throughout the century. Sudden or surreptitious fluctuations in the availability and cost of foodstuffs, textiles, and
other necessary items were believed to be directly attributable to the forces of
deregulation and the commercial imperatives of the emerging market economy.
In response, many communities turned violent and rioted in protest of these
changes in their local marketplaces. The turn to the so-called free market sig-
naled, for many of those who rioted, the erosion of local authority over matters
of trade and commerce as well as the eventual dissolution of customary, long-
held practices of buying and selling. Rather than capitulate, members of the
community found common cause in protecting their economic interests, and
through collective social action and popular protest, however loose or haphazard, offered some measure of resistance to the pressures of the free market.[21] As Adrian Randall and Andrew Charlesworth contend, contemporary
social and economic historians often ignore or downplay the extent to which
the development of a nationalized market economy was met with protest and
resistance, in the form of either regulatory laws and statutes or violent riots
when those laws and statutes failed to redress the inequities of the marketplace: "Rich and poor alike in the eighteenth century were the inheritors of
social and economic attitudes which stretched far into the past and which had
become deeply embedded into the popular culture. Those who wished to bring
about change did not by any means find the process an easy one. The confident
modernism of the Enlightenment found its advocates. But they also found
many more opponents, who . . . had little liking for the free market and unfettered capitalist world order they foresaw."[22] The moral and social strictures
that guided matters of trade and exchange were not, for many of the middling
and lower classes, an outmoded and largely irrelevant vestige from an earlier
time in the economic life of the nation; rather, they played an active and vital
role in shaping and regulating market activity, even as we enter the industrial
phase of capitalism when free markets were more widely accepted.

Jonathan Schmiechen and Kenneth Carls reinforce this point, arguing that
the eighteenth-century British marketplace is ultimately the product of the
dialectical tension between the centralization and decentralization of market
activity: "While on the one hand, the market was subject to increasing pressure as commercial and demographic growth pushed marketing outward from
the town center, on the other hand, the market was being forced by law and
tradition to remain in its centralized physical space. Markets were regulated
on the principle of the Roman maxim 'ubi est multitude, isi esse rector' (where
there is a crowd, someone should be responsible for its control); the need for
governance over market activities, including toll collection, drew these activities
toward the market center."[23] With the explosion in many urban populations
during the eighteenth century, these tensions would become even more apparent as the marketplace began to burst its seams, leading to public concerns over
crime, sanitation, and the deleterious effects of congestion in general. In response, we see a substantive reinvestment in locating and understanding where
and how exchange occurs in the hopes of providing some means of control
and containment. The response was not an abandonment of the traditional
marketplace but rather an attempt to improve upon that original structure in
the hopes of containing the forces that would potentially tear it apart, hence
the implementation of legal and administrative measures intended to regulate
and reconfigure the marketplace. In addition to these various legal measures
and provisions, maps, surveys, and chorographies may also be seen, in this
sense, as a strategy of containment in their subjection of the marketplace to a
compulsory visibility. The British marketplace is, I would contend, subject to
many of the same forces Sen notes as operating in colonial India, most notably
the construction of a geography of markets that would seemingly integrate and
homogenize intranational trade. More importantly, the production of such a
geography within England itself is no less subject to the same tensions and
conflicts the East India Company encountered when confronted with a multiplicity of sites of exchange whose localized practices often failed to cohere in a
smooth and, above all, profitable fashion. In fact, the subjugation of the English
marketplace to statist control in the form of regulative bodies that oversaw the
activities of market towns, a more centralized system of taxation and revenue
collection, and bureaucratic technologies of ordering, such as surveys, maps,
and chorographies, helped set the stage for similar endeavors in the colonial
margins, such as those Sen describes.

The consolidation of market activity through surveys, statistical accounts,
almanacs, and gazetteers represents an attempt to locate centers of trade and
commerce in order to transform the landscape from a disparate collection of
marketplaces into a coherent and integrated space for the production, distribution, and consumption of various goods and services. While many of these
localized markets were already dependent to some extent on the ebb and flow
of trade from other market centers, London in particular, the codification of

that relationship through the geography of the marketplace marks a turn in the economic life of the nation and the formation of capitalism more broadly. The very idea of trade on either a national or imperial scale is dependent on the construction of such a geography that can provide a reliable and consistent set of information as to distances between markets, days and hours of operation, types of commodities available, chief roads and byways for travel and transportation, and tolls for everything from the use of standardized weights and measures to passage over local bridges and roads. The geography of the marketplace becomes a critical tool for merchants and consumers alike in removing barriers to trade and providing a sense of continuity between areas that may hold fast to their own individuated customs and practices. Maps, surveys, and chorographies, in turn, contribute to this overriding sense of continuity by establishing a stable picture of the nation in which the gaps and discontinuities in and between marketplaces are displaced or elided altogether. The marketplace is thus subject to a degree of abstraction in the form of maps and surveys in order to provide a sense of cohesiveness that is putatively an accurate reflection of a unified and organic national body, created and sustained by legitimate forms of trade. The intended result is a homogenous, undifferentiated space that easily incorporates the marketplace into the working infrastructure of the nation.

## Maps, Markets, Nation

Among the numerous maps found in John Seller's *Anglia Contracta; or, A Description of the Kingdom of England & Principality of Wales* (1695), including surveys of Saxon and Roman Britain and current parish and county boundaries, we find a series dedicated to the geography of market towns and market activity in general.[24] Seller provides a convenient table that breaks down each county into "hundreds," a subdivision of the county or shire that has its own court, and then lists the name of the market town or towns located within the hundred (fig. 20).[25] Bedfordshire is thus divided up into eight hundreds, some of which contain multiple market towns and some that have none. Within Bedforshire, the Barford hundred possesses no market towns, while the Manshead hundred has no fewer than four: Leighton Boozard, Dwytable, Tuddington, and Hoborn. After the name of each market town, Seller includes an abbreviation of the specific day that particular marketplace is open (i.e., Dwytable W) since his text is not merely academic in nature, but rather a reference guide for traveler and merchant alike. To reinforce this more pragmatic function, Seller, whom I previously discussed with regard to his work as hydrographer to His Majesty, illustrates the table of hundreds and market towns with a county map on the following page. The maps are greatly reduced in scale given the compactness of the book and so are not very detailed, giving us only town names, the course of rivers, and a few small icons to denote topographical features, such as hills and forested areas. They do, however, give us a general sense of where the local

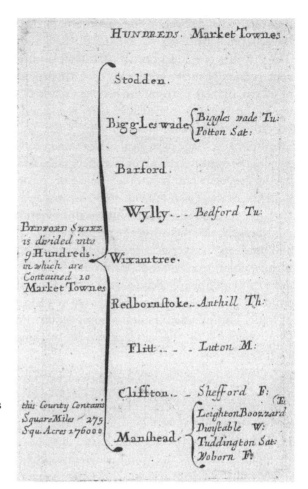

FIGURE 20. Table of hundreds
(*right*) and market towns
(*opposite*) for Bedfordshire,
John Seller, 1695. (© The British Library Board, shelfmark
Maps C.24.a.9.)

centers of trade and commerce were located with respect to the surrounding
towns that did not possess a market grant or charter. The geography of the
market town in Seller's text thus operates through a juxtaposition of table and
map to give us a more refined view of England's commercial life, stripping away
superfluous details in order to provide an integrated picture of county infrastructure. He does not inundate us with a lot of information, graphic or otherwise, but only that which is relevant to understanding, at least on the local level,
where and when markets operate in relation to the rest of the county.

While Seller is one of the most prominent figures to produce this kind of
work, he is by no means the first. Quantitative information regarding market towns was frequently available in various guidebooks, trade manuals, and
almanacs throughout the second half of the seventeenth century. For example, *A Book of the Names of All the Parishes, Market Towns, Villages, Hamlets,
and Smallest Places, In England and Wales* (1657) is, like Seller's text, a guidebook that contains a combination of charts, tables, and maps "for Travellers,

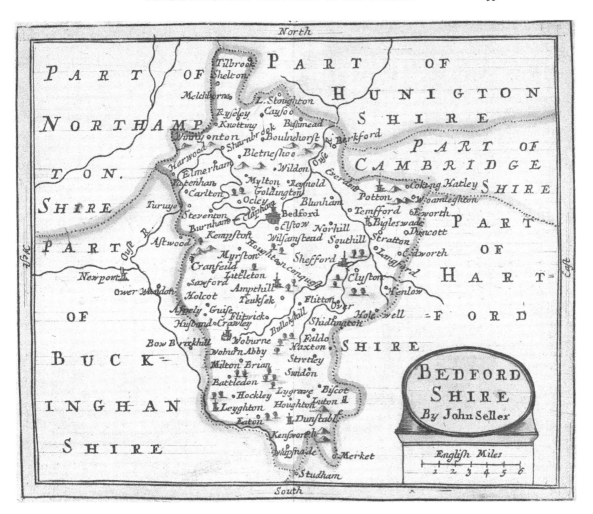

Quartermasters, Gatherers of Breefs, Strangers, Carriers, and Messengers with Letters, and all others that know the name of the place, but can neither tell where it is, nor how to goe unto it."[26] A chart is provided for each county, listing, as in Seller, the hundreds and their incorporated towns, including the market towns (fig. 21). In the left-hand margin, the town names are vertically arranged to correspond with the town names that are listed horizontally in the upper margin such that the distance between any two towns can be determined by finding their point of intersection within the table. Appended to the information found in the table is a small inset map that depicts the county and the surrounding area in order to provide a general sense of direction for the would-be traveler and "to know what market Towns lie in your way which way soever you travell."[27] The scale of the maps is greatly reduced, even more than Seller's, since they do not stand alone but rather are continuous with the table that they illustrate, yet in either instance, fidelity to the actual geography

| BEDFORD SHIRE | Bedforde | Ampthill | Tuddington | Dunstable | Leighton | Luton | Shefforde | Bigglesworth | Potton | Wooborne | Bletsher | Stowghton | Chellington | Oldwarden | Steuenton | Knotting | Oulney Northt | Newport Buck | Kymbalton Hunt | St Neots Hunt | Baldocke Hert | Hitching Hert | Melchborne | Berford | Merstone | |
|---|---|---|---|---|---|---|---|---|---|---|---|---|---|---|---|---|---|---|---|---|---|---|---|---|---|---|
| Temsforde N.E | 5 | 8 | 12 | 15 | 16 | 14 | 6 | 5 | 4 | 12 | 6 | 6 | 8 | 4 | 7 | 7 | 12 | 13 | 7 | 4 | 11 | 12 | 7 | 17 | 14 | 8 |
| Merstone. S. | 4 | 4 | 6 | 10 | 8 | 10 | 6 | 6 | 10 | 5 | 7 | 11 | 8 | 6 | 7 | 10 | 7 | 6 | 13 | 11 | 12 | 10 | 11 | 12 | 7 | 48 |
| Berforde N.E | 4 | 7 | 11 | 15 | 15 | 14 | 5 | 6 | 5 | 11 | 5 | 6 | 7 | 4 | 6 | 7 | 10 | 12 | 8 | 5 | 11 | 11 | 7 | 16 | 30 | |
| Mergate. S. | 15 | 11 | 7 | 3 | 8 | 3 | 12 | 14 | 16 | 10 | 10 | 26 | 19 | 13 | 16 | 21 | 19 | 16 | 24 | 20 | 10 | 7 | 22 | 42 | | |
| Melchborne N. | 7 | 12 | 16 | 20 | 19 | 20 | 12 | 11 | 11 | 13 | 4 | 3 | 5 | 11 | 7 | 2 | 9 | 12 | 4 | 6 | 18 | 18 | 27 | | | |
| Hitching Hert. E | 11 | 8 | 7 | 7 | 11 | 4 | 6 | 8 | 10 | 9 | 13 | 17 | 15 | 8 | 13 | 17 | 16 | 15 | 10 | 15 | 4 | 32 | | | | |
| Baldocke Hert | 12 | 9 | 10 | 11 | 14 | 7 | 6 | 6 | 8 | 12 | 15 | 16 | 16 | 8 | 14 | 19 | 18 | 17 | 19 | 13 | 45 | | | | | |
| St Neots Hunt N.E | 7 | 11 | 15 | 19 | 19 | 17 | 9 | 7 | 5 | 15 | 7 | 4 | 9 | 7 | 9 | 13 | 15 | 5 | 40 | | | | | | | |
| Kymbalton Hun N | 10 | 14 | 19 | 22 | 21 | 21 | 13 | 12 | 11 | 17 | 7 | 2 | 8 | 11 | 10 | 5 | 12 | 15 | 42 | | | | | | | |
| Newport Buck S.W | 8 | 8 | 10 | 14 | 9 | 17 | 12 | 14 | 15 | 7 | 9 | 13 | 7 | 12 | 6 | 11 | 4 | 50 | | | | | | | | |
| Oulney Northt W | 7 | 9 | 12 | 15 | 14 | 15 | 15 | 14 | 14 | 9 | 6 | 11 | 4 | 11 | 4 | 7 | 42 | | | | | | | | | |
| Knotting. N | 7 | 11 | 15 | 19 | 18 | 19 | 12 | 12 | 11 | 12 | 3 | 4 | 10 | 6 | 50 | | | | | | | | | | | |
| Steuenton N.W | 3 | 6 | 11 | 14 | 14 | 17 | 9 | 9 | 10 | 8 | 3 | 9 | 3 | 7 | 49 | | | | | | | | | | | |
| Oldewarden S.E | 4 | 5 | 9 | 12 | 13 | 11 | 2 | 3 | 5 | 9 | 7 | 9 | 43 | | | | | | | | | | | | | |
| Chellington N.W | 5 | 9 | 13 | 16 | 14 | 16 | 11 | 11 | 11 | 11 | 2 | 7 | 39 | | | | | | | | | | | | | |
| Stowghton N | 7 | 12 | 16 | 20 | 19 | 19 | 11 | 10 | 9 | 13 | 5 | 33 | | | | | | | | | | | | | | |
| Bletshoe. N.W | 4 | 9 | 13 | 16 | 15 | 16 | 9 | 9 | 9 | 11 | 42 | | | | | | | | | | | | | | | |
| Wooborne S.W | 8 | 5 | 4 | 6 | 4 | 8 | 11 | 13 | 44 | | | | | | | | | | | | | | | | | |
| Potton. E | 7 | 9 | 13 | 15 | 9 | 13 | 5 | 3 | 36 | | | | | | | | | | | | | | | | | |
| Bigglesworth E | 6 | 7 | 10 | 13 | 17 | 11 | 13 | 35 | | | | | | | | | | | | | | | | | | |
| Shefford S.E | 6 | 4 | 8 | 10 | 14 | 10 | 33 | | | | | | | | | | | | | | | | | | | |
| Luton S.E | 12 | 7 | 7 | 4 | 8 | 28 | | | | | | | | | | | | | | | | | | | | |
| Leighton S.W | 2 | 8 | 5 | 5 | 23 | | | | | | | | | | | | | | | | | | | | | |
| Dunstable S | 13 | 8 | 4 | 28 | | | | | | | | | | | | | | | | | | | | | | |
| Tuddington S | 9 | 5 | 31 | | | | | | | | | | | | | | | | | | | | | | | |
| Ampthill. S | 5 | 34 | | | | | | | | | | | | | | | | | | | | | | | | |

Henlow, *Clifton.*
Hide East, *Flit.*
Hide west, *Flit.*
Higham goben, *Flit.*
Hill, *Wixam.*
Hockecliffe, *Manf.*
Holcott, *Manf.*
Holme, *Biggle.*
Houghton conquest, *Redborne.*
Houghton Kings, *Manf.*

Howell, *Clifton.*

**K**
Kempston, *Redb.*
Knotting, *Stod.*

**L**
Lanford, *Biggle.*
Legenho, *Redb.*
LEIGHTON buzard, *Manfh.*
Ligrave, *Flitt.*

Limbene, *Flitt.*
Littleton, *Redb.*
LUTON, *Flitt.*

**M**
Mauldon, *Redb.*
Margatt, *Manfh.*
Melchborne, *Stod.*
Mepfhall, *Clifton.*
Merfton morton, *Redb.*
Milbrook, *Redb.*
Milhoe, *Biggle.*
Mil ton

B

FIGURE 21. "Bedfordshire," anonymous, 1657. (General Collection, Beinecke Rare Book and Manuscript Library, Yale University) remains somewhat skewed given that both guidebooks' primary purpose is to facilitate trade and commerce between market towns rather than offer an accurate and reliable representation of the physical topography. That is, these thematic mappings organize the landscape with a strict eye toward the location and distribution of market towns within and between the various counties of England and Wales; they are the logical extension of intranational trade in which the market town is *the* hub of commercial activity, a projection of the national body as a constellation of markets that can be readily accessed through recourse to these texts.

More simplified versions of this geography of the marketplace, often devoid of maps, may be seen in works such as John Playford's *Vade Mecum; or, The Necessary Companion* (1679), a handy reference book that contains, among other items, "A Catalogue of the Counties, Cities, Market-Towns, and Parishes, in England and Wales."[28] Rather than a compendium of routes, distances, and directions between market towns, as in Seller, Playford offers only a table listing the number of cities, market towns, and parishes in each county (fig. 22). This kind of information was also routinely available in almanacs, such as Thomas Trigge's *Calendarium Astrologicum; or, An Alamanack for the Year of Our Lord 1690*. His "Table of all the Bishopricks in England and Wales With the Number of Cities, Market-Towns, and Parishes therein, at this Day" is nearly identical in form and content to Playford's, the only difference being that Trigge computes for us the total number of market towns, which he estimates at 639 throughout England and Wales (fig. 23). We find a similar approach in *England's Golden Treasury: or, The True Vade Mecum* (1694), a trade manual that provides a "Catalogue of the Markets, and the days they are kept on" in addition to a host of tables covering a wide variety of topics relevant to matters of commerce, such as interest and monetary rates, wages, expenses, bills of exchange, and weights and measures.[29] Robert Lewes's *The Merchant's Map of Commerce* (1671), likewise provides useful and necessary information geared toward expediting matters of trade not only in England but also with foreign markets in the Americas, Africa, Asia, and Europe, maps of which are included in Lewes's text (fig. 24).[30] Not all market geographies, however, were so strictly business oriented. The location of market towns was routinely included in more general works intended to catalog all civil and ecclesiastical municipalities. For example, John Adams's *Index Villaris: or, An Alphabetical Table of All the Cities, Market-Towns, Parishes, Villages, and Private Seats, in England and Wales* (1680) situates the market town as one destination among many, as its title suggests, and provides their respective longitude and latitude, yet like all of these works, the basic idea remains the same: the market, as a physical space, is an integral and important part of the nation and so must be mapped, charted, and graphed in order to provide a proper context for market activity.

Almanacs, guidebooks, and trade manuals present a generalized picture of market infrastructure as well as an integrated and comprehensive sense of

*A Catalogue of the Counties, Cities, Market-Towns, and Parishes, in England and Wales.*

| Counties in England. | Cities. | Mark. T. | Parishes. | Counties in England. | Cities. | Mark. T. | Parishes. |
|---|---|---|---|---|---|---|---|
| Bedford | | 10 | 116 | Salop | | 13 | 170 |
| Berks | | 11 | 140 | Somerset | 3 | 29 | 385 |
| Buckingham | | 11 | 185 | Stafford | 1 | 12 | 130 |
| Cambridge | . | 8 | 163 | Suffolk | | 18 | 575 |
| Chester | 1 | 13 | 68 | Surrey | | 7 | 140 |
| Cornwall | | 23 | 161 | Sussex | 1 | 18 | 312 |
| Cumberland | 1 | 9 | 58 | Warwick | | 15 | 158 |
| Darby | | 8 | 106 | Westmorland | | 4 | 26 |
| Devon | 1 | 40 | 324 | Wilts | 1 | 21 | 304 |
| Dorset | | 18 | 248 | Worcester | 1 | 7 | 132 |
| Durham | 1 | 6 | 118 | York | 1 | 16 | 563 |
| Essex | 1 | 21 | 415 | | | | |
| Glocester | 1 | 25 | 280 | Counties in Wales. | | | |
| Hantshire | 1 | 18 | 253 | | | | |
| Hertford | | 18 | 120 | Anglesey | | 2 | 74 |
| Hereford | 1 | 8 | 176 | Brecknock | | 3 | 61 |
| Huntington | | 6 | 78 | Cardigan | | 4 | 64 |
| Kent | 2 | 17 | 398 | Carmarthen | | 6 | 87 |
| Lancaster | | 15 | 36 | Carnarvan | | 5 | 68 |
| Leicester | 1 | 12 | 200 | Denbigh | | 3 | 57 |
| Lincoln | 1 | 30 | 630 | Flint | | 3 | 28 |
| Middlesex | 2 | 18 | 73 | Glamorgan | | 6 | 118 |
| Norfolk | 1 | 27 | 660 | Merioneth | | 3 | 37 |
| Northampton | 1 | 11 | 326 | Monmouth | | 6 | 127 |
| Northumberl. | | 5 | 47 | Montgomery | | 6 | 47 |
| Nottingham | | 8 | 168 | Pembrook | | 5 | 145 |
| Oxford | 1 | 10 | 280 | Radnor | | 5 | 52 |
| Rutland | | 2 | 47 | | | | |

FIGURE 22. "A Catalogue of the Counties, Cities, Market Towns, and Parishes, in England and Wales," John Playford, 1679. (© The British Library Board, shelfmark 523.a.29.(2))

how one goes about utilizing that infrastructure. While the information can be somewhat static in nature, a mere collection of numbers and figures, each attempts, in its own way, to think synthetically about the ways in which the interdependence of market towns organizes national space and so bring market and nation into some degree of formal coherence. This image of an active and stable market economy is perhaps best represented in *Mr. Ogilby's and William Morgan's Pocket Book of the Roads, With their Computed and Measured Distances, and the Distinction of Market and Post-Towns* (1671). In the fourth edition of this popular guidebook, published in 1689, Ogilby and Morgan expand on their description of roads to include "A Table of the Market-Towns, and their distance from London, &c.," an emendation that indicates the increasing centrality of market towns to the economic livelihood of the nation and the need for accurate and reliable information in order to promote and sustain that activity (fig. 25). We do not find individual maps for each

## A Table of all the *Bishopricks* in *England* and *Wales*. With the Number of Cities, Market-Towns, and Parishes therein, at this Day.

| Names of Bishopricks, | Cities. | Market T. | Parishes. | N. of Bishopr. | Cities. | Market T. | Parishes. |
|---|---|---|---|---|---|---|---|
| 1 Canter. A. B. ⎫ 2 Rochester ⎬ | 2 | 17 | 398 | 14 Hereford | 1 | 8 | 176 |
| | | | | 15 Oxford | 1 | 10 | 208 |
| 3 London | 2 | 43 | 1165 | 16 Glocester | 1 | 24 | 246 |
| 4 Lincoln | 1 | 68 | 1214 | 17 Peterboro. | 1 | 13 | 373 |
| 5 Winchester | 1 | 26 | 398 | 18 Bristol | 1 | 8 | 248 |
| 6 Ely | 1 | 8 | 163 | 19 S. Davids | 0 | 23 | 416 |
| 7 Salisbury | 1 | 31 | 445 | 20 Llandaff | 0 | 12 | 245 |
| 8 Chichester | 1 | 18 | 322 | 21 S. Asaph | 0 | 13 | 691 |
| 9 Exeter | 1 | 59 | 555 | 22 Bangor | 0 | 7 | 142 |
| 10 Bath and Wells | 3 | 53 | 385 | 23 York, A.B. | 1 | 57 | 731 |
| 11 Norwich | 1 | 54 | 1132 | 24 Chester | 1 | 17 | 111 |
| 12 Worcester | 2 | 22 | 310 | 25 Carlisle | 1 | 13 | 84 |
| 13 Lichfield & Coven. | 1 | 34 | 416 | 26 Durham | 1 | 11 | 118 |

The Number of Bishopricks in *England* and *Wales*, are 26; whereof two are Arch-bishopricks.

The Number of Market-Towns in all the aforesaid Bishopricks, are 639.

The Number of Parishes in *England* & *Wales* are 10260.

The Number of Cities in the several Dioceses are 26, equal to the Number of Bishopricks.

*Another useful Observation.*

In the Year are ⎰ 52 ⎱ Weeks. ⎰ 365 ⎱ Days. ⎰ 8860 ⎱ Hours.

*Time* shews the way, Of *Lifes* decay.

FIGURE 23. "A Table of the All the Bishopricks in England and Wales. With the Number of Cities, Market Towns, and Parishes therein, at this Day," Thomas Trigge, 1690. (© The British Library Board, shelfmark General Reference Collection C.142.a.10.(3))

county as we do in Seller's *Anglia Contracta*. Instead, a portable sheet map of England is appended to the book with the name of every market town in italics in order to distinguish them from other forms of settlement. Perhaps the most significant change here is the computation of distances in relation to London, the center from which all trade emanates and returns, in addition to the standard "Cross Roads" between market towns: "We begin our Measures of the Roads at the Standard in Cornhill, London, and continue them through every Town, which makes the Measure so much exceed the Computation. The Cross Roads are such as lead from one City or great Town to another, and have no Repetition or Reference: They are placed Alphabetically, where the Town that Road takes place, as the Town that ends the Road doth in those from London; but the Table direct you readily to find either."[31] Rather than representing the geography of market towns as localized fragments, whether in the form of hundreds, parishes, or counties, Ogilby and Morgan organize their measurements with respect to London in order to suggest that the life

FIGURE 24. "A New and most Exact map of America," Robert Lewes, 1671. (Lawrence H. Slaughter Collection, Lionel Pincus and Princess Firyal Map Division, New York Public Library, Astor, Lenox, and Tilden Foundations)

of any individual market town is ultimately dependent on its proximity to the metropolitan center. The inclusion of a map of England and Wales, rather than county maps, further reinforces this more holistic and integrated conception of a nationalized market economy.[32] Efforts such as that of Ogilby and Morgan would continue to be the trend as we move into the eighteenth century and witness the production of larger, more encompassing maps and chorographies that situate the role and function of the market town in relation to the national and even imperial bodies. Without necessarily thematizing the market town or marketplace exclusively, these works nevertheless further delineate and refine the economic geography of the nation by incorporating the market town into an ever-expanding network of roads, towns, villages, and cities.

James Brome's *An Historical Account of Mr. Rogers' Three Years Travels over*

## Explanation.

Towns and their Distances, till you come to the place where you leave the Great Road, you are referred to the Road out of which each Branch issues.

As in the Road from London to Buckingham you are directed to Num. 1. fol. 13. for the Way as far as Uxbridge, and in the Road from London to Montgomery, you are referred to Num. 1. fol. 13. for the Way as far as Worcester, where the Road to Aberistwith, and the Road to Montgomery part, and so of the rest.

We begin our Measures of the Roads at the Standard in Cornhill, London, and continue them through every Town, which makes the Measure so much exceed the Computation.

The Cross Roads are such as lead from one City or great Town to another, and have no Repetition or Reference: They are placed Alphabetically, where the Town that begins the Road takes place, as the Town that ends the Road doth in those from London; but the Tables direct you readily to find either.

For Distinction Cities are in CAPITALS, Market-Towns in *Italick*; (a) and Post-Towns markt thus *, as fol. 13. * Waltham-Cross is a Post, and not a Market-Town; Hodsdon is a Market, and not a Post-Town; * Ware is both Market and Post, &c.

(a) But fol. 14. Hounslow, fol. 18. Glamford, fol. 19. Darleston, and fol. 20. Chidleigh, are by mistake in Roman.

*A Table*

---

## A Table of the Market Towns, and their distance from London, &c.

The Numbers under C. is the Computed Distance, under M. F. the Measure by Miles and Furlongs; for Example, against *Barwick*, under C. M. F. you have 262, 339, 2; that is to say, from London to *Barwick* is by Computation 262 Miles, by Measure it is 339 Miles, and 2 Furlongs. The figure before the Name directs you to fol. 13. where you have the Road to *Barwick*, and the distance of each Town; and so of the rest.

| fol | LONDON | C | M. F. | fol | LONDON | C | M. F. |
|---|---|---|---|---|---|---|---|
| 17 | to Aberavon | 150 | 193-7 | 19 | to Bagshot | 23 | 29-0 |
| 19 | Aberconway | 174 | 229-5 | 21 | Baldock | 29 | 38-0 |
| 16 | Abergaveny | 111 | 142-3 | 18 | Barnet | 10 | 11-7 |
| 13 | Aberistwith | 146 | 199-2 | 18 | Barton | 73 | 94-0 |
| 18 | Abington | 46 | 55-3 | 14 | Barwick | 262 | 339-2 |
| 18 | St. Albans | 20 | 21-5 | 19 | Basingstoke | 39 | 48-1 |
| 14 | Alnwick | 238 | 309-7 | 15 | Bath | 87 | 108-1 |
| 22 | Alresford | 47 | 59-7 | 14 | Bautry | 117 | 147-0 |
| 22 | Alton | 39 | 50-1 | 13 | Beaconsfield | 22 | 27-1 |
| 15 | Amersham | 24 | 29-5 | 19 | Beaumaris | 184 | 241-5 |
| 21 | Amesbury | 65 | 80-5 | 24 | Beckles | 83 | 106-5 |
| 19 | Andover | 55 | 66-2 | 22 | Bedford | 40 | 49-1 |
| 13 | Arundel | 46 | 55-4 | 23 | Bermingham | 88 | 109-5 |
| 18 | Ashford | 41 | 57-2 | 18 | Beverley | 141 | 179-0 |
| 20 | Ashburton | 153 | 191-0 | 21 | Bigleswade | 34 | 45-7 |
| 22 | Atleborough | 80 | 93-5 | 20 | Bishops Cast. | 116 | 156-2 |
| 20 | Axmister | 119 | 146-4 | 24 | Blandford | 85 | 107-2 |
| 15 | Aylesbury | 34 | 44-1 | 15 | Boston | 90 | 114-3 |
|  | Aborsbury | 106 | 129-7 | 17 | Born | 76 | 93-4 |
|  | Aberforth | 139 | 191-0 | 16 | Brecknock | 123 | 161-1 |
|  | Aldborough | 76 | 87-5 | 14 | Brentford | 8 | 10-1 |
|  | Alesham | 99 | 118-2 | 20 | Brent | 159 | 198-6 |
|  | Alford | 107 | 134-1 | 19 | Brickhill lit. | 37 | 43-7 |
|  | Alfreton | 100 | 133-0 | 23 | Bridgnorth | 108 | 135-6 |
|  | Alston more | 209 | 276-2 | 21 | Bridgwater | 116 | 143-3 |
|  | Altrincham | 137 | 181-0 | 15 | Bristol | 94 | 115-2 |
|  | Amblefide | 206 | 267-3 | 23 | Bromley | 6 | 9-5 |
|  | Ampthill | 36 | 43-2 | 13 | Bromyard | 96 | 124-4 |
|  | Appleby | 217 | 279-4 | 21 | Bruton | 93 | 115-5 |
|  | Appledore | 54 | 59-7 | 15 | Buckingham | 44 | 60-6 |
|  | St. Asaph | 159 | 212-0 | 14 | Buntingford | 27 | 31-6 |
|  | Ashborn | 108 | 133-0 | 18 | Burlington | 161 | 205-4 |
|  | Ashby | 89 | 105-2 | 24 | Burntwood | 15 | 17-6 |
|  | Askrig | 175 | 251-3 | 14 | Borough br. | 160 | 204-4 |
|  | Atherston | 84 | 103-6 | 16 | Burton | 195 | 244-4 |
|  | Auburn | 56 | 81-2 | 24 | Bury St. Ed. | 64 | 75-0 |
|  | Aukland | 184 | 254-1 |  | Bakewell | 115 | 141-6 |
|  | Aulcester | 72 | 91-4 |  | Bala | 145 | 184-1 |
|  | St. Auslel | 203 | 248-0 |  | Bampton De. | 56 | 66-3 |
|  | Autre | 133 | 161-5 |  | Bampton | 134 | 167-4 |
|  | Axbridge | 105 | 130-3 |  | Banbury | 53 | 74-5 |
|  | Aye | 74 | 91-4 |  | Bangor | 180 | 236-5 |

Figure 25. "A Table of the Market Towns, and their distance from London," John Ogilby, 1689. (General Collection, Beinecke Rare Book and Manuscript Library, Yale University)

*England and Wales* (1694), according to its title page, provides a wealth of descriptive detail concerning "the chiefest cities, town, and corporations . . . together with the antiquities, and places of admiration, cathedrals, churches of note in any city." Appended to his text is a map of England and Wales that illustrates his travels and, more importantly, enables the reader to see the distribution of market towns in relation to the surrounding towns and cities. Brome's geography of the market town becomes part of a more detailed excavation of the countryside, including the history of its growth and development extending back to antiquity. On a more intimate level, John Kirby's *The Suffolk Traveller; or, A Journey Through Suffolk* (1735) gives us a similar instance of travel literature that incorporates the geography of market towns as a necessary and critical feature of the landscape. While the scale is reduced to the county level, Kirby's turn to the local allows him to flesh out his understanding of the market town by giving his reader not only "the true Distance in the roads, from *Ipswich* to every Market Town in Suffolk, and the same from Bury St. Edmund's" but also "a Short Historical Account of the Antiquities of every Market Town." The market town thus becomes subject to a kind of archeology in which an understanding of its geography cannot be separated from local history and the history of England in general; the market town is in fact a critical node within that history. Similarly, John Badeslade's *Chorographia Britanniae; or, A New Set of Maps of All the Counties in England and Wales* (1742) accounts for every market town both through maps and "an alphabetical index, of all the cities, boroughs, & market towns, properly distinguish'd from each other, and in which country they are situate." The context here is, as announced in the title, Britannia, and so the maps and tables reflecting market activity are included alongside those depicting general points of interest, such as churches, universities, and monuments, as well as the topographical features of the land and coasts. Emanuel and Thomas Bowen's *Atlas Anglicanus* (1777) also provides relevant information regarding the time and place of markets and is "illustrated with historical extracts, relative to natural produce, trade, manufactures &c. both entertaining and instructive." This final qualifier suggests that the maps indeed serve the purposes of trade, but they also take on the quality of general reading material intended for mass consumption. The market town is thus saturated with additional layers of context such that its geography becomes, by extension, one element in a larger, more encompassing description of Britain.

To be sure, maps, almanacs, trade manuals, and gazetteers in the eighteenth century continue to represent the geography of market towns for specialized audiences such as merchants, wholesalers, and shopkeepers, yet we also see in these various travel narratives an appeal to a more general readership. Rather than make the marketplace and market town their sole focus, they incorporate it into a much more thorough and comprehensive view of the nation in order to suggest a degree of temporal and spatial continuity between the market and the nation. That is, the marketplace is no longer viewed only in terms of its locality or its immediate relationship to the surrounding region; it becomes instead an increasingly vital and important place within the national landscape and so must be situated within that context in order to understand just how the operations of the market coincide with and support the interest of the nation. This approach can be seen quite starkly in Daniel Defoe's *A Tour Thro' the Whole Island of Great Britain,* whose mapping of the nation is, like the texts previously mentioned, geared toward making trade and commerce visible by outlining the features of Britain's marketplaces and market towns. In the *Tour,* Defoe often includes lists of the active market towns throughout England and Wales, usually appended in the form of table. For example, while in Norfolk, Defoe provides the following information regarding nearby markets, which is set off from the main body of the text:

| | | |
|---|---|---|
| Thetford, | Hingham, | Harleston, |
| Dis, | West Deerham, | E. Deerham, |
| Harling, | Attleboro', | Watton, |
| Bucknam, | Windham, | Loddon, &c. |

The kind of information on offer here bears a direct relationship to the tables, maps, and charts found in other standardized atlases, trade manuals, gazetteers, and almanacs of the period. As Pat Rogers points out, Defoe frequently relied heavily on secondary sources in his writing of the *Tour,* including maps depicting areas with which he was unfamiliar. For example, Rogers cites Robert Morden's *Britannia* (1695), John Senex's *Atlas* (1721), and Herman Moll's *Set of Fifty New and Correct Maps of England and Wales* (1724) as critical sources for Defoe's *Tour,* recycling their findings within his text, often with little regard to their truth or accuracy.[33] J. H. Andrews also reveals that significant portions of Defoe's *Tour* were not necessarily the product of firsthand experience but rather derived from preexisting sources: "Almost all the 'Tour's' original observations could have been made by a traveller of Queen Anne's rule or earlier."[34] We also know that Defoe kept later editions of *The Merchant's Map of Commerce* (1671) and *A Book of the Names of All the Parishes, Market Towns, Villages, Hamlets, and Smallest Places, In England and Wales* (1657) in his library, along with a collection of almanacs dating from 1691 to 1711, though this fact, in and of itself, proves little.[35]

While direct evidence that Defoe relied on the preexisting corpus of seventeenth- and eighteenth-century market geographies is wanting in this instance, his text nevertheless bears a striking resemblance to them in terms of the kinds of information included, the manner in which that information is presented, and their overall intent to facilitate and promote trade and commerce. However, rather than simply provide raw data to be used in a pragmatic fashion, we are also given a sense of the market's relative importance to, as the title implies, the "whole island of Great Britain." The graphic information no

longer stands alone, as in previous attempts to compile and organize a geography of the marketplace, but it is now framed by the itinerary of a narrator who
can make sense of and interpret that information. As Betty Schellenberg notes,
Defoe's mapping of the nation is the product of a narrator who is able to comprehend these larger patterns of trade and commercial activity and translate
them into the form of a travel narrative, utilizing the itinerary as the primary
means of organizing and animating his geography of the market.[36] He provides
not only the name and location of and relative distances between market towns
but also a sense of how they fit together into a picture of a nation whose identity is rooted in market activity. The narrator thus supplements his table with
an explanation of the market town's vital role in sustaining the surrounding
countryside: "When we come into Norfolk, we see a face of diligence spread
over the whole country. . . . This side of Norfolk is very populous, and thronged
with great and spacious market-towns, more and larger than any other part
of England so far from London, except Devonshire, and the West-Riding of
Yorkshire. . . . Most of these towns are very populous and large; but that which
is most remarkable is, that the whole country round them is so interspersed
with villages, and those villages so large, and so full of people, that they are
equal to market-towns in other counties."[37] The size and population density
of the various market towns he encounters and their surrounding villages serve
as an indicator of the overall prosperity of the region, yet the narrator is also
making an explicit argument that a well-integrated system of markets encourages industry to spread from one market town to another. The very health of
the nation, as the narrator is careful to point out, is dependent on the intimate
relationship between marketplaces either nearby or further away from one another. The close proximity of marketplaces, at least on the county scale, can
only have beneficial consequences in terms of the economic impact on their
neighbors, a kind of shared energy that is readily and easily transferred across
the landscape.

  We see this same logic applied as the narrator journeys through the country
east of London and, again, inserts a small chart containing the names of the
counties and their respective market towns:[38]

| | | |
|---|---|---|
| Somersetshire | } | Frome, Pensford, Phillip's Norton, Bruton, Shepton, Mallet Castle Carey, and Wincanton. |
| Wiltshire | } | Malmsbury, Castlecomb, Chippenham, Caln, Devizes, Bradford, Trubridge, Westbury, Warminster, Meer. |
| Doresetshire | } | Gillingham, Shaftesbury, Bemister, and Bere, Sturminster, Shireborn. |
| Gloucester | } | Cirencester, Tetbury, Marshfield, Minchinghampton, and Fariford. |

Defoe notes that "some of the market towns are equal to cities in the bigness and superior to them in number of people" in order to underscore the correlation between high population density and economic prosperity, a common assumption throughout most of the eighteenth century.[39] The narrator then details the "innumerable villages, hamlets, and scattered houses" that have emerged in the interstices of the market towns as a result of the clothing trade, the staple industry for that area, concluding that the promotion of trade within the market towns has had a reciprocal effect on the entire region:

> The increasing circumstances of this trade, are happily visible by the great concourse of people to, and increase of buildings and inhabitants in these principal clothing towns where this trade is carried on, and wealth of the clothiers. The town of Froom, or, as it is written in our maps, Frome Sellwood, is a specimen of this, which is so prodigiously increased within these last twenty years or thirty years, that they have built a new church, and so many new streets of houses, and those houses are so full of inhabitants, that Frome is now reckoned to have more people in it, than the city of Bath, and some say, than even Salisbury itself, and it is very likely to be one of the greatest and wealthiest towns in England.[40]

As the narrator carefully notes, Frome Sellwood is as large and as vital as any other urban center, in this case, Bath and Salisbury, suggesting that its marketplace is, in many ways, just as critical an indicator of national prosperity as its much larger counterparts. Given its innumerable effects on the region, some of which may or may not be immediately recognizable or evident, the clothing trade is necessarily identified with its sites of production and distribution in order to fix it spatially and provide a representation that is consistent and normative in some sense. Frome Sellwood thus offers an exemplary marketplace whose success informs Defoe's thinking about the space of the nation as an extended market.

Defoe's purpose in the *Tour* is to map, describe, and analyze the geography of the British marketplace in order to make the case that trade and commerce are vital to the health of the nation. The emphasis here, as in most of Defoe's text, is on the visible signs of prosperity and their adequate representation. The marketplace must be made legible in order to facilitate trade and commerce, and so delineating its geography becomes a critical way of locating, or placing, trade in a manner that is comprehensible to both the general reader and England's merchant class. Like its seventeenth-century predecessors, the *Tour* is committed to providing geographic information that is useful and relevant to trade within and between markets, yet by incorporating that information into the form of a travel narrative, Defoe is also able to show the reader just how the marketplace feeds and sustains the economic life of the nation. As Christopher Parkes argues, "Defoe saw in the discourse of thematic cartography the ability to transform physically and psychologically the landscape of Britain into a blueprint for economic development."[41] Thomas Keith Meier reinforces this point, arguing that the *Tour* should be read as an extended defense of trade and commerce in keeping with, and in some ways, superior to Defoe's other economic writings. The *Tour*, he correctly insists, "is as much a catalogue of Defoe's attitudes toward business as it is a collection of geographical facts about Britain."[42] I would refine Meier's point somewhat to suggest that geography and business are not separate considerations for Defoe but rather are intimately bound up with one another. As Defoe himself remarks in the second part of *The Compleat English Tradesman*, vol. 2 (1727): "Trade is an ocean, the best and most experienc'd Sailor needs his Pilot books, his navigating Instruments, his Cross-Staff, Quadrant, Compass, &c. to steer by, and take his observations, and it may be with Truth said, the Mathematicians on shore make all the Ships sail at sea, for 'tis by their Rules, their Scales, their Tables of Lines and Tangents, by their Problems, and Experiments, that the expert Seamen direct their Ships, keep their Reckonings, and perform their voyages."[43] Defoe's analogy here links trade with the discipline of navigation, which is dependent on the precise and accurate measurement of the world's oceans and rivers; however, this set of metaphors may also be understood literally in terms of the need to survey and map the geographic distribution and disposition of England's market towns and marketplaces. Defoe is making the point that the instruments and methods associated with navigation, and surveying for that matter, are perhaps best utilized in furthering our understanding of trade and commerce on a national scale.

Trade, in this sense, is not simply a loose collection of local customs and practices irreducible to quantification and analysis but is in fact a science composed of objectively knowable rules and propositions that govern its motions and determine its outcomes. Toward that end, Defoe embraces both cartographic and chorographic methods, the map and the itinerary, in order to integrate the subjective details and impressions of the citizen/traveler into a comprehensive and equitable image of the nation. In contrast to travel narratives that preceded it, such as Celia Fiennes's *Journeys* (1702) or John Macky's *Journey through England in Familiar Letters* (1714–23), Defoe's *Tour* utilizes the notion of shifting perspectives between the map and the itinerary in order to provide a sufficient level of detail and description without getting overly bogged down in minutiae such that he loses sight of his primary subject, the whole island of Great Britain. Through the text's formal design, both narrator and reader simultaneously experience the nation cartographically as a defined and knowable place and as a series of discrete movements in and through that place. Pat Rogers and others have argued this very point in their treatment of the *Tour*. According to Rogers, Defoe's reliance on the circuit, or tour, as a means of organizing the text arises from the need to represent the fluidity of national space in ways that bolster his own economic and political agenda while at the same time giving some degree of shape and coherency to this perpetual flux: "Not only does he maintain a clear itinerary, with the progress from one county to another carefully charted, but he also employs a number of shifts to give the reader a sense of movement. Prospects unfold as we pass through the country; landscapes emerge before our gaze and fall away; contrasting scenes follow one another in smooth succession."[44] Rogers concludes that Defoe's use of the circuit as the structural principle of his *Tour* "manages to make his journeys not just intelligible, but even sequential and to some degree cumulative."[45] Terence Bowers, echoing Rogers's arguments regarding the temporal and spatial dynamics of the *Tour*, states that "visually and syntactically, Defoe represents a landscape of *interchangeability* where things can be moved and yet *not* be out of place."[46] For Bowers, the reader is asked to constantly negotiate between the prospect of the narrator as he travels throughout Britain and the larger "imagined community" to which they supposedly belong.

Edward Copeland characterizes Defoe's strategy here as "mapped perspectives," or the juxtaposition and synthesis of cartographic and progressive viewpoints embodied within a single narrative voice. It is a technique, according to Copeland, that informs a number of Defoe's works, including, among others, *A Journal of the Plague Year:* "As an historian, H. F. uses a bird's-eye view to report the plague's advance, parish by parish, across the map of London. And, as an in-the-street observer, he descends from this mapping height to walk the streets, to join with the urban inhabitants, who, he observes, are 'prisoners' of the map."[47] The simultaneity of these two perspectives presents a powerful model for conceiving and representing the space of the nation. For Rogers, Bowers, and Copeland, the itinerary and the map supplement each other in ways that can harmonize the landscape by providing a consistent and regular mode of representing space that effectively allows for the perspectives of both traveler and surveyor alike. Change over time is thus folded into a more stable picture of the land and vice versa. Defoe moves from the narrative perspective of the itinerary to a holistic representation of the national economy more akin to the map; the *Tour* is essentially always oscillating back and forth between both perspectives: the situated traveler moving from place to place and the cartographer who charts that itinerary and gives it some semblance of context. Map and itinerary are thus superimposed upon one another at every stage of the *Tour* in order to theorize the national economy in expressly spatial and geographic terms and to mediate the movement between the perspectives of Defoe and his narrator. As Defoe himself notes, a gentleman "may make himself master of the geography of the Universe in the maps, attlasses, and measurements of our mathematicians" and "make all distant places near to him in his reviewing the voiages of those that saw them." And while "those travellers, voiagers, surveyors, soldiers, etc., kno' but every man his share, and that shar but little, according to the narrow compass of their own actings," the gentleman, nevertheless, "receives the idea of the whole at one view" by taking in their various itineraries, however flawed or compromised, in the aggregate.[48]

This is something of a delicate balancing act, however, and one that, I would argue, Defoe's text does not always pull off successfully. Rogers, Bowers, and Copeland unwittingly assume the complementary nature of these "mapped perspectives" rather than attend to the ways in which they remain antagonistic at different points in Defoe's text. That is, they fail to recognize the way in which Defoe's use of the map and the itinerary in the *Tour* offers different, competing views of the nation that are not always easily reconciled, even though they are ostensibly the product of a single authorial voice. As Cynthia Wall contends, the rapid pace of economic, political, and social change since the Restoration, and the Great Fire of 1666 in particular, demanded a mode of representation that could somehow encompass the mutability of space, its ability to change over time in response to these respective forces. Defoe's text stands, for Wall, as an exemplary moment in the emergence of this new genre: "Defoe's *A Tour Thro' the Whole Island of Great Britain*, published in 1724–26, differs strikingly from earlier descriptions of London in its grammar, its imagery, and implications, and the differences both depend on and reflect a new consciousness of space—topographical, commercial, and even structural—as fluid, shifting, unreliable, unpredictable. Borrowing from the vocabulary of surveying and the grammar of motion, Defoe's *Tour* offers new generic strategies for a cultural and textual remapping of uncanny modern space."[49] Wall then juxtaposes this fluid "grammar of space" against more rigid and static depictions of Britain found in various maps and atlases available since the Renaissance in order to suggest that the latter fails to articulate a vision of the nation adequate to a more modern spatial and temporal hermeneutics.[50] The cartographic projection is seen as an inadequate form for expressing the vicissitudes of time on the life of the nation; it can only express a simultaneous present that is perhaps inaccurate or, at worst, a form of mystification. The *Tour*, in this sense, stands against the map because it is unable to account for the kinds of changes Defoe's narrator observes in the course of his travels, including the inevitable fluctuations and movements of the British marketplace. Defoe, however, does not wish to displace or bracket the map as somehow an inadequate mode of representing the oscillations of a functioning national economy. Rather, I would argue that he requires both the perspectives of map and itinerary in order to stabilize these competing definitions of the marketplace as place and as process.

Defoe's "need to impose some organizing principle upon the chaotic detail" of Great Britain assumes the marketplace as a critical site in that mapping, yet the marketplace often proves difficult to chart in a regular and consistent fashion.[51] Defoe offers the following observation regarding trade in the second part of *The Compleat English Tradesman* (1727): "As habits and the form of clothing are chang'd by the fancies and fashions of Men, so Trade is necessarily bound to follow the customs which the same fashions and fancies introduce."[52] He reiterates the point, here and elsewhere, that it is the nature of trade to be constantly changing and moving, often in ways that are not immediately recognized or understood: "Trade is quite altered.... The methods are chang'd, the course of things is chang'd, the manner both of buying and selling is altered; the Manufactures are chang'd, the very places where they are made are chang'd, the Manufacturers remove from town to town, and the place knows them no more; the Markets remove where they are sold, and even the demands of them both abroad and at home, the very Nations to which they were exported, take none now."[53] Markets appear and disappear from the landscape due to the natural vicissitudes of trade; the forces of supply and demand, increases or decreases in population, and changes in transportation create markets where none had existed previously and, in the same breath, eliminate others, even those that had once flourished and thrived. As an abstraction, the market is tied to a particular place, but perhaps only provisionally and as long as conditions permit. Sandra Sherman reinforces this point regarding Defoe's appreciation for "the irrationality of the market" in *The Compleat English Tradesman,* as well as a number of his other economic writings and fictional works.[54]

Sherman argues that Defoe neither resists nor ignores the market's inherent volatility; rather, he understands that the market is "a site of indeterminacy" and epistemological opacity that necessarily defies our ability to negotiate and "account" for its mysterious operations. The opacities, ambiguities, and uncertainties engendered and disseminated by the market are covered over and displaced by the creation of what Sherman terms "fictions of stability," or methods of accounting and representing, including narratives, that are intended to make sense out of the market and market relations.[55] Defoe, according to Sherman, often presents us with narrators who reject and overturn such fictions in order to suggest to his reader that we too should reject them and, instead, accommodate ourselves to a world of uncertainty, or in other words, the world as defined by the market.[56] I would take some issue with this reading however. Sherman, by her own admission, acknowledges that "[Defoe] is tied to a market that demands certainty, and a *real* tradesman—such as Defoe—cannot ignore the market," yet it is strange, in my estimation, to conclude that Defoe, speaking through the voice of his narrator, disavows his real-world commitments to certainty and legibility in matters of trade and commerce.[57] I would argue just the opposite is true in fact. Rather than reject fictions of stability, Defoe's narrators reveal to us why such fictions are necessary and important in the first place. That is, Defoe dramatizes the precarious nature of the market, as Sherman rightly contends, but he does so in order to justify and legitimate the need for more scrupulous and accurate methods of accounting that will provide for the kind of stability that both Defoe the author and Defoe the tradesman desire. These are still fictions of stability to be sure, but as Defoe demonstrates, they are always provisional, contingent, and subject to perpetual revision given the volatile and constantly changing face of the market. This is not an argument, as Sherman would have it, for the irrelevance of fictions of stability, but rather, for their importance *as fictions* whose plasticity allows for a more accurate and realistic representation of the market.

Defoe's construction of a geography of the marketplace thus arises from the need to at once understand the mechanisms that help foster and shape Britain's marketplaces yet also to lend some measure of stability to that which is, by definition, prone to considerable change and flux. The result is a bifurcated and somewhat conflicted vision of the nation as a mobile and kinetic space defined principally by commercial activity and as a stable and regimented assembly of markets that facilitate, yet also delimit, the range of this activity. Defoe's interest in the geography of Britain's marketplaces and market towns is thus born of a profound understanding of the ways in which trade and exchange in general are prone to fluctuation, yet he also wishes to offer a measure of containment and control in response to the fluid and unstable nature of trade itself. The very mobility of the market makes charting its place more, not less, important in Defoe's estimation. Rather than celebrate or encourage this mobility, the freedom of the market as it were, Defoe wishes to warn us about the potential downsides if market activity is not limited to those places specifically designated for the buying and selling of commodities. In *A Brief State of the Inland or Home Trade, of England* (1730), Defoe launches into an extended critique of private and illegitimate marketing that circumvents and, in his estimation, impedes the flow of trade through England's legally proscribed marketplaces. This "Invasion of Hawkers, Peddlers and other Clandestine Traders," according to Defoe, disrupts the proper circulation of goods and services, takes business away from what he terms "Fair Traders," and ultimately distorts the marketplace for both producers and consumers alike. They violate the original market charters as well as those legal provisions intended to secure the public marketplace and limit where and when trade may occur: "Instead of the Customers going to the Shop, they carry the Shop to the Customers; instead of the Country Inhabitants frequenting the Markets, which are the proper places of Trade, they make the Markets walk about to the Inhabitants, calling upon them at their Doors."[58] Defoe's personification of the market here unmoors trade from its fixed place within the sanctioned market town and allows it to wander about, arriving finally at the doors of the private home, where, as Defoe makes abundantly clear, it does not and should not belong.[59]

Throughout the text, Defoe frequently aligns the aims of these peddlers and hawkers who bring the market home, as it were, with smugglers and pirates who evade, or subvert, existing laws regarding trade and commerce and, in the process, draw money away from legitimate shopkeepers, merchants, and wholesalers, as well as the local municipalities and the government who are dependent on the revenues generated by trade: "The selling Pedlar robs the fair Trader of his ready Money Customers; and the Smuggling Pedlar robs him of his buying to Advantage: They buy of the Smugglers, who by robbing the Government of the Customs, bring in Goods from the Foreigner, and the Profit (at least the great Part of it), goes away to Strangers; they have the market, and we the Loss."[60] Fair trade, in Defoe's estimation, is necessarily tied to the traditional marketplace. Private marketing and piracy are considered illegitimate forms of trade because they evade the policies and regulations that govern the legitimate marketplace. More importantly, they are particularly resistant to any kind of geographic inscription, whether in the form of a map or chorography, because they have no proper place, which is a problem that Defoe believes must be acknowledged and ameliorated in some fashion. The idea of the free market in which trade transpires literally anywhere at any time is far from a positive development in his eyes; rather, it is a point of concern that must be addressed. For Defoe, the irrationality of the market needs to be checked or contained in order to protect the national interest against the likes of pirates, peddlers, smugglers, and other illegitimate traders, those who would distort and pervert the marketplace's proper role as the engine of Britain's future wealth and power. Defoe's geography of the marketplace is thus a strategy of containment, a fiction of stability if you will, in that it seeks to rationalize trade and commerce by delimiting its activity spatially while at the same time recognizing that this may in fact be an impossible task. As I am suggesting, we should not read this ambivalence on Defoe's part as favoring one outcome or the other; rather, Defoe needs and requires the "otherness" of the marketplace, abstract, elastic, and unknowable, in order to further justify and legitimate projects that seek to quantify and rationalize trade, such as his own survey of Britain's evolving market economy and its relationship to the nation as a whole.

We need, then, to examine the *Tour* not only as a part of Defoe's larger project of representing national space but also in terms of the ways in which the geography of the marketplace and market activity both contribute to and disrupt the production of that space. That is, we must not assume the complementary nature of nation and market in the *Tour*, as if these spaces were already one and the same. Rather, we should attend to the disparities and tensions that exist between them that make a text like the *Tour* such a vital and necessary project for Defoe. The dual perspective that structures Defoe's text is way of creating a unified and unifying representation of the national body; however, the marketplace, as the heterotopic locus of the text, emerges as the site around which antagonisms between the cartographic and progressive conceptions of the nation manifest themselves, creating a rupture within the *Tour*'s mapping of the nation. As Betty Schellenberg remarks, "Whatever Defoe's public vision of the nation is, there seems to be a nightmare hidden in the shadows behind it."[61] This nightmare, I would contend, is not an external threat to the marketplace and the economic prosperity it promises but rather emerges from within the very logic of the marketplace itself. Defoe's desire to construct a comprehensive and integrated picture of national space defined by trade and commercial activity is an implicit recognition that the market-place may not, in fact, be a stable referent for economic prosperity and national health. The heterogeneity of the British marketplace, like Sen's colonial landscape, legitimates the cartographic impulse behind Defoe's survey of the nation, yet it also forecloses the possibility of his success.

## The Limits to the Market

In Defoe's *Tour*, the marketplace continually resists assimilation into a coherent picture of the nation, which is announced as the chief aim of the book. The difficulty Defoe encounters time and again is his inability to understand the mechanisms by which certain markets flourish, often to the point of growing out of control, while others decay and eventually die out altogether. His descriptions of Britain's various markets, from local village to regional center to London itself, provide a wealth of information concerning the relative economic health of the nation, including the type and volume of trade that transpires in a given marketplace. However, the visible "face of trade" does not always signify economic prosperity and a progressive vision of the nation, nor does the absence of trade in a once prosperous market town necessarily mean destitution, malaise, and failure, though that possibility remains a concern for Defoe. The disconnect, rather, stems from the narrator's inability to reconcile the itinerary, or the perspective of the individual traveler, with the map that might provide a wider context for understanding the ebb and flow of trade within and between Britain's marketplaces. Despite his stated goal of locating and charting Britain's diverse market towns and marketplaces, Defoe's narrator discovers in the course of his travels that the market, given its highly unstable and precarious nature, often eludes his attempts to map its whereabouts in an accurate and reliable fashion. The surreptitious motions of the market-place thus confound Defoe's narrator, forcing him to contend with his own interpretive inadequacies. The empirical evidence gathered in the course of travel thwarts his attempts to define and theorize trade on a national scale. The doubling of the market as both an identifiable place on the map and as one in a succession of sites encountered through the itinerary thus mirrors Defoe's perhaps antithetical desire to stabilize the marketplace as a referent for commercial activity and to animate the marketplace as a brief fluctuation in the overall movement of goods and services. Map and itinerary often fail to cohere, and Defoe is quite pointedly dramatizing that failure in order to suggest measures of reform that may bring them into alignment. That is, Defoe, unlike so many of his contemporaries, does not seek to achieve a degree of transparency between the literal and figurative elements of his travels, a kind of pure description that levels all difference. Contrary to Pat Rogers's assertion that a "major part of the *Tour*'s rhetorical energy is expanded in the ambition to make Defoe's pen follow his foot," I would argue that Defoe stages their difference in order to place himself in the position of the reformer who must somehow reconcile the map and the itinerary, and it is the production of these different and disparate spaces that is the very precondition of the traveling subject.[62]

The city of Bristol, for example, has all the markers of a great and flourishing center of trade. As the narrator notes, "The shopkeepers in Bristol . . . have so great an inland trade among all the western counties, that they maintain carriers just as the London tradesmen do."[63] Trade in Bristol is comparable to that of London, both in terms of the volume of internal trade with other local and regional markets as well as the thriving international trade resulting from its role as one of Britain's largest port cities. Despite Bristol's ability to exploit its geographic advantages and its subsequent impact on the nation as a whole, its own marketplace exhibits a disturbing trend toward overcrowding and congestion that actually hinders trade: "The Tolsey of this city, (so they call their Exchange where their merchants meet,) has been a place too of great business, yet so straitened, so crowded, and so many ways inconvenient, that the merchants have been obliged to do less business there, than indeed the nature of their great trade requires. They have therefore long solicited, a sufficient authority of Parliament, empowering them to build a Royal Exchange; but there is not much progress yet made in this work, though if finished, it would add much to the beauty of the city of Bristol."[64] Trade moves outward from the urban center in response to the proliferation of trade in the city's marketplace, or exchange. The visible signs of prosperity in Bristol contain the potential seeds of its undoing in the form of unregulated and unmanaged urban space that curtails trade rather than facilitates its further growth and expansion. These pressures on the market infrastructure represent a failure on the part of city officials and local authorities to implement policy that would relieve congestion and create a more orderly environment for business, a fact that seems utterly lost on them but not the narrator. The reason for the oversight is clear. It is the "tenacious folly of its inhabitants" that unduly restricts trade to only subjects of the city, forcing many freemen to inhabit the areas outside the city gate in a haphazard fashion and increasing the population burden on those living within the city where space has become limited. A growing population and active trade, normally signs of wealth and prosperity, turn out to be entropic in nature due to poor planning and a failure to consider the ramifications of these policies.[65]

The narrator explicitly argues that fewer restrictions should be placed on who can and cannot trade within the city proper, that appropriate structures, such as a new exchange, need to be built in order to manage trade, and that the available housing market should be expanded to prevent surreptitious forms of cohabitation to spring up wherever they may. In order to make that case, however, he needs to argue against the prevailing logic that all is well in Bristol and that this will continue to be the trend in the future. Thus he reverses the signs and demonstrates that what appears to be prosperity may, in fact, be just the opposite if appropriate steps are not taken.[66] A similar instance of this semiotic instability appears in the town Halifax, another very prosperous market center whose influences are ambivalent at best. The country surrounding Halifax is very much a working landscape according to Defoe. He comments on the "goodness and wholesomeness" of the country that results from "their being constantly employed," which leads, in turn, to physical health and longevity as well as national health.[67] When he does finally arrive in Halifax, the narrator notes its prodigious size and population despite its geography, which, unlike Bristol, makes international trade impracticable: "In short, it is a monster, I mean, for a country parish, and a parish so far out of the way of foreign trade, courts, or sea ports."[68] The reason for its size, the narrator explains, is its function as a market center for the counties immediately adjacent: West Riding, Lincoln, Nottingham, Cheshire, Warwickshire, Lancashire: "Thus this one trading, manufacturing part of the country supports all the countries around it, and the numbers of people settle here as bees about a hive. As for the town of Halifax itself, there is nothing extraordinary except on a market-day, and then indeed it is a prodigious thing."[69] Even a town as relatively small as Halifax, and one without the same geographic advantages of other major cities, aspires to a kind of monstrosity due to its role as a market center, increasing the size of the local population and the boundaries of the city itself in such a short period of time. The narrator seems almost startled by this discovery so that he must immediately proffer some reason to explain it and, in turn, shift his perspective to the entire region in order to theorize the changes there. Monstrosity is thus a subjective experience that requires a reciprocal gesture of containment through recourse to the map.

London offers perhaps the best example of this strategy, given the fact that it is the single largest market in Britain and the center from which all commercial activity radiates and returns. As Defoe remarks in *A Brief State of the Inland or Home Trade, of England* (1730), "Nature and the Course of Business has made *London* the Chief or Principal Market," which is largely due to its location with respect to the rest of the nation and the world.[70] It is also "necessary there should be a Chief Market" according to Defoe because it is, and will be, beneficial for all of England: "Here the Main stream will run as to the Center, as the River to the Ocean, and as the Blood to the Heart; and it is certainly for the Health of the whole Body of Trade."[71] However, as Defoe acknowledges in his *A Plan of the English Commerce* (1728), this analogy may easily run in the other direction: "As the Veins may be too full of Blood, so a Nation be too full of Trade."[72] Likewise, "the fine fresh Rivers, when they run with a full and gentle stream, are the Beauty and Glory of a Country . . . but when swell'd by sudden and hasty showers . . . then they turn frightful and dangerous, drown the Country, and sometimes the People."[73]

In the *Tour*, we see this point dramatically illustrated as London resists being mapped precisely because it has, following Defoe's metaphor, overflowed its banks and glutted the body's circulatory system; its borders, both literal and figurative, elude quantification for Defoe's narrator: "It is the disaster of London, as to the beauty of its figure, that it is thus stretched out in buildings, just as the pleasure of every builder, or undertaker of buildings, and as the convenience of the people directs, whether for trade, or otherwise; and this has spread the face of it in a most straggling, confused manner, out of all shape, uncompact, and unequal; neither long or broad, round or square; whereas the city of Rome, though a monster for its greatness, yet was, in a manner, round, with very few irregularities of shape."[74] The narrator is thus faced with the daunting task of describing and mapping something that appears to defy such a project. He apologizes and stresses the provisional nature of his survey in comparison to a cartographic projection of the same area: "I have, as near, as I could, caused a measure to be taken of this mighty, I cannot say uniform, body; and for the satisfaction of the curious, I have here given as accurate a description of it, as I can do in so narrow a compass . . . or as I can do without drawing a plan, or map of the places."[75] The narrator's gesture to the map here implies the contingent and incomplete status of his own account, yet it also points to the map's inability to register the monstrous and shifting quality of the urban environment as it grows beyond its original borders, despite its promise of a more comprehensive picture of London. Edward Copeland notes this disjunction as Defoe's narrator juxtaposes the irregular and chaotic space of present-day London against "an imagined ideal of urban order," embodied by the cartographic image of a Renaissance walled city, which becomes the locus of nostalgic identification.[76] Neither the chorography nor the map is sufficient by itself in rendering an accurate representation of London, the implication being that perhaps, together, both could achieve a much higher degree of verisimilitude; however, I would argue that Defoe intentionally dramatizes the inability of his narrator to mediate the conceptual disparities and gaps that exist between both genres of geographic representation. Thus the possibility of coordinating his detailed description of the city with its cartographic projection is doomed to failure and necessarily so. The monstrousness of London, or Halifax for that matter, signals at once the need to synthesize both perspectives as a mode of containment and the very impossibility of its actualization.

The semiotic instability Defoe encounters in Britain's larger urban marketplaces also extends to its smallest towns and villages, some of which were, at one time, thriving commercial centers, while others have yet to realize their true economic potential. He encounters numerous decaying market towns whose trade has shifted elsewhere for a variety of reasons: poor transportation, competition from other markets at home and abroad, shrinking demand, lack of raw materials and natural resources, declining population, and so forth. However, the visible signs of decay are perhaps unreliable signs of a market's ultimate fate, since its situation is always capable of remediation, or at least that is the hope. In Ipswich, for example, the narrator remarks that it was once "the greatest town in England for large colliers or coal-ships" before the Dutch

Wars but is now destitute as result of the coal trade moving to London and Yarmouth and the use of Dutch flyboats, which proved to be a larger, cheaper, and more efficient mode of transportation.[77] Despite the dire situation that confronts him and the facts that have contributed to that situation, the narrator still refuses to acknowledge the legitimacy, or relevance, of the facts, stating that "the loss or decay of this trade, accounts for the present *pretended* decay of the town of Ipswich [italics mine]." The decay he finds in Ipswich is not real but pretended, and he suggests, or hopes rather, that at some future date the town will remove the veil, shake off the ruins, and emerge as the healthy and prodigious market it always was and always will be. Even after explaining the material causes for this apparent decay, he concludes, "I believe this must be owned for the true beginning of their decay, if I must allow it to be called a decay."[78] Decay is the only word available to describe the events in Ipswich, but the word is insufficient and inaccurate. It does not reflect the true state of the market, only its present appearance.[79]

The narrator then launches into a vigorous defense of Ipswich as an ideal port for the Greenland fishery, which the South Sea Company proposed to revive during the 1720s, after the Bubble, though it never successfully got off the ground. He catalogs the salient features of the town that would make such a venture profitable: cheap labor, good storage facilities, convenience of port, proximity to the oil market, among others, and concludes with the promise that Ipswich will inevitably return to its former glory one way or another: "What I have said, is only to let the world see what improvement this town and port is capable of. . . . The time will some time or other come (especially when considering the improving temper of the present age) when some peculiar beneficial business may be found out, to make the port of Ipswich as useful to the world, and the town as flourishing, as nature had made it proper and capable to be."[80] The figuration of the marketplace here takes on an abstract and even metaphysical cast, as the fate of Ipswich is subject to the workings of Providence. The external signs of decay are in need of explication and a proper context in order to negate and overturn an overly convenient reading that would suggest irrecoverable loss and ruin. Market status is clearly dependent on the material forces that shape patterns of trade and commerce, including the geographic disposition of a given marketplace, yet whether times are good or bad, whether trade flourishes or is deferred in some fashion, the market, as a concept that is as yet unrealized, remains thoroughly intact. Thus Defoe is able to play abstract and material definitions of the marketplace off one another in order to provide an ostensibly complete picture of the nation. The market remains situated and site specific, in this instance, the town of Ipswich, yet the articulation of its future potential, its untapped energy, requires the invocation of a more abstract conception of market relations as a means of explaining, and explaining away, the natural cycles of growth and decay that result from the circulation of capital.

Southampton stands out as another instance in which we encounter a town decaying due to the lack of trade, yet these signs also prove unreliable. The expansion of London as the commercial center of the nation has, as in Ipswich, devastated the local economy and reduced trade to the buying and selling of wine and "much smuggling." Southampton, however, is surrounded by lush and dense woodlands that, for reasons unclear to the narrator, remain untouched despite the presence of a once thriving timber industry that supplied the building of the Royal Navy. He wonders at the folly of nearby estates at not taking advantage of such a resource, noting that a significant portion of the trees have grown so decayed and old that they were "no longer serviceable to their country," a lamentable situation for Southampton, which would clearly benefit from its use: "These in my opinion are no signs of the decay of our woods, or of the danger of our wanting timber in England; on the contrary, I take leave to mention it again, that if we were employed in England, by the rest of the world, to build a thousand sail of three deck ships, from 80 to 100 guns, it might be done to our infinite advantage, and without putting us in any danger of excluding the nation of timber."[81] The overgrowth of timber in conjunction with the absence of trade in Southampton only *appear* to be the manifestation of decay when, in fact, the signs point to a thriving timber industry that will revive Southampton and the southern half of Hampshire county as well as contribute to the overall economic power of Great Britain. The level of prognostication here goes well beyond the mere description of place found in the chorography or the map. The inherent unreliability of description and the cartographic projection, their ability to present signs and images that are not true indicators of national wealth and vitality, requires that the author/traveler go beyond these modes of geographic representation and offer the reader an adequate context for those signs. The market and its geography is that context, yet the logic of the market is also the very source of this semiotic instability that precipitates the need for such a context in the first place. This is the fundamental antinomy at the heart of Defoe's representation of the nation as a unified and coherent body.

This antagonism is most visible when Defoe comes to the treatment of Scotland at the end of the text. Scotland does not present the reader with once thriving markets whose physical presence in the landscape denotes future prosperity. With the exception of Edinburgh and some of the larger towns and cities, we are confronted, in many instances, by the absence of a marketplace altogether, a fact that perplexes the narrator given the abundance of signs that would suggest otherwise. Upon entering Kirkubright, a coastal town, he says that the place "is a surprise to a stranger." The surprise results from his conflicting observations of, on the one hand, a "people without business" and a "port without trade" and, on the other, all the materials and "opportunities" for trade, including a navigable river, a deep bay with an island to protect it from the sea, a large salmon population as well as other varieties of fish with which to build a sustainable fishing industry. The narrator, however, has difficulty reconciling the two realities: "In a word, it is to me the wonder of all the towns of North-Britain; especially being so near England, that it has all the invitations to trade that Nature can give them, but they take no notice of it. A man might say to them, that they have the Indies at their door, and will not dip into the wealth of them; a gold mine at their door, and will not dig it."[82] To his credit, Defoe does not rationalize the problem by laying the blame directly on the Scots themselves and insinuating that their natural predisposition to indolence is the primary cause for the state of Kirkubright, though he does acknowledge those detractors who explain the reasons for poverty in just these terms. Instead, he reverses the formula to argue that indolence is an effect of poverty, not the other way around, and that the reasons for poverty are more complex in nature and thus harder to get at through mere description. Again, the signs are reliable, but only up to a point. He comments that the people not only *are* poor, but they *look* poor as well, implying that appearances are, to an extent, a reliable indicator of the real conditions in Scotland. However, the sober, grave mien of the townspeople, their general look of malaise and seriousness, may also be the surest sign that they could be a productive and diligent source of labor, if the conditions were right.[83]

Schellenberg's "nightmare" is then the possibility that this will not happen, that the people of Kirkubright will never *see* the signs of their own salvation and remain forever outside the chain of trade and commerce that sustains all of Great Britain. More importantly, the reasons behind that possibility not only elude Defoe, despite the thoroughness of his investigation, but the Scots themselves. As the narrator comments after visiting the capital city of Air, "What the reason of the decay of trade here was, or when it first began to decay, is hard to determine; nor are the people free to tell, and, perhaps, do not know themselves."[84] Both observer and observed fail to comprehend the mechanisms of the marketplace, how it is created, how it is sustained, and how it decays and dies. A survey, such as the *Tour*, is one method of enabling them to see by dramatizing the importance of seeing in the first place and teaching the proper way to see in the second. The improvement of Scotland is dependent on this very operation, which Defoe realizes is the fulcrum of economic growth and development. The material requirements for a marketplace are plainly visible, yet without the ability to conceptualize market relations, to understand the mechanisms of exchange and their vital role in the consolidation of the national body, these resources lie fallow. It is a knowledge the narrator possesses, yet the failure to implement that knowledge continually frustrates his improving gaze.

Defoe's conditional survey of Scotland, the sense of promise visible in the physical landscape, despite its lack of use, is clearly a plea for improvement and the further integration of English and Scottish trade in order to substantiate and legitimate the Act of Union. The semiotic instability of the marketplace enables Defoe to make his case for developing Scotland and maintain his fidelity to descriptive accuracy. The markers of prosperity and decay are carefully observed and transcribed in the course of his travels, yet those same markers easily transform into one another in order to sustain the improving ideology that guides the *Tour* and most of Defoe's economic writings. As I have been arguing, this strategy is predicated on a differential sense of spatial relations in which the market as abstract process and market as material place are opposed to one another and, in turn, constitute the principle of difference that undergirds his attempts to theorize space on a national scale. Markets exist where no market is clearly visible to the observing eye. They cannot be delineated or represented in either a map or a chorography, but for Defoe, they exist nevertheless, if only one can read the signs properly, a difficult task given the many slippages in signification that accrue to the marketplace as a site of exchange and transformation. Conversely, even where a marketplace clearly exists and is visible for all to see, its prodigious nature, its monstrousness, defies the narrator's ability to describe and outline its topography despite his attempts to do otherwise. Either way, whether successful or decaying, the marketplace is subject to an increasing degree of abstraction that resists inscription and stands against the map and the chorography as inadequate modes of geographic representation.

That is not to say, however, that the physical location of the marketplace is of no concern to Defoe, nor are efforts to understand market activity geographically necessarily useless given the difficulties in fixing its boundaries and limits. Clearly, the *Tour* is engaged in this project in a fairly direct fashion. Rather, as I am arguing, the market as a definable and knowable space is of even greater importance given its inherent instabilities and elusive nature. Map and survey still play a critical role here in terms of the need to make exchange regular and normative. Thus material and figurative definitions of the market remain in play, but their failure to coincide with one another allows for the creation of a narrative voice that must dramatize and perform this sense of disjunction in order to make the case for nation as that which will resolve the contradiction and bring market and nation into some sort of formal coherence. Without the invocation of the market as an ambivalent space, there is no force behind Defoe's rhetoric of improvement. Without the fundamental tension between the consolidation of trade in certain geographic locations and the abstraction of exchange into the notion of a placeless market, there is no reason to insist on reforms that will coordinate the two and, subsequently, channel trade toward national ends. It is the imperative to reform market activity, to make it more responsive to national concerns, as well as limit and contain its more harmful effects on the social body, that precipitates the further investment of the state in the physical sites of exchange even as more abstract notions of the market gain wider currency. While Defoe's reformist agenda is predicated on bringing the two into alignment so that theory and practice cohere, he must further exploit and exacerbate their differences in order to justify and legitimate his

economic and political philosophies, which can only be realized through recourse to the market as a heterotopia.

Defoe's redefinition of the market as both place and precept is dependent
on a certain conception of nation whose identity is shaped and determined
by its physical geography, the whole island of Great Britain as it were, and
by knowing and understanding that geography in ways possible only through
chorographic and cartographic practices. Market activity, in Defoe's *Tour*, is
no longer a local or provincial matter, but rather is incorporated into a larger
geography of trade and commerce that is coterminous with, if not identical
to, the nation itself. To survey the nation is to survey its places and patterns
of trade; to know and understand the geography of the market is to know and
more fully understand the nation and oneself as a national subject. Nation, as
a unique and identifiable geography, provides Defoe an important context for
framing and giving shape to the ever-changing landscape of Britain's markets,
as well as containing and, in some sense, regulating the often volatile, unpredictable ebbs and flows of trade in and between those marketplaces. It is, in
fact, the ebbs and flows of the market, its uneven and combined developments,
which make necessary a text, like Defoe's *Tour*, that visually and narratively locates the market and its modes of exchange in order to promote and contribute
to the nation's future wealth and prosperity. All trade and commerce conducted
on British soil is, for Defoe, always already national in purpose and scope, if
properly regulated and channeled. Defoe was certainly not alone in embracing
this line of mercantilist thought, nor was he the only person to emphasize
issues of geography and geographic representation in the pursuit of national
wealth and prosperity. The *Tour* represents just one such means of regulating
and channeling market activity toward national ends; the maps, surveys, charts,
and chorographies of the British marketplace, which I discussed earlier, are,
of course, another. Collectively, these works are technologies of space critical
to the formation of capital on a national scale, hence their increasing presence
and use throughout the seventeenth and eighteenth centuries. The modern
nation-state is thus dependent on the map, not only as a symbolic icon with
which people may identify, as Anderson or Helgerson would have it, but as a
practical tool for the maintenance and control of markets and their integration
into the fabric of national life.

# This Old House and Samuel Johnson's Scotland

It is surprising how people will go a distance for what they may have
at home.

—SAMUEL JOHNSON, from Boswell's
*The Journal of a Tour to the Hebrides* (1785)

## SCOTIA ANTIQUA, SCOTIA MODERNA

In the years after its publication, the commercial ideology we see at work in
Defoe's *Tour Thro' The Whole Island of Great Britain* and other topographical
works of its kind was embraced and enacted by prounion government officials,
entrepreneurs, merchants, allied tradespeople, and agrarian reformers, all of
whom helped to radically transform Scotland into a productive and relatively
compliant part of an integrated Great Britain. The material effects of these
transformations to Scotland and its geography from the early to the latter half
of the eighteenth century have been well-documented: vast tracts of land, especially in the lowlands, were enclosed and improved, estates were consolidated into large-scale agricultural concerns, new roads and byways were built,
markets expanded with a greater variety and volume of goods and services
available, towns and villages grew rapidly in kind along with the continued
development of Scotland's major urban areas, Edinburgh and Glasgow most
notably, and textile manufacturing, fishing, and timber became staple industries.[1] While some of these changes were already evident prior to 1750, according to T. M. Devine, the most rapid growth in Scotland's agrarian and
market economies can be found after 1760, with the most significant changes
coming after 1780: "The speed of Scottish rural transformation is one of its
most remarkable characteristics. Arguably, nowhere else in western Europe
was agrarian economy and society altered so quickly and rapidly in the eighteenth century."[2] These dramatic changes within rural Scotland were accompanied by concurrent revolutions in the industrial and manufacturing sectors

of its urban centers, whose growing populations, in turn, drove the demand for food and other agricultural products. The reciprocity between country and city was in large measure responsible for the extraordinary pace of Scotland's commercial expansion, an expansion whose effects on the landscape were clearly visible by the end of the eighteenth century. Defoe's strategic deployment of the marketplace as the organizing principle of his tour, I would also suggest, played an invaluable role in promoting the further development of Scotland as both a practical endeavor and as a matter of policy. The modernization of Scotland, in fact, cannot be properly understood without considering the contributions of texts, such as Defoe's *Tour*, that served to facilitate both intra- and international trade, helped regulate and contain, if not eradicate, illegitimate forms of trade, and perhaps most importantly, shaped public perceptions of Scotland, especially after the 1707 Act of Union.

Defoe's text, however, was hardly the first, or even the most influential, example of topographical writing on Scotland dedicated to its further economic development. The work of William Camden, Timothy Pont, Joan Blaeu, Robert and James Gordon, Robert Sibbald, and Martin Martin, collectively, helped contribute to the burgeoning genre of economic geography over the course of the previous century, articulating many of the same goals and aspirations in Defoe's *Tour* with respect to Scotland's prospects for trade and commerce.[3] That said, trade and commerce were rarely if ever the sole focus of these earlier attempts to survey and map Scotland, which instead broached a wide range of topics, including Scotland's origins and antiquity, the history of its civil and ecclesiastical institutions, the genealogy and ethnic makeup of its inhabitants, its ancient customs and laws, and the natural history of the landscape itself.[4] Economic geography had not fully emerged as a genre in its own right but rather was one element of many in these early topographies of Scotland. We do begin to see, however, an emerging split between those works exclusively committed to charting Scotland's present circumstances, such as Defoe's *Tour*, and those more focused on its ancient past toward the end of the seventeenth century, which will only continue to thrive and flourish throughout the eighteenth century, albeit in maps and chorographies dedicated solely to that particular subject. The more discursive and eclectic approach found in many seventeenth-century topographies of Scotland thus gives way to two different and not always complementary ways of representing its geography. As I will argue in the following chapter, the generic divide between these respective approaches to *Scotia moderna* and *Scotia antiqua*, to borrow the proposed subtitles for Robert Sibbald's failed atlas of Scotland, offers an important context for understanding Samuel Johnson's respective critiques of eighteenth-century commercial and antiquarian topographies of Scotland and his attempt to reconcile and resolve the conflicting interests inherent to mapping both ancient and modern Scotland in *A Journey to the Western Islands of Scotland* (1775).[5] Johnson, as I contend, posits a vision of a unified Great Britain in the *Journey* that is neither the product of conquest and dominion, military, commercial, or otherwise, nor the excavation and conservation of the past, but rather one that finds common ground in the minute details and particularities of domestic life throughout Scotland's history. As the empirical traveler abroad, Johnson assiduously documents and comments on the virtues and failings of the various homes he encounters and constructs a history in which the Scottish home comes to mark the evolution and progress of civilization itself, from its primitive shelters and habitations to the solid and dignified forts and castles of the feudal period and, lastly, to the genteel, refined environs of the modern home. Johnson's secret history of domesticity thus enables us to witness and chart the gradual yet lengthy process by which a nation moves inexorably from barbarity to civility. The creation of a truly civil society, in Johnson's estimation, is something that cannot be imposed on Scotland through the exercise of force or sheer will or, by extension, a map; rather, it must and will emerge as a matter of course from within the modalities of domestic life. That is, the home, as both material place and abstract ideal, unifies and binds England and Scotland into a single nation, or homeland, whose identity is rooted in the universal and universalizing experience of domestic labor and familial community. The home, in this sense, represents a critical heterotopic locus within the Scottish landscape for Johnson in that it typically falls outside of the general purview of economic and antiquarian topographic writings, either because it is not deemed a significant or legitimate topic of discussion or because its presence challenges the political and cultural assumptions that inform their respective mappings of Scotland, which are more overtly imperial in nature.

John Adair, a Scottish surveyor and cartographer, was a critical figure in this regard and an important precursor to Defoe's *Tour* in his insistence on the production of mathematically and geometrically rigorous maps of Scotland as a necessary and invaluable tool in the promotion of trade and commerce, the cultivation of industry and agriculture, and the development of its urban centers. As Charles Withers notes, while Adair certainly had his antiquarian proclivities, "The emphasis in [his] work was decidedly on mapping and the accurate delineation of the nation."[6] In 1686, Adair was commissioned by the Privy Council to survey all of Scotland in order to provide "Exact Geographical Descriptions of several Shires within this Kingdom . . . and the Hydrographical Description of the Sea-Coast, Isle, Crieks, Firths, and Lochs" (fig. 26). As the official act states, "The want of such exact Maps, having occasioned great Losses in time past: and likewise, thereby Forraigners may be invited to Trade with more security on our Coasts."[7] Unfortunately, the money for the survey, along with the Privy Council itself, dried up with the official unification of the English and Scottish Parliaments in 1707. In a somewhat desperate appeal for money and materials to complete his work, Adair wrote the secretary of state, the Earl of Mar, in June of 1713 with the hope of having his funding restored: "The Surveys of the South and West coasts and Firth of Clyde, are

FIGURE 26. "A true and exact Hydrographical description of the Sea coast and Isles of Scotland," John Adair, 1703. (Reproduced by permission of the National Library of Scotland)

in the greatest forwardness, an so wil require the least time, and expence to finish them. *They are very necessare for carrying on trade,* and with the descriptions wil make compleit part of Volume, which in my humble opinion, wil plea better, and be of greater use, than the publishing separated maps [italics mine]."[8] Adair clearly understands the value of trade and its importance to the government and is savvy, if not entirely sincere, to frame his request in these terms.[9] We later see Adair echo these sentiments regarding the importance of cartography to trade in his posthumously published essay appended to Herman Moll's *A Set of Thirty-Six New and Correct Maps of Scotland Divided into Shires* (1725). The preface, entitled "Of Scotland in General," reinforces his linking of Scotland's future prosperity to an understanding of its complex geography: "So that, considering the Goodness and Conveniency of the Ports, the many People, their Hardiness, Strength, and easy Temper, *Scotland,* in a few Years, if encouraged and assisted by the Government, might easily be Master of the Fishing Trade in *Europe.*" The inclusion of Adair's prefatory comments directs our subsequent reading of Moll's collection of maps, which illustrate and graphically reinforce both men's shared sympathies for a more robust fishing industry in Scotland.[10]

For both Adair and Defoe, an accurate and rigorous approach to the mapping of Scotland would, in theory, redress the historical imbalances between England and Scotland's respective economies and help to realize, if not immediately then at least in the near future, a level of productivity not possible by either nation on its own. It is an approach that we see again and again in the work of many eighteenth-century Whig topographers, as Thomas Curley refers to them, whose maps and surveys helped coordinate the movement of labor, raw materials, finished goods, and capital between towns, cities, and nations.[11] These so-called Whig topographies of Scotland, however, were not simply the practical instruments of economic reform and improvement; they also served a symbolic function by framing the nation in such a way as to suggest that commercial activity was the natural and inevitable extension of the land itself. It is as if Scotland, given its abundance of natural resources, its willing and able labor force, and of course, its proximity to English markets, is always already poised for future economic appropriation and exploitation, and it is simply the work of the topographic writer or cartographer to chart how the land and its people may best be improved and managed. Whig topographers thus sought to legitimate trade and commerce as activities central to the identity of Great Britain, and their respective representations of Scotland reflect this political and ideological agenda.

Herman Moll's "Map of the North West Part of the Western Islands" (1725), for example, offers this brief gloss in the margin: "These islands are of all others most capable of Improvements in the Fishery" (fig. 27). He then goes on to blame Charles II and "some crafty Merchants" for driving Dutch settlers, who had up until that point been quite successful fisherman, out of the village

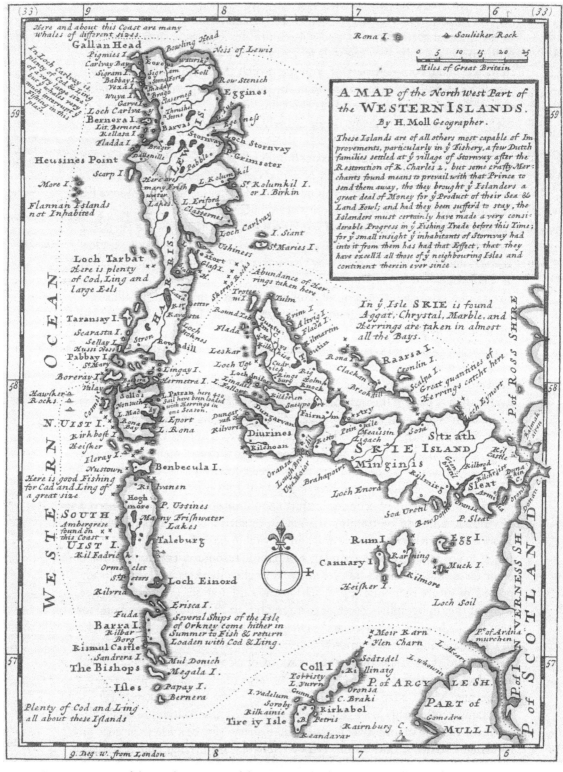

Figure 27. *Map of the North West Part of the Western Islands*, Herman Moll, 1725. (Reproduced by permission of the National Library of Scotland)

of Stornvay after the Restoration, setting back the entire region in terms of its future economic progress. Moll, like his friend and colleague Adair, placed economic concerns at the forefront of his work, including his seminal 1714 map *The North Part of Great Britain called Scotland* (fig. 28): "Its manifest by this Map, which is founded upon undoubted Authority, how easy it would be to settle the most advantageous Fishery in the World here, and also with a small Charge to make Rivers navigable, for Carrying timber to the Sea side, for there grows excellent good Fir &c in these parts, so that if things were rightly managed, there would be occasion to go to Norway for Wood or to New-foundland for fish; seeing North Britain can plentifully furnish us with both."[12] The inclusion of such marginalia suggests that Moll's advocacy for Scotland's improvement cannot be separated from his commitments as a cartographer. Text and graphics work together to press the map's "undoubted Authority" into the service of his particular brand of mercantilist ideology. It should also be recalled that Moll's maps were used to illustrate both Defoe's *Robinson Crusoe* and *A Tour Thro' The Whole Island of Great Britain* and that Defoe's own contributions to the *Atlas Maritimus & Commercialis* (1728) were loosely based on Moll's *Atlas Geographus* (1711–17).[13] Both Moll and Defoe, along with Adair, clearly shared a belief that an expanded geographic knowledge of Scotland served the interests of all of Great Britain, and they were deeply committed to fostering ties between geography and commerce as a matter of state policy and national identity.

These links between trade, geography, and imperialism become even more explicit by the second half of the century as further surveys, maps, and chorographies are produced with an express eye toward the commercial improvement of the nation. Like the earlier works of Defoe, Adair, and Moll, these geographies of Scotland often served a variety of practical functions, such as identifying current and potential sites of production and manufacturing, marking roads, stages, and distances necessary for transportation and distribution, and facilitating commercial activity in general. However, they were also increasingly deployed to legitimate such commercial activity as necessary, just, and right. John Knox's *A Commercial Map of Scotland* (1782), for example, utilizes the margins of his map in a manner similar to Moll to make the case that Scotland's and England's economic fates are hopelessly intertwined: "The experience of half a century proves, that the prosperity of this part of the island contributes, ultimately, to the prosperity of the other, and that the interest of Scotland, is in all respects, the interest of England" (fig. 29). Knox's comments here are appended to a direct plea for the formation of a unified "commercial parliament" that would eliminate barriers to trade between Scotland and England. While his plan never went into effect, Knox's advocacy for political solutions to matters of trade remains a prominent theme in his own work and that of other Whig topographers, many of whom were funded, either directly or indirectly, by the state. John Smeaton's *Report . . . Concerning the Practicability*

FIGURE 28. *The North Part of Great Britain called Scotland*, Herman Moll, 1714. (Reproduced by permission of the National Library of Scotland)

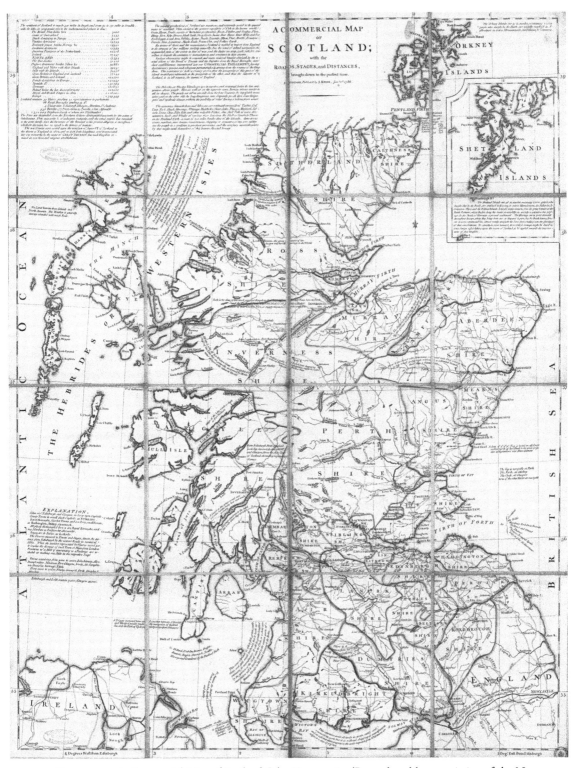

FIGURE 29. *A Commercial Map of Scotland*, John Knox, 1782. (Reproduced by permission of the National Library of Scotland)

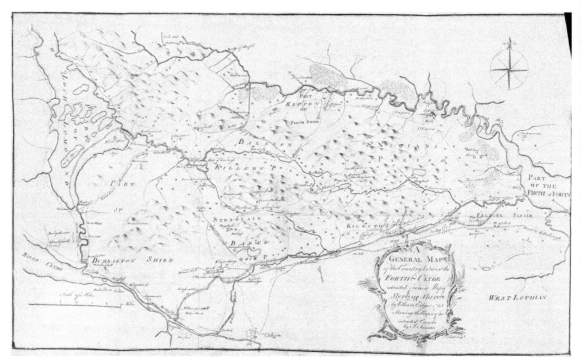

FIGURE 30. "A General Map of the Country Betwixt the Forth & Clyde," John Smeaton, 1767. (Special Collections Research Center, University of Chicago Library)

*and Expense of joining the Rivers Forth and Clyde by a Navigable Canal* (1767), for one, was commissioned by Scotland's Board of Trustees for Fisheries, Manufactures, and Improvements, which had been established by an Act of Parliament in 1727. The *Report* includes a variety of maps produced by Smeaton outlining the parameters and geographic feasibility of his proposed project, which then served as the basis for the construction of the canal that, while not finished until 1790, was intended to (and did for a time) aid merchants in the transportation of labor, finished goods, and raw materials (fig. 30).[14]

Likewise, James Anderson's *Account of the Present State of the Hebrides and Western Coasts of Scotland* (1785) was essentially a report to the Lords of the Treasury and the House of Commons' Committee of Fisheries that lauds this part of Scotland as a vast natural resource but argues, lamentably, that it is not being properly managed and regulated:

It has long afforded matter of astonishment to neighbouring nations, that Britain, whose shores are surrounded by greater shoals of fish than those of any other country on the Globe, should have so long remained inactive herself with regard to fisheries, while others have been enriched by the treasures they have derived by this source. . . . Yet the fisheries on her own coast . . .

have still been suffered to remain in such a languid state, as neither to employ the industry of the People, augment the wealth of the Nation, nor add to the revenue and resources of the State.[15]

In response, the *Account* proposes to explain "the circumstances that have hitherto repressed the industry of the Natives" and to offer suggestions "for encouraging the fisheries, and promoting other improvements in those countries." The bulk of Anderson's text thus meticulously describes the Hebrides and Western Islands with these issues regarding commercial improvement always at the forefront. He includes with the *Account* a map, entitled "A New Map of Scotland," that incorporates information from his surveys and is professed by Anderson to be more accurate than existing cartographies, including the highly regarded work of Adair and, more recently, Murdoch Mackenzie (fig. 31).[16] In the right margin of the map, Anderson includes a column for his "remarks" that identify sites critical to the development of Scotland's as yet untapped resources: mineral deposits, pasturage for the raising of livestock, sheep in particular, forests able to supply timber to the Royal Navy, and of course, harbors, inlets, shoals, and rivers ideally suited for the development of the fishing industry. More importantly, this information, according to Anderson, will contribute to the employment of the people, the wealth of the nation, and an increase in state revenues. His text thus frames the development of the Hebrides and Western Islands of Scotland as an issue of both local and national interest in order to make those interests appear reasonable, logical, and above all, inevitable. In turn, Anderson's appeal to the nation, like Knox's, serves to authorize and legitimate the kinds of information provided by his text and other Whig topographies. Collectively, their work succeeded in consolidating the union by transforming Scotland into a more economically stable and viable part of the nation by the end of the eighteenth century. They also helped to establish economic geography and cartography as a necessary tool of British imperialism and, in time, a legitimate genre in its own right.

The proliferation of Whig topographies over the course of the eighteenth century, as I am contending, represents a form of occupation and expropriation of Scottish territory, both literally and figuratively, as they not only served a pragmatic function but also helped to shape and define Scotland in the English imagination during the tumultuous period following the 1707 Act of Union. Their efforts, however, must be considered alongside the production of maps and chorographies whose vision of the nation differed sharply from that of the Whig topographers and their progressive vision of Scotland rooted in agrarian improvement and commercial development. More specifically, I would like to consider in the remainder of this section those cartographers and topographical writers who eschewed the interests of the Whig topographers and economic matters altogether by focusing exclusively on matters regarding Scottish antiquity.[17] This generic split between economic and antiquarian geographies,

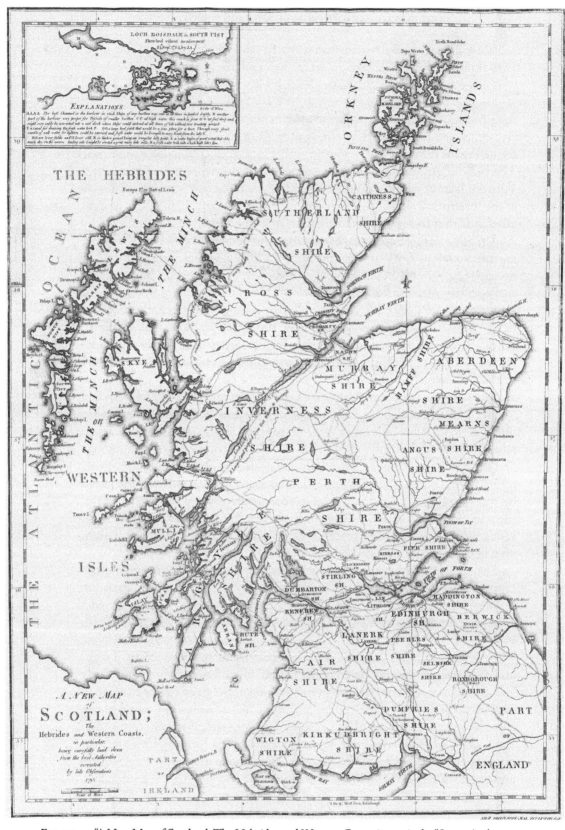

Figure 31. "A New Map of Scotland; The Hebrides and Western Coasts in particular," James Anderson, 1785. (Harvard Map Collection, Harvard Library)

as I will contend, is reflective of larger conflicts and tensions within British national identity, both prior to and after the Act of Union, between those advocates of the Union desirous to exploit Scotland's vast natural resources and to establish stronger commercial ties with England and those critics of the Union who see the excavation of Scotland's past as a bulwark against the forces of modernization and assimilation. Rather than resolve this rift, the Act of Union, as well as the rebellions of 1715 and 1745, only further deepened the gulf separating these competing definitions of Scottish territory, thus driving a burgeoning market for both antiquarian and economic maps, surveys, atlases, travel narratives, and chorographies throughout the eighteenth century. The marketplace for either genre, as I am suggesting, cannot properly be understood separately; rather, each must be seen as a reaction and response to the other and to Scotland's continued integration into the Union. While the division between strictly economic and antiquarian geographies only continues to grow over the course of the eighteenth century, both approaches to the mapping of Scotland ultimately rely on many of the same cartographic practices and technologies to legitimate their competing claims on the land. That is, their differences aren't as much methodological as they are politically and ideologically motivated by, on the one hand, a desire to document and preserve something of Scotland's past and, on the other, the need to cultivate and improve on its present circumstances.

As I noted previously, antiquarian fare was routinely included in many seventeenth-century topographies of Scotland, although it was often just one subject among many. However, as Jeremy Black notes, antiquarian mapping, as a distinct and separate genre, emerges around the late seventeenth century in conjunction with a broader interest in historical geography, including maps of the biblical, classical, and medieval worlds. "If locating the present came to be of greater importance to politicians and estate-owners and of interest to readers, the same was also true of the past. Maps came to play an integral role in the presentation of the past, indeed to be a way in which the past could be presented."[18] These antiquarian maps were not re-creations or reproductions of older maps. Rather, they resembled contemporary maps in their emphasis on scientific objectivity and cartographic accuracy, removing any ornamental embellishments entirely in order to present a more rationalized view of the past. The map, however, functions somewhat differently for the antiquarian scholar whose purpose is chiefly the display of information for the education and entertainment of his reader as opposed to an object of immediate, utilitarian value. In many respects, the map is a fitting vehicle for the dissemination of antiquarian knowledge in that it ordered and spatialized information in much the same fashion as the collector's cabinet filled with curious and surprising objects. The map provides a sense of context, a container if you will, for the details and descriptions to follow but provides little guidance in terms of the explanation or explication of those details. As Susan Manning puts it,

"The taxonomic and fragmented language of things offered by antiquarians lacked the connecting parts of articulated speech that made a single coherent narrative possible, and the 'progression' into the Anglophone homogeneity of Civil Society inevitable."[19] The contiguous logic of the map, its ability to juxtapose a concatenation of places within a delimited space, is thus ideally suited to the epistemology of the antiquarian. Time is flattened out and projected onto the two-dimensional space of the map in order to make the past present and, more importantly, to transform the past into an object of knowledge that can be appropriated, possessed, and arranged as the antiquarian topographer sees fit.

This form of antiquarian occupation is, I would argue, no less an act of territorial expropriation and subjugation than the economic maps of the Whig topographers or, for that matter, the military surveys of the Highlands conducted by the Ordnance Survey following the uprising at Culloden. I refer to such mappings as "occupations" in order to convey a sense of the quasi-professional status of antiquarian studies during the eighteenth century while also underscoring its affinities with the military and economic mappings of Scotland, endeavors more readily associated with acts of conquest, appropriation, and occupation. In a metaphorical sense, antiquarian maps are no different than these other modes and genres of cartography in their shared desire to graphically occupy and define the land in particular ways, even though those images of Scotland may differ greatly. The form and method of their presentation may be similar, but their respective ideological goals and ambitions regarding Scotland are certainly not. Thus, in opposition to the rationalized projections of so-called Whig topographers, we see the creation of a countervailing image that locates Scottish antiquity as a regular feature of its present landscape, in turn giving that sense of the past an aura and presence that cannot and will not be eradicated by the forces of improvement. Antiquarian mappings of Scotland in effect collapse time and space in order to mobilize the *idea* of Scottish antiquity as a political and ideological weapon in debates regarding British national identity post-1707. The promotion of Scotland's past through the production of antiquarian maps is not so much a historical exercise as it is an attempt to define the present state of the nation.[20]

While seventeenth- and eighteenth-century antiquarian topographers of Scotland covered a wide range of historical periods and subjects, including its primitive origins and the Middle Ages, more often than not, their efforts centered on the excavation and mapping of the vestiges of the Roman occupation of Britain, including forts, walls, battlements, roads, camps, and ports.[21] As Philip Ayres notes in his *Classical Culture and the Idea of Rome in Eighteenth-Century England*, "At the same time that classical civic ideals were being adapted to current political purposes, the classical temperament was naturalized in a still profounder dimension by an intense focusing on Britain's own Roman past."[22] Ayres argues that the excavation of Roman Britain should rightly be seen as part of a larger effort to legitimate the classical virtues of *libertas* and *civitas* as the ideological cornerstones of England's aristocracy following the Glorious Revolution of 1688. In response to the overtly commercial and imperial ambitions of an emergent bourgeois class, England's ruling elite instituted what Ayres refers to as an "oligarchy of virtue" that was meant to effectively stem the perceived tide of greed and avarice, which they felt was destroying the principles of legitimate government as well as eroding their own social and political authority. The bodying forth of the ruins and remains of Rome's occupation of Britain in the form of antiquarian topographies and maps thus established a direct and evidentiary connection between modern Britain and ancient Rome, or as Ayres puts it, "The British had become genetically Roman."[23] Maps of Roman Britain are meant to literalize this genealogy by offering supposedly scientific and objective proof of such a link while at the same time metaphorically superimposing the image of Roman colonization over that of modern Britain. It is an image that would have a substantial effect on the British national imaginary for much of the eighteenth century; however, the nature and force of its impact shifts somewhat when we turn specifically to Scotland as the site of these antiquarian occupations.

The analogy of Britain as a latter-day Rome takes on different cast when we consider England's own efforts to colonize Scotland and bring it into the Union as a compliant and productive part of the empire. In this extended analogy, England is likened to the Roman military seeking to subdue and pacify a group of entrenched clans and tribes unwilling to cede their power while Scotland is, in either scenario, the object of conquest. Regardless of the historical context, the Roman Empire or eighteenth-century England, Scotland forever remains that territory desperately in need of civilization and improvement, and antiquarian scholars actively fostered and encouraged such analogies, however tenuous, as a part of their own imperial designs for Scotland. Given the perception that Scotland's feudal past remained a very real stumbling block to its modernization and integration into the Union, it is not coincidental that many antiquarians wished to return to that period, prior to the Middle Ages, when the Roman forces of Agricola had defeated the Caledonians and consolidated their rule over Scotland, save for the Highlands and Western Islands, which were never fully subdued. By marginalizing its medieval past in favor of Roman antiquity, antiquarian scholars were able to emphasize Scotland's classical, as opposed to gothic, origins and, in turn, the possibility of its future remediation as part of a homogeneous and more virtuous Great Britain. The Scots are thus, in reality, no different than their English counterparts; they both have common roots in Roman antiquity, and despite the differences in their subsequent histories, Scotland will, as a matter of course, rightly reclaim its ancient heritage. The unification of Scotland and England is, in this sense, not viewed so much as an act of imperial aggression as it is the inevitable restoration and rebirth of the Roman republic, albeit in a modern and perhaps more perfect form, including the subjugation of the northern Scotland. However, while the antiquarian adamantly opposes such imperial ambitions in favor of a society and government guided by republican virtue, they nevertheless are reliant on the very same technologies of empire, including maps, charts, graphs, illustrations, and chorographies, that the Whig topographers utilize in the service of expanding trade and commerce. The imperial visions of the antiquarians may differ in critical ways from that of Defoe, Moll, Adair, and others, but their use of these technologies suggests an underlying similarity in that they require the illusion of objectivity and rational inquiry in order to legitimate their particular claims on Scotland. The map thus becomes an especially potent rhetorical strategy that is frequently deployed in many antiquarian topographies of Roman Britain.

Antiquarian scholars are in fact even more dependent on the map in this sense, given the myriad uncertainties and ambiguities that routinely present themselves as part of any historical investigation, much less one that reaches back well over a thousand years. The often speculative or conjectural nature of their findings, a common point of criticism and ridicule in literature satirizing antiquarianism, makes the need for illustrative supplements, such as maps, plans, and charts, all the more necessary. As Robert Sibbald acknowledges in his *Historical Inquiries, Concerning the Roman Monuments and Antiquities in the North Part of Britain called Scotland* (1707), "The long interval of Time, betwixt the time we live in, and that in which the *Romans* were here, has occasioned Difficulties in the tracing them," and as a result, "it is hard to fix certainly the places where the *Roman* Walls, Ports, Colonies, and Forts were."[24] Despite these obstacles, Sibbald promises to refrain from offering conjectures in instances where evidence is lacking, stating that "when I have not such proofs, I shall most willingly submit my Conjectures to the Learned, that they may Accept, or Reject them, as they think Good." Sibbald is all too aware of the problems and pitfalls of his proposed inquiry and so must shore up the limits of conjectural knowledge by offering the disclaimer in his preface. However, his promise to hold himself to a higher standard is already an admission that there are those readers who would cast doubt on his text and its findings, thus precipitating Sibbald's decision to also include an attenuated map, *The Roman Wall betwixt the Firths of Clyd and Forth*, along with detailed plans of the wall's layout and structure (fig. 32). The map, in conjunction with the illustrations, serves to further authenticate Sibbald's inquiry by making the Roman past visible and presenting to his reader a form of evidence that is, to some extent, self-legitimating. It is also an effective means of offering the reader the vicarious pleasures of the antiquarian scholar as he gazes upon and experiences these ruins, artifacts, and relics firsthand. The graphic inscription of the past, whether in the form of a map, plan, chart, or illustrative drawing, appeals, on the one hand, to the rational intellect that demands the materiality

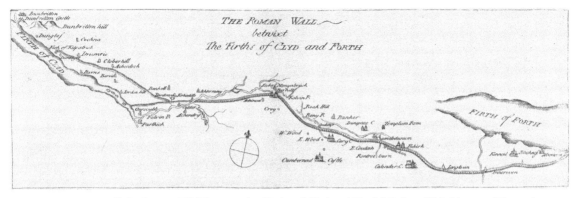

FIGURE 32. "The Roman Wall betwixt the Firths of Clyd and Forth," Robert Sibbald, 1707. (Harvard Map Collection, Harvard Library)

of historical evidence and is wary of speculation and conjecture and, on the other, to the polite, gentlemanly reader who consumes antiquarian texts in the much the same fashion as the reader of novels, for the purposes of pleasure, entertainment, and moral education. For Sibbald, the map appears to mediate the demands of both constituencies, simultaneously allaying fears of bias and rank amateurism while making Roman antiquity visible in a new and engaging manner. The logic behind Sibbald's use of the map, its ability to appeal to a range of different audiences, also informs the deployment of maps in many other antiquarian topographies of Roman Scotland throughout the eighteenth century; however, as we will see, it is a precarious balancing act and one that is not always successful.

Like Sibbald, William Stukeley, perhaps the most influential figure in eighteenth-century antiquarian studies, also used maps regularly to supplement and flesh out his various surveys of Scottish antiquities.[25] For example, his 1720 *Account of Roman Temple, and Other Antiquities, Near Graham's Dike in Scotland* contains a map entitled *Vallum Barbaricum vulgo Graham's Dike* (fig. 33). The map, authored by Stukeley himself, presents us with a decidedly Roman topography, complete with Latin toponyms and markers indicating the sites of the antiquities that he will further describe and illustrate in his text. The map uses very little ornamentation and forgoes color altogether in order to provide a starkly objective view of the area of his antiquarian investigations. Stukeley also applies this carto-antiquarian methodology to a number of his other works, including his compendious *Itinerarium Curiosum; or, An Account of the Antiquitys and Remarkable Curiositys in Nature or Art, Observ'd in Travels thro' Great Britain* (1724). As in his prior work, Stukeley includes a variety of illustrations to accompany his extensive textual descriptions of Scotland's notable antiquities, including a chart of the Caves of Hawthornden (plate 38), yet he also includes a much more extensive map entitled *Ingratiam Itineran-*

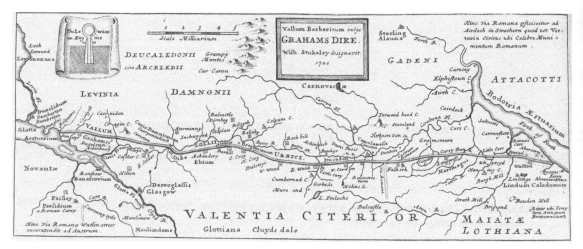

FIGURE 33. "Vallum Barbaricum vulgo Graham's Dike," William Stukeley, 1720. (James Marshall and Marie-Louise Osborn Collection, Beinecke Rare Book and Manuscript Library, Yale University)

*tium Curiosorum, Antonini Aug. itinerarium per Britanniam,* which depicts the Roman road system in Britain throughout England and Wales (plate 56).[26] A somewhat similar, but more refined and detailed map of Roman Britain, this time including Scotland and Ireland, appears in Stukeley's *An Account of Richard of Cirencester, Monk of Westminster, and of his Works: With his Antient Map of Roman Britain; and the Itinerary Thereof* (1757). However, despite Stukeley's exacting and scrupulous methods, the revised map was later revealed to be based on bogus information culled from manuscripts written by Charles Bertram under the guise of Richard of Westminster (fig. 34).

Stukeley, however, was not the only author to be taken in by Bertram. Alexander Gordon, a native Scot, also incorporated the information from Bertram's forged manuscript into the map that prefaces his *Itinerarium Septentrionale: or, A Journey Thro' most of the Counties of Scotland, and Those in the North of England* (1726) (fig. 35). Like Stukeley, Gordon is principally interested in charting the locations of Roman buildings, forts, walls, and other structures. As he states in the preface, "I confess, I have not spar'd any Pains in tracing the Footsteps of the Romans, and in drawing and measuring all the Figures in the following Sheets from the Originals; having made a pretty laborious Progress through almost every Part of Scotland for Three Years successively."[27] His willingness to accept the findings of Bertram's forgery, however, suggests that his philoromanism perhaps compromised the integrity of his study. As Philip Ayres notes, despite his "pro-Caledonian bias," Gordon's appreciation for the virtues of Roman antiquity rivals that of Stukeley.[28] Despite the fact that Stukeley and Gordon's map was based on misinformation, conjecture, and speculation, they published it nevertheless in the belief that they were serving

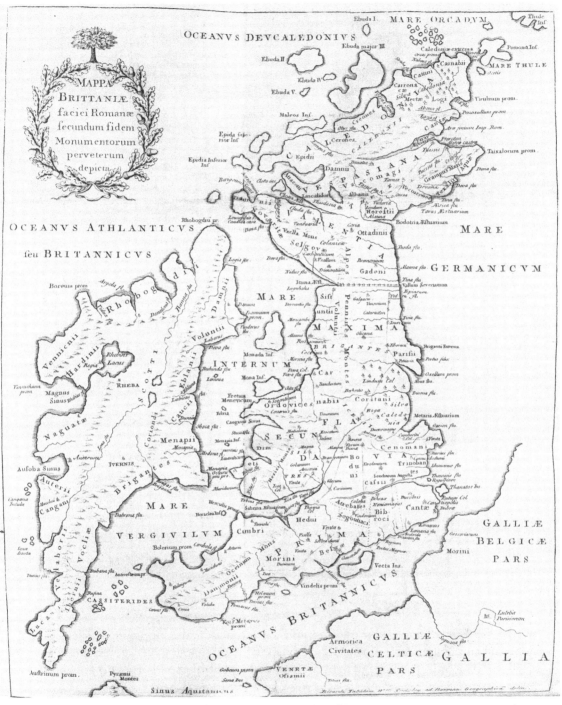

Figure 34. "Mappa Brittaniae faciei Romanae secundum fidem Monumentorum perveterum depicta," William Stukeley, 1757. (General Collection, Beinecke Rare Book and Manuscript Library, Yale University)

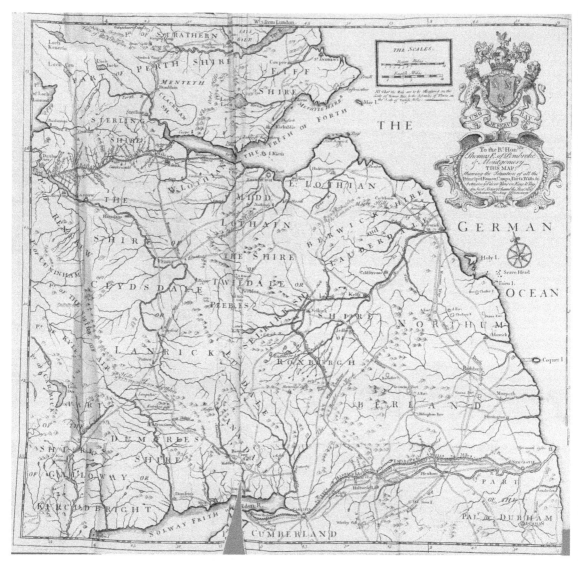

FIGURE 35. *Itinerarium Septentrionale: or, A Journey Thro' most of the Counties of Scotland, and Those in the North of England,* Alexander Gordon, 1726. (General Collection, Beinecke Rare Book and Manuscript Library, Yale University)

a higher, more noble purpose; in their estimation, the inevitable deficiencies and inaccuracies in the factual details of their topographies are permissible and understandable in light of the moral and ideological purpose that guides their inquiries.

John Horsley vigorously defends his own text, *Britannia Romana: or, the Roman Antiquities of Britain in Three Books* (1732), against a similar set of accusations:

What signifies that knowledge . . . which brings no real advantage to mankind? And what is it to anyone, whether the Roman walls pass'd this way or
that? or whether such a Roman inscription is to be read this way or another?
To this I would answer: There is that beauty and agreeableness in truth, even
supposing it to be merely speculative, as always affords on the discovery of it
real pleasure to a well turned-mind: and I will add, that it not only pleases,
but enriches and cultivates too. . . . There are a multitude of places in the
unknown parts of the world, whose very names we should be pleased to
know, though it is hard to say, what we should be better for this knowledge.[29]

Horsley makes the point that the location of Roman walls is important even
if that bit of knowledge is a matter of speculation rather than verifiable fact
and suggests that the value of antiquarian topography is not entirely based on
its fidelity to precise and accurate measurements but rather on whether or not
that knowledge accords with the truth. Paradoxically, while Horsley disparages
the latter in his preface, the ensuing text practically fetishizes the map as the
standard of objectivity and historical truth. His extensive use of maps depicting the geography of Roman Britain suggests someone who believes, contrary
to his previous statements, that they are not useless knowledge but rather the
standard by which historical truth should rightly be judged.

In book I of his text, for example, Horsley includes a series of ten maps
collectively entitled *A general map of the Roman walls in the north of England*,
with the first containing an overview of the entire area of his proposed topography and the subsequent maps providing more detailed views (fig. 36).
He later offers another series of maps, five in total, detailing Antoninus Pius's
wall in Scotland, all of which are accompanied with extensive and detailed
descriptions. The entirety of book III of this prodigious work is dedicated
specifically to the geography of Roman Britain, beginning with an essay on
Ptolemy's *Geography* accompanied by two illustrative maps, *A Corrected Map of
Britain according to Ptolemy, or Ptolemy's Britain Rectified* and *Britain according
to Ptolemy, taken from Mercator*. He then moves on to the familiar *Britannia
Romana, according to Antonine's Intinerary* and concludes with *Britannia Romana, according to the Notitia*, a map based on the Roman imperial document
the *Notitia Dignitatum*, as well as a reproduction of the *Peutinger Table*, which
is an itinerarium depicting the Roman road system in a three-quarters, or
bird's eye, view. Regarding this last item, Horsley compares its topography of
Roman Britain to that found in the *Antonine Intinerary* in order to highlight
their many discrepancies as well as document their similarities: "It would not
indeed have been amiss, if, in settling the stations of the of the Itinerary, I had
compared more exactly the numbers there with these in this table. I confess I
have not much light or benefit from the comparison, now that I have made it
with what diligence and accuracy I could; but perhaps an abler hand may strike
more light of it."[30] Horsley readily admits that these two maps often present

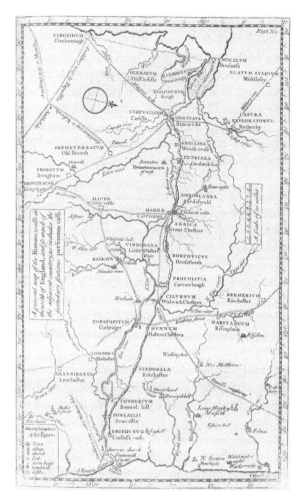

FIGURE 36. "A general map of the Roman walls in the north of England," John Horsley, 1732. (General Collection, Beinecke Rare Book and Manuscript Library, Yale University)

very different pictures of Britain, thus his inability to reconcile them with one another; however, despite the fact that he can draw no certain conclusions as to why these maps differ from one another or determine the source of their errors, his comparison nevertheless is conducted under the aegis of "diligence" and "accuracy" *as if* such an answer might be forthcoming, perhaps not from him but from some other antiquarian scholar.

Horsley's defense of speculative knowledge as useful and virtuous is, in this respect, not entirely antithetical to those topographies of modern-day Scotland. Rather, he shares their commitment to empirical rigor and cartographic accuracy in his recognition that ancient maps of Roman Britain are rife with errors and in his subsequent desire to correct and remediate those inconsistencies through the scrupulous collection and evaluation of any and all relevant evidence. In fact, Stukeley's and Horsley's emphasis on greater scientific rigor in the production, reproduction, and analysis of antiquarian maps and topographies only takes on increased urgency as we move into the latter half of the eighteenth century when the expanding market for such texts continues to foment further attacks against their perceived lack of veracity and authenticity. William Roy's *The Military Antiquities of the Romans in Britain* (1793) is perhaps one of the most detailed and rigorous of all the antiquarian topographies in this regard. Following the Jacobite uprising at Culloden in 1745, Roy served as the chief surveyor and mapmaker for the English Ordnance Survey from 1747 to1755, and his military surveys of Scotland afforded Roy's *Military Antiquities* with a degree of accuracy and legibility in his maps that was unprecedented. As Roy notes in the preface, "The study of Antiquity was but little the object of the young people employed in that service, yet it was not wholly neglected; many sketches of Roman works having been made in the ordinary course of other observations."[31] While carrying out his responsibilities as a military surveyor, Roy, a native Scotsman, continued to make sketches of Roman works and to plot their locations so that he could easily return to them in order to take more precise measurements and flesh out his analysis with more detail than his initial surveys afforded. However, as Yolande O'Donoghue notes, Roy's work was interrupted for nearly ten years when professional commitments forced him to leave Scotland for the south of England.[32] Undaunted, he resumed the project again in 1764 and began transforming his original, somewhat imperfect sketches into fully realized manuscript illustrations. The book was completed by 1773, though it wouldn't see publication until 1793, and Roy was shortly thereafter made a Fellow of the Society of Antiquaries in 1776.

As for the book itself, the *Military Antiquities* is broken into four sections that deal with, respectively, the military history of the Romans in Britain, the institution of the Roman militia and the layout of their camps, a description and analysis of the campaigns of Julius Agricola, and lastly, a reevaluation of the "ancient geography of North Britain," along with a detailed account of the writings of Richard of Cirencester, who was also the dubious subject of Stukeley's earlier work. For each section, Roy provides detailed sketches of ancient military roads, fortifications, camps, works, and battlefields, all of which are accompanied by extensive commentary. In addition to the sketches, the text includes numerous maps, including three large-scale maps depicting the whole of Scotland and Great Britain as they would have appeared during the time of the Roman conquest. The first plate, entitled *Mappa Britannae Septentrionalis Facei Romnae Secundum Fidem Monumentorum*, dramatizes this ancient view of Scotland by juxtaposing modern toponyms with their Latin equivalents and giving us a scale that enables readers to move easily between English and Roman measurements. Roy offers a similar act of translation later in his text by providing charts that give us columns of ancient place-names alongside their modern names as well as distances between places in both English and Roman miles.[33] Both the maps and charts thus seek to give us, like previous antiquarian cartographies, a modern version of ancient Scotland. That is, the methodologies and technologies employed to survey Scotland are quite modern, the product of military expediency in the wake of the Jacobite rebellion, yet those modern practices are placed in the service of rendering a more accurate and faithful picture of the ancient past. The result is a depiction of Scottish antiquity superimposed on top of the geography of eighteenth-century Great Britain in a way that suggests their simultaneity.

Given Roy's background in military surveying and cartography, it is no coincidence that his antiquarian investigations in Scotland would also center on military activity, however far removed in time. In his preface, Roy defends his desire to excavate the geography of Roman imperial conquest on just these grounds, implying that antiquarian studies of Scotland during this period can only rightfully be undertaken by someone with his degree of military training and knowledge:[34]

> Among those studies which some proportion at least of the speculative part of mankind are imperceptibly led into, for private amusement only, Antiquity is one which hath always commanded a considerable share of the attention such as have engaged it: each, according to his particular taste, inquiring into that favorite branch that pleases him most; and in this choice he seems generally to be directed by the relation which it bears to his ordinary employments in life. Hence it is that military men, especially those who have been much accustomed to observe and consider countries in the way of their professions . . . are naturally led to compare present things with past; and being thus insensibly carried back to former ages, they place themselves among the ancients, and do, as it were, converse with the people of those remote times.[35]

Given the fact that most histories centered on wars and armed conflict, Roy's antiquarian and military interests would seem to coincide naturally; however, he does recognize that that his *Military Antiquities*, while of little value to the practice of modern warfare, will provide for "the relief of the contemplative mind" and the "lubrications of his leisure hours."[36]

Roy's defense of his own work as "true" in both senses of the word resembles similar arguments constructed by Stukeley, Horsley, and others who actively embrace and participate in the cartographic and chorographic discourses of the Whig topographers yet who wish to differentiate themselves from the strictly economic motives behind their efforts, which they feel devalue and displace Scotland's past, including its Roman history, in favor of its present and future development. Roy's desire to separate his antiquarian pursuits from his employment as a military surveyor and cartographer thus seems a bit disingenuous in that he fails to recognize any similarity or connection between the two. Roy's penchant for mathematical and geometric precision certainly informs and shapes his antiquarian mapping of Scotland, giving it an unprecedented degree of authority, but he stops short of conflating the intent and purpose of his survey of Roman military antiquities with his military survey of Scotland, or his later work on the Ordnance Survey, the methods and details of which are outlined in a separate text, *An Account of the Trigonometrical Operation, Whereby the Distance between the Two Meridians of the Observatories of Greenwich and Paris Has Been Determined* (1790).

However, it is critical that *we* do not accede to Roy's questionable distinction and instead view maps intended to facilitate the armed pacification of the Highlands and maps whose purpose is to delineate the Roman conquest of Scotland as two sides, if you will, of eighteenth-century attitudes and responses to the unification of England and Scotland. As I have previously argued, antiquarian topographies of Roman Scotland must be read and interpreted in the same context as any other imperial cartography, whether military or economic in nature. While these maps certainly differ in focus and emphasis, each genre represents a figurative "occupation" of the land that provides an ideological justification and rationale for that occupation. The military and economic mappings of Scotland are, in this sense, more than merely the pragmatic instruments of conquest and colonial subjugation; as icon and symbol, they help to legitimate acts of imperial aggression by providing a homogeneous and rationalized view of the territory in question, one that is uniquely able to project the idea of an ordered and, above all, civilized space. Scotland is thus emptied of its otherness and transformed into a single indivisible nation. Antiquarian occupations of Scotland function in much the same manner, yet their shared belief in republican virtue and classical ideals puts them at odds with the more overtly imperial agenda of the Whig topographers and their economic maps. Hence, they choose to provide a counterimage that defines its utility not in terms of expropriation and incorporation but instead as a vehicle for moral contemplation and edification. Rather than an instrument for the carving up of territory and the delineation of property, the antiquarian topography of Scotland utilizes the map to collapse the temporal gap between the Roman period and modern Britain so as to make the point that Scotland is always already British territory. This truth is perhaps covered up by the detritus of history, but the antiquarian map, in a sense, peels back the layers to reveal what was essentially there all along, the remnants of a common and shared past.

## Geography, History, and Empire

Two years after his extensive tour of Scotland, Samuel Johnson's *A Journey to the Western Islands of Scotland* (1775) confronts us with a place that resembles, in many ways, those descriptions and images projected in both economic and antiquarian topographical writings, a number of which I have discussed in the previous section. Rather than favor one of these approaches to the geography of Scotland over the other, Johnson instead chooses to incorporate elements of

both in order to affirm the value of understanding the often complex relationship between ancient and modern Scotland, despite the general trend toward
separating and analyzing them within a single, discrete work. The inclusive
nature of Johnson's *Journey* thus represents something of an anomaly among
eighteenth-century topographical writings on Scotland in that it doesn't seem
to hew to the conventions of one genre or the other. However, Johnson's decision to examine both ancient and modern Scotland in a single work does not
contradict the underlying reality of an ever-widening gulf between topographical works that are specifically geared toward antiquarian studies and those that
take trade, commerce, and improvement as their primary focus. Rather, as I
will argue, Johnson uses his travels in Scotland as an opportunity to articulate
and dramatize this very tension and to address what he sees as the imbalances
and distortions that emerge when either perspective on the Scottish landscape,
whether historical or contemporary in nature, is uncoupled from the other.
For Johnson, to sever our consideration of the geography of ancient Scotland
from its modern counterpart allows for all manner of political and ideological
prejudices to corrupt and pervert what Johnson believes should be the proper
aim of any geographical inquiry, an objective and empirically verifiable picture
of the land itself. Not that such a task is so easy or readily achievable in his
estimation. While Johnson remains largely sympathetic to the purposes and
goals of antiquarian and improver alike, Johnson also reveals, quite intentionally, the many difficulties he has trying to reconcile these competing interests.
His advocacy for the modernization and economic development of Scotland
is often at odds with his admiration and reverence for its ancient character,
its history, manners, customs, architecture, and, perhaps most importantly, its
forms of domestic economy, and Johnson spends a considerable portion of the
*Journey* making his reader aware of that internal conflict, often in an overt and
demonstrative fashion. We see Johnson, in true antiquarian fashion, proffering
moral lessons and insights as he dolefully meditates on the ruins of Scotland's
past, but in the very next moment, he is extolling the modern conveniences
and amenities that trade with England has fortunately brought to an otherwise
primitive and savage people.

Johnson, it would seem, is hopelessly caught between Scotland's potential
futures and its possible pasts. Unable to reconcile or mediate these competing ideological demands, he can only affirm his commitments to progress and
improvement while simultaneously professing an abiding, somewhat romanti-
cized nostalgia for a past that is no longer available, if it ever truly was. Johnson's ambivalence, however, must also be seen as characteristic of the larger
split within eighteenth-century approaches to the mapping of Scotland and
topographical writing that I outlined previously. The *Journey* mirrors the very
same generic and ideological split between those eighteenth-century topographies of Scotland principally dedicated to matters of trade and commerce and
those invested in the study and analysis of Scottish antiquities, Roman Britain

most notably. This divide, as I have argued, is driven largely by the various tensions surrounding the integration of Scotland into the union and conflicts over territorial control and national identity following the Highland uprisings of 1715 and 1745. In response to these tumultuous events, antiquarian and economic topographers deployed a shared set of chorographic and cartographic methods and technologies in order to put forth their respective image of the nation with the purpose of defining Scotland's place within an integrated Great Britain. Johnson's *Journey* is no different in this respect. However, rather than exclusively participate within one tradition or either, his text remains firmly situated between both in its desire to address both economic and antiquarian matters, even though these agendas often appear to be at cross purposes. In this sense, the *Journey* comes to embody both traditions of mapping Scotland, as well as giving voice to their many contradictions and ironies.

While not quite as enthusiastic or rabid a proponent of growth as Defoe and other Whig topographers, Johnson frequently echoes his support for agrarian and market reforms in the *Journey*, as well as professing an ardent belief in the material benefits that economic progress afforded to otherwise "barbaric" nations. As Nicholas Hudson notes, Johnson was quite aware of "the liberating and civilizing impact of commerce on society."[37] Quoting Johnson's review of Soame Jenyns's *Free Inquiry into the Nature and Origin of Evil* (1757), Hudson shows that Johnson, far from unequivocally supporting the social hierarchies implicit in the Great Chain of Being, believed in the kind of social mobility found only in a commercial society. To think otherwise would, according to Johnson, contradict "the maxims of a commercial nation, which always suppose and promote a rotation of property, and offer every individual a chance of mending his condition by his diligence."[38] This kind of progressive ideology then extends itself to the *Journey* and Johnson's reflections on the evolution of Scotland after 1707: "Since they have known that their condition was capable of improvement, their progress in useful knowledge has been rapid and uniform. What remains to be done they will quickly do, and then wonder, like me, why that which was so necessary and so easy was so long delayed. But they must be for ever content to owe to the English that elegance and culture, which if they been vigilant and active, perhaps the English might have owed to them."[39] Johnson's imperial "Englishness" is certainly in evidence here as he reveals a deep appreciation for the impact trade and commerce with England has had on the material life of the Scots.[40] Even in those sections dealing with the remotest corners of the Highlands and Western Islands, Johnson manages to present the realities of daily life while still stressing the positive aspects of commercialization. He notes, for example, that the lack of commerce in these geographically isolated areas has led to gross disparities between nominal and real values such "that hardly any thing has a known or settled rate."[41] Johnson is critical of these fluctuations in price because they lead to dishonesty and deception on the part of merchants eager to fleece unsuspecting travelers, including

Johnson and Boswell. However, rather than view this situation as simply a moral failing on the part of the Scots, Johnson's critique implicitly makes the case for the establishment of a "common measure" of value between England and Scotland's respective economies and the creation of a shared commercial language in order to eliminate future misunderstandings and conflicts. While he finds this common measure wanting at present, Johnson nevertheless holds out hope that such a standard will soon come to pass. As much as Johnson believed that "life improves but by slow degrees," he still felt compelled to acknowledge that "there was perhaps never any change of national manners so quick, so great, and so general, as that which has operated in the Highlands, by the last conquest, and the subsequent laws."[42] Johnson is here referring to, of course, the defeat of Jacobite forces at Culloden in 1745, which was quickly followed by the demilitarization of the Highland clans and the introduction of laws to secure property rights, thus creating the conditions necessary for trade and commerce to flourish. Johnson openly welcomed these reforms to Scotland's juridical and governmental institutions because of their salutary effects on its economy.

The *Journey*, like Defoe's *Tour*, actively promotes the idea that Scotland is not only capable of improvement but that trade and commerce are the primary mechanisms by which Scotland will be transformed into a fully civilized and modern nation. Johnson remarks while touring Bamff: "As they approach to delicacy a nation is refined, as their conveniences are multiplied, a nation, at least a commercial nation, must be denominated wealthy."[43] However, despite pronouncements such as these, the *Journey* remains far from univocal or settled on the subjects of trade, commerce, and modernization. According to Hudson, Johnson believed that "the historical changes occurring in the Highlands and, at a later stage of development, in England and Lowland Scotland entailed social readjustments that were both irresistible and morally ambivalent."[44] While Johnson recognized the fact that modernization was dependent on Scotland's commercial expansion, he remained wary of the intended and unintended consequences of that expansion. As a result, Johnson often qualifies, if not contradicts outright, his pro-Union stance by including details that force his reader to appreciate the moral costs of gentrification. There are, of course, Johnson's lengthy digressions concerning the practice of rack-renting, the unfettered greed of many lairds, the displacement of tenants no longer able to pay higher rents, and the subsequent emigration of Scots to the colonies in pursuit of a better life, all of which suggest his painful awareness of the downsides of capitalist modernity as it insinuates itself throughout Scotland. In a discussion of rising ground rents and their impact on productivity, Johnson concludes that "universal plenty is to begin and end in universal misery. Hope and emulation will be utterly extinguished; and as all must obey the call of immediate necessity, nothing that requires extensive views, or provide for distant consequences, will ever be performed."[45] The natural abundance of the land is not realized in the form of capital to the tenant or the laborer but rather is siphoned off as profit by a landlord who cares little for the land's future productivity or the material benefits to the consumer. As a result, the tenant is reduced to labor merely in order to subsist, and consumers are denied the goods and services necessary for genuine and sustained economic improvement. It is a situation that Johnson believes will bankrupt the nation in the long run. While higher rents appear on the surface to be an indicator of progress, they are, in fact, the very means of Scotland's undoing, especially when coupled with the fact that many Scots would rather emigrate to the colonies than continue to exist under those harsh conditions. Johnson's apprehensions and misgivings regarding the effects of economic reform extend not only to the average laborer but also to those at the highest stations of Scottish society.

Johnson's commitment to improving Scotland's economy comes with a con-comitant understanding that, as Hudson puts it, "the increasing authority of wealth at the expense of rank" was "a necessary part of the modernization of society" and that this emergent form of authority and power comes with its abuses as well as its benefits.[46] As Deidre Lynch notes, Johnson feared that the "economic rationalization" following the uprising at Culloden would ul-timately "obliterate not only the distinction between the social ranks but also the idiosyncrasies that distinguished regions or national characters."[47] Martin Wechselblatt further argues that Johnson was critical of the highly fluid and variable nature of commercial values in Scotland (and England for that matter) because they ultimately debased and supplanted traditional moral and cultural values that Johnson thought should remain in place.[48] For example, Johnson expresses great admiration for the "kindness of consanguinity" and "reverence of patriarchal authority" he witnesses among the Highland clans, noting that "every duty, moral or political, was absorbed in affection and adherence to the chief."[49] However, he also recognizes that "to lose this spirit, is to lose what no small advantage will compensate."[50] One cannot but hear the note of lament, if not outright remorse, in Johnson's observation that the Highlanders "are now losing their distinction, and hastening to mingle with the general commu-nity."[51] The creation of common measures, common practices, and common institutions leads to the inevitable eradication of cultural differences, a fact that haunts Johnson throughout the *Journey*. Tellingly, after conveying his rev-erence for Scotland's patriarchal heritage, Johnson immediately asks "whether a great nation ought to be totally commercial?" His answer, not surprisingly, is a qualified no. Commercial interests are important to the nation and central to the progress of modernity, but other so-called modes of happiness, irre-ducible to the acquisition and consumption of goods and luxuries, must also find expression.

Johnson values, for example, the "true pastoral hospitality" he encounters in various domestic settings, often appearing astonished at the existence of civilized behavior under such hostile conditions.[52] While in Raasay, Johnson praises his hosts, Mr. Macleod and his family, for their generosity despite the barren and foreboding environment in which they live: "Such a feat of hospitality, amidst the wind and waters, fills the imagination with a delightful contrariety of images. Without is the rough ocean and the rocky land, the beating billows and the howling storm: within is plenty and elegance, beauty and gaiety, the song and the dance."[53] Johnson clearly admires this sort of altruistic exchange precisely because it does not accord with the kinds of relations found in a commercial society, such as England, which he finds less than charitable even under the best of circumstances. However, Johnson observes that perhaps the virtue of hospitality is gradually being upended by those who would seek to profit off unsuspecting English travelers. In the village of Auknasheals, an old woman provides Johnson and Boswell milk out of what he can only assume to be an authentic act of hospitality, and feeling an abiding sense of pity and compassion for her wretched living conditions, Johnson offers the old woman and other villagers bread, tobacco, and "a small handful of halfpence." Only later does Johnson discover from another Highland woman that the villagers were not, in fact, indigent at all and so less than deserving of he and Boswell's commiseration, prompting Johnson to comment, "Honesty is not greater where elegance is less."[54] Johnson comes to understand that the practice of hospitality is potentially undermined by the presence of the Englishman abroad who does not appreciate or understand its limits, including Johnson himself. Upon leaving the Hebrides, Johnson advises his reader that even though "more time would have given us a more distinct view . . . it was not proper to live too long upon hospitality, however liberally imparted."[55] Johnson never expounds further on the subject of proper versus improper behavior when receiving another's hospitality, only that he feels as if he has worn out his welcome and so must promptly take his leave.

Whether Johnson's decision is an expression of his sense of moral virtue, civic duty, or merely personal etiquette, the implication is that he must leave because he recognizes the proper limits of hospitality and understands that his remaining, like the old woman who falsely elicited his sympathy, threatens to transform a social good into an inauthentic and less-than-virtuous version of an otherwise venerable custom. As the practice of hospitality is being emptied of any meaning by native and tourist alike, it remains bound, like the martial spirit of the laird, to a vision of premodern Scotland that, for Johnson, is rapidly passing from view with the commercialization and industrialization of the nation. While he accepts the latter as inevitable, he nevertheless laments and mourns the passing of the former in the hopes of recuperating that vision in some fashion. Johnson's desire to articulate and dramatize this sense of loss is, I would suggest, directed at those topographical writers whose representations of Scotland only accentuate the positive, redeeming aspects of trade, commerce, and economic reform, while ignoring their negative implications, not only for Scotland itself but Great Britain as a whole. Johnson believes that true progress cannot be achieved by the often limited and limiting surveys, maps, and chorographies of the Whig topographers, whose ideological biases preclude what Johnson feels is the proper display of mourning and reverence for Scotland's arguably noble past. As expressions of empire, or imperial longing, they focus solely on that information that is relevant and necessary to the creation of a fully modern Scotland and, in the process, render a survey of the land that is divorced from a sense of the land's history and antiquity. For Johnson, however, questions of geography and history cannot and should not be separated from one another as doing so violates the classical order of knowledge in which both subjects are, in fact, a single, unified discipline. Those topographies and maps of Scotland that would only consider the nation's present and future circumstances do so at the expense of a more comprehensive and authentic representation of the nation, one that incorporates historical and antiquarian subjects rather than excluding them on the grounds that they are neither useful nor of value. Johnson's antiquarian pursuits must be seen then as a reaction to other modes of geographic representation for which the study of history is largely irrelevant and unnecessary.

Like many eighteenth-century antiquarian topographers, Johnson's anxieties about such a dramatic and irrevocable overturning of the old order precipitate his veneration of Scotland's past as a means of preserving something of its aura and character, as well as emphasizing its relevance to the identity of modern Britain. In contrast to those sections of the *Journey* that focus on Scotland's economic fortunes, Johnson devotes a significant portion of his text to assiduously documenting, describing, and analyzing those details of the Scottish landscape relevant to its ancient and feudal past: architectural ruins, both religious and secular, monuments and primitive artifacts, natural curiosities, local histories, customs, traditions, etymologies, place-names, family genealogies, and so forth. Johnson visits and comments on, for example, an ancient fort on the island of Inch Keith, a ruined cathedral at St. Andrews, and the remains of the monastery at Aberbrothick. He notes, on occasion, those vestiges of the Roman military conquest of Scotland as well as more pedestrian sites, such as duns, boroughs, caverns, and huts, all of which have fallen into disuse or decay over time. Johnson's turn toward antiquarian themes and topics in the *Journey* is, in part, a response to and critique of those surveyors, chorographers, and mapmakers who would, in the name of profits and progress, choose to marginalize or ignore altogether the ways in which Scotland's past remains a recalcitrant feature of its present landscape. Johnson thus effectively pits his investigation into Scotland's past against the Whig topographers' providential vision of a modernized, economically robust Scotland in order to qualify and contain the pernicious effects of that vision.

However, while Johnson shares many antiquarians' concerns and reservations about the overtly commercial intent and utilitarian nature of geographic representations of Scotland post-1707, it would be a mistake to place his *Jour-*

*ney* alongside the works of Robert Sibbald, William Stukeley, Alexander Gordon, John Horsley, or William Roy. Johnson is rightfully wary of the Whig topographers' claims on Scotland given the ideological and political biases inherent in their maps and chorographies, yet as many scholars have noted, Johnson finds antiquarian topographers no less suspect in this regard, regardless of their political affiliation.[56] I do not wish to rehash Johnson's vexed relationship to antiquarianism, save to reiterate the fact that Johnson's attitudes are certainly mixed, ranging from outright contempt to profound respect and admiration. As John Vance notes, "Whereas Johnson judged some of their activity useless and pedantic if not downright absurd, he approved of much of the antiquarians' work, enjoyed the friendship and respected the scholarship of many of them, and showed an interest himself in preserving and commenting on aspects of the past that the antiquarians held dear."[57] Johnson's career is marked by works that roundly satirize antiquarians and antiquarianism, such as *Marmor Norfolciense* (1739) and numerous essays in the *Rambler*.[58] However, he just as often praises their efforts in his unflinching belief that the study of antiquity is valuable and necessary for understanding and coping with the challenges of the present age. Vance goes on to argue that Johnson's ambivalence stems from the fact that, while he and the antiquarians may share the same artifacts, relics, and ruins as the objects of their respective historical inquiries, they often differ as to how those objects should be properly interpreted and understood. For Johnson, history is meant to illustrate and exemplify moral and ethical truths that are applicable to all ages; however, the allegorical function of history is too easily lost on those antiquarians whose obsessive attention to trivial minutiae and whose sheer delight in the act of "tracking down, preserving, and displaying relics of a bygone age" compromise the integrity of their studies.[59] Johnson was also a strident critic of the rampant speculation and high degree of incredulity found in many antiquarian works. Despite sharing ideological ground with antiquarian scholars and writers, Johnson nevertheless found much of their work seriously compromised by an overall lack of empirical rigor, both in terms of the geography and the history, and their tendency to offer conjecture where facts were wanting. Details deemed irrelevant or unnecessary to their particular branch of antiquarian studies would be excised in much the same fashion as those commercial topographers whom Johnson criticized for being too selective in what they did and did not choose to present. Johnson's steadfast belief that the study of antiquity only has value and meaning when pursued in a meticulous and thoughtful manner leads him, consequently, to criticize those antiquarians who are less than scrupulous in their methods or who fail to observe and absorb the lessons of the past.

As Johnson states in a letter to Hester Thrale, dated August 15, 1773, just prior to setting off on his journey, "There are indeed minute discriminations both of places and of manners, which perhaps are not unworthy of curiosity, but which a traveler seldom stays long enough to investigate and compare. The dull utterly neglect them, the acute see a little, and supply the rest by fancy and conjecture."[60] Johnson here rails at travelers who fail to properly observe and record differences of place and manner either because they are too "dull" to recognize them or because their sights remain too focused and narrow due to certain disciplinary and ideological constraints, which invites all manner of speculation in order to cover the gaps of their respective surveys. It is a problem that he directly addresses in his preface to Alexander MacBean's *A Dictionary of Ancient Geography* (1773), published the same year he embarked on his travels through Scotland. There, Johnson insists on the need for objective methods and standards when dealing with the historical geography of any nation or territory, and he calls for improvements to our knowledge of modern geography so that we may infer back to antiquity and fill in the gaps, as it were: "I have in some degree enlightened ancient by modern Geography, having given the situation of places from later observation. Names are often changing, but place is always the same, and to know it exactly is always of importance."[61] Johnson suggests that a lack of objective standards has led to significant gaps in our understanding of the geography of the ancient world. In response, he advocates for modern methods of surveying so that we may correct and amend that picture, as well as obtain a more accurate sense of the world at present.[62] Johnson's entreaty here signifies his commitment to antiquarian topographies that display due diligence to empirical methods and protocols, yet he is also is tacitly addressing those antiquarians who he feels exchange true historical understanding for pleasure, profit, or politics. As a result of their misapprehension of the nature and value of history, they engage in unwarranted acts of speculation and romantic exaggeration in order to satisfy their penchant for collecting the strange and the curious. Johnson was particularly critical of those antiquarians who distorted Scotland's history in order to legitimate its further economic and military subjugation. By projecting images of wild and fantastic landscape populated by a debased, savage people, some antiquarian scholars, often politically affiliated with Whig interests, were able to mobilize a particular conception of Scotland's past that dramatized the dire need for economic reform and thus, in Johnson's estimation, compromised the historical intent of their surveys.[63]

According to Thomas Curley, Johnson strongly objected to texts such as Kenneth Macaulay's *History of St. Kilda* (1764) and John Campbell's *Political Survey of Britain* (1774) because of their zeal for economic reform and improvement, which he believed blinded them to those aspects of Scottish society and culture that were rapidly disappearing in the rush toward modernization.[64] Martin Martin's *A Description of the Western Islands of Scotland* (1695) and Thomas Pennant's *A Tour in Scotland and Voyage to the Hebrides* (1772) do not fare much better in this respect. While their surveys of Scotland were influential on Johnson's *Journey* in terms of the range of subjects he covers, including his interest in feudal Scotland, Johnson clearly wishes to distinguish himself from either text due to their Whig affiliations. As Curley notes, "Martin had actually cared little about preserving the memory of the Highland past and even supported economic reforms for turning the Hebrides into a trading community."[65] In response, Johnson comments on Martin at key points throughout the *Journey*, suggesting that his desire to promote and improve his native Scotland compromises the accuracy and legitimacy of his work: "But he probably had not the knowledge of the world sufficient to qualify him for judging what would deserve or gain the attention of mankind. The mode of life which was familiar to himself, he did not suppose unknown to others, nor imagined that he could give pleasure by telling that of which it was, in his little country, impossible to be ignorant."[66] His Whiggish sensibilities ultimately override his commitment to empirical protocols, a favorite theme of Dr. Johnson, and thus compromise his integrity as a surveyor and an author. Johnson finds Pennant somewhat more reliable than Martin, calling him "the best traveler I ever read" and defending the accuracy of his narration at various points throughout the *Journey*, as well as in Boswell's *Journal of a Tour to the Hebrides*. However, despite his occasional praise, Johnson still manages to hurl a few barbs at him. A supporter of economic reform, Pennant openly attacked the clan system in the Highlands as a hindrance to true progress, which prompted Johnson to respond, "He's a *Whig*, Sir, a *sad dog*."[67] On a number of occasions in the *Journey*, Johnson echoes his remarks about Martin in his assessment of Pennant's work, suggesting that he is equally prone to error due to his Whig sympathies. "We were at Col under the protection of the young laird, without any of the distresses, which Mr. Pennant, in a fit of simple credulity, seems to think almost worthy of an elegy by Ossian."[68] Pennant's desire to emphasize the "distresses" of Highland existence is here likened to MacPhereson's bogus epic, *Ossian*, in order to underscore both texts' overly romantic and, hence, fictitious nature. It is a charge he levels at Pennant and each of these authors because he sensed that their political ideology ultimately interfered with their judgment and ability to produce an accurate picture of Scotland as it was undergoing dramatic transformation. For Johnson, their competence and integrity as geographers were compromised by their overarching desire to implement Whig economic reforms, and the biases in their presentation would inevitably lead them to overlook or eliminate those elements of the land and its people that Johnson believed were worthy of recording.

While a strident critic of both improver and antiquarian alike, Johnson himself had to confront and reconcile this conundrum to some extent as he embarked on his own survey of Scotland or risk the same accusations of bias and distortion he would otherwise hurl at others. Johnson's desire to liberate himself from that paradox thus leads him to write the *Journey* against commercial and antiquarian topographies that, for him, promote England's imperial ambitions at the expense of a more authentic and integrated understanding of Scotland's past and present circumstances, as well as its future within a unified

Great Britain. While the creation of an objective and thoroughly rationalized picture of Scotland's geography is still a worthy goal in Johnson's estimation, the Whig topographers' relentless focus on the economic, political, and cultural assimilation of Scotland into the Union represents yet another instance of power masquerading as knowledge. Their putatively objective maps and chorographies, for Johnson, fail to draw any distinction between power and knowledge, or naïvely assume their difference, and thus constitute a form of territorial appropriation that, despite seeming innocuous on the surface, is no less destructive in its effects. The imperatives of profit and personal gain enable eighteenth-century commercial topographers of Scotland to map and describe its geography with an ever greater precision, yet despite their greater acceptance of and adherence to empirical methods (or because of it), they ignore certain features of the landscape that Johnson believed were deserving of note and further analysis. Whatever truths may or may not be gleaned from their findings remain largely unrecognized and unheralded in deference to charting modern-day Scotland for the purposes of trade and economic expansion ever northward. For Johnson, the study of geography should properly be seen as a vital and integral part of one's moral education and subsequent development into an enlightened "citizen of the world" rather than as an instrument of power and imperial aggression. As many critics have pointed out, Johnson vigorously opposed acts of imperial violence and aggression, preferring to view the world in terms of a universalizing humanism that extended to all peoples regardless of national origin, race, religion, or ethnicity.[69] Even though he failed to apply this enlightenment principle in an even and just manner, his reflections on Scotland being no exception, Johnson still remained an astute critic of England's imperial pretensions, especially with regard to the American colonies. Few scholars, however, have noted the extent to which Johnson's critique of imperialism, economic, military, or otherwise, is bound up with his unique understanding of the ways in which geographic knowledge too often serves the ends of empire.

In his introduction to *The World Display'd,* Johnson gives us a condensed history of European exploration and discovery, but he does so in order to make the point that advances in navigation and hydrography, since the time of Noah, have always been driven by the imperatives of territorial and commercial conquest. He cites the Romans' many contributions to expanding our geographical knowledge of the world and its oceans but notes that they "thought only on war and conquest" and that "their ships seem to have been of little other use than to transport soldiers."[70] He later discusses Portugal and the invaluable work of Prince Henry the Navigator in the "discovery" of Africa, only to later criticize his role, and that of the Portuguese, in the establishment of the slave trade there: "What mankind has lost and gained by the genius of this prince, it would be long to compare, and very difficult to estimate. Much knowledge has been acquired, and much cruelty been committed."[71] It is a critique he then extends to all European nations eager to "gratify avarice, and extend corruption; to arrogate dominion without right, and practice cruelty without right." Johnson speculates that had Prince Henry's designs "slept in his bosom," both oppressed and oppressor would today be much happier, but since Henry's influence continues to make itself felt, Johnson hopes that "out of so much evil some good may sometimes be produced." Johnson's ambivalence concerning the effects of imperial conquest pits the relative merits of an improved knowledge of the world's geography against the intentions and motivations of those seeking that knowledge. At times, Johnson appears to celebrate and applaud those who further the cause of geographic inquiry, whether explorer, tourist, surveyor, or antiquarian, yet on other occasions, he displays grave reservations about the depredations and outright violence made possible by that knowledge.

Johnson makes these connections between imperial conquest and geography explicit in his 1756 review of Lewis Evans's *Analysis of a General Map of the Middle British Colonies in America*. The map in question was published originally in 1749 but was republished in 1755 by Benjamin Franklin as a part of volume 1 of Evans's *Geographical, Historical, Political, Philosophical, and Mechanical Essays*.[72] The folded-in map, based on Evans's own survey of the Ohio valley, served as a useful and necessary instrument for any military action against French interests in the region and as a symbolic projection of the future boundaries of the British colonies.[73] In his review, Johnson offers mixed praise, commending the map's empirical rigor but also stating that it was hardly exemplary. More importantly, Johnson takes direct aim at the political and ideological motivations underpinning Evans's map, forcefully arguing against the westward expansion of the colonies and the subsequent need for émigrés from Great Britain, both of which he feels will only foment revolution abroad and depopulation at home. Johnson's critique, however, is not limited only to Evans and his supporters but is also leveled at those who would utilize maps and geographic knowledge in general for the purposes of war and conquest: "The last war between the Russians and Turks made geographers acquainted with the situation and extent of many countries little known before, in the north of Europe, and the war now kindled in America, has incited us to survey and delineate the immense wastes of the western continent by stronger motives than mere science or curiosity could ever have supplied, and enabled the imagination to wander over the lakes and mountains of that region, which many learned men have marked as the seat destined by Providence for the fifth empire."[74] Stated more succinctly, Johnson concludes, "Power is the constant and unavoidable consequence of learning."[75] Johnson clearly understands the extent to which the imperatives of capitalist accumulation have contributed to the growth of geography as a discipline and, conversely, the ways in which geography authorizes and legitimates conquest and empire. It is thus hard for Johnson to divorce the production of knowledge entirely from self-interest and power; the representation of the land is always somehow bound up with its possession in some form or another.

Johnson, quite understandably, finds antiquarian topographers more ame-nable in this regard. Unlike their commercial counterparts, they are able to assert the social, intellectual, and moral worth of geographic knowledge over and above the acquisition of property or territory and the conquest of foreign nations. However, as I noted previously, this humanistic ideal turns out to be something of a canard. William Roy's investments in military and antiquarian cartography are equally informed by an imperial ideology that seeks to or-der and control Scotland's past as much as its present landscape. Roy's maps, charts, and chorographies of Roman Scotland represent a form of spatial and temporal occupation that belie his overt claims of the moral and intellectual worth of geographic knowledge and the vicarious pleasure one receives from reading such antiquarian fare. This same note of justification and legitimation may also be seen in the collective works of Robert Sibbald, William Stuckeley, Alexander Gordon, and John Horsley, all of whom seek to frame and appro-priate Scottish antiquity in ways that are deeply political in their intent and ultimate effect on British national identity post-1707. While each professes a disinterested and humanistic view of geography in keeping with the classical tradition, the truth is that they are no different than those commercial topog-raphers who would justify their various efforts on the grounds of mere utility. Power remains a motive force behind and an abiding consequence of the pro-duction of geographic knowledge, antiquarian surveys and maps of eighteenth-century Scotland being no exception. The generic and ideological split between topographies of ancient and modern Scotland thus masks what Johnson sees as a fundamental continuity underlying their collective endeavors: the politici-zation of geography and history, which can only encourage and hasten further the process of disciplinary specialization and the division of knowledge itself.

Rather than improving our understanding of Scotland and its diverse spaces, the compartmentalization of geographic knowledge invariably serves the parti-san interests of commercial and antiquarian topographers and their particular claims on its territory; each is invested in translating Scotland's geography into terms and figures that make the exercise of power at once more efficient and more persuasive to their respective audiences, yet for Johnson, the value of their work remains suspect due to narrow disciplinary concerns that would sever ancient from modern Scotland and, more generally, geography from history. Johnson lamented what he saw as the increasing disconnect between geography and history in topographical works dedicated to either the study of ancient or modern Scotland, with the former co-opted by a misguided and often fallacious antiquarianism and the latter the province of those concerned solely with matters of trade, commerce, and economic development in general. The *Journey*, as Nicholas Hudson argues, provided Johnson an opportunity to redress this imbalance: "It was precisely this combination of progressive 'modern' nationalism with a romantic nostalgia for the past which is dramatized in the travel accounts of both Johnson and Boswell. This nationalism is significant because it constitutes the mortar of a quintessentially *British* nationalism blending (in sometimes unstable quantities) nostalgia for the past with pride in progress and modernity."[76] Hudson points here to the "unstable" blending of two seemingly contradictory impulses in the *Journey*, one toward a romantic veneration for the nation's past and the other toward a more progressive sense of its present and future circumstances. However, this formulation is not so much a contradiction for Johnson as it is a response to standard eighteenth-century representations of Scotland that, for him, separate geography from history and history from geography in their desire to forge an imperial Britain. Rather than recapitulate the modalities of commercial and antiquarian topographies, Johnson attempts to bring these two seemingly antithetical geographic discourses into some sort of formal coherence by attending to a site that is frequently overlooked or ignored in their various surveys, although one that is no less relevant or worthy of dissection in his estimation.

As I will argue in the remainder of this chapter, Johnson places the home against this existing corpus of maps, surveys, and chorographies of Scotland in order to posit a vision of a unified Great Britain that is not the product of conquest and dominion, military, commercial, or otherwise, but rather one that finds common ground in the minute details and particularities of domestic life. That is, the home, as both a material place and an abstract ideal, unifies and binds England and Scotland into a single nation, or homeland as it were, whose identity is rooted in the universal and universalizing experience of domestic labor and familial community. Johnson's attempt to reconceptualize the Union following the violent uprisings of 1715 and 1745 thus leads him to effectively replace the *arcana imperii* with the *arcana domus*, or the secrets of the state with the secrets of the home, in the hopes of establishing a more equitable, less tendentious relationship between center and periphery. Johnson unearths the covert intentions behind state and public efforts to construct a body of geographic knowledge that invariably serves their own partisan interests, yet this sustained critique of prior commercial and antiquarian topographies of Scotland cannot be fully understood unless we also consider Johnson's reciprocal desire to shed some light upon the mysteries of domestic life that have, in his estimation, gone largely unrecognized and unarticulated. As the empirical traveler abroad, Johnson assiduously documents and comments on the virtues and failings of the various homes he encounters, as well as noting the very real differences between domestic life in Scotland and England, which in the case of the Highlands and Western Islands are vast indeed. While Johnson's sympathies, by and large, remain with his native England when making such judgments, he nevertheless reconciles those differences by constructing a history in which the Scottish home comes to mark the evolution and progress of civilization itself, from its primitive shelters and habitations to the solid and dignified forts and castles of the feudal period and, lastly, to the genteel, refined environs of the modern home. Johnson's secret history of domesticity enables us to witness and chart the gradual yet lengthy process by which a nation, such as England, moves inexorably from barbarity to civility. More importantly, Johnson constructs such a progressive history in order to suggest that the home is the principle engine driving those changes over time. The creation of a truly civil society, in Johnson's estimation, is something that cannot be imposed on Scotland through the exercise of force or sheer will; rather, it must and will emerge as a matter of course from within the modalities of domestic life. The home thus offers Johnson a point of continuity that unites the ancient and modern worlds and so brings geography and history together in a meaningful way that will redefine the scope and boundaries of both disciplines going forward.

## HOME IMPROVEMENT

Johnson's decision to provide a detailed survey of domestic life in the *Journey* represents something of a departure from most commercial and antiquarian topographies of Scotland, which tend to consider subjects such as the home and domesticity in general to be of little intellectual or pragmatic value, as their interests tend toward public rather than private matters. Boswell's frequent objections to and apologies for Johnson's proclivity to discourse about trivial items, such as windows, eating utensils, linen cloth, and pudding, among others, reveal a set of attitudes and assumptions regarding the domestic that are typical of eighteenth-century topographies of Scotland. As Boswell famously quips at one point in their journey, "To apply his great mind to minute particulars, is wrong."[77] Even when such topics are broached, which is a rarity, home life is mostly given a cursory treatment; descriptions are brief, and few salient details are provided, save those that might be curious and surprising for English readers unfamiliar with the various forms of domestic economy in Scotland. Martin appears to show little interest in the workings of the Scottish home apart from noting its inhabitants' extraordinary resiliency in the face of otherwise harsh conditions and, of course, their generous and hospitable nature toward strangers such as himself. He does manage to offer odd tidbits and scraps of information regarding a variety domestic customs and habits, such as the preservation of solan geese in ashes, the making of beds from heath because they are "effectual for drying superfluous humours" and "strengthening the nerves," and the inculcation of poesy and song in the youth at an early age.[78] However, despite the overall positive tenor of Martin's descriptions, there is little sense of cohesion or continuity here. Like the entirety of his *A Description of the Western Islands of Scotland* (1695), domesticity is reduced to a catalog of engaging facts and observations rather than forming the philosophical basis for his travels and the subsequent narration of that journey. Martin does not suggest to his reader that the home is, in any way, a privileged or crucial site within the national landscape or a unique window into the character of its people as Johnson does; it is simply one place among many of either equal or greater importance.

Kenneth Macaulay's *History of the Island of St. Kilda* (1764), by contrast, delivers a bit more in the way of context and explanation than Martin for the current state of the Scottish home; however, what little time he does spend discussing domestic matters is mostly negative in tone and intent. He paints, for example, a rather squalid picture of the homes on St. Kilda, only to lay the blame for their inferior construction squarely on the island's inhabitants: "It will be readily expected that a race of men and women, bred in St. Kilda, must be a very slovenly generation, and every way inelegant.—I confess it is impossible to defend them from this imputation.—Their method of preparing a fort of manure, to them indeed of vast use, proves that they are very indelicate."[79] Macaulay views these homes made from turf and manure as inferior to the arguably sturdier and nobler stone habitations that were built generations, if not centuries, earlier, suggesting an overall decline in the quality of domestic life on St. Kilda: "It is plain that those who laid them (the stones) together, understood the rules of masonry much better than the *St. Kildians* of this age, and they must have been undoubtedly men of greater power."[80] Thomas Pennant, likewise, places the eighteenth-century Scottish home, especially those in the Highlands and Western Islands, within a larger history of domestic decline and decay, from the venerable castles, forts, and piles of ancient and feudal Scotland to the wretched huts, duns, and cottages that dot its current landscape. He describes the homes on the isle of Columba as "very mean, thatched with straw of bere pulled up by the roots, and bound tight on the roof with ropes made of heath."[81] Pennant does note that "some of the houses that lie a little beyond the rest seem to have been better constructed than the others, and to have been the mansions of the inhabitants when the place was in a flourishing state, but at present are in a very ruinous condition." For Pennant, the typical Scottish home, despite some redeeming qualities, is a place where poverty, indolence, and privation are most visible and most felt. His purpose, as well as that of Macaulay, in fabricating this brief history of domestic degradation is to substantiate and reinforce the notion that Scotland is a nation in decline and so is in need of further economic development and improvement to alleviate the systemic problems that continually crop up in the course of his travels. That is, both Pennant and Macaulay accentuate and exploit the vast differences between domestic life in Scotland and England in part to confirm well-engrained stereotypes already familiar to and accepted by their more refined, urbane readership while, in the same breath, eliciting their support and sympathy for economic reforms that they are convinced will ultimately benefit the entire nation. Implicit in their respective histories of domestic decline and devolution is the profound belief that current trends may be reversed and domestic life in Scotland ultimately remade in the image of its English neighbors. It is a belief that Johnson shares to some extent, although his conclusions as to how such a transformation may effectively be achieved differ sharply.

Johnson, as I have argued previously, remains largely sympathetic to the improving gaze of authors such as Macaulay and Pennant, despite his misgivings regarding their work, and like them, he is not reticent to discourse about the substandard living conditions, meager resources, and overall lack of amenities and luxuries when the opportunity presents itself. Certainly for the Englishman on tour, and a Londoner at that, many of the habitations Johnson and Boswell encounter leave much to be desired, and Johnson can't help but reflect and ruminate on the gross disparities between domestic life in Scotland and England. For example, in his *Journal of a Tour to the Hebrides*, Boswell recounts he and Johnson entering a hut near the castle at Col, which was inhabited by a poor family. The hut is filled with smoke due to a lack of windows or any proper ventilation, a common problem in this kind of structure, thus prompting Johnson to pronounce upon exiting, "Et hoc secundum sententiam philosophorum est esse beautus," or translated, "And this is what the philosophers call happiness." It is a statement clearly delivered with a good deal of sarcasm. Boswell responds that the "philosophers, when they placed happiness in a cottage, supposed cleanliness and no smoke," to which Johnson replies, "Sir, they did not think about either."[82] Johnson notes that the philosophers got it wrong because they ignore the actual living conditions in such places and instead choose to romanticize the primitive cottage as a place of happiness and sanctuary. In his desire to restore a sense of balance to these representations of Scotland, Johnson vigilantly reminds his reader that Scotland is inferior to England in most respects, especially with regard to their degenerate standards of domesticity. This applies not only to the rustic cottage but also to wealthier homes that can well afford modern conveniences such as windows. Despite their incorporation into the structure of the house, Johnson observes that Scots rarely open the window for the purposes of ventilation, mostly because they are difficult to move due to poor craftsmanship and a general lack of willingness to remedy the problem.[83] Johnson's criticism is so harsh, in fact, that Boswell offers an apology to his fellow Scots in his *Journal*, stating that Johnson overgeneralizes about matters that are, in essence, trivial and insignificant. Johnson's acerbic and brutally honest assessments of domestic life in Scotland thus mirror those of Macaulay and Pennant to some extent. As an English subject traveling through a land that, while formally incorporated into a unified Britain, still remains *terra incognita* in many respects, Johnson's survey of Scotland's domestic spaces cannot help but reflect on the many differences, economic, cultural, religious, and otherwise, that continue to divide the nation internally.

However, unlike many of his contemporaries, Boswell included, Johnson does not focus exclusively on those differences, or needlessly exaggerate them in order to engage and fascinate his reader. Rather, the home represents a site of unanimity and continuity, a common place if you will, that promises some degree of mediation and reconciliation between England and Scotland and the differences that would otherwise separate them, hence the amount of time and energy Johnson devotes to the subject in the *Journey*. Johnson's anthropological preoccupation with the domestic lives of both Scotland's Highland clans and lowland gentry is the logical extension of his belief that the nation's character is not revealed through "illustrious actions, or elegant enjoyments," but rather is best represented in the steady flow of "daily duties" and "petty pleasures," understood generally as the common life. As Johnson declares near the outset of his travels, "The great mass of nations is neither rich nor gay: they whose aggregate constitutes the people, are found in the streets, and the villages, in the shops and farms; and from them collectively considered, must the measure of general prosperity be taken."[84] The *Journey* thus includes a wealth of information regarding the varieties of domestic economy Johnson and Boswell encounter along the way. This information may include subjects such as the division of labor in the home, the patriarchal structure of authority, modes of subsistence, sleeping and eating arrangements, diet and methods of cooking, familial customs and rituals, and so forth. Johnson also demonstrates a keen interest in the architecture and physical structure of the home itself, the materials from which it is made, the technologies required for the purposes of building and maintenance, its relationship to the surrounding environment, and perhaps most importantly, the home's history and subsequent development. For Johnson, "Edifices, either standing or ruined, are the chief records of an illiterate people,"[85] and so he leaves himself ample opportunity to explore various primitive shelters, duns, and huts, located chiefly in the Highlands and Western Islands, as well as the more refined and civilized estates of Scotland's nobility and landed gentry. Johnson thus elevates the quotidian to a subject worthy of scholarly dissection and examination, even though, by his own admission, such topics may "take away something from the dignity of writing, and therefore are never communicated but with hesitation, and a little fear of abasement and contempt."[86] These reservations aside, Johnson nevertheless holds fast to the general maxim that the "true state of every nation is the state of common life," which then serves as one of the *Journey*'s guiding principles.[87]

The details of domestic, or private, life are worth surveying and recording for Johnson because they provide a window into the manners, habits, and customs of a people or nation, as well as help us to better understand the complexities of the human condition. As Howard Weinbrot argues, Johnson deploys the "domestic metaphor" in many of his works, fictional and otherwise, in order to assert that the home, properly understood in its more expansive sense as the Latin *domus*, should be viewed as a figure for the world itself.[88] In *Rambler* no. 161, for example, Johnson translates a maxim from Juvenal, "A single house will show what is done or suffered in the world," thus placing home and world in a metonymic relationship that is underwritten by the idea of common and universal humanity.[89] The home represents a microcosm that mirrors and distills all the possible varieties of experience available to each individual regardless of place, and so to survey the home, whether in Scotland or elsewhere, makes the entire world legible and comprehensible in a manner that is concrete and substantial. Robert Mayhew describes Johnson's general approach here as "anti-geographical" in that he qualifies and negates geographic differences in the belief that one's identity, or character, is formed irrespective of its particular place or locality: "Johnson's attack on the possibility that the environment regulated the mental and moral powers of mankind was patterned as a negative use of geographical information: looking across the globe, the moralist and Christian would find that the differences imposed by space alone did not alter the dilemmas of living a good and responsible life."[90] Johnson levels geographic difference so that he may foreground an immutable human nature that stands apart from and resists local, regional, and national forms of identification. The antigeographical principle underlying Johnson's humanistic approach to travel and travel writing transcends those boundaries while at the same time remaining absolutely local and specific with regard to the places in which his universal subject moves and operates, the minutiae and routines of domestic life being no exception.

It is an idea we also see expressed by Johnson in his letter to Hester Thrale, composed at the outset of his journey to Scotland: "One town, one country is very like another. Civilized nations have the same customs, and barbarous nations have the same nature."[91] There is a uniformity to the world and all of its inhabitants such that the only meaningful distinctions to be made, as Johnson implies, are those concerning their relative place on the historical continuum from barbarity to civility. The *Journey* then seeks to confirm and validate this theoretical premise in an experiential and methodical fashion, reasoning from observed facts rather than merely assuming their veracity or fabricating them outright, a dubious talent Johnson ascribes to many armchair philosophers and hacks who rarely if ever leave the polite confines of their homes in England.[92] The details he relates are objectively determined and empirically verifiable and so more meaningful for Johnson because they are not the product of a wayward, overzealous imagination marred by "antiquarian credulity, or patriotick vanity."[93] The *Journey* was unique in this respect, according to Thomas Curley. Johnson's text combined "the humanistic studies of early grand touring and the scientific principles of contemporary exploration" as a corrective to those maps and chorographies of Scotland that favored one approach at the expense of the other.[94] Mayhew concludes, along with Curley, that the *Journey* represents Johnson's attempt to reconcile his own brand of humanist inquiry with empirical methods and protocols such that "physical and human geography are seamlessly linked."[95] The home, I would add, is pivotal to achieving this balance between Johnson's commitment to empirical rigor and his reciprocal desire to fashion a text more akin to Bunyan's progress, one whose primary purpose is to provide moral instruction and guidance to the reader. Johnson's scrupulous attention to the minute details of domestic life in the *Journey* thus provides him a unique opportunity to expound upon general truths relevant to a nation shaped and defined by the fundamental universality of domestic experience.

The gross disparities in the quality and tenor of domestic life cannot, as result, be assessed in either absolute or overtly negative terms, but rather they must be viewed within the context of a general history of civilized development in which the nation naturally evolves, at varying and uneven rates, from a state of barbarity to one of civility. That is, Johnson assumes the home as the locus of a shared national identity whose common ancestry has its roots in the civilizing effects of domestic labor and activity. As Johnson himself states in his dedication to Thomas Percy's *Reliques of Ancient English Poetry* (1765), "No active or comprehensive mind can forbear some attention to the reliques of antiquity: It is prompted by natural curiosity to survey the progress of life and manners, and to inquire by what gradations barbarity was civilized, grossness refined, and ignorance instructed."[96] However, rather than limit his scope to only the "reliques" and ruins of antiquity, Johnson broadens his survey to include a history of the Scottish home and its place within that larger narrative of national progress and improvement. Martin Wechselblatt, for one, points out that Johnson, alongside Adam Smith, David Hume, and other historians of the period, embraced a stadial theory of civilizations in which "emergent societies depart from a rudimentary level of hunting and gathering, pass through pastoral and agricultural phases, to finally arrive at commercial activity, the stage at which trade makes possible an intellectual intercourse that results in the flowering of the liberal arts."[97] Johnson applies this four-stage schema not only to his understanding of the primitive origins and subsequent history of Scotland but to England as well, which is no longer seen as altogether different from Scotland but simply at a later stage in its development. Nicholas Hudson argues, along similar lines, that Johnson considered "the historical evolution of Scotland" and "the history of England" to be in fact the same history: "What Johnson believed he witnessed in the Highlands was not the imperial extension of 'English' manners over a foreign people. . . . Rather, Johnson thought that the Highlanders were merely emerging from a 'barbarous' to a 'civilized' state that represented the common and ideal destiny of all humanity."[98] For Johnson to travel through Scotland is, in this respect, to step back in time, as it were, and survey an earlier epoch in the life of the nation. Geographic difference is thus collapsed only to be replaced by the temporal divisions of Johnson's progressive theory of civilization, which helps to explain as well as legitimate the changes occurring in Scotland, and the Highlands in particular. Johnson, as Hudson suggests, does not view these changes within an imperial context but rather as the natural product of human evolution and the irrepressible forces of modernity to which both Scotland and England are subject.

Johnson's archeology of the home thus seeks to excavate and examine the history of the nation in order to reveal its foundations in the modalities of domestic life and, more importantly, to make the point that domesticity continues to inform and shape British national identity even into the present age. For example, while visiting Slanes Castle, near Aberdeen, Johnson takes the opportunity to explore a local natural wonder, the Buller of Buchan, "which no man can see with indifference, who has either sense of danger or delight in rarity."[99] It is a place of rare sublimity in Johnson's estimation with its steep rock walls, gloomy interior, and a "dark gulf of water" that flows in and out through an arch carved out by the sea located at the bottom of the cavity. As Johnson peers both downward into the buller from an opening at the top and upward from its watery bottom, he is initially filled with feelings of confinement and dread, especially at the prospect of falling on the rocks below or being drowned, yet such feelings soon give way to a more rational and contemplative mindset, eager not just to experience the place but also understand its history and purpose. We learn, for instance, that the buller and its many cavities served as a gathering place for groups of women during the summer and also as a storehouse for smugglers and pirates. Boswell also mentions in his account that, according their host, Mr. Boyd, people dined in the caves on occasion. Whether this is true at the present, Johnson does not offer comment, preferring instead to speculate on the cave's antiquity. Johnson notes, "It is hardly to be doubted but the pirates of ancient times often used them as magazines of arms, or repositories of plunder." He further adds that, given its natural fortifications and defenses, the buller perhaps functioned as a shelter from storms or as a retreat from pursuing enemies for Scotland's ancient mariners.[100] Either possibility seems a reasonable conjecture to Johnson, though he offers little other evidence or support for his views. He does, however, conclude his ruminations on the buller with a telling gesture to the "elegance" and "grandeur" of their reception at Slanes Castle, whose grounds were "neither uncultivated nor unfruitful" but "still all arable."[101] He remarks that there are no flocks or herds there either, but the land, he seems to suggest, could easily sustain such activity were there sufficient desire and incentive.

The juxtaposition of the cave and the castle here is not merely a fact of geographic proximity but rather is a strategic device Johnson deploys throughout the *Journey*. By placing the primitive shelter of the buller against the more elegant and modern accommodations of Slanes Castle, Johnson is able to offer a narrative of Scotland's progress and civilization in which the figure of the home becomes both a symbol of and motive force behind that change over time. The home signifies, for Johnson, as a space where Scotland's transformation can most readily be seen, hence his desire to document and describe homes in all their types and varieties, including very primitive shelters such as the buller. We again see the traces of this secret history of domesticity in Johnson's assessment of the various forms of home, both primitive and modern, he encounters

while in the Hebrides. Johnson, for example, organizes his discussion of the
Hebridean home into the general categories of house and hut, with the house
serving as the more civilized mode of domestic life and the hut, the ruder and
less cultivated: "The habitations of men in the Hebrides may be distinguished
into huts and houses. By a house, I mean a building with one story over the
other; by a hut, a dwelling with only one floor. The laird, who formerly lived in
a castle, now lives in a house; sometimes sufficiently neat, but seldom very spacious or splendid."[102] The laird, the tacksmen, and the ministers, as the most
prominent and influential figures in the community, tend to occupy houses
according to Johnson, yet even these are wanting. They tend to be overly small
and often overcrowded with provisions and other sundry items and, in Johnson's estimation, are not especially clean, although he is aware that, from the
perspective of his hosts, they are believed to be quite decent and habitable.
In comparison are the huts, which vary in quality from "murky dens, to commodious dwellings."[103] Johnson again surveys the architecture and building
materials used to fashion these huts, the more advanced of which utilize stone
walls, mortar, glass windows, and boarded floors, while the meaner ones tend
to resemble the aforementioned hut at Col: dirt floors, thatched walls and roof,
few or no windows for ventilation, and a lack of adequate furnishings. In a brief
relation about his unplanned stay in one such hut, Johnson notes that his sleeping accommodations contained "an elegant bed of Indian cotton, spread with
fine sheets," a fact that both surprises and delights him, yet this feeling is short
lived when his feet sink into the muddy floor beneath his bed, apparently a frequent occurrence following a long, soaking rain.[104] Houses, he points out, are
able to avoid such problems, given their more modern construction, although
they too can be highly variable in their overall appearance and character.

More important here is Johnson's brief observation that, in former times,
the laird resided in a castle but now lives in a house. While he offers no direct
comment on the laird's change of habitation, I would argue that this passage
should be read in a manner similar to his experiences at Slanes Castle. In either instance, Johnson places the relative merits of a more primitive form of
habitation, a hut and cave respectively, against the figure of the castle, which
represents a later stage in the development of the Scottish people, although
one that is passing if not already moribund. At Dunvegan, for example, they
arrive at the home of Lady Macleod who, as Johnson observes, "had lived many
years in England" and "was newly come hither with her son and four daughters,
who knew all the arts of southern elegance, and all the modes of English economy."[105] The household thus displays a considerable degree of assimilation in
its conformity to English conventions and standards of taste, a development
that Johnson looks upon favorably. The house, however, has not entirely lost
all traces of its antiquity. As Johnson notes, the house, which is "built upon the
rock, and looks upon the water," is "partly old and partly modern," meaning that
it is a curious amalgamation of architectural forms and designs drawn from the

nation's feudal past as well as the present age. Johnson uses the occasion to provide further context in order that we understand just how the house embodies and preserves that larger history of civilized growth and development: "[The house] forms two sides of a small square: on the third side is the skeleton of a castle of unknown antiquity, supposed to have been a Norwegian fortress, when the Danes were masters of the islands. It is so nearly entire, that it might have been made habitable, were there not an ominous tradition in the family, that the owner shall not long outlive the reparation. The grandfather of the present laird, in defiance of prediction, began the work, but desisted in a little time, and applied his money to worse uses."[106] Johnson goes on to explain how fortresses and castles are specific to a time when wars, either with rival clans or some outside invader, were more prevalent and more frequent, and so requiring structures, such as the abandoned fortress, that could adequately withstand such an attack. The "disorderly state of insular neighbourhood," as Johnson characterizes this period of time in Scotland's history, required a mode of habitation that could meet and satisfy domestic needs and wants while at the same time providing protection and defense against armed conflict, and the fortress at Dunvegan evokes, in rather dramatic fashion, this violent and turbulent period, which Johnson assures us has long since passed. In its place, we now find the significantly more genteel and civilized home of Lady Macleod and her family, whose canny interpolation of English manners and customs marks the telos of this particular history or, at the very least, a later stage of national development in which the need to prepare for and wage war has given way to more private and domestic concerns.

To be sure, Johnson displays great veneration and admiration for the ancient fortress, and he laments the fact that the laird's family has chosen not to put any more money toward its future improvement, as well as their foolish adherence to superstition and nonsensical traditions that keep them from doing so. However, his nostalgia for the ancient castle should in no way obscure his fundamental belief that a modern nation is defined by the extent to which its domestic arts and practices have been cultivated and improved over time, as opposed to its martial skills. In Boswell's version of these same events, he mentions a dispute with Lady Macleod over the possibility of her building a new home on a farm just five miles from the castle. Boswell argues against such a move, insisting that "the seat of the family should always be on the rock of Dunvegan," a point with which Johnson wholeheartedly agrees, although he advises her to proceed with her plans to build a secondary, or "jointure," house which is a common practice, he insists, among the "great families of England."[107] Johnson proves himself sympathetic to Lady Macleod's need for a garden and land able to provide sustenance for her and her family, as well as a certain measure of comfort and enjoyment. Boswell, however, will not hear of such compromise and boldly asserts that, were he the laird, he would never leave his ancestral estate, preferring the noble profile of the castle perched on the rocky outcrop to Lady Macleod's more pastoral and domestic landscape. Johnson appears to confirm Boswell's "resolute feudal enthusiasm" in his response that "an ancient family residence ought to be a primary object," but rather than entirely dismiss the seriousness of Lady Macleod's arguments, he proposes that "when the family is again in opulence, something may done by art" to make the castle a more hospitable and convenient place to live.[108] Again, Johnson strives to restore some sense of balance between Boswell's and Lady Macleod's respective ideas of what does and what does not constitute a proper home for a laird, yet in this instance, rather than propose a secondary residence, Johnson argues that the castle can be, with time and money, domesticated and so retain its ancient character while still fulfilling its duties as a modern home, one more in keeping with the style and manner of those in England.

Domesticity, as a progressive and even revolutionary ideal, thus emerges as a sign of Scotland's future remediation and potential assimilation into a unified Britain. Johnson articulates a more genteel vision of empire in which the modern home serves as the universal embodiment of a virtuous and civilized domesticity whose codes of conduct and habits of mind Scotland must somehow internalize and reproduce, or at least approximate, if they are ever to fully and truly assimilate into the national body. As Johnson is keen to point out on a number of occasions, this sense of identification and affiliation with the nation requires a reciprocal breaking away from patterns of domesticity that have traditionally structured Scottish society, most notably, the clan system found in the Highlands and Western Islands. For example, at Lochbuy, home to a "true Highland laird, rough and haughty, and tenacious with his dignity," Johnson takes an equally dim view of the ancient castle there, which he comments, in a somewhat critical tone, was a product of "mere necessity . . . built only for safety, with little regard to convenience, and with none to elegance or pleasure."[109] As long as the laird could protect his family from enemies and other hostile forces, the castle was a more than sufficient habitation, but as Johnson concludes, "that they are not large nor splendid is no wonder" given the scarcity of resources and labor required to construct a more stately and noble edifice. His opinion of the modern home the laird has built near the castle, however, is considerably more favorable: "Lochbuy has, like other insular chieftans, quitted the castle that sheltered his ancestors, and lives near it, in a mansion not very spacious or splendid. I have seen no houses in the islands much to be envied for their convenience or magnificence, yet they bear testimony to the progress of the arts and civility, as they shew that rapine and surprise are no longer dreaded, and are much more commodious than then ancient fortresses."[110] Despite the less than satisfactory conditions he finds in the laird's mansion, Johnson nevertheless views it as a decided improvement over the castle, whose presence can only underscore the relative modernity of the home that has, for the better, been erected next to it. Johnson thus situates the laird's home within a larger history of domestic progress and improvement that will, in time, bring

Scotland and England into a more complementary and reciprocal relationship with one another.

Johnson reserves similar comments for the changes found at Boswell's ancestral home at Auchinleck. He praises Lord Auchinleck's efforts "to make improvements in his patrimony," such as planting trees on the estate's fertile grounds, even though he is "not wholly at leisure for domestick business or pleasure" given his responsibilities as "one of the Judges of Scotland."[111] And like Lochbuy and Lady Macleod, he has even managed to build a "house of hewn stone, very stately, and durable" in close proximity to the ruined castle of his ancestors, as well as a "very agreeable and commodious summerhouse" not too far from the house. As before, Johnson finds these improvements admirable and necessary, leading him to conclude, "Such opportunities of variety it is judicious not to neglect."[112] Johnson does remark at one point that he was "less delighted with the elegance of the modern mansion than with the sullen dignity of the old castle," the ruins of which he then goes on to describe in some detail; however, I would suggest that his somewhat nostalgic comment here does not so much contradict his overall positive assessments of Lord Auchinleck's estate, but rather it needs to be read and interpreted in light of those passages in which Johnson attempts to strike a delicate balance between the kind of romantic patriotism evinced by Boswell and the more progressive, domestic sensibility advocated by Lady Macleod.[113] In the *Journal*, Boswell objects to the changes he discovers upon returning to his ancestral home and laments the fact that material from an ancient chapel on the estate was used subsequently to build a house that had once served as the family's primary residence "till my father erected that 'elegant modern mansion,' of which Dr. Johnson speaks so handsomely."[114] Johnson, as Boswell notes, lauds these improvements even as he displays an abiding appreciation for the ruins of the old castle, whose dignity, in Johnson's terms, only emerges against the backdrop of domestic improvement and the continued modernization of Scotland. That is, the castle signifies, for Johnson, the marker of a particularly violent and conflicted stage of civilization that has since given way to a period in which the demands and concerns of the modern home have become tantamount. Hence, Johnson's nostalgia for ancient and feudal Scotland, a point emphasized by many scholars and critics, is revealed to be, in fact, a means of domesticating the past rather than championing its alterity.

Johnson continually pits the virtues of the modern home against the more primitive and retrograde structures of Scotland's past in order to demonstrate the extent to which its inhabitants have already begun to assimilate themselves to English domestic values and practices, which is the inexorable and inevitable telos of this particular history. Johnson wishes to assure his reader that Scotland has begun to integrate itself into the Union in a meaningful and productive way and, more importantly, that this progress in national manners and character is most evident in its emergent forms and modes of domesticity.

Johnson's interest in constructing a history of domesticity, in this sense, is to assert the relevance and importance of the home in the subsequent development and modernization of Scotland. However, Johnson's survey of the various forms and modes of domesticity in Scotland is a means of addressing not only its future place within a unified Britain but also that of England as well. While in Raasay, for example, Johnson describes the laird's house as being of a "neat modern fabrick," despite the fact that access to the house is difficult, given that the steps are made of roughly hewn stone.[115] Once inside, Johnson finds great "civility, elegance, and plenty" and a "general air of festivity," complete with music and dancing for the evening's entertainment, which he admits is somewhat surprising given its remoteness from the traditional "mansions of pleasure" found in England and London more specifically.[116] Nevertheless, Johnson finds the two comparable in many ways, leading him to conclude, "More gentleness of manners, or a more pleasing appearance of domestick society, is not found in the most polished countries."[117] Johnson here suggests that domestic life in Scotland is at least equal to, if not better than, that found in more refined and civilized nations, such as England, thus negating the differences that geography and physical distance have otherwise imposed on the development of Scotland. Johnson draws a similarly positive assessment of the Scottish home while traveling through Lough Ness. The first Highland hut Johnson and Boswell encounter, as we learn, is made entirely from loose stones arranged in a somewhat circular fashion and situated in a manner so as to avoid the destructive effects of wind and water. The entire structure is capped off by a series of rafters and covered by a thatched roof made from heath, which is then secured to the walls by rope made from the same material, and a small hole is made in the roof in order to provide some light and allow smoke to vent but still protect those inside as well as the dirt floor. Johnson notes that the hut is typical for "one of the nations of this opulent and powerful island"; however, he then draws a favorable comparison between the huts he observes in the Highlands to the noble palaces with which he is already familiar: "Huts however are not more uniform than palaces; and this which we were inspecting was very far from one of the meanest, for it was divided into several apartments; and its inhabitants possessed such property as a pastoral poet might exalt into riches."[118] By placing the hut and the palace on somewhat equal footing here, Johnson is able to reveal the extent of his admiration for the domestic lifestyle of the Highland family, their hospitality and resourcefulness most importantly.

Johnson's relativistic assessment of domestic life in Scotland enables him to bring the cottage and the palace into a metaphorical relationship with one another and so dispense with the kinds of prejudiced judgments that he believes too often color and distort public perceptions of Scotland, however untrue. In *Rambler* no. 168, Johnson deploys the very same analogy in an attempt to explain how the meaning of a given word is determined by the context in which it is uttered and the particular disposition of its hearer: "No word is naturally or intrinsically meaner than another; our opinion therefore of words, as of other things arbitrarily and capriciously established, depends wholly upon accident and custom. The cottager thinks those apartments splendid and spacious, which an inhabitant of palaces will despise for their inelegance; and to him who has passed most of his hours with the delicate and polite, many expressions will seem sordid, which another equally acute, may hear without offense."[119] The meanings and associations assigned to the cottage and the palace respectively are revealed here to be nothing more than arbitrary in nature; hence the differences that would separate the two are neither fixed nor absolute but rather are equally arbitrary in nature. As a result of this insight, Johnson is able to expose those differences as the inevitable product of the flaws and biases inherent to our perceptions of Scotland and, in turn, assert the underlying continuity between the cottage and the palace, or any form of domestic habitation for that matter. Later in his travels, Johnson returns to this comparison between the relatively primitive homes found throughout much of Scotland and the opulent palaces of the so-called civilized world. On the island of Inch Kenneth, Johnson offers the following description of the cottage of Sir Allan: "We all walked together to the mansion, where we found one cottage for Sir Allan, and I think two more for the domesticks and the offices. We entered, and wanted little that palaces afford. Our room was neatly floored, and well lighted; and our dinner, which was dressed in one of the other huts, was plentiful and delicate."[120] Johnson informs his reader that Sir Allan "lives not only with plenty, but with elegance, having conveyed to his cottage a collection of books, and what else is necessary to make his hours pleasant." The cottage on Inch Kenneth is not merely a place of survival and subsistence but rather one of leisure and education as well as religious devotion and "domestick worship," a practice upon which Johnson looks quite favorably.

The juxtaposition of Sir Allan's cottage with the unspecified image of a palace allows Johnson to extol the virtues of domestic life on Inch Kenneth, which in no way suffers in comparison with the arguably more venerable homes associated with the courts of England and Europe. In fact, it is, in some respects, superior because free from the social and political entanglements that necessarily accompany public life and the kind of absolute power and authority that the palace is intended to symbolize here. In *Rambler* no. 20, for instance, Johnson offers the following analogy between the man who rises "by common understanding steadily and honestly applied" and the man who is given to affectation and pretension in the hopes of improving his public reputation: "The state of the possessor of humble virtues, to the affecter of great excellencies, is that of a small cottage of stone, to a palace raised with ice by the Empress of Russia; it was for a time splendid and luminous, but the first sunshine melted it into nothing."[121] The architectural metaphor highlights the familiar distinction in Johnson between the substantiality of common experience and the corresponding insubstantial and ephemeral nature of public life.[122] The ice palace is

associated here with the ostentatious trappings of imperial power and authority, which are perhaps beautiful and dazzling at first glance, but beneath the
"light" of reasoned inquiry, are revealed to be little more than a cunning fiction.
The cottage, on the other hand, is given the weight and substance of stone,
lending a degree of permanence and meaningfulness to common, domestic experience. Johnson's domestic allegory thus serves to break down the differences
between Scotland and England by suggesting that the home, regardless of its
particular geography, offers a critical moral supplement to the deleterious and
dissipating effects of the public sphere and the social and political institutions
on which it rests. In this sense, Johnson's investment in domesticity is revealed
to be a useful and productive heterotopia for addressing a set of moral problems and social ills that are relevant not only to present-day Scotland but also
to his native England.

We see this narrative played out in *Idler* no. 63 as Johnson illustrates the
various grades and qualities of domestic habitation found at each stage of civilized development, from "rudeness to convenience, from convenience to elegance" and, finally, "from elegance to nicety."[123] He begins with the savage who,
due to necessity, "shelters himself in the hollow rock, and learns to dig a cave
where there was none before."[124] Over time, the savage moves outward from
the primitive shelter to open pastures where "he forms a thicket for himself,
by planting stakes at proper distances, and laying branches one to another,"
and then eventually succeeds in the building of a house, which is continually
improved and refined "till ease in time is advanced to pleasure." Once released
from "the importunities of natural want," the house is subjected to the formal rules of architecture and design, which raise it to a state of elegance and,
eventually, luxury. It is this last transition that pricks Johnson's sense of moral
outrage as domestic improvement devolves into "gilt cornices, inlaid floors, and
petty ornaments, which shew rather the wealth than the taste of the possessor."[125] Johnson's comment, or criticism rather, is directed at the excesses that
he believes have, within the course of the last century, begun to debauch and
corrupt English society, thus drawing a somewhat ominous conclusion to a
history characterized chiefly by incremental progress and improvement. The
English home, in this last stage of civilized development, is emptied of its moral
and aesthetic worth by its wealthy proprietors, who have "improved" it beyond
all good taste in a misguided attempt to cultivate status and credit among their
neighbors and the public at large. The home thus serves as a synecdoche for a
nation that has somehow deviated from the path its forebearers, whose simpler,
more primitive forms of domestic habitation were, in Johnson's estimation,
devoid of the vanity and pride that necessarily come with the rapid accumulation of wealth and power and the increased consumption of luxury items.
Johnson's progressive modernism reaches its limit here as the home is no longer
viewed as the bastion of civility, decorum, and modesty it once was, at least in
Johnson's eyes.

The *Journey* offers a literal variant of this narrative in its various representations of Scotland's primitive homes, which for Johnson embody and preserve the unadulterated virtues of domesticity, including the practice of hospitality and civility toward others, ingenuity and self-reliance under adverse conditions, respect for and adherence to patriarchal authority, and an abiding sense of affection and sympathy for one's family members. Johnson's moral landscape figures the home as a privileged space in which behaviors are shaped, the mind educated, and the soul invigorated, but just as importantly, it is where these values are preserved and reproduced from one generation to the next and protected from the onslaughts and indignities of public life, which are an inevitable and unavoidable reality. A place such as the Highlands of Scotland does not present such conflicts, however, because there is little to no real distinction to be drawn between the domestic and public spheres; they are, in essence, the same, which, I would argue, is the source of its value and meaning for Johnson. Rather than place the private and public spheres at cross-purposes, as he does in many of his periodical writings on domestic matters, Johnson instead projects an idealized and somewhat reductive image of Scotland in which the private and public interest are virtually one and the same, home as nation, nation as home. In so doing, Johnson not only offers what he believes to be an important historical insight into the patriarchal origins of all mankind, England included, but he posits, as well, a model for a unified Britain in which the cares and concerns of the domestic sphere have a greater role to play in the shaping of the national character. That is, Johnson's conflation of home and nation in his analysis of primitive societies, such as in the Highlands, is as much an image of the future as it is a condition of the past. The home becomes, in this sense, the heterotopic locus for a social critique that is directed primarily at his English audiences; the virtues of domesticity represent an alternative moral and ethical system to the excesses and appetites endemic to the public sphere, and so they provide a check on those behaviors Johnson deemed socially disruptive and harmful as well as a means for reforming them when necessary.

Johnson's turn to the domestic metaphor, as Howard Weinbrot argues, enables him to interject questions of private moral conduct into public affairs and to promote the virtues of domestic life and their salutary effects on an otherwise corrupt and licentious nation. As Johnson himself states in *Rambler* no. 68, "To be happy at home is the ultimate result of all ambition, the end to which every enterprise and labour tends, and of which every desire prompts the prosecution."[126] Johnson concludes that true happiness may only be found at home, yet his pronouncement also betrays an anxiety that ambition, labor, and desire may not in fact result in domestic felicity but rather tend toward other, less savory ends. Eithne Henson makes a similar point in her argument that, for Johnson, "the domestic sphere, marriage and family life, rather than the traditional world of male action, is where the human being becomes most profoundly her or his full moral self."[127] While the responsibilities and duties of the domestic sphere are largely relegated to women during the eighteenth century, Johnson represents something of a departure from those norms in his presentation of a more balanced and egalitarian conception of the home and its role in shaping one's true moral character, irrespective of gender, wealth, or social standing.[128] The routine cares and concerns of the domestic sphere are democratizing forces that level, if not eliminate outright, the customary differences and discriminations that structure and define public life and, in Johnson's estimation, obscure the true condition of humanity. As Johnson states in *Idler* no. 51, "The petty cares and petty duties are the same in every station to every understanding, and every hour brings some occasion in which we all sink to the common level. We are all naked till we are dressed, and hungry till we are fed; and the general's triumph, and sage's disputation, end, like the humble labours of the smith or plowman, in a dinner or a sleep."[129] This premise also informs Johnson's reservations regarding biographies that place undue emphasis on heroic or dramatic public deeds while ignoring the private and domestic lives of their subjects. In *Rambler* no. 60, for example, Johnson roundly criticizes historians and biographers who "rarely afford any other account than might be collected from publick papers."[130] Rather, a proper biography should, according to Johnson, "lead the thoughts into domestick privacies, and display the minute details of daily life, where exterior appendages are cast aside, and men excel each other only by prudence and by virtue."[131] The suggestion here is that biographers inundate the reader with many diverting and engaging facts that are perhaps relevant to understanding their subjects' public selves, but they are merely "appendages" that draw our attention away from the kinds of instruction and wisdom afforded by a more thorough vetting of their domestic lives.

Johnson thus valorizes the home, as the literal and abstract locus of common life, precisely because he wished to provide a marked contrast to the worldly ethos that he believed attended public life as a matter of course; it is a site that resists, to some extent, the social and cultural forces that would otherwise tear it apart. Nicholas Hudson argues that Johnson believed that it is "the virtue exercised in the humble circumstances of common life, not the splendid displays of the rich, that constitutes the real and durable fabric of social well being."[132] Like many authors of the period, Johnson accords to the home an authenticity and legitimacy that is simply unavailable within the realm of politics and the public sphere in general. As Hudson notes, "Johnson's moral writings have remained resistant to political analysis because he so determinedly distanced moral, religious, and aesthetic discourse from the language of politics, dwelling consistently on the realm of private life. As he wrote in *Rambler* no. 68, 'It is, indeed, at home that every man must be known by those who make a just estimate of his virtue or felicity.' It was in private that people, men and women equally, seem to become merely 'human' rather than actors on a public stage."[133] The authentic self only emerges for Johnson within a domestic realm stripped of the inducements to fame and publicity. As James N. D. Bush observes, "The idea of the domestic functions . . . as a metaphor for the 'attainable good' in human affairs . . . available to any persons wise enough to discipline their ambitions of transcendent greatness and the 'excessive curiosity' that is the intellectual analogue of such ambition."[134] Home takes on a moral cast that is central to Johnson's trenchant critique of power and the arrogance, pride, and vanity that too often flow from its unchecked and unlimited exercise. The home is, in this sense, not so much a disengaged and isolated refuge from the world, such as Cowper's pastoral retreats.[135] Rather, it is a place *in* the world that affords us a unique vantage point on the public sphere and its inability to foster and inculcate the moral self. Johnson's deployment of the home as a rhetorical strategy thus enables him to establish an authorial voice that is putatively free from the prejudices and biases endemic to public life while still providing him the opportunity to address its failures and shortcomings in a skeptical and critical fashion. For Johnson, the home, as a heterotopic space, is simultaneously a part of, yet separate from, the public sphere; it shapes and influences the public sphere in a positive fashion without necessarily being absorbed by it or corrupted by its vices and inherently profligate nature. Whether in England or Scotland, this idealized notion of domesticity serves as an instrument of moral and social reform that will ultimately benefit the entire nation and its efforts to forge a lasting union.

Like Bunyan's neighborhood, Behn's use of the scene, Swift's country of the mind, and Defoe's conception of the market, the home represents a space that is conceived against the map, at once continuous with the nation of which it properly is a part yet, at the same time, completely other with respect to those public social, religious, and political bodies that Johnson believes pose a threat to private virtue and domestic felicity in one way or another. Viewed in this context, Johnson's decision to make the home and domesticity a central feature of his survey of Scotland is, in part, a response to the conundrum posed by those commercial and antiquarian topographers for whom geographic knowledge is always an extension of an imperial vision informed by the will to power. Johnson asserts, on the one hand, that the details and facts of domestic life in the *Journey* are neither trivial in nature nor a degraded form of knowledge, as Boswell often charges. Rather, he must counter such false assumptions and elevate the domestic to a subject worthy of examination and dissection by showing that the private home and the public world beyond its immediate borders are intimately connected to one another, both materially and philosophically; to invest oneself in the observation and recording of domestic knowledge is to understand the world in a manner that is more profound and substantive than any existing map or topographical work on the subject of Scotland. However, Johnson's turn to the domestic as a critical feature of his survey is also a means of liberating himself from the instrumentalization of geographic knowledge that he finds all too common in eighteenth-century commercial and antiquarian topographies of Scotland. As a space that is, in Johnson's estimation, separate from and antagonistic toward the public interest, the home represents the possibility of constructing a geography that is disinterested and impartial with respect to the value and purpose of the knowledge generated by such a survey. Its inclusion in the *Journey* does not ostensibly further the commercial and economic imperatives of the fiscal-military state or its desire to acquire territory in pursuit of those goals, nor does it provide any political or ideological justification for the unilateral conquest and expropriation of a foreign nation or its people. Johnson thus differentiates the acquisition and analysis of domestic knowledge from the production of geographic knowledge for the purposes of the state or mere public consumption and use in order to legitimate his own survey of Scotland as a model of reasoned geographic inquiry, one that eschews the dictates and allures of power in favor of a more enlightened view of the world and the varieties of place it contains.

# The Neighborhood Revisited

I BEGAN THIS book with the proposal that the neighborhood functions as a site that resists and opposes the cartographic imperatives of the state and its desire, after 1660, to eradicate any and all forms of religious dissent. For Bunyan, the neighborhood comes to embody and articulate that sense of conflict between the community of the godly and the repressive governments of Charles II and James II, purposively marking off a space that is different from, or other to, the state, while at the time offering an alternative way of imagining the national landscape, one that is not the product of political arithmetic and cartographic thinking, but rather is informed by scriptural truths and the affective practices of "heart-religion." This particular understanding of neighborhood as an alternative or dissenting space, however, fades somewhat as we move into the eighteenth century and nonconformity finds greater political, social, and cultural acceptance and, in turn, a genuine and secure sense of place within Great Britain. Rather than disappear after the Restoration period, Bunyan's concept of neighborhood in fact takes on newfound significance with that acceptance and begins to shape and define the national geography in ways that Bunyan could only imagine. Unmoored from its origins in seventeenth-century radical Protestant theology, the neighborhood loses, to some extent, its sense of being a religious or spiritual space and instead comes to function principally as a secularized means of classifying, mapping, and differentiating the local, although in a manner unlike its ecclesiastical and governmental equivalents: the parish, the county, the shire, the hundred, the ward, and so forth. The neighborhood, in this regard, is no longer a space that is in opposition to or outside of the national interest; rather, it is one that is seen as pivotal to the realization of authentic national community.

During the eighteenth century, the neighborhood becomes a widely recognized term signifying an area or district whose identity is predicated on the specific racial, ethnic, linguistic, religious, or class makeup of its inhabitants.[1] This more modern conception of neighborhood emerges in part from the spatial logic of agrarian and industrial capitalism: the increased concentration of capital in major urban centers and the subsequent expansion of the labor pool in those centers engendered a proliferation of new and varied urban spaces, including the subdivision of the neighborhood, in response to those geographic and demographic pressures. The term was also used to describe local forms of rural community whose collective identity remained to some degree stable and homogenous during this period of rapid and drastic change. Over time, the neighborhood, in both its rural and urban contexts, was assimilated into the British vernacular landscape such that it became an indispensable part of the way in which subjects and citizens processed and assembled their world, as well as their sense of nation. This secularized version of the neighborhood, however, does not represent a complete break from Bunyan and his fragmented vision of local community; rather, it shares some distinct affinities with its seventeenth-century predecessor. The modern understanding of neighborhood has its origins in the dissenting movements and ideologies of seventeenth-century Britain and, consequently, traces of that history are readily visible in later articulations of neighborhood that emphasize the importance of neighborly feeling and conduct, as well as the virtues of secular, as opposed to religious, community. That is, the idea of neighborhood continues to carry with it a set of meanings and associations already evident in the works of Bunyan and other nonconformist theologians who believed, as did Edmund Burke, that feeling and sympathy play a critical role in the formation of social bonds and the creation of authentic community. Rather than a site of resistance to the nation and a world that was seen as hostile to their cares and concerns, the neighborhood is transformed into a place where we can freely participate in and adopt forms of national identification that are no longer antagonistic toward but rather in concert with local customs, interests, and history.

The neighborhood is thus reimagined and reconceived by many eighteenth-century social theorists: the Earl of Shaftesbury, Adam Ferguson, Samuel Johnson, and Edmund Burke, most notably, as a space that is integral to the formation what Deidre Lynch refers to as "local nationhood."[2] As Lynch argues, national consciousness begins, for these authors, with local attachments forged through sympathetic identification and long-held customary practices, and they each share in the belief that England is "more successful than other countries at soliciting patriot love precisely because it makes feelings fostered in such parochial spaces 'the first link in the series' that leads to an attachment to the state."[3] The nation is, according to this line of thought, the natural and inevitable extension of neighborly sentiments and local sympathies that have been fostered and sustained within these smaller, organic communities. For Adam Ferguson, it is the "little district" that best inculcates and promotes the virtues of fellow feeling and a more intimate, private understanding of the social body, yet this turn, or return, to the local is not viewed as antithetical to the process of national identification but rather a strategic step toward its realization.[4] We see this idea also articulated by Edmund Burke in his *Reflections on the Revolution in France* (1790), where he admonishes the reader "to be attached to the subdivision, to love the little platoon we belong to in society."[5] As many have noted, Burkean nationalism is fundamentally local in its orientation and deeply romantic in its ideology. The neighborhood is understood by Burke as an ideal model for national relations and as a synecdoche for a distinctly English brand of community that reaches consensus not through the use of reason or the intellect but rather through the display of feeling, sympathy, and care for one's fellow citizens, regardless of whether they live next door or hundreds of miles away. Where Bunyan's neighborhood was provincial and insular in nature, Burke's neighborhood is a place that successfully mediates the local and the national, the private and the public, in a balanced and harmonious fashion and, in so doing, binds the nation together into a single, cohesive body. Burke's articulation of neighborhood differs from Bunyan's in this respect; however, both possess a common understanding of the ways in which social bonds are forged and maintained, at least on the local level. More importantly, Burke also appears to share Bunyan's criticisms and reservations regarding the state and its promotion of a rationalized, cartographically derived image of the national body. Burke's sentimental revaluation of local community as central to a distinctly British national identity is in part a response to those, like the French revolutionaries, who would view and represent their nation strictly in terms of the map, a development Burke argues cannot and should not manifest itself with respect to his native England.

Among Burke's chief objections to the proposed realignment of the local and general legislatures following the French Revolution was the geometrical and, in his estimation, entirely bogus method of carving up France into divisions and subdivisions of governance. The architects of the new commonwealth planned to fashion eighty-three "regularly square" *departments*, and these would, in turn, be broken down into *communes*, which would themselves be divided further into *cantons*. Each respective unit was to adhere strictly to the principle of "square measurement" in an effort to reorganize the very basis of civil representation and, consequently, redistribute power along supposedly more equitable lines. For Burke, however, this new tripartite structure and its attendant geography was a fiction that ignored the many discrepancies between territory and polity. The imposition of such a grid on the ancient and customary territorial boundaries that marked France prior to the revolution was, at best, aesthetically uninspired, requiring "nothing more than an accurate land surveyor, with his chain, sight, and theodolite."[6] It did not require any degree of ingenuity when compared to the "ebb and flow of various properties and jurisdictions" predicated on nothing more than tacit consensus and fortuitous accident. At worst, the planned grid was the logical extension of a "juridical metaphysics" in which the geometrical principle of equivalence served to both reshape the physical geography of France and to announce a profound shift in the political arithmetic of the nation.[7] Equality in all things was the order of the day, including the remapping of France itself; however, the desire to trans-

form the land into the material embodiment of this progressive ethos failed
to consider the quite real territorial differences that would remain entrenched
despite every effort to the contrary. As Burke remarks, "It was evident, that the
goodness of the soil, the number of people, their wealth, and the largeness of
their contribution, made such infinite variations between square and square as
to render mensuration a ridiculous standard of power in the commonwealth,
and equality in geometry the most unequal of all measures in distribution of
men."[8] Burke objects to the proposed geometrical grid on practical grounds,
noting the many inequities in the quality of the land, the distribution of the
population, and the ability of a given segment of that population to contribute
to the wealth and vitality of the nation.

However, beyond these many obstacles to effective governance, Burke's real
fear here is the dissolution of older, well-established ecclesiastical and secular
jurisdictions, which were more efficacious not only in their ability to coordinate the flow of power between the state and the local but also in the sense
that they bound the nation together in a much more organic and harmonious
manner. That is, the problem is not merely bureaucratic in nature but rather
involves questions of filiation, incorporation, and identification on both the
local and national level. Burke asserts that "no man ever was attached by a sense
of pride, partiality, or real affection, to a description of a square measurement.
He will never glory in belonging to the Checquer, No 71, or to any other badge-
ticket."[9] The tripartite system of departments, communes, and cantons thus
threatens the very mechanisms by which we pledge our allegiance to our local
community and, by association, the nation as a whole. Rather than produce
a sense of equality, the grid of jurisdictions and municipalities literally hacks
up France into pieces that are no longer bound to one another by tradition,
custom, and habit. Feeling and affection are subsumed and effaced altogether
by a cartographic rationality that does not adequately account for the ways in
which communitarian bonds are forged and maintained.

Burke's romantic nostalgia for these ancient connections, both here and
throughout the text, certainly informs his extended critique of the grid and
its inevitable impact on the very stability of France itself, yet it also serves as
a means of articulating a more positive, albeit conservative, geography of the
nation, one in which the neighborhood plays a decisive role. Burke states: "We
begin our public affections in our families. No cold relation is a zealous citizen.
We pass on to our neighbourhoods, and to our habitual provincial connections. These are inns and resting-places. Such divisions of our country as have
been formed by habit, and not by a sudden jerk of authority, were so many little
images of the great country in which the heart found something it could fill."[10]
Burke establishes a continuum of affective relations that begins in the home
and then extends outward to the neighborhood as an "inn" or "resting-place" on
our way toward a national sentiment that is no longer merely local in its orien-

tation. Burke posits a Johnsonian sense of home, and not the civic or juridical institutions promulgated by the revolutionary party, as the site where such sentiments are ultimately cultivated; however, his use of the picaresque metaphors here also suggests that the neighborhood is a critical mediating space in the translation of domestic feeling into a deep and abiding affection for and attachment to the national body. The neighborhood is, as he suggests, the image of the nation in miniature and so able to bind together home and nation in a way that does not disrupt or corrupt the circulation of affect so critical to Burke's social and political epistemology.

While the cartographic rationality that informs the revolution in France perhaps threatens the viability of the neighborhood, its place and value within England, for Burke, is relatively assured, or so he hopes. His critique of France's political geography is in many ways predicated on his belief that the neighborhood is a critical space in the creation and maintenance of a uniquely *British* national identity that resists the French mode of map, survey, and census which emerges following the revolution. Like Bunyan, Burke understands the neighborhood as a space that is against the map in its refusal of abstraction, quantification, and mensuration, yet Burke departs from Bunyan in his extrapolation of that resistance into a first principle of national community. In short, Burke's romantic brand of nationalism is inherently anticartographic. Contra Benedict Anderson, the map is, for Burke, always an insufficient and inadequate form for representing the nation because it does not elicit our sympathies, it does not stir our emotions, it does not stimulate the moral sense, and as a result, it provides no real or meaningful sense of connection to the national body. Rather, the map serves as a means of exclusion, as in the case of *Mansfield Park* when Maria and Julia Bertram ridicule Fanny Price for not being able to "put the map of Europe together."[11] There, Fanny's lack of familiarity with maps marks her as an outsider within the Bertram family and the community at Mansfield Park more generally, but rather than laugh along with Maria and Julia, Austen would have us sympathize with Fanny and even admire her lack of concern with worldly matters, such as the names of the rivers in Russia or how to get to Ireland. That kind of knowledge, Austen suggests, is rightfully the province of the Bertram sisters, who place a high value on the possession of geographic knowledge as a means of differentiating themselves from those, like Fanny, who, in their eyes, lack taste, proper cultivation, and refinement. Rather than an image of inclusivity and consensus, the map is represented here as an object that threatens the formation of familiar and social bonds at Mansfield. Austen frequently echoes Burke in this regard and provides a narrative example, however brief, of this anticartographic principle in action, and like Burke, Austen finds in the idea of neighborhood a more genuine and authentic sense of community that is the product of local affections and sympathies rather than the political arithmetic of the state. Thus Austen affirms and validates many of Burke's assumptions about the value and meaning of neighborhood, in particular, its ability to cultivate proper sentiment and so bind home and nation together in a meaningful way.

To return to *Mansfield Park*, the Burkean view that the local ties of the neighborhood mediate our relationship to the nation is articulated in the novel most emphatically by Edmund Bertram, a figure whose very name is meant to reinforce this connection. Austen gives voice to Burke via Edmund as he expresses his thoughts and feelings about the neighborhood of Mansfield Park; it is a subject to which Edmund returns quite often. In a protracted debate between Edmund and Mary Crawford over the value of clergymen and their moral influence on society, Miss Crawford asserts that preaching two sermons a week from the pulpit can hardly be deemed important when the audience is small at best. She degrades the clergy as an essentially worthless profession based on her own experiences, to which Edmund replies, "*You* are speaking of London, *I* am speaking of the nation at large."[12] Indeed, Miss Crawford speaks from the assumption that London is "a pretty fair sample of the rest," but Edmund promptly points out the error in her logic by telling her that "we do not look in great cities for our best morality." Against Miss Crawford's metropolitan sensibilities, Edmund offers in its place the value of exercising his clerical duties within the confines of the parish and the neighborhood: "A fine preacher is followed and admired; but it is not in fine preaching only that a good clergyman will be useful in his parish and his neighbourhood, where the parish and neighbourhood are of a size capable of knowing his private character, and observing his general conduct, which in London can rarely be the case."[13] Edmund agrees that preaching is in fact of limited use, as Miss Crawford suggests, when it is the sole form of contact between a clergyman and a parishioner, but this only occurs in London where the clergy are "known to the largest part only as preachers."[14] However, within the context of the neighborhood, there is greater opportunity to observe the "conduct" and "good principles" of the clergyman outside of the pulpit and so afford him the opportunity to shape and influence his parishioners in a much more direct and profound manner. Edmund's recourse to the neighborhood here suggests that a greater intimacy between himself and his flock will enable him to effectively teach by example and not merely precept.

The geography of the neighborhood is perceived by Edmund to be more conducive to the exercising of his clerical duties, yet he also points out that the beneficial effects of his chosen profession are not merely registered on the local level but instead have an impact on the entire nation. As stated previously, Mary Crawford's assessment of the clergy is based primarily on her knowledge of their activities, or lack thereof, in London, while Edmund, on the other hand, draws his conclusions about the value of local preaching on his assessment of the nation as a whole. He emphasizes that the character and identity of the nation are determined in large measure on the behavior of its clergy: "It will, I believe, be every where found, that as the clergy are, or are not what they ought to be, so are the rest of the nation."[15] Edmund's position here is neither provincial nor insular, but like Burke, he sees a necessary and organic link between the constitution of the neighborhood and the moral worth of the nation. However, he asserts the circulation of affect from home to neighborhood to nation even as that sense of continuity is disturbed and perhaps undermined by Mary Crawford's very line of questioning. That is, her presence in Mansfield Park represents something of a challenge to Edmund's idealization of the neighborhood, which only emerges when placed in stark contrast to the urban ethos of Miss Crawford. Austen here suggests that the communitarian bonds forged by the neighborhood may not translate to places such as London, and so the moral and ethical values that Edmund promotes and embodies never move beyond the neighborhood but instead find their terminus there. In Burkean terms, the neighborhood is no longer an inn or resting place; it is the de facto end of the journey. Not only does London present a problem for Edmund, but Miss Crawford, as its representative, remains an implicit threat to the creation of a harmonious neighborhood centered in and around Mansfield Park. Her newfound status as a neighbor to Edmund and the rest of Mansfield's inhabitants further destabilizes the neighborhood as a place of virtue and piety and jeopardizes its integrity and sense of identity. However, despite his protestations regarding her views on religion and preaching, Edmund never suggests that Miss Crawford does not somehow belong to the neighborhood of Mansfield Park and, due to his romantic sympathies, remains myopic to the possibility that her presence there directly contradicts his overtly Burkean position.

The neighborhood is thus represented as an ambivalent space in *Mansfield Park*. In one sense, it serves to promote the virtues of home, religion, and rural community, yet Austen also wishes to warn us, as in Bunyan, that neighbors can often be an impediment to the actualization of those virtues. As a result, there is a great deal of discussion and hand-wringing in the novel about who may be included in the neighborhood setting of Mansfield Park without fundamentally compromising the integrity and identity of its community. The boundaries of the neighborhood prove to be fluid and porous and so the need to vigilantly monitor precisely who is "in" and who is "out," to borrow Austen's own language. While figures such as Humphry Repton and Mr. Yates are clearly marked as outsiders, the status of Henry and Mary Crawford, as well as Dr. and Mrs. Grant, are much more problematic in that they are neighbors who threaten the very ideals that the neighborhood is meant to embody and uphold, as Burke would have it. Their physical presence within the neighborhood suggests to us a sense of belonging, yet their continued influence over those at Mansfield only serves to forestall the emergence of a more authentic sense of neighborhood that we see in Burke. We certainly see this in the case of Henry Crawford, whose presence in Mansfield potentially compromises the integrity and identity of the neighborhood in ways that are not always imme-

diately apparent. Like his sister's desire to join those in and around Mansfield through marriage to Edmund, Henry also has designs to infiltrate the
neighborhood, at first of his own accord and later through a proposed union
with Fanny.

After a game of whist, Henry Crawford turns to Fanny and announces his
plans to rent a home at Thornton Lacey, a modest property close to Mansfield Park that was intended for Edmund: "Henry Crawford was in the first
glow of another scheme about Thornton Lacey, and not being able to catch
Edmund's ear, was detailing it to his fair neighbour with a look of considerable earnestness. His scheme was to rent the house himself the following
winter, that he might have a home of his own in that neighbourhood."[16] Henry
does not address this matter at first to either Edmund or Sir Thomas, both
of whom would be a more proper audience than his "fair neighbour" Fanny,
to whom he speaks because she is the person standing closest to him. However, the scene foreshadows the fact that Fanny represents a potential means
of admittance into the neighborhood of Mansfield Park, and so, by appealing
to her in some fashion, he will be allowed to remain there as more than just a
mere guest. Henry states his intentions to this effect: "His attachment to the
neighbourhood did not depend upon one amusement or one season of the
year: he had his heart set upon having something there that he could come
to at any time, a little homestall at his command where all the holidays of his
year might be spent, and he might find himself continuing, improving, and
*perfecting* that friendship and intimacy with the Mansfield Park family which
was increasing in value to him every day."[17] The feeling with which Henry addresses the subject of his taking up a residence at Thornton Lacey reinforces
the connection between the neighborhood and the circulation of affect, and his
rhetoric here about improving and perfecting intimacy within the neighborhood setting clearly echoes Burke. However, that sense of shared feeling is not
reciprocated by either Fanny or Sir Thomas, who happen to be listening in on
their conversation. Fanny remains "proper and modest, so calm and uninviting"
in her response to Henry's proposal.[18] Sir Thomas is simply "not offended" by
the subject.

Sir Thomas's reaction, as well as Fanny's, is guarded at best and permissive
at worst. Even after directly telling Sir Thomas, "I want to be your neighbour,"
and asking his permission to take up residency at Thornton Lacey, Henry is
met again with nothing but politeness and civility, even as his request is summarily denied. Sir Thomas replies, "It is the only way, sir, in which I could *not*
wish you established as a permanent neighbour; but I hope, and believe, that
Edmund will occupy his own house at Thornton Lacey."[19] Sir Thomas's justification for his refusal echoes Edmund's earlier statements regarding the value
and necessity of the local clergy to reside as permanent residents in their parish and neighborhood rather than serving as a merely nominal inhabitant. He
faults Henry for not having considered this point before making his request,

though he also suggests that it is "perfectly natural" that he did not do so be-forehand, given his lack of familiarity with such matters. In fact, despite his faux pas, Sir Thomas does not entirely reject the idea that Henry resides in the neighborhood; he only asks that Henry not reside at Thornton Lacey and interfere with Edmund's professional duties. Edmund naturally concurs with his father and invites Henry to stay with him every winter as a friend, yet even after Henry concedes their objections to taking up a residency there, Sir Thomas still feels the need to repeat that "Thornton Lacey is the only house in the neighbourhood in which I should *not* be happy to wait on Mr. Crawford as an occupier."[20] The repetition here seems to confirm that Henry, like his sister, represents some kind of threat to the moral fabric on the neighborhood, but despite Sir Thomas's and Henry's objections, the possibility of his inclusion in the neighborhood of Mansfield Park is not foreclosed by any means. In fact, his future residence there appears to be welcomed by both. Their ambivalence is, as Austen suggests here and elsewhere, indicative of the problem with neighbors and neighborhoods, at least as Burke understands them. Figures such as Henry and Mary Crawford cannot be neatly assimilated into the neighborhood with-out fundamentally compromising its integrity and identity as a site of affective identification. They represent a threat from within the neighborhood itself that is hard to detect, much less expunge. Even the supposedly principled and religiously minded Edmund fails to fully register the implications of the Craw-fords' inclusion in their little circle of friends and family.

Fanny displays a similar ambivalence regarding Henry despite her many ob-jections to him throughout the novel. When Henry's plans to reside at Thorn-ton Lacey are thwarted, he turns to a potential union with Fanny as a means of gaining access to the neighborhood. He informs Miss Crawford that once he weds Fanny, they will settle in Northamptonshire at Stanwix Lodge, another property in close proximity to Mansfield. Miss Crawford is overjoyed at this prospect, especially given her own reservations about being forever isolated at Thornton Lacey, but when Henry reveals his intentions to Fanny during her stay in Portsmouth, she has deep reservations yet fails to voice them at that time. As in his earlier entreaty, Henry tells her that "he had a great attach-ment to Mansfield" and that "he looked forward with the hope of spending much, very much of his time there—always there, or in the neighbourhood."[21] However, he then qualifies his comments by hinting at his future plans to settle down with her and begin a family: "'Mansfield, Sotherton, Thornton Lacey,' he continued, 'what a society will be comprised in those houses! And at Michaelmas, perhaps, a fourth may be added, some small hunting-box in the vicinity of everything so dear—for as to any partnership in Thornton Lacey, as Edmund Bertram once good-humouredly proposed, I hope I foresee two objections, two fair, excellent, irresistible objections to that plan.'"[22] Henry obliquely refers to Fanny and their future offspring, but she remains silent at his suggestion, wishing he had not said it yet not objecting to his proposal at the same time. Her regret stems from the fact that, while she does not wish to encourage Henry, she finds herself somewhat struck by the overall improvement in his character and temperament, so much so that, like Edmund's own romantic inclinations toward Miss Crawford, she fails to see that his inclusion in the neighborhood of Mansfield Park undermines the very principles of local attachment and affective community that Fanny articulates throughout the novel. The irony, of course, is that, like Henry and Mary Crawford, Fanny was, at one point, an outsider with respect to Mansfield, and because she too is not proper to that place, her presence is initially viewed with a good deal of suspicion, if not contempt. Rather than a figure vigilantly policing the margins of the neighborhood, as she does later in the novel, she is represented as an interloper who threatens the very integrity of the Bertram family, a concern raised early on by Sir Thomas.

At the outset of the novel, Sir Thomas and Mrs. Norris are debating whether or not Fanny's inclusion in the neighborhood is warranted. Mrs. Norris argues on Fanny's behalf: "A niece of our's Sir Thomas, I may say, or at least of *your's*, would not grow up in this neighbourhood without many advantages."[23] Here, the neighborhood is posited as a place of cultivation and improvement where Fanny will be exposed to all kinds of beneficial influences, including, as Mrs. Norris's flattery hints, Sir Thomas himself. However, while neighborhood is offered here as a site of inclusion that will supposedly promote the virtues of civility, propriety, and taste in Fanny, it also raises Sir Thomas's concerns that Fanny will not remain merely a neighbor but rather will infiltrate their home further by falling in love with and marrying either Tom or Edmund. That is, her position as Tom's and Edmund's cousin is not nearly as problematic as the fact that, as another denizen of the neighborhood, her close physical proximity to Sir Thomas's sons may lead to an intimacy that he does not find suitable. Fanny's status here as both cousin and neighbor appears to be the cause of much of Sir Thomas's anxiety, despite Mrs. Grant's belief that it won't be a problem in the least. Fanny is, like Henry and Mary Crawford, yet another figure who potentially threatens to infiltrate and compromise the neighborhood as it is understood by Burke. Sir Thomas's fears are later realized by Fanny's marriage to Edmund; however, it seems that, on closer inspection, Mrs. Grant wins the debate about Fanny's future role within Mansfield Park. Their union, rather than a destructive force, only serves to improve Mansfield by blurring the categories of home and neighborhood in ways that facilitate and affirm Burke's sense of affective community, which is at the core of Austen's own conception of neighborhood and its role in the formation of national identity.

As noted previously, Burke sees the neighborhood as a necessary link between home and nation; it is the place where local and national attachments are mediated and ultimately reconciled. This same schema, I would argue, should be applied to a reading of *Mansfield Park*. Like Burke, and Bunyan for that matter, Austen's neighborhood is a place in which affective relations and domestic virtues are cultivated and where our intellectual, moral, and spiritual senses are developed in concert with those living within the locality. In this sense, the marriage of Fanny and Edmund and the subsequent exclusion of Henry and Mary Crawford, as well Maria Bertram, brings the neighborhood into alignment with Austen's vision of the nation, which is profoundly local in its orientation. As a result, the nation always appears off in the distance throughout much of *Mansfield Park*; we catch glimpses of it but solely through the lens of the neighborhood. From Sir Thomas's frequent trips to the West Indies to Fanny's exile in Portsmouth to Yates's transforming the house into his personal version of the London stage, Austen's novel is careful to show us the ways in which the nation, and the empire, impinges upon and shapes the course of events within the community at Mansfield Park. The conflicts and tensions that arise from Britain's increased prominence on the world stage cannot be shut out or ignored, as they permeate the neighborhood of Mansfield, often in ways that potentially undermine Burke's vision of the neighborhood as a profoundly moral space.

As in *The Pilgrim's Progress*, the neighborhood, for Austen, is a space that is often "other" to the nation and, in that otherness, provides a critical and much-needed perspective on the nation. That is, Austen's novel bears traces of Bunyan's conception of the neighborhood in its acknowledgment of the conflicts and tensions that arise between local and national concerns and the ways in which the local provides a space of difference from which to critique the nation. However, Austen departs from Bunyan in that her neighborhood, rather than being a space of resistance or dissent, offers its reader a microcosm of the nation rooted in the practice and cultivation of "good neighborhood." With her closing image of the neighborhood restored in *Mansfield Park*, Austen ultimately rejects Bunyan's more provincial worldview and the idea that the neighborhood can no longer mediate our relationship to the nation, as Burke argues it must. Her conception of the neighborhood, in short, does not represent a form of retrenchment, a turning away from the world outside of Mansfield in deference to local concerns and small society. Rather, the moral condition and identity of the nation is, in some sense, dependent on the space of the neighborhood as an important means of reforming and improving the nation in general. Franco Moretti's mapping of Austen's Britain reveals to us the ways in which this particular geography of the nation informs not only *Mansfield Park* but her work in general.[24] The various settings of Austen's novels, collectively considered, confront us with a somewhat restricted image of the nation, what Moretti refers to as the "*intermediate* space of the nation-state," a phrase I evoked at the outset of this book in relation to Foucault's concept of the heterotopia.[25] I would amplify Moretti's point here and suggest that the neighborhood, as an intermediate and contingent space, is central to

Austen's representation of the nation. As he argues, "The novel functions as the symbolic form of the nation-state. . . . It's a form that (unlike an anthem, or a monument) not only does not conceal the nation's internal divisions, *but manages to turn them into a story.*"[26] Such a statement may indeed be applied to a novel like *Mansfield Park* in which the erecting, as well as violation, of those internal divisions, like the neighborhood, becomes a central focus of the narrative itself. Rather than view the neighborhood as a site that is, in some fashion, other to the nation, Moretti posits their complementarity and so aligns Austen, correctly in my opinion, with a particularly Burkean form of nationalism that emphasizes the continuity between the neighborhood and the nation. However, while I agree in general with Moretti's thesis, he fails to consider the ways in which the neighborhood, for Austen, also functions as a site of difference and alterity with respect to the nation, thus retaining that sense of resistance we see in Bunyan's writing. The cause of this oversight or elision, in my estimation, stems from the very method Moretti deploys in his analysis of Austen, specifically, the use of maps to "bring to light the *internal* logic of narrative: the semiotic domain around which a plot coalesces and self-organizes."[27]

Moretti argues here and elsewhere that the map, properly understood, can be an effective and valuable tool for understanding both the space of literature and literature in space: "Of maps, I mean, not as metaphors, and even less as ornaments of discourse, but as analytical tools: that dissect the text in an unusual way, bringing to light relations that would otherwise remain hidden."[28] He then goes on to "dissect" in this fashion the novels of Austen, Scott, and Goethe, among others, mapping their settings and locations in order to reveal the way in which the novel form symbolically figures (and reconfigures) public perceptions of the modern nation-state. Moretti's cartographic approach aids our understanding of the novel, as well as the history of its production and, in the process, changes and reorients our very understanding of what a map is, what it is capable of doing, and why we would want to use one to study literature in the first place. While the map does not answer or explain every question raised by the literary text, as Moretti reminds us, it does at least offer "a model of the narrative universe which rearranges its components in a non-trivial way" in order to "bring some hidden patterns to the surface."[29] He is careful to point out that the map is only a means of organizing and presenting data, and so he does not supply its own interpretation or meaning; it is, for him, merely a heuristic device whose claims on reality and the material world are always partial, contingent, and limited. Moretti's conclusions are certainly quite "novel" and worth further consideration; however, he does not fully consider the implications of his cartographic approach to the study of literature, nor does he view the map in its historical context or consider how the map has signified in different and even conflicting ways throughout the early modern period. It is an omission that potentially compromises the validity of his insights and, ultimately, our understanding of the texts in question.

For one, his carto-literary methodology naïvely assumes the map to be a more objective and rational form of analysis precisely because its findings are limited and contingent. That is, the provisional nature of the map offers a means of organizing information that is, in his estimation, value neutral because it stops short of drawing firm conclusions or decisive interpretations that may be ideologically or politically coded in some fashion. Moretti routinely professes to be merely providing geographic data, albeit assembled and presented in a highly creative and purposeful fashion, thus prompting his own explanations and thoughts as to what that data might mean. However, his self-reflexive insights and a confessional tone aside, does not Moretti's approach represent yet another instance of the cartographic fallacy? His apparent desire to dissociate the form that information and knowledge take from its potential meanings and implications has been a recurring motif within the history of the map from the early modern period onward, and I would argue that Moretti's work is essentially no different. It represents yet another instance of the cartographic fallacy at work and, in the process, misconstrues, if not distorts, the historical relationship between cartography and literature. For all of his interest in maps and charts as analytical tools, Moretti, paradoxically, fails to consider the ways in which maps themselves signified for these authors, or just how maps were received, processed, and understood by those who consumed them during the eighteenth and nineteenth centuries. He would subject a text, such as Austen's *Mansfield Park*, to a mapping that her narrative might otherwise refuse in its awareness of the map's ideological and social functions. Translating narrative space into cartographic space elides the reality that these two geographies are not commensurate with one another, nor do they cohere neatly. In fact, their relationship can be, more often than not, antagonistic and contradictory, a source of dissonance within the literary text that is at once problematic and compelling.

Austen's neighborhood resists cartographic inscription in that it is a space defined largely by feeling and the affective relations among a discrete group of individuals, not intersecting lines of longitude and latitude, as Moretti would have it. As a familiar and profound social space, the neighborhood remains a site of local identification that is able to resist incorporation into the national landscape, even as it transforms the very shape and contours of that landscape. We see this in the very movement from Bunyan's representation of the neighborhood to that of Burke, which is, in short, the movement from local to national forms of identification, or how the spaces of dissent and difference I have discussed in this book, such as scene, country, market, and home, become, over time, a way of imagining and "mapping" the nation itself. That is not to say that the neighborhood of the nineteenth century (or the twenty-first for that matter) does not retain some heterotopic residuum from its origins in seventeenth-century religious dissent. As Austen's text well demonstrates, the neighborhood can just as easily disarticulate our image of the nation as it can reflect back to us one that is uniform, harmonious, and pleasing. Its valence, as I have tried to show, moves and shifts with time and with its particular social, political, and economic context, but the principle of spatial difference and differentiation, the heterotopic conceit, always remains a formal possibility, not only on the margins of the empire but at its very center as well. It is a possibility that the map cannot acknowledge or register in any fashion, which is precisely the point.

# NOTES

## INTRODUCTION

1. See, for example, Black, *Maps and Politics*; Jacob, *The Sovereign Map*; Wood, *Power of Maps*; Petchenik, *Nature of Maps*; Harley, "Maps, Knowledge, and Power"; Scott, *Seeing like a State*; and Edney, "The Irony of Imperial Mapping."
2. Anderson, *Imagined Communities*, 164.
3. Anderson, *Imagined Communities*, 175.
4. Buisseret, *Monarchs, Ministers, and Maps*, 4.
5. Cormack, *Charting an Empire*, 1.
6. Helgerson, *Forms of Nationhood*, 111.
7. For a detailed examination of Saxton's frontispiece, see Helgerson, *Forms of Nationhood*, 108–24.
8. Helgerson, *Forms of Nationhood*, 114.
9. Helgerson, *Forms of Nationhood*, 122–24. See also Slack, *The Invention of Improvement*, 15–52.
10. Helgerson, *Forms of Nationhood*, 124.
11. In addition to Saxton's *Survey of England and Wales*, Helgerson examines William Camden's *Britannia* (1586–1607), John Norden's *Speculum Britanniae* (1593–98), John Speed's *Theater of the Empire of Great Britain* (1611), and Michael Drayton's *Poly-Olbion* (1612).
12. See Conley, *Self-Made Map*, 311n4. As Conley elaborates, the cartographer in the Elizabethan age, while remaining a loyal to the monarch, is, at the same time, "metamorphosed into a protodemocratic subject who . . . gains agency through increasing self-consciousness and mastery of the represented world that owes its existence to his many talents."
13. Applying Helgerson's thesis, Alyssa Connell argues that chorographic description continues to play a formative role in the "writing of Britain," as she terms it, during the late seventeenth and eighteenth centuries. See "Paper Kingdom."
14. See, for example, Mayhew, *Enlightenment Geography*, 37. As Mayhew argues, despite claims of impartiality and scientific objectivity, maps and geography books of the period were frequently employed in the legitimation of a particular political viewpoint to a wider audience: "The readership for geography . . . was split in two. First, there was a scholarly community of historians, classicists, and theologians, in other words, the community of humanist scholars. Secondly, there was a community of those needing a practical education. It is misleading to emphasize one tradition at the expense of the other or to ignore that both communities had political agendas and looked to geography books for both facts and narrative which bolstered these agendas." Mayhew's focus here on the plurality of political languages found in geographic texts during the later seventeenth and eighteenth centuries suggests a much more fragmented and divisive picture of the nation

than the earlier work of Buisseret, Cormack, and Helgerson, which tended to view the work of geography and cartography in more monolithic terms.

15. Pedley, *Commerce of Cartography*, 1.

16. Pedley, *Commerce of Cartography*, 1.

17. Wood, *Power of Maps*.

18. Miller, "Accounting and Objectivity," 75. Miller defines "calculable spaces" as abstract spaces that "cut across geographical and physical boundaries" in order to make visible "the hierarchical arrangement of persons and things." It is the space of order and knowledge that can be managed and changed depending on the mode of calculation and its purposes.

19. Brewer, *Sinews of Power*, 221. For a broader historical and geographical analysis of the ways in which information systems have served the imperatives of the state, see Black, *Power of Knowledge*.

20. See, for example, Withers, *Geography, Science and National Identity*; Edney, "Reconsidering Enlightenment Geography and Map Making"; and Gascoigne, "Joseph Banks, Mapping, and the Geographies of Natural Knowledge."

21. See Peluso, "Whose Woods Are These?"; Rundstrom, "Mapping, Postmodernism, Indigenous People and the Changing Direction of North American Cartography"; Orlove, "Mapping Reeds and Reading Maps"; Godlewska, "Resisting the Cartographic Imperative"; and Wood, *Rethinking the Power of Maps*.

22. Johnson, *Journey to the Western Islands of Scotland*, 148.

23. Edney, *Mapping an Empire*, 319. See also Sen, *Empire of Free Trade*; and Barrow, *Making History, Drawing Territory*.

24. Edney, *Mapping an Empire*, 325.

25. See Evers, "A Rough Game: Surveyors and Indians."

26. See Givens, "Maps, Fields, and Boundary Cairns."

27. Givens, "Maps, Fields, and Boundary Cairns," 2. Michael Yiakoumi was a goatherd who, along with a few others, overtly violated government prohibitions on goat herding within the forest limits. His actions were seen as an act of political dissent and, as Givens suggests, "deliberate disobedience."

28. Givens, "Maps, Fields, and Boundary Cairns," 20.

29. As Elizabeth Helsinger states, "Anderson's investigations tend to focus on the means of consensus rather than the practice of dissent." The nation is, in Anderson's view, the product of rational consensus rather than a composite of differing voices and spaces that "contest or reconstitute a national symbolic." *Rural Scenes and National Representation*, 11.

30. Another example of what Elizabeth Deeds Ermarth refers to as the "homogenizing media of experience," the map projects a "common horizon" that attempts to reconcile multiple and conflicting viewpoints within a unified field of perception. The map, as a static, neutral depiction of space, thus equalizes all perspectives and produces the illusion of rational consensus. Ermarth's point here echoes both Anderson and Helgerson to some extent, but her notion of consensus as a formal property within realist aesthetics does not necessarily imply the creation of national consensus. See *Realism and Consensus in the English Novel*.

31. Helgerson, *Forms of Nationhood*, 108. Helgerson theorizes the connections between visuality and the nation in relation not only to Benedict Anderson but

also J. R. Hale, who argues that, without maps, the individual cannot visualize the country to which he or she belongs. Helgerson merely takes the obverse of that statement to declare that maps are necessary to visualizing the nation and that the nation, in turn, is dependent on its being visible. See also Harley, "Meaning and Ambiguity in Tudor Cartography," 26.

32. See Lefebvre, *The Production of Space*; Harvey, *The Limits to Capital*; Sills, "Eighteenth-Century Cartographic Studies"; Andrews, "Introduction"; Edney, "The Origins and Development of J. B. Harley's Cartographic Theories"; and Black, *Maps and Politics*.

33. Pile and Keith, *Geographies of Resistance*, 30. See also Sharp et al., *Entanglements of Power*; and Paulston, *Social Cartography*.

34. Foucault, "Of Other Spaces," 352.

35. Foucault, "Of Other Spaces," 353.

36. Foucault believed that "a whole history of spaces has still to be written," suggesting that his own list of examples was far from comprehensive. Quoted in Pickles, *A History of Spaces*, xi.

37. Mary McLeod's criticizes Foucault for not taking common spaces into consideration in his discussion of heterotopias and suggests that "other" spaces may also be familiar spaces: "What are explicitly omitted from his list of 'other' spaces, however, are the residence, the workplace, the street, the shopping center, and the more mundane areas of everyday leisure, such as playgrounds, parks, sporting fields, restaurants, and so on." "'Other' Spaces and 'Others,'" 16–17.

38. Moretti, *Atlas of the European Novel*, 22. Moretti deploys the phrase in reference to the geography of Jane Austen's novels. He draws the second half of this quote from Kiernan, "State and Nation in Western Europe," 35.

39. Helsinger, *Rural Scenes*, 11.

## 1. JOHN BUNYAN, NEIGHBORHOOD, AND THE GEOGRAPHY OF DISSENT

1. See Watts, *Dissenters*, 272–76.

2. Watts, *Dissenters*, 267. Daniel Neal, in his *History of the Puritans*, also compiled the results in addition to the Evans manuscript, but his original accounting was lost and only survives in an incomplete copy made by Josiah Thompson. While gaps and errors in the Evans list have been noted since, the document still provides the most comprehensive picture of Dissenting churches prior to the mid-nineteenth century.

3. Watts, *Dissenters*, 270, 272. See Map 1, "Distribution of Presbyterians, 1715–1718."

4. Watts, *Dissenters*, 280.

5. Watts, *Dissenters*, 281–82. Congregationalism was also quite strong in south Wales and Monmouthshire, but this was due primarily to the sustained missionary work of figures like Vavasor Powell and Henry Maurice.

6. See Brewer, *Sinews of Power*.

7. See Acosta, "Spaces of Dissent and the Public Sphere in Hackney, Stoke Newington, and Newington Green."

8. Ashcraft, *Revolutionary Politics and Locke's Two Treatises on Government*, 26.

9. On the increasing politicization of the parish and its transformation from a unit

of ecclesiastical authority to an extension of both Crown and Parliament, see Eastwood, *Government and Community in the English Provinces, 1700–1800;* Trotter, *Seventeenth Century Life in the Country Parish;* Webb and Webb, *English Local Government from the Revolution to the Municipal Corporations Act;* and Corrigan and Sayer, *The Great Arch.*

10. Keeble, *Literary Culture of Nonconformity,* 68.
11. Eastwood, *Government and Community in the English Provinces,* 9.
12. Kent, "The Centre and the Localities," 376.
13. Kent suggests that we must not look at the evolution of local government in England simply as a process of the state imposing its will on the localities, a top-down model as it were, but rather as a combination of a growing bureaucracy and the desire and willingness on the part of local authorities to utilize that institutional framework to address questions of social policy, such as poor relief, control of migrant populations, and the criminal prosecution of vagrants. In short, the state was as much a resource for local authorities as the local authorities were for the state and its desire to extend its influence. The law and policies of the state and the needs of the localities often coincided not as a result of coercion by the state but rather based on a symbiotic reciprocity that mutually benefited both state and local interests.
14. Hill, *Tinker and a Poor Man,* 117.
15. See Anderson, *Imagined Communities.*
16. Bunyan's "neighborhood" is somewhat, although not explicitly, related to the concept of "Neighbours Fare," which Joanne Meyers defines as "the notion that one's own experiences and fortunes are inevitably bound to those of one's fellows." "Defoe and the Project of 'Neighbours Fare,'" 2.
17. Bunyan, *Christian Behaviour,* 43.
18. Quoted in Luxon, *Literal Figures,* 135.
19. Bunyan, *Christian Behaviour,* 43.
20. Bunyan, *Christian Behaviour,* 21.
21. Bunyan, *Saved By Grace,* 203–4.
22. This moral imperative to love your neighbor as yourself is also echoed frequently in the Gospels, among other places in the Bible. See, for example, Matthew 19:19, Mark 12:31, and Luke 10:27 (AV).
23. Gal. 5:14 (AV). Bunyan offers his extended commentary on this passage in his "Exhortation to Peace and Unity."
24. Bunyan, *Grace Abounding to the Chief of Sinners,* 14.
25. Bunyan, "A Few Sighs From Hell," 309.
26. Bunyan, "A Holy Life," 277.
27. Bunyan, *Pilgrim's Progress,* 5.
28. Bunyan, *Pilgrim's Progress,* 13.
29. Bunyan, *Pilgrim's Progress,* 14.
30. Bunyan, *Pilgrim's Progress,* 16.
31. Bunyan, *Pilgrim's Progress,* 173.
32. Bunyan, *Pilgrim's Progress,* 173–74.
33. Bunyan, *Pilgrim's Progress,* 174.
34. Luxon, *Literal Figures,* 160.

35. Fish, *Self-Consuming Artifacts*, 224–64.

36. Luxon, *Literal Figures*, 130–58.

37. Bunyan, *Pilgrim's Progress*, 40.

38. Fish, *Self-Consuming Artifacts*, 229.

39. Bunyan, *Pilgrim's Progress*, 32.

40. Fish pointedly omits the subject of allegory from his analysis, remarking triumphantly in the preface that the word does not even appear in the chapter on *The Pilgrim's Progress*. Such an omission enables Fish to skirt the question of allegorical representation altogether, which, as I am suggesting, damages his reading of Bunyan's text in terms of its geography and understanding of space in general.

41. On the seventeenth-century conflict between Cartesian and allegorical conceptions of space, see Martin, *Ruins of Allegory*. Working from Benjamin's definition of baroque allegory, Martin contends that Milton's fixation on the ruined fragment disrupts the totalizing effects of Cartesian space. Rather than the assured relationship of part to whole we get in Christian allegory, Milton's baroque allegory exalts the indeterminacy of signification that creates a rift between part and whole, thus opening up the possibility of relative spaces that resist incorporation into the planar order of neoclassical rationalism. See also Benjamin, *Origin of German Tragic Drama*.

42. See Turner, "Bunyan's Sense of Place."

43. For a historical overview of allegory and its discontents from its classical antecedents through its postmodern incarnation, see Kelley, *Reinventing Allegory*; Longxi, "Historicizing the Postmodern Allegory"; and Hirsch, "Transhistorical Intentions and the Persistence of Allegory." Each author reaches different conclusions about the transformations in the definition and use of allegory, but all agree on the general critique of allegory as a genre and mode of signification during the eighteenth century.

44. Pile and Keith, *Geographies of Resistance*, 1–32.

45. Greaves, "Organizational Response of Non-Conformity to Repression and Indulgence."

46. Watts, *Dissenters*, 224.

47. Greaves, "Organizational Response of Non-Conformity," 484.

48. Hill, *Tinker and a Poor Man*, 54.

49. Bunyan, *Christian Behaviour*, 11.

50. Bunyan, *Christian Behaviour*, 54.

51. Hill, *Tinker and a Poor Man*, 275–76. Hill here echoes E. P. Thompson's famous pronouncement in *The Making of the English Working Class* that, in Bunyan's writings, "we find the slumbering radicalism which was preserved throughout the eighteenth century, and which breaks out again in the nineteenth century." Thompson, *Making of the English Working Class*, 34.

52. N. H. Keeble offers a somewhat different take in his insistence that Bunyan's literary "genius" stems largely from the ability to accommodate his religious views to "the experience of defeat, repression and ridicule" that will characterize nonconformity during much of the Restoration. The point is neatly summarized in the maxim "political defeat was the condition of cultural achievement." *Literary Culture of Nonconformity in Late Seventeenth-Century England*, 22.

53. Hill, *Tinker and a Poor Man*, 129–30. According to Hill, Bunyan's program of good neighborhood is accompanied by an abiding awareness of class, which perhaps came from his reading of texts such as Richard Bernard's *The Isle of Man*. Bernard expressly connects a critique of the gentry and a preference for the poor with the desire for good neighborhood, yet I am not sure we can extend the same logic to Bunyan. I don't question that Bunyan was deeply aware of class and the problems it posed for religious community, but good neighborhood, in a sense, supersedes class distinctions, or rather, provides a much more generalized conception of the social through which inequities of many kinds may be remedied. Class fails to constitute, as Hill notes, an analytical category and thus is somewhat removed from its later Marxist invocation.

54. See MacPherson, *Political Theory of Possessive Individualism*.

55. Hill, *Puritanism and Revolution*, 152.

56. The use of the "map" as a metaphor for spiritual guidance and progress predates Bunyan's own map, but such metaphors were rarely literalized in the form of an actual map. See, for example, Teate, *A Scripture-Map of the Wildernesse of Sin, and Way to Canaan*.

57. Bunyan, *Pilgrim's Progress*, 41.

58. Jeffrey Peters's *Mapping Discord* discusses the relationship between allegory and cartography and, more specifically, the use of allegorical maps for subversive purposes.

## 2. Aphra Behn and the Colonial Scene

1. Jan Jansson's *Guinea* (1647) also bears a striking resemblance to Blaeu's original.

2. For similar examples of seventeenth-century Dutch cartography, see Frederik de Wit's *Atlas* (1680), Olfert Dapper's *Description de l'Afrique* (1686), and Jan Jansson's *Novus Atlas, sive Theatrum orbis terrarum* (1638).

3. Ogilby not only fails to identify his sources, which was common practice at the time, but he also fails to credit Montanus, whose text he more or less reproduced.

4. Ogilby, *America*, 304–5.

5. Ogilby, *America*, 376–77.

6. Ogilby, *America*, 368.

7. A second edition of Ligon's *A True and Exact History* was published in 1673. Ligon was a royalist who fled England for Barbados in 1647 due to financial hardship and political turmoil and lived there for over two years before returning to England because of a fever and declining health.

8. See, for example, Samuel Thornton's "Chart of the Sea Coasts of Europe, Africa, and America," which appears in *The Atlas Maritimus Novus*.

9. The OED contains the following entry for hydrography: "The science which has for its object the description of the waters of the earth's surface, the sea, lakes, rivers, etc., comprising the study and mapping of their forms and physical features, of the contour of the sea-bottom, shallows, etc., and of winds, tides, currents, and the like. (In earlier use, including the principles of Navigation.) Also a treatise on this science, a scientific description of the waters of the earth."

10. The original edition of Bosman's *A New and Accurate Description* was published, without Moll's map, in 1705.

11. The map had been reissued in Moll's *The World Described; or, A New and Correct Sett of Maps* (1709–20). For other examples of Moll's maps from this period, see his *Atlas Geographus: or, A Compleat System of Geography* (1711–17).

12. See Boulukos, "Olaudah Equiano and the Eighteenth-Century Debate on Africa."

13. For more on Postlethwayt's views on the slave trade, see Hudson, "'Britons Never Will Be Slaves'"; and Darity, "Eric Williams and Slavery."

14. The maps in question are reproduced from the originals created by Jean Baptiste Bourguignon d'Anville, who was at that time France's most prolific cartographer.

15. See, for example, Hayden, "'As Far as a Woman's Reasoning May Go.'" Hayden argues that Behn's novel represents her attempt to participate in the discourses of the New Science and to make the case for the relevancy of female voices within those discourses.

16. Gallagher, Introduction, 4.

17. For other texts that utilize the "triangular trade" as a model for understanding the Atlantic world of the seventeenth and eighteenth centuries, see Bean, *British Trans-Atlantic Slave Trade, 1650–1775*; Solow, *Slavery and the Rise of the Atlantic System*; Davis, *Rise of the Atlantic Economies*; Rawley, *Transatlantic Slave Trade*; Sheridan, "The Commercial and Financial Organization of the British Slave Trade, 1750–1807"; and Steele, *The English Atlantic, 1675–1740*.

18. Davies, *Royal African Company*, 187. Davies argues that there often were no goods, such as sugar, ginger, cotton, tobacco, and rum, to bring back to London markets, and so the contract was terminated in the West Indies. This is due either to the unavailability of these items or the fact that they were not of sufficient value in England to make their transport financially worthwhile. See also Rawley, *Transatlantic Slave Trade*, 154; and Bean, *British Trans-Atlantic Slave Trade*, 48–49.

19. For a further discussion on the role of shuttle routes during the period, see Walton, "New Evidence on Colonial Commerce."

20. Curtin, *Atlantic Slave Trade*, 95. While Curtin does not address the triangular trade model specifically, his text nevertheless demonstrates the difficulty of abstracting general patterns by which we may understand the slave trade as an integrated phenomenon.

21. See also Merritt, "The Triangular Trade"; Ostrander, "The Making of the Triangular Trade Myth"; and Sheridan, *Sugar and Slavery*.

22. See Anderson, *Imagined Communities*, 170–78.

23. Gilroy, *Black Atlantic*, 15.

24. Gilroy, *Black Atlantic*, 48.

25. Whether or not *Oroonoko* can be read as either a critique of the slave trade or England's colonial ambitions remains a matter of some debate, one that is hardly settled in my estimation. Some argue that the Restoration sees the emergence of a Tory ideology that is more amenable to trade and empire than previously thought. While I agree that there is some ambivalence regarding these issues, that does not preclude my general point here that Behn evinces a critical, if not skeptical, voice with regard to matters of colonial trade, slavery, and English imperialism. For further examples, see Hoxby, *Mammon's Music*; Gallagher,

"Oroonoko's Blackness"; Pacheco, "Royalism and Honor in Aphra Behn's *Oroonoko*"; Sussman, "The Other Problem with Women"; and Visconsi, "The Degenerate Race."

26. Behn, *Oroonoko*, 101.

27. Behn, *Oroonoko*, 103.

28. Behn, *Oroonoko*, 115.

29. Behn, *Oroonoko*, 117.

30. See Pigg, "Trying to Frame the Unframable"; Bratach, "Following the Intrigue"; Gallagher, "Who Was That Masked Woman?"; Ferguson, "Feathers and Flies"; and Zimbardo, "Aphra Behn."

31. Behn's *Oroonoko* was, not coincidentally, adapted for the stage by Thomas Southerne in 1696, likely because the novel was already predisposed to a theatrical re-creation.

32. Holland, *The Ornament of Action*, 41–42.

33. See *Works of Aphra Behn*, 5:158–59. In fact, the play was criticized heavily, its use of the scene notwithstanding, and did not fare well overall. The chief accusation was that Behn had lifted her play from an earlier Spanish work entitled *Don Fenise*, authored by Francisco de Quintana. Janet Todd agrees that Behn certainly drew from the play, which was really a collection of shorter stories, but her handling of the subject matter is distinctively Behn.

34. See Visser, "Scenery and Technical Design." I do not mean to suggest that this model applies in every situation. Rather, it is a reductive accounting intended to underscore some salient features common to the scenic stage as it was configured during the Restoration.

35. Southern, *Changeable Scenery*, 17.

36. Visser, "Scenery and Technical Design," 80.

37. Visser, "Scenery and Technical Design," 74–75. Dryden's *Albion and Albanius* (1685) utilizes these upper shutters, as noted in the following stage direction: "*The farther part of the Heaven opens and discovers a Machine; as it moves forwards the Clouds which are before it divide, and shew the Person of* Apollo" (II.18).

38. Lewcock, "More for Seeing Than Hearing," 66–67.

39. *Works of Aphra Behn*, 5:3. Dawn Lewcock provides a more detailed reading of the play's use of the scenic stage. See Lewcock, "More for Seeing Than Hearing," 71–75.

40. Behn, *The Forc'd Marriage*, 11.

41. Behn, *The Forc'd Marriage*, 22.

42. Behn, *Oroonoko*, 89.

43. Behn, *Oroonoko*, 95.

44. Behn, *Oroonoko*, 95.

45. Oroonoko is often caught between the imperative to heroic action and the civilizing impulse of either the spoken or written word, both of which Oroonoko is meant to embody but problematically so. That is, he cannot successfully mediate discourse and action, and thus the tragic flaw. The tension between discourse and action is also, as we have seen, one central to debates about the theater where the text is lauded above the action on the stage, which I would extend to the action of scene changing.

46. Behn, *Oroonoko*, 98.
47. Behn, *Oroonoko*, 112.
48. Behn, *Oroonoko*, 106.
49. Behn, *Oroonoko*, 113.
50. Behn, *Oroonoko*, 134.
51. Gallagher, Introduction, 12–13. See also Dunn, *Sugar and Slaves*; Price, *Guiana Maroons*; and Stedman, *Five Years Expedition against the Revolted Negroes of Surinam* (1796).
52. Quoted in Frohock, "Violence and Awe," 448. As Frohock notes, Behn lamented losing Surinam to the Dutch and thus losing a key foothold in South America.
53. See also Behn, *The Widow Ranter* (1689).
54. Behn, *Oroonoko*, 133–34.
55. Behn, *Oroonoko*, 127.

### 3. Surveying Ireland and Swift's "Country of the Mind"

1. Buisseret, *Monarchs, Ministers, and Maps*, 4.
2. Andrews, *Plantation Acres*, 3. See also Smyth, *Common Ground*, 106.
3. See Mercator, *Angliae Scotiae et Hiberniae Nove Descriptio* (1564); Ortelius, *Hiberniae Britannicae insulae nova descriptio* (1573); Goghe, *Hibernia, insulae non procul ab Anglia vulgare Hirlandia vocata* (1567); and Nowell, *A General Description of England and Ireland* (1564–65).
4. Smyth, *Map-Making, Landscape and Memory*, 23. Smyth notes the map's undue emphasis on Ireland's eastern coast in contrast to the relatively sparse amount of information and detail to the west, signifying the gap between England's imperial ambitions and its ability to realize those ambitions.
5. J. H. Andrews notes that the idea of an "all-Ireland cadastre" remained something of an elusive "Utopian dream" for many politicians and surveyors alike during the sixteenth and seventeenth centuries, but it was a dream that was ultimately destined to fail given the myriad complexities and inherent difficulties of realizing such a grandiose project. *Plantation Acres*, 54. See also Andrews, "Geography and Government," 181, 190; and *A Paper Landscape*
6. For more on the map as a symbol of dynastic authority and power, see Klein, *Maps and the Writing of Space in Early Modern England*, 52–56; and Helgerson, *Forms of Nationhood*.
7. For more on the long history of the estate map, see Buisseret, *Rural Images*.
8. Raymond Gillespie argues that plantation surveys and maps were not exclusively devoted to the confiscation and redistribution of property but also were seen as technologies necessary to the creation of a new social and cultural order in Ireland, a commonwealth in its truest sense of the word. The notion of plantation mapping as a means of social reform, however, was less a factor during the Cromwellian and Restoration settlements, which were principally concerned with the transfer of land and title. See Gillespie, "The Problems of Plantations."
9. Smyth, *Map-Making, Landscape and Memory*, 37. Lythe's map also was the basis for Baptista Boazio's *Irelande* (1599) and John Speed's "The Kingdom of Ireland" from his atlas *Theatre of the Empire of Great Britain* (1610–11). For more detailed

analysis of Boazio, Speed, and their relationship to Lythe's work, see Klein, *Maps and the Writing of Space*, 117–18; and Andrews, *Shapes of Ireland*.

10. Smyth, *Map-Making, Landscape and Memory*, 40–41.

11. Quoted from Spenser's "A View of the State of Ireland" in Smyth, *Map-Making, Landscape and Memory*, 6n24.

12. Warham St. Leger to Lord Burghley, Cork, 20 April 1582, S.P. 63/93/41. Quoted in Andrews, *Plantation Acres*, 28n1.

13. Andrews, *Plantation Acres*, 29.

14. Smyth, *Map-Making, Landscape and Memory*, 48. Smyth discusses the "platte" of a proposed Munster seigniory and parish drawn up in 1586 that utilizes a geometric grid as the basis for manorial settlement and argues that, while such plans were successfully implemented in North America, it was "rarely if ever achieved on the ground either in Munster or elsewhere in Ireland." J. H. Andrews suggests that Robins was likely the surveyor for the "platte" of the proposed Munster seigniory and parish. *Plantation Acres*, 31–32. See also Andrews, "Geography and Government," 180.

15. Smyth, *Map-Making, Landscape and Memory*, 48. See also Andrews, "Geography and Government," 189.

16. Smyth, *Map-Making, Landscape and Memory*, 58.

17. "Robins the surveyor's bill" [11 September 1587], S.P. 63/131/14. Quoted in Andrews, *Plantation Acres*, 39n35.

18. Andrews, *Plantation Acres*, 39.

19. Smyth, *Map-Making, Landscape and Memory*, 115.

20. Delle, "'A Good and Easy Speculation,'" 21.

21. Andrews, *Plantation Acres*, 41.

22. Andrews, *Plantation Acres*, 39. Andrews argues emphatically that "the failure of the Munster surveys—for failure it was—extended to almost every aspect of the work."

23. As J. H. Andrews notes, these older forms of surveying do not disappear entirely after the sixteenth century; rather, they coexist, in various ways, with more modern approaches to surveying and mapping throughout the seventeenth and eighteenth centuries both in Ireland and England. *Plantation Acres*, 1–27. For more on the transformation of surveying and surveyors during the Tudor period, see also McRae, *God Speed the Plough*, 169–97; and Montaño, *Roots of English Colonialism in Ireland*, 154–212.

24. Klein, *Maps and the Writing of Space*, 43–44. See also Andrews, *Plantation Acres*, 17–19, and Smyth, *Map-Making, Landscape and Memory*, 15.

25. Andrews, *Plantation Acres*, 20–21.

26. McCrae, *God Speed the Plough*, 170.

27. McCrae, *God Speed the Plough*, 186. See also Klein, *Maps and the Writing of Space*, 42–60.

28. McCrae, *God Speed the Plough*, 186.

29. Quoted in Montaño, *Roots of English Colonialism in Ireland*, 161.

30. Klein, *Maps and the Writing of Space*, 112.

31. Smyth, *Map-Making, Landscape and Memory*, 12.

32. Smyth, *Map-Making, Landscape and Memory*, 58.

33. Netzloff, "Forgetting the Ulster Plantation," 321. Speed's map, like Boazio's, is believed to be based on the surveys of Robert Lythe.

34. Netzloff, "Forgetting the Ulster Plantation," 331.

35. Smyth, *Map-Making, Landscape and Memory*, 41–43.

36. Smyth, *Map-Making, Landscape and Memory*, 54.

37. Quoted in Andrews, *Shapes of Ireland*, 104. See also *Plantation Acres*, 44.

38. Andrews, *Plantation Acres*, 103–4; Smyth, *Map-Making, Landscape and Memory*, 54.

39. Quoted in Hayes-McCoy, *Ulster and Other Irish Maps*, xii. See also Andrews, *Shapes of Ireland*, 23.

40. Smyth, *Map-Making, Landscape and Memory*, 49–50.

41. Smyth, *Map-Making, Landscape and Memory*, 50.

42. Smyth, *Map-Making, Landscape and Memory*, 51.

43. Andrews, "Geography and Government," 179–80.

44. Andrews, "The Maps of the Escheated Counties of Ulster, 1609–10," 139–40. See also Smyth, *Map-Making, Landscape and Memory*, 68.

45. Smyth, *Map-Making, Landscape and Memory*, 73.

46. The Strafford Survey was overseen by Dr. William Gilbert and Rev. John Johnson.

47. See Margey, "Representing Plantation Landscapes," 152–53.

48. Klein, *Maps and the Writing of Space*, 128. For more on the Irish Commission of 1622, see also Margey, "Representing Plantation Landscapes," 156–64.

49. Andrews, *Plantation Acres*, 74–75.

50. Andrews, "Maps and Mapmakers," 103; and *Plantation Acres*, 83.

51. Andrews, *Plantation Acres*, 90–92, 97.

52. Andrews, *Plantation Acres*, 89, 114–15.

53. Buisseret, *The Mapmaker's Quest*, 178. See also Kearns, "Bare Life, Political Violence, and the Territorial Structure of Britain and Ireland."

54. Andrews, *Plantation Acres*, 64–65, 69–70. According to Andrews, two of Petty's chief innovations was to hire and train Cromwell's soldiers as surveyors in order to expedite such a massive undertaking, while lowering overall costs, and to exact a measure of revenge against those professional surveyors who objected to his methods.

55. Larcom, *A History of the Survey of Ireland Commonly Called the Down Survey by Doctor William Petty, A.D. 1655–6*, 376–77. Quoted in Smyth, *Map-Making, Landscape and Memory*, 170n10.

56. The title of surveyor general existed throughout Ireland's plantation period, but as J. H. Andrews notes, the position was largely administrative and political in nature, as most of Ireland's surveyor generals possessed little in the way of professional training or experience in actual surveying. See Andrews, *Plantation Acres*, 55–57, 61. An adventurer is a general term designating those "English merchants, guild-members, parliamentarians, and other town-dwellers" who had "invested money in the pacification of Ireland."

57. Smyth, *Map-Making, Landscape and Memory*, 172–73. See also Andrews, *Plantation Acres*, 61.

58. Andrews, *Plantation Acres*, 69.

59. Mary Poovey estimates his total assets in 1652 to be around £500, but by 1685, they were approximately £6,700, with property holdings in Ireland around 50,000 acres. *A History of the Modern Fact*, 122. See also Smyth, *Map-Making, Landscape and Memory*, 187–88; and Slack, *The Invention of Improvement*, 98.

60. Poovey, *History of the Modern Fact*, 123.

61. Poovey, *History of the Modern Fact*, 138–39.

62. Poovey, *History of the Modern Fact*, 136.

63. For more of the book history of Petty's *Hiberniae delineatio*, see Andrews, *Shapes of Ireland*, 118–52.

64. Andrews, *Shapes of Ireland*, 149, 135–36. Andrews contends elsewhere that one possible reason for the long gap between the completion of the Down Survey and the publication of the atlas was that Petty felt that his original survey was incomplete and that his maps were simply too flawed for public consumption. He also suggests that, given his other interests and duties, Petty may have simply lost interest in the project and so was more than happy to leave the entire matter to Taylor, which is, in effect, what happened.

65. Kohl, *Travels in Ireland*, 289. Quoted in Andrews, *Shapes of Ireland*, 148, n.53.

66. Andrews, *Shapes of Ireland*, 122.

67. Andrews, *Plantation Acres*, 146–47.

68. Cox, "Regnum Corcagiense," 67. Quoted in Andrews, *Plantation Acres*, 150n23.

69. Andrews, "Maps and Mapmakers," 103–06.

70. Andrews, "Maps and Mapmakers," 103.

71. Andrews, *Plantation Acres*, 151.

72. Andrews, *Plantation Acres*, 154.

73. Andrews, *Plantation Acres*, 163. See also Andrews, *Henry Pratt, Surveyor of the Kerry Estates*; and Andrews, "New Light on Three Eighteenth-Century Cartographers."

74. Andrews, *Shapes of Ireland*, 162.

75. Smyth, *Map-Making, Landscape and Memory*, 387–89.

76. For examples of their most significant mercantilist writings, see Sir William Petty, *Political arithmetick* (1690) and *A treatise of taxes and contributions* (1662); Sir William Davenant, *Discourses on the public revenues, and on the trade of England* (1698) and *An essay on the East India trade* (1696); John Graunt, *Natural and political observations . . . made upon the bills of mortality* (1662); and Josiah Child, *Brief observations concerning trade and interest of money* (1668) and *A new discourse of trade* (1693).

77. For more on Swift's knowledge and critique of the writings of Petty, Graunt, Davenant, and Child, see Wittkowsky, "Swift's Modest Proposal"; Briggs, "John Graunt, William Petty, and Swift's *A Modest Proposal*"; and Landa, "'A Modest Proposal' and Populousness" and "Swift's Economic Views and Mercantilism."

78. Wittkowsky, "Swift's Modest Proposal," 95.

79. See Sussman, "The Colonial Afterlife of Political Arithmetic," 107–9, 104–5, 111–13, 120.

80. Swift, "A Tale of a Tub," 105. Colin Kiernan links this formulation to Swift's broader rejection of Newtonian science and its conception of absolute time and space. See "Swift and Science."

81. Swift, "On Poetry: A Rhapsody," 573–74.
82. Swift, "On Poetry: A Rhapsody," 574. Defoe appears to reference Swift's senti-
    ment in his *Tour Thro' the Whole Island of Great Britain* while traveling though
    the Highlands: "Our geographers seem to be almost as much at a loss in the de-
    scriptions of this north part of Scotland, as the Romans were to conquer it; and
    they are obliged to fill it up with hills and mountains, as they do the inner parts
    of Africa, with lions and elephants, for want of knowing what else to place there.
    Yet this country is not of such difficult access, as to be passed undescribed, as if
    it were Impenetrable." Defoe, *Tour*, 663.
83. For more on European attempts to map the African continent, see Heawood, *A
    History of Geographical Discovery in the Seventeenth and Eighteenth Centuries*. The
    exploration of Africa had been pursued somewhat during the sixteenth century,
    mostly by the Portuguese, but this activity was quite limited, providing only the
    necessary details of the coastal areas where centers of trade and commerce were
    located. Some maps depicted features of the interior, though this information
    was often highly suspect. Many cartographers simply relied on unsubstantiated
    accounts of travels there or prior maps that reinforced and perpetuated these
    initial errors. The lack of empirical data severely compromised the validity of
    maps of Africa, a fact that Swift exploits in his poem in order to comment on the
    deceptive quality of all maps. The vast majority of the African continent would
    remain unexplored and unsurveyed in any regular fashion until the end of the
    eighteenth century, when imperial expansion demanded greater knowledge of
    the soon-to-be-colonized territory.
84. See Edney, "Reconsidering Enlightenment Geography and Map Making."
85. For a more thorough discussion of the relationship between empiricism and geo-
    graphy, see Bowen, *Empiricism and Geographical Thought*.
86. Frank Boyle offers a similar argument in the context of Swift's broader critique
    of modernity and narcissism. See *Swift as Nemesis*.
87. Helgerson, "The Folly of Maps and Modernity," 242. Helgerson examines at
    length the association between maps and worldliness in many seventeenth-
    century Dutch paintings, where their inclusion is often an iconographic clue to
    the viewer that the subject being depicted is, too, a figure of worldliness and so
    should be looked upon critically. Helgerson contends that this negative interpre-
    tation of the map coexists in tension with its more positive reading as a symbol
    of national identity and pride. Both readings are possible within a single painting,
    and this undecidability surrounding the map becomes a central thematic in the
    Dutch tradition. See also Helgerson, *Adulterous Alliances*.
88. A number of scholars have taken up Swift's critique of maps as a technology of
    empire, including Hawes, "Three Times around the Globe," and Neill, *British
    Discovery Literature and the Rise of Global Commerce*.
89. Wagner, *Reading Iconotexts*, 54.
90. For further discussion of the use of maps in *Gulliver's Travels*, see Moore, "The
    Geography of *Gulliver's Travels*," and Bracher, "The Maps in *Gulliver's Travels*."
    Both Moore and Bracher acknowledge a satirical strain in Swift's use of maps
    in *Gulliver's Travels*; however, Moore asserts that some of his "errors" may have
    been unintended, the product of a faulty or incomplete knowledge of the world's

geography, while Bracher comes closer to Wagner in his argument that Swift intentionally distorts the facts and confuses his reader in order to satirize contemporary literature of travel and discovery.

91. Swift, *Gulliver's Travels*, 41.

92. Swift, *Gulliver's Travels*, 100.

93. Swift, *Gulliver's Travels*, 100.

94. Swift, *Gulliver's Travels*, 40.

95. McKeon, *Origins of the English Novel, 1600–1740*, 350.

96. Swift, *Gulliver's Travels*, 40.

97. Neill discusses the relativity of Gulliver's rational and rationalizing view of the world, as well as his blindness to his own place in that world. See *British Discovery Literature and the Rise of Global Commerce*, 104–19.

98. Conley, *Self-Made Map*, 6.

99. Fabricant, *Swift's Landscape*, 1.

100. Fabricant, *Swift's Landscape*, 18–19. Fabricant discusses some of the salient differences between Swift's approach to representing the landscape and that of his Tory compatriots and friends, including Pope.

101. Fabricant, *Swift's Landscape*, 17. As Fabricant later notes in reference to Addison's man in a dungeon, "For those deprived beings who are trapped in their surroundings, detached aesthetic contemplation is at best laughable, a sign of self-delusion and blindness rather than superior perception or visual discernment" (175).

102. Williams, *The Country and the City*, 46–47. Quoted in Fabricant, *Swift's Landscape*, 40.

103. Fabricant, *Swift's Landscape*, 20–23.

104. Fabricant, *Swift's Landscape*, 155.

105. Fabricant, *Swift's Landscape*, 180. As she argues here and elsewhere, Swift was critical of the so-called "long view" because such distances allowed the observer to overlook or ignore the harsh, unpleasant realities of the Irish landscape. See also 182–83.

106. Fabricant, *Swift's Landscape*, 94. For more on Swift's attention to the "short view," see 186–87, 91.

107. On the connection between the Yahoos from *Gulliver's Travels* and Ireland, see Fabricant, *Swift's Landscape*, 35–36.

108. Fabricant, *Swift's Landscape*, 42.

109. See Bunn, "The Tory View of Geography," 154–55. Bunn goes on to argue that the traditional "Tory view" of the land as the true source of political power and authority is not antithetical or hostile to the notion of trade and commerce overseas, or imperial expansion for that matter. Citing James Harrington's *Oceana* (1656), Bunn suggests that it was simply a matter of which took precedence and that the country party widely embraced Harrington's idea of an "imperial republic" whose identity and moral character remained tied, first and foremost, to the land. Trade and commerce were seen, in this sense, as the means by which the republic naturally extended itself geographically, while, at the same time, preserving the integrity and value of those rural virtues and country house ideals that defined the Tory's vision of a greater Britain.

110. See Fabricant, *Swift's Landscape*, 95–96, 114–16, 123. When Swift does articulate

and advocate for the country house ideal, it is often from a position of an outsider who is alienated from its comforts and beauties.

111. Fabricant, *Swift's Landscape*, 84–85.

112. Fabricant, *Swift's Landscape*, 106.

113. Fabricant, *Swift's Landscape*, 73. Fabricant notes that, in the pastoral, the world of the country is often threatened by those who reside in the city, but for Swift, both the country and the city are already dominated by the commercial interest. Thus the Tory ideal of a virtuous country opposition no longer holds.

114. Fabricant, *Swift's Landscape*, 75.

115. Fabricant, *Swift's Landscape*, 171.

116. Fabricant, *Swift's Landscape*, 157.

117. Fabricant, *Swift's Landscape*, 160.

118. Swift, "Addison, Joseph," 252.

119. Swift, as a Tory, does believe emphatically in service to the king, but as he clarifies in the sermon "Doing Good," "By love of country, I do not mean loyalty to our King, for that is a duty of another nature" (233).

120. Richard Helgerson locates the emergence of this ambiguity regarding the meaning of "country" within the early seventeenth century when maps, surveys, and chorographies began to place a greater emphasis on land, rather than the monarch, as the primary point of national identification. As I am suggesting, the map may play a critical role in the rise of nationalism, as Helgerson argues, but perhaps not patriotism, which is more related to the idea of country rather than the nation. See *Forms of Nationhood*, 133.

121. During, "Literature—Nationalism's Other?," 140. See also Cunningham, "The Language of Patriotism, 1750–1914." Cunningham argues that Bolingbroke's brand of patriotism, while rooted in Greek and Roman antiquity, comes to him largely via the Italian humanists, Machiavelli most notably.

122. Bolingbroke, *Contributions to the Craftsman*, 18. Quoted in During, "Literature—Nationalism's Other?," 141.

123. *The Complete Works of William Hazlitt*, 4:67–68. Quoted in During, "Literature—Nationalism's Other?," 138.

124. Swift, "Doing Good," 233.

125. Swift, "On the Testimony of Conscience," 155–56. We see a similar formulation in Swift's "Cadenus and Vanessa" (1713), where he asserts that "*Greeks* and *Romans* understood," more so than their modern English counterparts, that "to perish for our Country's Good" is the noblest virtue (123). Furthermore, the epigraph with which I opened this chapter invokes this nostalgic longing for patriotic virtue, as "Great, Good and Just, *was once apply'd* / To One who for his Country died" but, unfortunately, is no longer (italics mine).

126. Ian Higgins identifies Lycurgus Sparta as the principle source for Swift's notion of patriotism, in particular, his emphasis on conformity and obedience in matters of state and the need for balanced government that adheres to constitutional law. Swift's High Anglican Toryism is, according to Higgins, a modified version of Spartan principles of governance. See Higgins, "Swift and Sparta." Apart from Lycurgus Sparta, we must also consider a variety of classical, mostly Roman, sources for Swift's musings on the purpose and value of patriotism, including,

among others, Cato, Cinna, and Cicero, to whom Swift once referred as "that consummate philosopher, and noble patriot," in "Mr. Collin's Discourse of Free-Thinking," 44.

127. Swift, "On the Irish Club," 428.

128. Swift, "A Project for the Advancement of Religion and the Reformation of Manners," 61. See also "The Sentiments of a Church-of-England Man," in which Swift states that "to sacrifice the Innocency of a Friend, the Good of our Country, or our own Conscience to the Humour, or Passion, or Interest of a Party; plainly shews that either our Heads or our Hearts are not as they should be" (1).

129. Swift, "A Project for the Advancement of Religion," 62. Swift goes on to argue that the moral authority of the Crown has been usurped to some extent by men whose fidelity to the queen and the church is suspect, if not entirely lacking.

130. Swift, "The Sentiments of a Church-of-England Man," 1. See also "On False Witness," in which Swift criticizes those who, due to their allegiance to party rather than king and country, resort to bearing false witness in order to take down their political enemies (180–89).

131. Swift, "The Sentiments of a Church-of-England Man," 2.

132. Swift, "A Letter to the Right Honourable the Lord Viscount Molesworth," 92.

133. Swift, "Doing Good," 236.

134. Swift, "Doing Good," 236.

135. Swift, "A Letter to the Lord Chancellor Middleton," 108.

136. Conversely, in "A Letter to Mr. Harding the Printer," Swift calls those who support Wood and his coin "betrayers of their country" who "would sell their Souls and their Country" (15, 22).

137. Swift, "A Letter to the Lord Chancellor Middleton," 113.

138. Vincent, *Nationalism and Particularity*, 114–15. Vincent sums up this distinction: "Patriotism is the great lost, liberty-based language of the ancients, nationalism is a modern aberration."

139. Swift, "The Advantages Proposed by Repealing the Sacramental Test," 248.

140. Swift, "A Letter to the Whole People of Ireland," 63.

141. Swift, "An Humble Address to Both Houses of Parliament," 136.

142. Swift, "An Humble Address to Both Houses of Parliament," 136–37. We see the same sentiment leveled at the Anglican clergy in Swift's "A Preface to the Bishop of Sarum's Introduction to the Third Volume of the History of the Reformation of the Church of England" (1713). Paraphrasing Burnet's text, Swift declaims, *"The Bulk of the Clergy, and one Third of the Bishops are stupid Sons of Whores, who think of nothing but getting Money as soon as they can: If they may but procure enough to supply them in Gluttony, Drunkenness, and Whoring, they are ready to turn Traytors to God and their Country, and make their Fellow Subjects Slaves"* (69).

143. See Griffin, *Patriotism and Poetry in Eighteenth-Century England*; Hill, "The English Revolution and Patriotism"; Colley, "Radical Patriotism in Eighteenth-Century England"; Furtado, "National Pride in Seventeenth-Century England"; and Cunningham, "The Language of Patriotism."

144. The title "the Hibernian Patriot" had been given to Swift by George Faulkner. See McGinn, "A Weary Patriot."

145. See Mahony, "The Irish Colonial Experience and Swift's Rhetorics of Percep-

tion in the 1720s." Mahony argues elsewhere that many Irish Catholics remained skeptical of, if not outright hostile to, Protestant claims on Swift as a true Irish patriot throughout the eighteenth and nineteenth centuries. In fact, it is not until the twentieth century that revisionist histories of the period began to embrace Swift as a champion of Ireland's poor and oppressed, regardless of their religious orientation. See also Mahony, *Jonathan Swift.*

146. See Hill, *From Patriots to Unionists*, 57–62.

147. Swift's antagonism toward Dissent, in all of its forms, is well documented in sources too numerous to mention here. However, with respect to his views on Dissent and its relationship to patriotism, see Holmes, "James Arbuckle and Dean Swift," and Hayton, *Ruling Ireland, 1685–1742.*

148. Hayton observes that Whigs in Ireland and England were united ideologically and politically after 1688; however, they eventually split over the issue of Dissent, with England largely in support of their cause and Irish Whigs demanding loyalty to the Anglican Church. Protestant patriotism and High Church Toryism begin to unite at this period as many Whigs join the Tory Party, especially in Ireland, over the question of Dissent's future role within government and the republic at large. Hayton, *Ruling Ireland*, 68, 70–71, 90–95.

149. Swift, *The History of the Four Last Years of the Queen*, 7:106. The act was officially titled "An Act that the Solemn Affirmation and Declaration of the People Called Quakers, Shall be Accepted, Instead of an Oath in the Usual Form" (1696).

150. Swift, *History of the Four Last Years of the Queen*, 107.

151. Swift, *History of the Four Last Years of the Queen*, 107.

152. Their refusal to swear the oath of allegiance to the king, the country, and its laws is one such instance not far from Swift's mind in recounting this particular bit of history. The result was the Quaker Act of 1662, which made not taking the oath illegal, and the Conventicle Act of 1664, which outlawed all Quaker meetings because they refused the oath of allegiance.

153. Swift, *Examiner*, "No. 14, November 9, 1710," 10.

154. Swift, *Examiner*, "No. 13, November 2, 1710," 5.

155. Swift, *Examiner*, "No. 13, November 2, 1710," 6.

156. Swift, "The Sentiments of a Church-of-England Man," 7.

157. Swift, "*Horace*, Book I, Ode XIV, *O navis, referent, &c.* Paraphrased and inscribed to *Ireland*," 283.

158. Swift, "The Answer of the Right Honourable William Pulteney, Esq; to the Right Honourable Sir Robert Walpole," 119.

159. Swift, "Short Remarks on Bishop Burnet's History," 268.

160. Swift, "Short Remarks on Bishop Burnet's History," 345.

161. Swift, *A Modest Proposal*, 118.

162. Swift, *A Modest Proposal*, 113.

163. Swift, *A Modest Proposal*, 116.

164. Swift, *Gulliver's Travels*, 52.

165. Swift, *Gulliver's Travels*, 58.

166. Swift, *Gulliver's Travels*, 53.

167. Swift, *Gulliver's Travels*, 55.

168. Swift, *Gulliver's Travels*, 70.

169. Swift, *Gulliver's Travels*, 96.
170. Swift, *Gulliver's Travels*, 116.
171. Swift, *Gulliver's Travels*, 120.
172. Swift, *Gulliver's Travels*, 122.
173. Swift, *Gulliver's Travels*, 116.
174. Swift, *Gulliver's Travels*, 183.
175. Swift, *Gulliver's Travels*, 186–87.
176. Swift, *Gulliver's Travels*, 186.
177. Swift, *Gulliver's Travels*, 188.
178. Swift, *Gulliver's Travels*, 186–87.
179. Swift, *Gulliver's Travels*, 268, 269, 271.
180. Swift, *Gulliver's Travels*, 240.
181. Swift, *Gulliver's Travels*, 274. For more on the Houyhnhnms' relationship to republican virtue, see Higgins, "Swift and Sparta."
182. Swift, *Gulliver's Travels*, 273.
183. Swift, *Gulliver's Travels*, 273.

## 4. Daniel Defoe and the Limits to the Market

1. Sen, *Empire of Free Trade*, 11–12.
2. Sen, *Empire of Free Trade*, 3.
3. See also Edney, *Mapping an Empire*.
4. Sen, *Empire of Free Trade*, 91.
5. Sen, *Empire of Free Trade*, 91–95. A critical figure in producing this "geography of order" was James Rennell, a military engineer and surveyor general of the East India Company. He helped organize the colony into a manageable space for military and financial exploitation in his *Bengal Atlas* (1782) and *Description of the Roads in Bengal and Bahar* (1778), both of which ignore the sacred and secular features of more traditional geographies. Sen, quite rightly, aligns Rennell's work with that of William Roy and John Sinclair's efforts to order and map Scotland.
6. Sen, *Empire of Free Trade*, 15. Chapter 1, "Passages of Authority," provides a general description of India's precolonial marketplace as "a world of exchange characterized by multiple domains" and governed by "overlapping authorities and obligations." In this sense, the marketplace was not a singular entity but rather pluralistic in its various cultural and social uses.
7. Sen, *Empire of Free Trade*, 7–8.
8. The primary target of Sen's critique is Immanuel Wallerstein's "world systems" theory as it is outlined in his *The Modern World System: Capitalist Agriculture and the Origins of the European World Economy in the Sixteenth Century* (1974) and *The Modern World System II: Mercantilism and the Consolidation of the European World-Economy, 1600–1750* (1980). Wallerstein and others who ascribe to his model of economic relations merely reproduce the geography of colonial expansion rather than offering a substantive critique of its bias toward industrializing nations rather than the colonial margins.
9. Sen, *Empire of Free Trade*, 129.
10. See Richard Cantillon, *Essai sur la nature du commerce en général* (1759); Francois

Quesnay, *Tableau économique* (1758); and David Ricardo, *On the Principles of Political Economy and Taxation* (1817).

11. Agnew, *Worlds Apart*, 56.
12. Agnew, *Worlds Apart*, 43–46. Agnew relates this etymological change to Marx's distinction between use and exchange value within the commodity form. The marketplace is identified here with the circulation of useful and necessary commodities, with money as the principle medium of exchange, which is expressed in the formula C-M-C. In the transition to capitalism, this equation would be inverted so that commodities become the medium of exchange for the circulation of money, or M-C-M. Subsequently, the market loses its shape and definition as exchange value, figured in terms of the liquidity of money, now defines capitalist social relations in ways that cannot be neatly circumscribed.
13. The integration of trade on a national scale is dependent on a high degree of specialization within both local and regional marketplaces throughout the seventeenth and eighteenth centuries. See Everitt, *Landscape and Community in England.*
14. Agnew, *Worlds Apart*, 41.
15. Hilton, "Lords, Burgesses and Hucksters," 6. The emergence of regional, or cardinal, marketplaces after 1570, such as Exeter, York, Shrewsbury, Canterbury, Maidstone, and Northampton, among others, occurs for a variety of reasons, including declining regional populations, lack of adequate roads and bridges, competition from larger markets, and the concentration of capital in a small but stable population of rural landowners. See also Everitt, *Landscape and Community in England*, 111.
16. Agnew, *Worlds Apart*, 50.
17. See Everitt, "The Marketing of Agricultural Produce, 1500–1640," 577–86. A proclamation of 1619 expanded the duties of the clerk to include punishing those who violated the laws of the marketplace, inspecting the system of weights and measures to make sure there was no abuse, checking the quality of merchandise, and mediating fluctuations in price, supply, and demand.
18. See Chartres, "The Marketing of Agricultural Produce, 1640–1750," 495–501.
19. Everitt, "The Marketing of Agricultural Produce, 1500–1640," 486.
20. The OED defines the common beam as "the transverse bar from the ends of which the scales of a balance are suspended; the public standard balance formerly in the custody of the Grocers' Company of London; *fig.* an authorized standard." As Alan Everitt points out, the construction of market halls arose out of the "statutory obligation" to provide a "common beam," or a regular system of weights and measures to guarantee a certain degree of uniformity in all transactions. Tolls were then exacted for the use of the common beam, which became an important source of revenue for the town. "The Marketing of Agricultural Produce, 1500–1640," 31–32.
21. See Randall and Charlesworth, *Markets, Market Culture and Popular Protest in Eighteenth-Century Britain and Ireland.*
22. Randall and Charlesworth, *Markets, Market Culture and Popular Protest*, 24.
23. Schmiechen and Carls, *The British Market Hall*, 8. See also Smith, "The Market Place and the Market's Place in London, c. 1660–1840."

24. Seller produced terrestrial maps in addition to the *Anglia Contracta,* including the *Atlas Minimus; or, A Book of Geography: Shewing All the Empires, Monarchies, Kingdomes, Regions, Dominions, Principalities, and Countries in the Whole World* (1679). Seller's interest in maps extended into more general texts on the subjects of navigation and geography, such as *A Pocket Book: Containing Severall Choice Collections in Arithmetick, Astronomy, Geometry, Surveying, Dialling, Navigation, Astrology, Geography, Measuring, Gageing* (1677), *A New Systeme of Geography* (1685), and *Practical Navigation; or, An Introduction to the Whole Art* (1672).

25. The OED provides the following commentary on the history and usage of the term. "Most of the English counties were divided into hundreds; but in some counties *wapentakes,* and in others *wards,* appear as divisions of a similar kind. The origin of the division into hundreds, which appears already in OED. Times, is exceedingly obscure, and very diverse opinions have been given as to its origin. 'It has been regarded as denoting simply a division of a hundred hides of land; as the district which furnished a hundred warriors to the host; as representing the original settlement of the hundred warriors; or as composed of a hundred hides, each of which furnished a single warrior' (Stubbs *Const. Hist.* I.v. §45). 'It is certain that in some hundred instances the hundred was deemed to contain exactly 100 hides of land.' (F. W. Maitland). The hundred, OHG. (Alemannisch) *huntari, huntre,* was a subdivision of the *gau* in Ancient Germany; but the connexion between this and the English *hundred* is not clearly made out."

26. *A Book of the Names of All the Parishes, Market Towns, Villages, Hamlets, and Smallest Places, In England and Wales* (London: M.S., 1657), title-page. This text is an expanded version of an earlier work, *A Direction for the English Traveller* (1643), whose author also remains unidentified.

27. *A Book of the Names,* 2.

28. Playford, Vade *Mecum; or, The Necessary Companion,* 25.

29. *England's Golden Treasury; or, The True Vade Mecum,* 63.

30. The map of the Americas included in Lewes's text is John Overton's "A New and Most Exact Map of America" (1671), which had also been published separately the same year.

31. Ogilby and Morgan, *Mr. Ogilby's and William Morgan, Pocket Book of the Roads.* The quote is drawn from the "Explanation" that precedes the table.

32. As Robert Mayhew argues, Ogilby's placement of London at the center of his road maps reflects a royalist bias that sought to stress connections between the monarch and the land. While this is perhaps true of Ogilby's *Britannia* (1675), its predecessor, the *Pocket Book of the Roads,* appears more utilitarian than ideological in its recognition of London as the de facto center of trade and commerce. See Mayhew, *Enlightenment Geography: The Political Languages of British Geography, 1650–1850,* 66–85. For a further discussion of Ogilby's road maps, see also Wall, *The Prose of Things,* 53–59.

33. Defoe also includes maps by Herman Moll at the beginning of each letter in the *Tour.* See Rogers, "Defoe's Use of Maps of Wales," and "Further Notes on Defoe's *Tour Thro' Great Britain.*"

34. Andrews, "Defoe and the Sources of his *Tour,*" 272.

35. See Heidenreich, *The Libraries of Daniel Defoe and Phillips Farewell: Oliver Payne's Sales Catalogue* (1731). My evidence is admittedly somewhat tenuous given the fact that we cannot distinguish between what exactly belonged to Defoe and what belonged to Farewell, but it is a fact still worthy of note given the subject of my analysis.

36. Schellenberg, "Imagining the Nation," 297.

37. Defoe, *Tour*, 85.

38. Defoe, *Tour*, 260.

39. Defoe, *Tour*, 260.

40. Defoe, *Tour*, 261.

41. Parkes, "'A True Survey of the Ground,'" 396. Parkes's essay contends that Defoe plays a critical role in the development of "thematic cartography" and the discipline of economic geography specifically. He thus correctly reinserts exchange and market activity back into Defoe's own thinking about the space of the nation. Most scholarship on the *Tour*, however, fails to acknowledge this fact by characterizing Defoe as something of an armchair scientist and dilettante who applied facts and figures for the purposes of fiction rather than the furthering of geographic knowledge.

42. Meier, *Defoe and the Defense of Commerce*, 57.

43. Defoe, *The Compleat English Tradesman*, 2:2–3.

44. Rogers, *Text of Great Britain*, 46.

45. Rogers, *Text of Great Britain*, 57.

46. Bowers, "Great Britain Imagined," 161.

47. Copeland, "Defoe and the London Wall," 413. Copeland quotes Michel de Certeau, "Practices of Space," 122–45. The use of "mapped perspectives," Copeland notes, can also be seen in Defoe's *Robinson Crusoe* (1719), *Captain Singleton* (1720), *Moll Flanders* (1722), *Colonel Jack* (1722), and *Roxana* (1724).

48. Defoe, *The Compleat English Gentleman*, 225–26. See also Edney, "Irony of Imperial Mapping," 24–25.

49. Wall, "Grammars of Space," 389.

50. Wall, "Grammars of Space," 387–412. Wall's essay forms the basis for her more extended treatment of Defoe in *The Literary and Cultural Spaces of Restoration London*.

51. Schellenberg, "Imagining the Nation," 297.

52. Defoe, *Compleat English Tradesman*, 2:3–4.

53. Defoe, *Compleat English Tradesman*, 2:3.

54. Sherman, *Finance and Fictionality*, 10.

55. Sherman, *Finance and Fictionality*, 130–31.

56. Jesse Edwards makes a similar argument, claiming that such "uncertainty" should be properly read as signs of the wondrous and miraculous with respect to trade and commerce, a kind of an "economic sublime." See "Defoe the Geographer."

57. Sherman, *Finance and Fictionality*, 154–55.

58. Defoe, *A Brief State of the Inland or Home Trade*, 29–30.

59. We see this idea echoed in Defoe's *A Journal of the Plague Year* (1724) when servants break down the boundaries between the market and the domestic space, collapsing any real distinction between either sphere. The incorporation of home

and market, of household and urban economies, is predicated on and exacer-
bated by the plague itself. See Sherman, "Servants and Semiotics."

60. Defoe, *A Brief State of the Inland or Home Trade*, 59–60.

61. Schellenberg, "Imagining the Nation," 305.

62. Rogers, *Text of Great Britain*, 48. Rogers spends a great deal of time showing
how the *Tour* appropriates and mirrors Defoe's travels, arguing that, in effect,
the actual journey and its figuration achieve a kind of simultaneity that is at the
heart of Defoe's vision of the nation. However, even Rogers admits that Defoe,
at times, deploys a Shandean self-consciousness in order to dramatize the act of
making the literal and figurative mirror one another, which suggests that the *Tour*
departs in crucial ways from this supposed goal of transparency.

63. Defoe, *Tour*, 262.

64. Defoe, *Tour*, 263. As we are told in a brief note, Bristol's Tolsey was replaced by a
new exchange house built by John Wood the Elder in 1741–43.

65. Steve Poole argues that "the paternalistic nature of Bristol's civic tradition" in fact
prevented the city from experiencing riots on the scale of many other English cities and towns during the same period. Rather than capitulate entirely to market
forces, Bristol sought to control and regulate market activity in a way that would
stem the tide of popular protest and promote social harmony. See "Scarcity and
the Civic Tradition."

66. See Sherman, "Servants and Semiotics." For Sherman, servants function as
"reversible," or unstable, signs within a credit-based economy since they must
mediate, like texts themselves, between abstract participants engaged the act of
exchange and the circulation of capital. It is the impersonality of the market that
requires this form of mediation, yet Defoe is wary of the servants' ability to resist
signification due to their volatile and mobile nature.

67. Defoe, *Tour*, 491.

68. Defoe, *Tour*, 495.

69. Defoe, *Tour*, 497.

70. Defoe, *A Brief State of the Inland or Home Trade*, 15.

71. Defoe, *A Brief State of the Inland or Home Trade*, 17.

72. Defoe, *A Plan of the English Commerce*, 255.

73. Defoe, *A Plan of the English Commerce*, 256.

74. Defoe, *Tour*, 286–87.

75. Defoe, *Tour*, 288.

76. Copeland, "Defoe and the London Wall," 414.

77. Defoe, *Tour*, 66.

78. Defoe, *Tour*, 67.

79. Defoe, *Tour*, 68. Defoe strongly criticizes Macky's account of Ipswich, arguing
that it is not quite as decayed as he made it out. He faults his facts and his powers of observations, commenting that "superficial observers, must be superficial
writers, if they write at all."

80. Defoe, *Tour*, 70.

81. Defoe, *Tour*, 154.

82. Defoe, *Tour*, 596.

83. Alistair Duckworth offers a similar reading of this passage in "'Whig' Landscapes

in Defoe's *Tour*," 459. Duckworth argues that Defoe appropriates the classical topos of "unbought provisions" found in many country house poems of the seventeenth century and simply applies it to the Scottish marketplace.

84. Defoe, *Tour*, 601.

## 5. THIS OLD HOUSE AND SAMUEL JOHNSON'S SCOTLAND

1. For more on the rapid growth of Scotland's economy during the eighteenth century, and in particular the material effects of that growth on its geography, see Turnock, *The Historical Geography of Scotland since 1707*; Whyte and Whyte, *The Changing Scottish Landscape, 1500–1800*; Devine, *The Transformation of Rural Scotland*; and Hamilton, *An Economic History of Scotland in the Eighteenth Century*.

2. Devine, *Transformation of Rural Scotland*, 61.

3. Some relevant examples include Camden, *Britannia* (1607); Pont, "The Pont Maps of Scotland" (1583–1614); Blaeu, *Theatrum Orbis Terrarum Sive Atlas Novus*, vol. 5 (1654); Gordon and Gordon, "The Manuscript Maps of Robert & James Gordon, ca. 1636–1652"; Martin, *A Description of the Western Islands of Scotland* (1703); and Sibbald, *Scotia Illustrata sive Prodromus Historiae Naturalis* (1683–84), and *A Collection of Several Treatises concerning Scotland* (1739).

4. For more on the relationship between antiquarian topography and Scottish national self-image, see Withers, "How Scotland Came to Know Itself," and *Geography, Science and National Identity*.

5. In 1683, Robert Sibbald, geographer royal to Charles II, proposed a general atlas of Scotland, to be divided into two sections, *Scotia Antiqua* and *Scotia Moderna*, reflecting his interest in both ancient and modern Scotland. See Sibbald, *Account of the Scottish Atlas, or Description of Scotland Ancient and Modern* (1683).

6. Withers, "Reporting, Mapping, Trusting," 516. For examples of Adair's antiquarian work, see his *Queries in order to a True Description: And, an Account of the Natural Curiousitys, and Antiquities* (1694), as well as his drawings of Arthur's O'on, a Roman structure located near the Antonine wall.

7. Quoted in Withers, "Reporting, Mapping, Trusting," 515.

8. Moir and Inglis, *The Early Maps of Scotland to 1850*, 1:75.

9. Moir and Inglis, *The Early Maps of Scotland to 1850*, 1:65–78. While Adair had previously worked on Sibbald's ill-fated *Atlas Scotiae*, due to his contractual obligations to Sibbald and numerous financial hardships, many of Adair's surveys and maps were not published until the early eighteenth century. His 1686 survey of the coast of Scotland first appeared in his *The Description of the Sea-Coasts and Islands of Scotland, with Large and Exact Maps for the Use of Seamen* (1703).

10. Moll notes that his maps are based on various surveys by Adair as well as other seventeenth-century geographers, such as Timothy Pont and Robert Gordon.

11. Curley, *Samuel Johnson and the Age of Travel*, 208, 216. Curley defines Whig topographers as those who "looked to Britain's future prosperity rather than Scotland's past glory and championed modern progress, trade, and industry."

12. Moll offers similar comments about the abundance of fish and livestock next to an inset map of the Shetland Islands and also St. Kilda.

13. Moll and Defoe knew one another personally and professionally, and it is widely suspected that Defoe took the title of his novel *Moll Flanders* from the book *A History of Flanders with Moll's Map*. See Reinhartz, *The Cartographer and the Literati*.

14. Apart from its practical applications, the *Report*, like many of the other Whig geographies, evinces strong nationalistic overtones, such as when Smeaton compares his canal to the Canal Royal de Languedoc in France and concludes that the French efforts are neither geographically nor economically sound: "That the same toll which will hardly keep the *French* canal in repair, will make this a very beneficial undertaking to the *British* adventurers" (15). By playing on anti-French sentiment, Smeaton is able to advocate the canal as beneficial to Great Britain as a whole, and not Scotland exclusively.

15. Anderson, *Account of the Present State of the Hebrides and Western Coasts of Scotland*, i–ii.

16. The subject of appendix IX of Anderson's *Account* is "Observations on Mr. Murdoch Mackenzie's charts of the Hebrides and Western Coasts of Scotland, by the same" (403–16). Anderson takes Mackenzie and his maps, many of which were published between 1775 and 1776, to task for being inaccurate and filled with errors. In response, Mackenzie published a defense of his maps entitled *Justification of Mr. Murdoch McKenzie's Nautical Survey of the Orkney Islands and Hebrides, in Answer to the Accusations of Doctor Anderson* (1785).

17. See Sweet, *Antiquaries*; Woolf, *The Social Circulation of the Past*; Piggott, *Ancient Britons and the Antiquarian Imagination*; Jacks, *The Antiquarian and the Myth of Antiquity*; and Levine, *Humanism and History*.

18. Black, *Maps and History*, 17–18.

19. Manning, "Antiquarianism, the Scottish Science of Man, and the Emergence of Modern Disciplinarity," 68.

20. Eric Gidal makes a similar argument with respect to the various attempts of antiquarian scholars to substantiate the poetry of Ossian using maps, topographical descriptions, and statistical data. See *Ossianic Unconformities*, 55–124.

21. For further analysis of the connection between cartography and the creation of Roman Britain, see Hingley, "Projecting Empire."

22. Ayres, *Classical Culture and the Idea of Rome*, 84.

23. Ayres, *Classical Culture and the Idea of Rome*, 86.

24. Sibbald, *Historical Inquiries, Concerning the Roman Monuments and Antiquities in the North Part of Britain called Scotland* (1707), iii.

25. For further information on William Stukeley, see Hancock, *William Stukeley*, and Piggott, *William Stukeley*.

26. The map is attributed to Herman Moll, who also included it in his own *A set of fifty new and correct maps of England and Wales* as well as *A new description of England and Wales, with the adjacent islands* (1724), both of which were published the same year as Stukeley's text.

27. Gordon, *Itinerarium Septentrionale: or, A Journey Thro' most of the Counties of Scotland, and Those in the North of England* (1726), vii.

28. Ayres, *Classical Culture and the Idea of Rome*, 100–102. Ayres points out that Gordon was considered a bit too sympathetic to his native Scotland by his fellow

antiquaries. His chosen name as a member of the Society of the Roman Knights, a group of antiquarians dedicated to the study of Roman Britain founded by Stukeley, was Galgacus, the name of the leader of the Caledonian forces that fought and were defeated by Agricola at Mons Graupius in 84 AD. However, Gordon's identification with Scottish nationalism was complimentary with his belief that Rome had been a civilizing influence on his native country.

29. Horsley, *Britannia Romana*, ii.

30. Horsley, *Britannia Romana*, xxx.

31. Roy, *Military Antiquities*, iv–v.

32. O'Donoghue, *William Roy, 1726–1790*, 19–20.

33. Roy, *Military Antiquities*, 142–47.

34. The title page of *Military Antiquities* states that Roy was "Major-General of his Majesty's Forces, Deputy Quarter-Master General, and Colonel of the Thirtieth Regiment of Foot."

35. Roy, *Military Antiquities*, i.

36. Roy, *Military Antiquities*, ii. For a more detailed analysis of Roy's work, see Hodson, "The Lucubrations of His Leisure Hours"; Macdonald, "General William Roy and His 'Military Antiquities of the Romans in North Britain'"; and Andrews, *Maps in Those Days*.

37. Hudson, *Samuel Johnson and the Making of Modern England*, 22.

38. Hudson, *Samuel Johnson and the Making of Modern England*, 22. Quoted from Johnson's *Works* (1825), 6:56.

39. Johnson, *Journey*, 52.

40. Johnson, *Journey*, 51. See also Law, "Samuel Johnson on Consumer Demand, Status, and Positional Goods."

41. Johnson, *Journey*, 147.

42. Johnson, *Journey*, 73.

43. Johnson, *Journey*, 48. Robert Mayhew notes that Johnson appreciated the value of geographic knowledge in matters of trade and commerce and cites Johnson's prefaces to *The Preceptor* (1748), Rolt's *Dictionary of Trade* (1671), and MacBean's *Dictionary of Ancient Geography* (1773) as evidence of his support for the commercial value of geography. See Mayhew, *Geography and Literature Historical in Context*, 12–17.

44. Hudson, *Samuel Johnson and the Making of Modern England*, 23.

45. Johnson, *Journey*, 96.

46. Hudson, *Samuel Johnson and the Making of Modern England*, 23.

47. Lynch, "Beating the Track of the Alphabet," 379. As I have noted, the "economic rationalization" of Scotland begins prior to 1745, though the pace of change certainly becomes more rapid after that point.

48. See Wechselblatt, "Finding Mr. Boswell." Wechselblatt points out that Johnson's criticism of Scotland's commercialization, in fact, mirrors his criticisms of the same process simultaneously unfolding at home in England: "In a sense, what Johnson 'finds' in Scotland, recognizes in the other, is the commercialization of *England*, the motor-force driving the geopolitical realization of Enlightenment outward" (141).

49. Johnson, *Journey*, 94.

50. Johnson, *Journey*, 99.

51. Johnson, *Journey*, 66.

52. Johnson, *Journey*, 55.

53. Johnson, *Journey*, 80.

54. Johnson, *Journey*, 62.

55. Johnson, *Journey*, 146.

56. For critical works that discuss Johnson's vexed attitudes toward antiquarianism, literary antiquarianism in particular, see Harrison, "Samuel Johnson's Folkloristics"; Kaminski, "Johnson and Oldys as Biographers"; Lipking, *The Ordering of the Arts in the Eighteenth Century*; Lynch, *The Age of Elizabeth in the Age of Johnson*; and Vance, *Samuel Johnson and the Sense of History*.

57. Vance, *Samuel Johnson and the Sense of History*, 63.

58. Vance cites *Rambler* nos. 82, 83, 161, and 177 as examples of Johnson's critical attitudes toward antiquarianism.

59. Vance, *Samuel Johnson and the Sense of History*, 82.

60. *The Letters of Samuel Johnson*, 1:340. Pat Rogers notes that the letter was likely composed on August 12 based on a postscript from Johnson mentioning that he had written the letter but forgot to send it. See Rogers, *Johnson and Boswell*.

61. Johnson, preface to *A Dictionary of Ancient Geography*, by Alexander MacBean (1773), iv.

62. See Johnson, *An Account of an Attempt to Ascertain the Longitude* (1755). The original text was published under the pseudonym Zachariah Williams.

63. My thanks to Paul Baines for his insight regarding antiquarianism and its various political affiliations. While Whigs generally supported the production of economically themed geographies and Tories embraced more antiquarian fare, such broad categorizations don't always hold when confronted with a publication history that reveals varying ideological and political motivations on either side of the divide. As Baines notes, Tory figures, such as George Hickes, Richard Rawlinson, Thomas Hearne, Brown Willis, and Humphrey Wanley, all professed an interest in antiquarian studies, yet many Whigs also displayed antiquarian tendencies, including White Kennett, Edmund Gibson, Roger Gale, and William Stukeley.

64. Curley, *Samuel Johnson and the Age of Travel*, 209. In Boswell's *Journal of a Tour to the Hebrides*, Macaulay gives Johnson a copy of his book, for which he thanks him, commenting "it was a very pretty piece of topography" (222). Johnson's politeness in this instance, however, does not contradict his overall reservations regarding Macaulay's text, which also serves as the basis for Johnson and Boswell's route through the Highlands.

65. Curley, *Samuel Johnson and the Age of Travel*, 207.

66. Johnson, *Journey*, 78–79.

67. Boswell, *Life of Johnson*, 3:274. Quoted in Curley, *Samuel Johnson and the Age of Travel*, 210. Thomas Pennant identified himself as a "moderate Tory" who was, like many Whigs of the period, an ardent supporter of the 1707 Act of Union and a staunch critic of Jacobitism. Pennant, however, feared populism in all its forms, whether Roman Catholic or Puritan in nature. See Mayhew, *Enlightenment Geography*, 143–51.

68. Johnson, *Journey*, 125.

69. For more on Johnson's ambivalent views on imperialism, see Hawes, "Johnson and Imperialism"; Scherwatzky, "Johnson, Rasselas, and the Politics of Empire"; Curley, "Johnson and the Irish"; Hudson, "The Material and Ideological Development of the British Empire," in *Samuel Johnson and the Making of Modern England*, 170–220; and Aravamudan, "The Despotic Eye and Oriental Sublime" in *Tropicopolitans: Colonialism and Agency, 1688–1804*, 190–229.

70. Johnson, "Introduction to *The World Display'd*," 209.

71. Johnson, "Introduction to *The World Display'd*," 220.

72. Franklin's 1755 edition was reprinted in London by Dodsley.

73. For more on Evans's and Johnson's relationship to his work, see the brief introduction that accompanies Johnson's "Review of Lewis Evans."

74. Johnson, "Review of Lewis Evans," 200.

75. Johnson, "Review of Lewis Evans," 201.

76. Hudson, *Samuel Johnson and the Making of Modern England*, 150.

77. Boswell, *Journal*, 239. As many have noted, Boswell's Johnson frequently conflicts with the image of Johnson we receive in the *Journey*. While Johnson acknowledges that many of his observations may appear trivial and unworthy of note, he routinely defends his choice of subjects as vital to producing a more accurate picture of Scotland. Boswell, conversely, has little patience for Johnson's preference for the mundane and commonplace, believing that such interests are beneath a man of his supposed dignity and repute. For more on Boswell's representation of Johnson in the *Journal*, see Radner, "Constructing an Adventure and Negotiating for Narrative Control," and Savage, "'Roving among the Hebrides.'"

78. Martin, *A Description of the Western Islands of Scotland*, 238.

79. Macaulay, *History of the Island of St. Kilda*, 44.

80. Macaulay, *History of the Island of St. Kilda*, 49.

81. Pennant, *A Tour in Scotland and Voyage to the Hebrides*, 237.

82. Boswell, *Journal*, 338.

83. Johnson, *Journey*, 47.

84. Johnson, *Journey*, 48.

85. Johnson, *Journey*, 85.

86. Johnson, *Journey*, 48.

87. As many critics have shown, Johnson's keen interest in domestic matters is not restricted only to the *Journey*. It is, in fact, a subject to which he returns quite frequently prior to his travels through Scotland, albeit in the context of his native England and the emerging public sphere discourse regarding the moral and social value of home. See Bogel, "The Rhetoric of Substantiality"; Bush, *Samuel Johnson and the Art of Domesticity*; Grundy, "Celebrare Domestica Facta"; Hart, "Everyday Life in Johnson," in *Samuel Johnson and the Culture of Property*; Henson, "Johnson and the Condition of Women"; and Weinbrot, "Samuel Johnson and the Domestic Metaphor."

88. Johnson often uses the local and the particular, in this instance, the home, in order to illustrate and expound upon more universal themes and subjects. For more on Johnson's descriptive and rhetorical techniques, see Edinger, *Johnson and Detailed Representation*; Edinger, "Johnson on Conceit"; and Donaldson, "Samuel Johnson and the Art of Observation."

89. Johnson, *Rambler* no. 161, 5:94.

90. Mayhew, *Samuel Johnson and Eighteenth-Century English Conceptions of Geography*, 29. Mayhew argues that Johnson's "anti-geographical" methodology can be seen in a number of his works, including *The Vanity of Human Wishes* (1749) and *The History of Rasselas, Prince of Abyssinia* (1759), as well as *Rambler* nos. 135, 204, and 205. See also Vance, *Samuel Johnson and the Sense of History*, 11–12. Mayhew further explores the relationship between Johnson's moral and empirical landscapes in his *Landscape, Literature and English Religious Culture, 1660–1800*, 127–308.

91. *The Letters of Samuel Johnson*, 1:340.

92. Johnson frequently criticizes those who remain idle at home and refuse to challenge their ideas and beliefs about the world through the enlightening experience of travel. As Johnson states in *Idler* no. 58, "A few miles teach him the fallacies of the imagination" (181). For other examples that address this issue, see also *Idler* no. 97 (295–300) and no. 101 (309–11).

93. Johnson, *Journey*, 143. Johnson applies these derogatory terms to their guide's description of the bishop's house at Iona, which he says cannot be trusted as a result.

94. Curley, *Samuel Johnson and the Age of Travel*, 193.

95. Mayhew, *Samuel Johnson and Eighteenth-Century English Conceptions of Geography*, 36.

96. Percy, *Reliques of Ancient English Poetry* (1765), viii–ix. The quote is from Johnson's dedication to Lady Northumberland.

97. Wechselblatt, "Finding Mr. Boswell," 128.

98. Hudson, *Samuel Johnson and the Making of Modern England*, 161. Hudson notes that Johnson himself thought that England had only recently emerged from its more barbaric state, beginning roughly during the Renaissance.

99. Johnson, *Journey*, 46.

100. Johnson offers a similar historical interpretation of the caves at Raasay "into which the rude nations of the first ages retreated from the weather." They were also used in the service of "piratical expeditions." *Journey*, 77.

101. Johnson, *Journey*, 47.

102. Johnson, *Journey*, 105.

103. Johnson, *Journey*, 105.

104. Johnson, *Journey*, 106.

105. Johnson, *Journey*, 81.

106. Johnson, *Journey*, 81.

107. Boswell, *Journal*, 291.

108. Johnson's hybridized image of a home that is at once ancient and modern, Scottish and English, is not unlike the one William Blackstone uses in the *Commentaries* to describe the nature of the common law and the grounds of its authority: "We inherit an old Gothic castle, erected in the days of chivalry, but fitted up for a modern inhabitant. The moated ramparts, the embattled towers, and the trophied halls, are magnificent and venerable, but useless. The inferior apartments, now converted into rooms of convenience, are chearful and commodious,

though their approaches are winding and difficult." Blackstone, *Commentaries on the Laws of England*, 3:268.

109. Johnson, *Journey*, 146.
110. Johnson, *Journey*, 144.
111. Johnson, *Journey*, 150.
112. Johnson, *Journey*, 151.
113. Johnson, *Journey*, 150.
114. Boswell, *Journal*, 396.
115. Johnson, *Journey*, 74.
116. Johnson, *Journey*, 74.
117. Johnson, *Journey*, 75.
118. Johnson, *Journey*, 55.
119. Johnson, *Rambler* no. 168, 5:126.
120. Johnson, *Journey*, 137.
121. Johnson, *Rambler* no. 20, 3:115.
122. Fredric Bogel discusses at length this dialectic in Johnson's writings as well as within eighteenth century thought more generally: "The rhetoric of substantiality ... permits us to designate aspects of common experience, and to ascribe value to them, without claiming that value is merely a subjective imposition or that it derives from a sphere—whether moral, aesthetic, or metaphysical—distinct from common experience itself." "The Rhetoric of Substantiality," 465.
123. Johnson, *Idler* no. 63, 2:196.
124. Johnson, *Idler* no. 63, 2:196.
125. Johnson, *Idler* no. 63, 2:197.
126. Johnson, *Rambler* no. 68, 3:360.
127. Henson, "Johnson and the Condition of Women," 67.
128. In Boswell's *Journal*, Johnson states that "no woman is the worse for sense and knowledge" than a man, a comment that Boswell believes at first to be merely a courtesy to his hosts but, later, is confirmed by Johnson to be taken quite seriously (294).
129. Johnson, *Idler* no. 51, 2:159. See also Bush, *Samuel Johnson and the Art of Domesticity*, 12–13.
130. Johnson, *Rambler* no. 60, 3:322.
131. Johnson, *Rambler* no. 60, 3:321.
132. Hudson, "Samuel Johnson, Urban Culture, and the Geography of Postfire London," 588. Hudson's emphasis is less concerned with Johnson's views on domesticity than he is with his critique of London's extravagant and opulent architecture, which he viewed as overt symbols of vanity and decadence. In contrast, Boswell notes that Johnson expressed a preference for London's "innumerable lanes and courts" and "the multiplicity of human habitations which are crowded together" (589). See Boswell, *Life of Johnson*, 1:421–22.
133. Hudson, *Samuel Johnson and the Making of Modern England*, 107.
134. Bush, *Samuel Johnson and the Art of Domesticity*, 17–18.
135. In *Rambler* no. 6, Johnson decries Cowper's preference for isolation and retreat as a response to the folly and vanity of mankind, suggesting that, while he may

change his place of abode, he will only succeed in compounding his own un-happiness (3:30–35). In addition, Johnson addresses the problematic tendency toward domestic isolation and provincialism in *Rambler* nos. 51, 135, and 138, as well as *Idler* no. 51 and *Adventurer* no. 102. See also Bush, *Samuel Johnson and the Art of Domesticity*, 15–16.

## Conclusion

1. The OED would appear to confirm this point. There, we find the following defi-nitions for neighbourhood (n.): "a. The people living near to a certain place or within a certain range; neighbours collectively," and "b. A district or portion of a town, city, or country, esp. considered in reference to the character or circum-stances of its inhabitants." The date chart for both entries places its usage, in this sense, at or near the end of the seventeenth century, with its appearances growing more frequent from the eighteenth through the twentieth centuries.

2. See Lynch, "Social Theory at Box Hill."

3. Lynch, "Social Theory at Box Hill," 4. Lynch here quotes Burke, *Reflections on the Revolution in France*, 135.

4. See Ferguson, *An Essay on the History of Civil Society.*

5. Burke, *Reflections on the Revolution in France*, 135.

6. Burke, *Reflections on the Revolution in France*, 286.

7. Burke, *Reflections*, 287.

8. Burke, *Reflections on the Revolution in France*, 287.

9. Burke, *Reflections on the Revolution in France*, 315.

10. Burke, *Reflections on the Revolution in France*, 315.

11. Austen, *Mansfield Park*, 15.

12. Austen, *Mansfield Park*, 83.

13. Austen, *Mansfield Park*, 84.

14. Austen, *Mansfield Park*, 84.

15. Austen, *Mansfield Park*, 84.

16. Austen, *Mansfield Park*, 222.

17. Austen, *Mansfield Park*, 222.

18. Austen, *Mansfield Park*, 223.

19. Austen, *Mansfield Park*, 223.

20. Austen, *Mansfield Park*, 224.

21. Austen, *Mansfield Park*, 370.

22. Austen, *Mansfield Park*, 370.

23. Austen, *Mansfield Park*, 4.

24. See Moretti, *Atlas of the European Novel*, 19, 21.

25. Moretti, *Atlas of the European Novel*, 22.

26. Moretti, *Atlas of the European Novel*, 20.

27. Moretti, *Atlas of the European Novel*, 5.

28. Moretti, *Atlas of the European Novel*, 3.

29. Moretti, *Graphs, Maps, Trees*, 53–54.

# BIBLIOGRAPHY

## Primary Sources

Adair, John. *The Description of the Sea-Coasts and Islands of Scotland, with Large and Exact Maps for the Use of Seamen.* Edinburgh, 1703.

———. *Queries in order to a True Description: And, an Account of the Natural Curiousitys, and Antiquities.* Edinburgh, 1694.

Adams, John. *Index Villaris: or, An Alphabetical Table of All the Cities, Market-Towns, Parishes, Villages, and Private Seats, in England and Wales.* London: G. Godbid and J. Playford, 1680.

Anderson, James. *Account of the Present State of the Hebrides and Western Coasts of Scotland.* Edinburgh: C. Eliot, 1785.

Andrews, John. *Historical Atlas of England; Physical, Political, Astronomical, Civil and Ecclesiastical, Biographical, Naval, Parliamentary, and Geographical; Ancient and Modern; From the Deluge to the Present Time.* London: J. Smeaton, 1797.

Austen, Jane. *Mansfield Park.* Oxford: Oxford UP, 1999.

Badeslade, John. *Chorographia Britanniae; or, A New Set of Maps of All the Counties in England and Wales.* London: W. H. Toms, 1742.

Behn, Aphra. "The Forc'd Marriage, Or the Jealous Bridegroom." In *The Works of Aphra Behn,* vol. 5, *The Plays, 1671–1677,* edited by Janet Todd. Columbus: Ohio State UP, 1996.

———. *Oroonoko, The Rover and Other Works.* Edited by Janet Todd. New York: Penguin, 1992.

———, ed. *The Works of Aphra Behn.* Vol. 5, *The Plays, 1671–1677,* edited by Janet Todd. Columbus: Ohio State UP, 1996.

Blackstone, William. *Commentaries on the Laws of England.* 4 vols. New York: W. E. Dean, 1844.

Blaeu, Joan. *Atlas Major, sive Cosmographia Blaviana.* Amsterdam: Joan Blaeu, 1662–65.

———. *Theatrum Orbis Terrarum Sive Atlas Novus.* Vol. 5. Amsterdam: Joan Blaeu, 1654.

Bolingbroke, Henry St. John Viscount. *Contributions to the Craftsman.* Edited by Simon Varey. Oxford: Clarendon, 1982.

*A Book of the Names of All the Parishes, Market Towns, Villages, Hamlets, and Smallest Places, In England and Wales.* London: S.S., 1657.

Bosman, William. *A New and Accurate Description of the Coast of Guinea.* London: Knapton, D. Midwinter, Lintot, Strahan, Round, and Bell, 1721.

Boswell, James. *The Journal of a Tour to the Hebrides.* Edited by Peter Levi. New York: Penguin, 1984.

———. *Life of Johnson.* 6 vols. Edited by G. B. Hill. Oxford: Clarendon, 1934–50.

Bowen, Emanuel, and Thomas Bowen. *Atlas Anglicanus.* London: T. Kitchen, 1777.

Brome, James. *An Historical Account of Mr. Rogers' Three Years Travels over England and Wales*. London: J. Moxon and B. Beardwell, 1694.

Bunyan, John. *Christian Behaviour; Being the Fruits of Christianity*. In *The Miscellaneous Works of John Bunyan*, vol. 3, edited by J. Sears McGee. 1663. Oxford: Clarendon, 1987.

———. "Exhortation to Peace and Unity." In *The Miscellaneous Works of John Bunyan*, vol. 5, edited by Graham Midgley. 1688. Oxford: Clarendon, 1986.

———. "A Few Sighs From Hell." In *The Miscellaneous Works of John Bunyan*, vol. 1, edited by T. L. Underwood. 1658. Oxford: Clarendon, 1980.

———. *Grace Abounding to the Chief of Sinners*. Edited by James Thorpe. 1666. Boston: Houghton Mifflin, 1969.

———. "A Holy Life: The Beauty of Christianity." In *The Miscellaneous Works of John Bunyan*, vol. 9, edited by Richard L. Greaves. 1658. Oxford: Clarendon, 1981.

———. *Mapp Shewing the Order & Causes of Salvation & Damnation*. In *The Miscellaneous Works of John Bunyan*, vol. 7, edited by Graham Midgley. 1663. Oxford: Clarendon, 1989.

———. *The Pilgrim's Progress*. Edited by Roger Pooley. 1678. New York: Penguin Books, 1987.

———. *Saved By Grace*. In *The Miscellaneous Works of John Bunyan*, vol. 8, edited by Richard L. Greaves. 1676. Oxford: Clarendon, 1979.

———. "A Vindication of Some Gospel Truths Opened." In *The Miscellaneous Works of John Bunyan*, vol. 1, edited by T. L. Underwood. 1657. Oxford: Clarendon, 1980.

Burke, Edmund. *Reflections on the Revolution in France*. New York: Penguin, 1986.

Burton, William. *A Commentary on Antoninus, his Itinerary, or Journies of the Romane Empire, so far as it concerneth Britain*. London: T. Roycroft, 1658.

Camden, William. *Britannia, sive florentissimorum regnorum Angliae, Scotiae, Hiberniae, et insularum adiacentium ex intima antiquitate chorographica descriptio*. 6th ed. London: George Bishop, 1607.

Cox, Richard. "Regnum Corcagiense: or a Description of the Kingdom of Cork." *Journal of the Cork Historical and Archeological Society*, 2nd series, 8.54 (1902): 65–83.

Dapper, Olfert. *Description de l'Afrique*. Amsterdam: Wolfgang, Waesberge, Boom and van Someren, 1686.

Defoe, Daniel. *A Brief State of the Inland or Home Trade, of England*. London: Tho. Warner, 1730.

———. *The Compleat English Gentleman*. Edited by Karl D. Bülbring. 1729. London: D. Nutt, 1890.

———. *The Compleat English Tradesman*. Vol. 2. London: C. Rivington, 1727.

———. *A Plan of the English Commerce*. London: C. Rivington, 1728.

———. *A Tour Thro' the Whole Island of Great Britain*. Edited by Pat Rogers. New York: Penguin, 1986.

*England's Golden Treasury: or, The True Vade Mecum*. London: T. Lacy, 1694.

Ferguson, Adam. *An Essay on the History of Civil Society*. Edinburgh: A. Kincaid and J. Bell, 1767.

Goghe, John. *Hibernia, insulae non procul ab Anglia vulgare Hirlandia vocata*. 1567.

Gordon, Alexander. *Itinerarium Septentrionale: or, A Journey Thro' most of the Counties of Scotland, and Those in the North of England*. London: A. Gordon, 1726.

Gordon, Robert, and James Gordon. "Manuscript Maps by Robert & James Gordon, ca. 1636–1652." Edinburgh: The National Library of Scotland. https://maps.nls.uk /mapmakers/gordon.html.

Gough, Richard. *Anecdotes of British Topography*. London: W. Richardson and S. Clark, 1768.

Hazlitt, William. *The Complete Works of William Hazlitt*. Vol. 4. Edited by P. P. Howe. London: Dent, 1930–34.

Horsley, John. *Britannia Romana: or, the Roman Antiquities of Britain in Three Books*. London: J. Osborn and T. Longman, 1732.

Jansson, Jan. *Novus Atlas, sive Theatrum orbis terrarum*. Amsterdam, 1638.

Johnson, Samuel. *An Account of an Attempt to Ascertain the Longitude*. London: R. Dodsley and J. Jeffries, 1755.

———. *The Idler* and *The Adventurer*. In *The Yale Edition of the Works of Samuel Johnson*, vol. 2, edited by W. J. Bate, John M. Bullitt, and L. F. Powell. New Haven, CT: Yale UP, 1963.

———. "Introduction to *The World Display'd*." In *The Works of Samuel Johnson*, vol. 2, edited by Arthur Murphy. 1759. London: Luke Hansard and Sons, 1810.

———. *A Journey to the Western Islands of Scotland*. Edited by Peter Levi. New York: Penguin, 1984.

———. *The Letters of Samuel Johnson*. Vol. 1, edited by R. W. Chapman. Oxford: Clarendon, 1952.

———. *The Rambler*. In *The Yale Edition of the Works of Samuel Johnson*, Vols. 3–5E, edited by W. J. Bate and Albrecht B. Strauss. New Haven, CT: Yale UP, 1969.

———. "Review of Lewis Evans, *Analysis of a General Map of the Middle British Colonies in America*." In *The Yale Edition of the Works of Samuel Johnson*, Vol. 10, edited by Donald J. Greene. 1756. New Haven, CT: Yale UP, 1977.

Kirby, John. *The Suffolk Traveller; or, A Journey Through Suffolk*. London: J. Bagnall, 1735.

Knox, John. *A Commercial Map of Scotland*. London: J. Knox, 1782.

Kohl, J. G. *Travels in Ireland*. London: Bruce and Wyld, 1844.

Larcom, Thomas, ed. *A History of the Survey of Ireland Commonly Called the Down Survey by Doctor William Petty, A.D. 1655–6*. Dublin: Irish Archeological Society, 1851.

Leach, John. "A Map of the River Gambra from its Mouth to Eropina." In *A New General Collection of Voyages and Travels*, vol. 2, edited by Thomas Astley. 1732. London: T. Astley, 1745–47.

Lewes, Robert. *The Merchant's Map of Commerce*. London: R. Horn, 1671.

Ligon, Richard. *A True and Exact History of the Island of Barbados*. London: Humphrey Moseley, 1657.

Macaulay, Kenneth. *History of the Island of St. Kilda*. London: T. Becket and P. A. De Hondt, 1764.

MacBean, Alexander. *Dictionary of Ancient Geography*. London: G. Robinson and T. Carell, 1773.

Martin, Martin. *A Description of the Western Islands of Scotland*. London: Andrew Bell, 1703.

Mercator, Gerard. *Angliae Scotiae et Hiberniae Nove Descriptio*. Duisburg, 1564.

Moll, Herman. *Atlas Geographus: or, A Compleat System of Geography*. London: J. Nutt, 1711–17.

———. *A Set of Thirty-Six New and Correct Maps of Scotland*. London: T. and J. Bowles, 1725.

———. *A Set of Twenty New and Correct Maps of Ireland*. London: H. Moll, 1728.

———. *The World Described; or, A New and Correct Sett of Maps*. London: Tho. Bowles, 1709–20.

Montanus, Arnoldus. *De nieuwe en onbekende Weereld*. Amsterdam: Jacob Meurs, 1671.

Neal, Daniel. *The History of the Puritans, or, Protestant Non-conformists*. London: R. Hett, 1732.

Nowell, Lawrence. *A General Description of England and Ireland*. London, 1564–65.

Ogilby, John. *America: Being the Latest, and Most Accurate Description of the New World*. London: J. Ogilby, 1671.

———. *Britannia*. London: J. Ogilby, 1675.

Ogilby, John, and William Morgan. *Mr. Ogilby's and William Morgan, Pocket Book of the Roads, With their Computed and Measured Distances, and the Distinction of Market and Post-Towns*. London, J. Ogilby, 1679.

Ortelius, Abraham. *Hiberniae Britannicae insulae nova descriptio*. Antwerp, 1573.

Pennant, Thomas. *A Tour in Scotland and Voyage to the Hebrides*. London: B. White, 1772.

Percy, Thomas. *Reliques of Ancient English Poetry*. London: J. Dodsley, 1765.

Petty, William. *Hiberniae delineatio: quoad hactenus licuit*. London, 1685.

Playford, John. *Vade Mecum; or, The Necessary Companion*. London: A.G. and J.P., 1679.

Pont, Timothy. "Pont Maps of Scotland, ca. 1583–1614." Edinburgh: The National Library of Scotland. https://maps.nls.uk/pont/.

Post, Frans, and Georg Marggraf. "Praefecturae Paranambucae pars Borealis." In *Rerum per octennium in Brasilia et alibi nuper gestarum*, edited by Caspar van Baerle. Amsterdam: Joan Blaeu, 1647.

Postlethwayt, Malachy. *The Africa Trade the great Pillar and Supporter of the British Plantation Trade in America*. London: 1745.

———. *Britain's Commercial Interests Explained and Improv'd*. London: D. Browne, 1757.

———. *Great Britain's True System*. London: A. Millar, 1757.

———. *The National and Private Advantages of the African Trade Considered*. London: J. and P. Knapton, 1746.

———, trans. *The Universal Dictionary of Trade and Commerce*. London: J. and P. Knapton, 1751–55.

Pratt, Henry. *Tabula Hiberniae novissima et emendatissima*. London: Henry Pratt, 1705.

Pratt, Samuel Jackson. *Humanity; or, The Rights of Nature*. London: T. Cadell, 1788.

Roy, William. *The Military Antiquities of the Romans in Britain*. London: W. Bulmer, 1793.

Seller, Jeremiah, and Charles Price. *The English Pilot. The Fifth Book*. London: J. Thornton, 1701.

Seller, John. *Anglia Contracta; or, A Description of the Kingdom of England & Principality of Wales*. London, 1695.

———. *Atlas Maritimus; or, The Sea-Atlas.* London: J. Darby, 1675.

———. *Atlas Minimus; or, A Book of Geography: Shewing All the Empires, Monarchies, Kingdomes, Regions, Dominions, Principalities, and Countries in the Whole World.* London, J. Seller, 1679.

———. *The Coasting Pilot.* London: J. Seller, 1673.

———. *The English Pilot. The First Book.* London: W. Mount and T. Page, 1671.

———. *The English Pilot. The Second Book.* London: G. Crane, T. Brown, J. Moor, 1671

———. *The English Pilot. The Third Book.* London: J. Darby, 1675.

———. *Hydrographia Universalis; or, A Book of Maritime Charts.* London: J. Seller, 1690.

———. *A New Systeme of Geography, designed in a most plain and easy method for the better understanding of that science.* London, 1685.

———. *A Pocket Book: Containing Severall Choice Collections in Arithmetick, Astronomy, Geometry, Surveying, Dialling, Navigation, Astrology, Geography, Measuring, Gageing.* London, J. Seller and C. Price, 1677

———. *Practical Navigation; or, An Introduction to the Whole Art.* London: J. Darby, 1672.

Sharrock, Roger, gen. ed. *The Miscellaneous Works of John Bunyan.* 13 vols. Oxford: Clarendon, 1976–94.

Sibbald, Robert. *Account of the Scottish Atlas, or Description of Scotland Ancient and Modern.* Edinburgh: D. Lindsay, J. Kniblo, J. van Solingen, and J. Colmar, 1683.

———. *A Collection of Several Treatises concerning Scotland.* Edinburgh: Hamilton and Balfour, 1739.

———. *The Description of the Sea-Coasts and Islands of Scotland, with Large and Exact Maps for the Use of Seamen.* Edinburgh, 1703.

———. *Historical Inquiries, Concerning the Roman Monuments and Antiquities in the North Part of Britain called Scotland.* Edinburgh: James Watson, 1707.

———. *Scotia Illustrata sive Prodromus Historiae Naturalis.* London: J. Kniblo, J. van Solingen, and J. Colmar, 1683–84.

Sinclair, John. *The Statistical Account of Scotland. Drawn up from the communications of the Ministers of the different parishes.* Vol. 1. Edinburgh: William Creech, 1791.

Smeaton, John. *Report of John Smeaton, engineer, and F. R. S. concerning the practicability and expense of joining the rivers Forth and Clyde by a navigable canal, and thereby to join the east sea and the west.* Edinburgh: John Balfour, 1767.

Snelgrave, William. *A New Account of Some Parts of Guinea, and the Slave Trade.* London: P. Knapton, 1734.

Spenser, Edmund. *A View of the Present State of Ireland.* Edited by Andrew Hadfield and Willey Maley. Oxford: Oxford UP, 1997.

Stedman, John Gabriel. *Five Years Expedition against the Revolted Negroes of Surinam.* London: J. Johnson and J. Edwards, 1796.

Swift, Jonathan. "Addison, Joseph: The Freeholder, 1715–6." In *Miscellaneous and Autobiographical Pieces, Fragments, and Marginalia,* edited by Herbert Davis, vol. 5 of *The Prose Works of Jonathan Swift.* Oxford: Basil Blackwell, 1969.

———. "The Advantages Proposed by Repealing the Sacramental Test." In *Irish Tracts, 1728–1733, and Sermons,* edited by Herbert Davis, vol. 12 of *The Prose Works of Jonathan Swift.* 1732. Oxford: Basil Blackwell, 1955.

———. "The Answer of the Right Honourable William Pulteney, Esq; to the Right Honourable Sir Robert Walpole." In *Miscellaneous and Autobiographical Pieces, Fragments, and Marginalia*, edited by Herbert Davis, vol. 5 of *The Prose Works of Jonathan Swift*. 1730. Oxford: Basil Blackwell, 1969.

———. "Cadenus and Vanessa." In *Swift: Poetical Works*, edited by Herbert Davis. 1713. London: Oxford UP, 1967.

———. "Doing Good: A Sermon, on the Occasion of Wood's Project." In *Irish Tracts, 1720–1723, and Sermons*, edited by Herbert Davis and Louis Landa, vol. 9 of *The Prose Works of Jonathan Swift*. 1724. Oxford: Basil Blackwell, 1963.

———. *The Examiner*, "No. 13., November 2, 1710." In *The Examiner and Other Pieces Written in 1710–11*, edited by Herbert Davis, vol. 3 of *The Prose Works of Jonathan Swift*. Oxford: Basil Blackwell, 1966.

———. *The Examiner*, "No. 14., November 9, 1710." In *The Examiner and Other Pieces Written in 1710–11*, edited by Herbert Davis, vol. 3 of *The Prose Works of Jonathan Swift*. Oxford: Basil Blackwell, 1966.

———. *Gulliver's Travels*. Edited by Claude Rawson. 1726. Oxford: Oxford UP, 2005.

———. *The History of the Four Last Years of the Queen*. Edited by Herbert Davis, vol. 7 of *The Prose Works of Jonathan Swift*. 1758. Oxford: Basil Blackwell, 1964.

———. "Horace, Book I, Ode XIV, paraphrased and inscribed to Ireland." In *Swift: Poetical Works*, edited by Herbert Davis. 1726. London: Oxford UP, 1967.

———. "An Humble Address to Both Houses of Parliament." In *The Drapier's Letters and Other Works, 1724–1725*, edited by Herbert Davis, vol. 10 of *The Prose Works of Jonathan Swift*. 1735. Oxford: Basil Blackwell, 1966.

———. "A Letter to the Lord Chancellor Middleton." In *The Drapier's Letters and Other Works, 1724–1725*, edited by Herbert Davis, vol. 10 of *The Prose Works of Jonathan Swift*. 1724. Oxford: Basil Blackwell, 1966.

———. "A Letter to Mr. Harding the Printer." In *The Drapier's Letters and Other Works, 1724–1725*, edited by Herbert Davis, vol. 10 of *The Prose Works of Jonathan Swift*. 1724. Oxford: Basil Blackwell, 1966.

———. "A Letter to the Right Honourable the Lord Viscount Molesworth." In *The Drapier's Letters and Other Works, 1724–1725*, edited by Herbert Davis, vol. 10 of *The Prose Works of Jonathan Swift*. 1724. Oxford: Basil Blackwell, 1966.

———. "A Letter to the Whole People of Ireland." In *The Drapier's Letters and Other Works, 1724–1725*, edited by Herbert Davis, vol. 10 of *The Prose Works of Jonathan Swift*. 1724. Oxford: Basil Blackwell, 1966.

———. *A Modest Proposal*. In *Irish Tracts, 1728–1733, and Sermons*, edited by Herbert Davis and Louis Landa, vol. 12 of *The Prose Works of Jonathan Swift*. 1729. Oxford: Basil Blackwell, 1955.

———. "Mr. Collin's Discourse of Free-Thinking." In *A Proposal for Correcting the English Tongue, Polite Conversation, Etc.*, edited by Herbert Davis, vol. 4 of *The Prose Works of Jonathan Swift*. 1713. Oxford: Basil Blackwell, 1964.

———. "On False Witness." In *Irish Tracts, 1720–1723, and Sermons*, edited by Herbert Davis and Louis Landa, vol. 9 of *The Prose Works of Jonathan Swift*. 1715. Oxford: Basil Blackwell, 1963.

———. "On the Irish Club." In *Swift: Poetical Works*, edited by Herbert Davis. 1723. London: Oxford UP, 1967.

———. "On the Testimony of Conscience." In *Irish Tracts, 1720–1723, and Sermons,* edited by Herbert Davis and Louis Landa, vol. 9 of *The Prose Works of Jonathan Swift.* 1744. Oxford: Basil Blackwell, 1963.

———. "On Poetry: A Rhapsody." In *Swift: Poetical Works,* edited by Herbert Davis. 1733. London: Oxford UP, 1967.

———. "A Preface to the Bishop of Sarum's Introduction to the Third Volume of the History of the Reformation of the Church of England." In *A Proposal for Correcting the English Tongue, Polite Conversation, Etc.* edited by Herbert Davis, vol. 4 of *The Prose Works of Jonathan Swift.* 1713. Oxford: Basil Blackwell, 1964.

———. "A Project for the Advancement of Religion and the Reformation of Manners." In *Bickerstaff Papers and Pamphlets on the Church,* edited by Herbert Davis, vol. 2 of *The Prose Works of Jonathan Swift.* 1709. Oxford: Basil Blackwell, 1939.

———. *The Prose Works of Jonathan Swift.* Edited by Herbert Davis et al., 16 vols. Oxford: Basil Blackwell, 1939–74.

———. "The Sentiments of a Church-of-England Man, with Respect to Religion and Government." In *Bickerstaff Papers and Pamphlets on the Church,* edited by Herbert Davis, vol. 2 of *The Prose Works of Jonathan Swift.* 1708. Oxford: Basil Blackwell, 1939.

———. "Short Remarks on Bishop Burnet's History." In *Miscellaneous and Autobiographical Pieces, Fragments, and Marginalia,* edited by Herbert Davis, vol. 5 of *The Prose Works of Jonathan Swift.* 1726. Oxford: Basil Blackwell, 1969.

———. "A Tale of a Tub." In *A Tale of a Tub with Other Early Works, 1696–1707,* edited by Herbert Davis, vol. 1 of *The Prose Works of Jonathan Swift.* 1704. Oxford: Basil Blackwell, 1965.

———. *Swift: Poetical Works.* Edited by Herbert Davis. London: Oxford UP, 1967.

———. "To His Grace the Archbishop of Dublin, A Poem." In *Swift: Poetical Works,* edited by Herbert Davis. 1724. London: Oxford UP, 1967.

Teate, Faithful. *A Scripture-Map of the Wildernesse of Sin, and Way to Canaan; or, The Sinners Way to the Saints Rest.* London: G. Sawbridge, 1655.

Thornton, John. *The English Pilot. The Fourth Book.* London: J. Thornton and W. Fisher, 1698, 1706.

Thornton, Samuel. "Chart of the Sea Coasts of Europe, Africa, and America." In *The Atlas Maritimus Novus, or the New Sea-Atlas.* 1683? London: R. Mount and T. Page, 1708–15.

Trigge, Thomas. *Calendarium Astrologicum; or, An Alamanack for the Year of Our Lord 1690.* London: B. Griffin, 1690.

Wit, Frederik de. *Atlas.* Amsterdam: 1680.

## Secondary Sources

Abbeele, Georges Van Den. *Travel as Metaphor: From Montaigne to Rousseau.* Minneapolis: Minnesota UP, 1992.

Acosta, Ana. "Spaces of Dissent and the Public Sphere in Hackney, Stoke Newington, and Newington Green." *Eighteenth-Century Life* 27.1 (Winter 2003): 1–27.

Agnew, Jean-Christophe. *Worlds Apart: The Market and the Theater in Anglo-American Thought, 1550–1750.* Cambridge: Cambridge UP, 1986.

Anderson, Benedict. *Imagined Communities: Reflections on the Origin and Spread of Nationalism*. London: Verso, 1983.

Andrews, John Harwood. "Defoe and the Sources of His *Tour*." *Geographical Journal* 126.3 (1960): 268–77.

———. "Geography and Government in Elizabethan Ireland." In *Irish Geographical Studies in Honour of E. Estyn Evans*, edited by Nicholas Stephens and Robin E. Glasscock, 178–91. Belfast: Queen's University.

———. *Henry Pratt, Surveyor of the Kerry Estates*. Tralee: Kerry Archeological and Historical Society, 1980.

———. "Introduction: Meaning, Knowledge, and Power in the Map Philosophy of J. B. Harley." In Laxton, *The New Nature of Maps*, 2–32.

———. "Maps and Mapmakers." In *The Shaping of Ireland: The Geographical Perspective*, edited by William Nolan, 99–110. Dublin: Mercier, 1986.

———. *Maps in Those Days: Cartographic Methods before 1850*. Dublin: Four Courts, 2009.

———. "The Maps of the Escheated Counties of Ulster, 1609–10." *Proceedings of the Royal Irish Academy* 74C (1974): 133–70.

———. "New Light on Three Eighteenth-Century Cartographers: Herman Moll, Thomas Moland, and Henry Pratt." *Bulletin of the Irish Georgian Society* 35 (1992/93): 17–24.

———. *A Paper Landscape: The Ordnance Survey in Nineteenth-Century Ireland*. Dublin: Four Courts, 1975.

———. *Plantation Acres: An Historical Study of the Irish Land Surveyor and His Maps*. Belfast: Ulster Historical Foundation, 1985.

———. *Shapes of Ireland: Maps and Their Makers, 1564–1839*. Dublin: Geography Publications, 1997.

Aravamudan, Srinivas. *Tropicopolitans: Colonialism and Agency, 1688–1804*. Durham, NC: Duke UP, 1999.

Ashcraft, Richard. *Revolutionary Politics and Locke's Two Treatises on Government*. Princeton, NJ: Princeton UP, 1986.

Ayres, Philip. *Classical Culture and the Idea of Rome in Eighteenth-Century England*. Cambridge: Cambridge UP, 1997.

Barrow, Ian J. *Making History, Drawing Territory: British Mapping in India, c. 1756–1905*. New Delhi: Oxford UP, 2003.

Bean, Richard Nelson. *The British Trans-Atlantic Slave Trade, 1650–1775*. New York: Arno, 1975.

Benjamin, Walter. *The Origin of German Tragic Drama*. Translated by John Osborne. New York: Verso, 1977.

Black, Jeremy. *Maps and History: Constructing Images of the Past*. New Haven, CT: Yale UP, 1997.

———. *Maps and Politics*. Chicago: U of Chicago P, 1997.

———. *The Power of Knowledge: How Information and Technology Made the World*. New Haven, CT: Yale UP, 2014.

Bogel, Fredric. "The Rhetoric of Substantiality: Johnson and the Later Eighteenth Century." *Eighteenth-Century Studies* 12.4 (1979): 457–80.

Boulukos, George. "Olaudah Equiano and the Eighteenth-Century Debate on Africa." *Eighteenth-Century Studies* 40.2 (2007): 241–55.

Bowen, Margarita. *Empiricism and Geographical Thought: From Francis Bacon to Alexander von Humboldt.* Cambridge: Cambridge UP, 1981.

Bowers, Terence N. "Great Britain Imagined: Nation, Citizen, and Class in Defoe's *Tour Thro' the Whole Island of Great Britain.*" *Prose Studies* 16.3 (1993): 148–78.

Boyle, Frank. *Swift as Nemesis: Modernity and Its Satirist.* Stanford, CA: Stanford UP, 2000.

Bracher, Frederick. "The Maps in *Gulliver's Travels.*" *Huntington Library Quarterly* 8.1 (Nov. 1944): 59–74.

Bratach, Anne. "Following the Intrigue: Aphra Behn, Genre and Restoration Science." *Journal of Narrative Technique* 26.3 (1996): 209–27.

Brewer, John. *Sinews of Power: War, Money and the English State, 1688–1783.* London: Unwin Hyman, 1989.

Briggs, Peter. "John Graunt, William Petty, and Swift's *A Modest Proposal.*" *Eighteenth-Century Life* 29.2 (2005): 3–24.

Buisseret, David. *The Mapmaker's Quest: Depicting New Worlds in Renaissance Europe.* Oxford: Oxford UP, 2003.

———. *Monarchs, Ministers, and Maps: The Emergence of Cartography as a Tool of Government in Early Modern Europe.* Chicago: U of Chicago P, 1992.

———. *Rural Images: Estate Maps in the Old and New Worlds.* Chicago: U of Chicago P, 1996.

Bunn, James. "The Tory View of Geography." *Boundary 2* 7.2 (Winter 1979): 149–67.

Bush, James N. D. *Samuel Johnson and the Art of Domesticity.* Ottawa: National Library of Canada, 2003.

Certeau, Michel de. "Practices of Space." In *On Signs,* edited by Marshall Blonsky, 122–45. Baltimore: Johns Hopkins UP, 1985.

Chartres, John. "The Marketing of Agricultural Produce, 1640–1750." In *The Agrarian History of England and Wales, 1640–1750,* vol. 5, part 2, edited by Joan Thirsk, 406–502. Cambridge: Cambridge UP, 1990.

Clingham, Greg, ed. *The Cambridge Companion to Samuel Johnson.* Cambridge: Cambridge UP, 1997.

Colley, Linda. "Radical Patriotism in Eighteenth-Century England." In Samuel, *Patriotism,* 169–87.

Conley, Tom. *The Self-Made Map: Cartographic Writing in Early Modern France.* Minneapolis: Minnesota UP, 1996.

Connell, Alyssa L. "Paper Kingdom: Travel Literature, Chorography, and the Writing of Britain, 1660–1770." Ph.D. diss., University of Pennsylvania, 2015.

Copeland, Edward. "Defoe and the London Wall: Mapped Perspectives." *Eighteenth-Century Fiction* 10.4 (July 1998): 407–28.

Cormack, Lesley. *Charting an Empire: Geography at the English Universities, 1580–1620.* Chicago: U of Chicago P, 1997.

Corrigan, Philip, and Derek Sayer. *The Great Arch: English State Formation as Cultural Revolution.* Oxford: Blackwell, 1985.

Cunningham, Hugh. "The Language of Patriotism." In Samuel, *Patriotism,* 57–89.

Curley, Thomas M. "Johnson and the Irish: A Postcolonial Survey of the Irish Literary Renaissance in Imperial Great Britain." *Age of Johnson: A Scholarly Annual* 12
(2001): 67–197.

———. *Samuel Johnson and the Age of Travel.* Athens: U of Georgia P, 1976.

Curtin, Phillip. *The Atlantic Slave Trade: A Census.* Madison: Wisconsin UP, 1969.

Darity, William, Jr. "Eric Williams and Slavery: A West Indian Viewpoint?" *Callaloo*
20.4 (1997): 801–16.

Davies, K. G. *The Royal African Company.* London: Longmans, 1957.

Davis, Ralph. *The Rise of the Atlantic Economies.* London: Weidenfeld and Nicolson,
1973.

Delle, James A. "'A Good and Easy Speculation': Spatial Conflict, Collusion and Resistance in Late-Sixteenth Century Munster Ireland." *International Journal of Historical Archeology* 3.1 (1999): 11–35.

Devine, T. M. *The Transformation of Rural Scotland: Social Change and the Agrarian
Economy, 1660–1815.* Edinburgh: Edinburgh UP, 1994.

Donaldson, Ian. "Samuel Johnson and the Art of Observation." *ELH* 53.4 (1986): 779–99.

Duckworth, Alistair M. "'Whig' Landscapes in Defoe's *Tour.*" *Philological Quarterly*
61.4 (Fall 1982): 453–65.

Dunn, Richard S. *Sugar and Slaves: The Rise of the Planter Class in the English West
Indies, 1624–1713.* Chapel Hill: U of North Carolina P, 1972.

During, Simon. "Literature—Nationalism's Other?" In *Nation and Narration,* edited
by Homi K. Bhabha, 138–53. London: Routledge, 1990.

Eastwood, David. *Government and Community in the English Provinces, 1700–1800.*
New York: St. Martin's, 1997.

Edinger, William. *Johnson and Detailed Representation: The Significance of Classical
Sources.* Victoria: University of Victoria, 1997.

———. "Johnson on Conceit: The Limits of Particularity." *ELH* 39.4 (1972): 597–619.

Edney, Matthew H. "The Irony of Imperial Mapping." In *The Imperial Map: Cartography and the Mastery of Empire,* edited by James R. Akerman, 11–45. Chicago: U
of Chicago P, 2009.

———. *Mapping an Empire: The Geographical Construction of British India, 1765–1843.*
Chicago: U of Chicago P, 1997.

———. "The Origins and Development of J. B. Harley's Cartographic Theories." *Cartographica* 40.1/2 (2005): Monograph 54.

———. "Reconsidering Enlightenment Geography and Map Making: Reconnais-
sance, Mapping, Archive." In *Geography and Enlightenment,* edited by David N.
Livingstone and Charles W. J. Withers, 165–98. Chicago: U of Chicago P, 1999.

Edwards, Jesse. "Defoe the Geographer: Redefining the Wonderful in *A Tour Thro' the
Whole Island of Great Britain.*" In *Travel Narratives, the New Science, and Literary
Discourse, 1569–1750,* edited by Judy Hayden, 179–96. Abingdon: Routledge, 2012.

Ermarth, Elizabeth Deeds. *Realism and Consensus in the English Novel.* Princeton, NJ:
Princeton UP, 1983.

Everitt, Alan. *Landscape and Community in England.* London: Hambledon, 1985.

———. "The Marketing of Agricultural Produce, 1500–1640." In *The Agrarian History of England and Wales, 1500–1640,* vol. 4, edited by Joan Thirsk, 466–592. Cambridge: Cambridge UP, 1967.

Evers, Alf. "A Rough Game: Surveyors and Indians." In *The Catskills: From Wilderness to Woodstock*, 59–64. New York: Doubleday, 1972.

Fabricant, Carole. *Swift's Landscape*. Baltimore: Johns Hopkins UP, 1982.

Ferguson, Margaret. "Feathers and Flies: Aphra Behn and the 17th Century Trade in Exotica." In *Subject and Object in Renaissance Culture*, edited by Margreta de Grazia, Maureen Quilligan, and Peter Stallybrass, 235–59. Cambridge: Cambridge UP, 1996.

———. "Juggling the Categories of Race, Class and Gender: Aphra Behn's *Oroonoko*." *Women's Studies* 19.2 (1991): 159–81.

Fish, Stanley. *Self-Consuming Artifacts: The Experience of Seventeenth-Century Literature*. Berkeley: U of California P, 1972.

Foucault, Michel. "Of Other Spaces: Utopias and Heterotopias." In *Rethinking Architecture*, edited by Neil Leach, 350–56. New York: Routledge, 1997.

———. *The Order of Things: An Archeology of the Human Sciences*. New York: Vintage Books, 1994.

Frohock, Richard. "Violence and Awe: The Foundations of Government in Aphra Behn's New World Settings." *Eighteenth Century Fiction* 8.4 (1996): 437–52.

Furtado, Peter. "National Pride in Seventeenth-Century England." In Samuel, *Patriotism*, 44–56.

Gallagher, Catherine. Introduction to *Oroonoko; or, The Royal Slave*, by Aphra Behn, 3–25. Boston: Bedford-St. Martin's, 2000.

———. "Oroonoko's Blackness." In Todd, *Aphra Behn Studies*, 235–58.

———. "Who Was That Masked Woman? The Prostitute and the Playwright in the Comedies of Aphra Behn." In Hunter, *Rereading Aphra Behn*, 65–85.

Gascoigne, John. "Joseph Banks, Mapping, and the Geographies of Natural Knowledge." In *Georgian Geographies: Essays on Space, Place, and Landscape in the Eighteenth Century*, edited by Charles Withers and Miles Ogborn, 151–73. Manchester: Manchester UP, 2004.

Gidal, Eric. *Ossianic Unconformities: Bardic Poetry in the Industrial Age*. Charlottesville: U of Virginia P, 2015.

Gillespie, Raymond. "The Problems of Plantations: Material Culture and Social Change in Early Modern Ireland." In Lyttleton and Rynne, *Plantation Ireland*, 43–60.

Gilroy, Paul. *The Black Atlantic: Modernity and Double Consciousness*. Cambridge, MA: Harvard UP, 1993.

Givens, Michael. "Maps, Fields, and Boundary Cairns: Demarcation and Resistance in Colonial Cyprus." *International Journal of Historical Archeology* 6.1 (March 2002): 1–22.

Godlewska, Anne. "Resisting the Cartographic Imperative: Giuseppe Baggeti's Landscapes of War." *Journal of Historical Geography* 29.1 (2003): 22–50.

Greaves, Richard L. "The Organizational Response of Non-Conformity to Repression and Indulgence: The Case of Bedfordshire." *Church History* 44 (1975): 473–84.

Griffin, Dustin. *Patriotism and Poetry in Eighteenth-Century England*. Cambridge: Cambridge UP, 2002.

Grundy, Isobel. "Celebrare Domestica Facta: Johnson and Home Life." *New Rambler* D.6 (1990–91): 6–14.

Hamilton, Henry. *An Economic History of Scotland in the Eighteenth Century*. Oxford: Clarendon, 1963.

Hancock, David Boyd. *William Stukeley: Science, Religion and Archeology in Eighteenth-Century England*. Woodbridge: Boydell, 2002.

Harley, J. B. "Maps, Knowledge, and Power." In Laxton, *The New Nature of Maps*, 52–81.

———. "Meaning and Ambiguity in Tudor Cartography." In *English Map-Making, 1500–1650*, edited by Sarah Tyacke, 22–45. London: British Library, 1983.

Harrison, Phyllis. "Samuel Johnson's Folkloristics." *Folklore* 94.1 (1983): 57–65.

Hart, Kevin. *Samuel Johnson and the Culture of Property*. Cambridge: Cambridge UP, 1999.

Harvey, David. *The Enigma of Capital and the Crises of Capitalism*. Oxford: Oxford UP, 2010.

———. *The Limits to Capital*. London: Verso, 1999.

Hawes, Clement. "Johnson and Imperialism." In Clingham, *Cambridge Companion to Samuel Johnson*, 114–26.

———. "Three Times around the Globe: Gulliver and Colonial Discourse." *Cultural Critique* 18 (1991): 187–214.

Hayden, Judy. "'As Far as a Woman's Reasoning May Go': Aphra Behn, *Oroonoko*, and the New Science." In *Travel Narratives, the New Science, and Literary Discourse, 1569–1750*, edited by Judy Hayden, 123–42. Abingdon: Routledge, 2012.

Hayes-McCoy, G. A., ed. *Ulster and Other Irish Maps*. Dublin: Stationery Office for the Irish Manuscript Commission, 1964.

Hayton, D. W. *Ruling Ireland, 1685–1742: Politics, Politicians and Parties*. Woodbridge: Boydell, 2004.

Heawood, Edward. *A History of Geographical Discovery in the Seventeenth and Eighteenth Centuries*. New York: Octagon Books, 1965.

Heidenreich, Helmut, ed. *The Libraries of Daniel Defoe and Phillips Farewell: Oliver Payne's Sales Catalogue*. 1731. Berlin: H. Heidenreich, 1970.

Helgerson, Richard. *Adulterous Alliances: Home, State, and History in Early Modern European Drama and Painting*. Chicago: U of Chicago P, 2000.

———. "The Folly of Maps and Modernity." In *Literature, Mapping, and the Politics of Space in Early Modern Britain*, edited by Andrew Gordon and Bernhard Klein, 241–62. Cambridge: Cambridge UP, 2001.

———. *Forms of Nationhood: The Elizabethan Writing of England*. Chicago: U of Chicago P, 1992.

Helsinger, Elizabeth. *Rural Scenes and National Representation: Britain, 1815–1850*. Princeton, NJ: Princeton UP, 1996.

Henson, Eithne. "Johnson and the Condition of Women." In Clingham, *Cambridge Companion to Samuel Johnson*, 67–84.

Higgins, Ian. "Swift and Sparta: The Nostalgia of *Gulliver's Travels*." *Modern Language Review* 78.3 (1983): 513–31.

Hill, Christopher. "The English Revolution and Patriotism." In Samuel, *Patriotism*, 159–68.

———. *Puritanism and Revolution: Studies in Interpretation of the English Revolution of the 17th Century*. New York: St. Martin's, 1997.

———. *A Tinker and a Poor Man: John Bunyan and His Church, 1628–1688.* New York: Knopf, 1988.

Hill, Jacqueline. *From Patriots to Unionists: Dublin Civic Politics and Irish Protestant Patriotism, 1660–1840.* Oxford: Oxford UP, 1997.

Hilton, R. H. "Lords, Burgesses and Hucksters." *Past and Present* 97 (1982): 3–15.

Hingley, Richard. "Projecting Empire: The Mapping of Roman Britain." *Journal of Social Archeology* 6.3 (2006): 328–53.

Hirsch, E. D. "Transhistorical Intentions and the Persistence of Allegory." *New Literary History* 25 (1994): 549–67.

Hodson, Yolande. "The Lucubrations of His Leisure Hours: William Roy's *Military Antiquities of the Romans in Britain* 1793." *Scottish Geographical Journal* 127.2 (June 2011): 117–32.

Holland, Peter. The *Ornament of Action: Text and Performance in Restoration Comedy.* Cambridge: Cambridge UP, 1979.

Holmes, Richard. "James Arbuckle and Dean Swift: Cultural Politics in the Irish Confessing State." *Irish Studies Review* 16.4 (November 2008): 431–44.

Hoxby, Blair. *Mammon's Music: Literature and Economics in the Age of Milton.* New Haven, CT: Yale UP, 2002.

Hudson, Nicholas. "'Britons Never Will Be Slaves': National Myth, Conservatism, and the Beginnings of British Anti-Slavery." *Eighteenth-Century Studies* 34.4 (2001): 559–76.

———. *Samuel Johnson and the Making of Modern England.* Cambridge: Cambridge UP, 2003.

———. "Samuel Johnson, Urban Culture, and the Geography of Postfire London." *Studies in English Literature, 1500–1900* 42.3 (2002): 577–600.

Hunter, Heidi, ed. *Rereading Aphra Behn: History, Theory, and Criticism.* Charlottesville: Virginia UP, 1993.

Jacks, Phillip Joshua. *The Antiquarian and the Myth of Antiquity: The Origins of Rome in Renaissance Thought.* Cambridge: Cambridge UP: 1993.

Jacob, Christian. *The Sovereign Map: Theoretical Approaches in Cartography throughout History.* Translated by Tom Conley, edited by Edward H. Dahl. Chicago: U of Chicago P, 2006.

Kaminski, Thomas. "Johnson and Oldys as Biographers: An Introduction to the Harleian Catalogue." *Philological Quarterly* 60.4 (1981): 439–53.

Kearns, Gerry. "Bare Life, Political Violence, and the Territorial Structure of Britain and Ireland." In *Violent Geographies: Fear, Terror, and Political Violence,* edited by Derek Gregory and Allan Pred, 7–35. Abingdon: Routledge, 2007.

Keeble, N. H. *The Literary Culture of Nonconformity in Late Seventeenth-Century England.* Leicester: Leicester UP, 1987.

Kelley, Theresa. *Reinventing Allegory.* Cambridge: Cambridge UP, 1997.

Kent, Joan R. "The Centre and the Localities: State Formation and Parish Government in England, circa 1640–1740." *Historical Journal* 38.2 (1995): 363–404.

Kibbey, Ann. *The Interpretation of Material Shapes in Puritanism: A Study of Rhetoric, Prejudice and Violence.* Cambridge: Cambridge UP, 1986.

Kiernan, Colin. "Swift and Science." *Historical Journal* 14.4 (Dec. 1971): 709–22.

Kiernan, V. G. "State and Nation in Western Europe." *Past & Present* 31.1 (July 1965): 20–38.

Klein, Bernhard. *Maps and the Writing of Space in Early Modern England.* New York: Palgrave Macmillan, 2001.

Landa, Louis. "'A Modest Proposal' and Populousness." *Modern Philology* 40.2 (1942): 161–70.

———. "Swift's Economic Views and Mercantilism." *ELH* 10.4 (1943): 310–35.

Law, Peter J. "Samuel Johnson on Consumer Demand, Status, and Positional Goods." *European Journal of Economic Thought* 11.2 (2004): 187–207.

Laxton, Paul, ed. *The New Nature of Maps: Essays in the History of Cartography.* Baltimore: Johns Hopkins UP, 2001.

Lefebvre, Henri. *The Production of Space.* Oxford: Blackwell, 1991.

Levine, Joseph. *Humanism and History: Origins of Modern English Historiography.* Ithaca, NY: Cornell UP, 1987.

Lewcock, Dawn. "More for Seeing Than Hearing: Behn and the Use of Theatre." In Todd, *Aphra Behn Studies,* 66–83.

Lipking, Lawrence. *The Ordering of the Arts in the Eighteenth Century.* Princeton, NJ: Princeton UP, 1970.

Longxi, Zhang. "Historicizing the Postmodern Allegory." *Texas Studies in Literature and Language* 36.2 (1994): 212–31.

Luxon, Thomas. *Literal Figures: Puritan Allegory and the Reformation Crisis in Representation.* Chicago: U of Chicago P, 1995.

Lynch, Deidre. "Beating the Track of the Alphabet: Samuel Johnson, Tourism, and the ABC's of Modern Authority." *ELH* 57.2 (1990): 357–405.

———. "Social Theory at Box Hill: Acts of Union." In *Re-reading Box Hill: Reading the Practice of Reading Everyday Life,* edited by William Galperin, Romantic Circles Praxis Series (April 2000). http://www.rc.umd.edu/praxis/boxhill/lynch/lynch.html.

Lynch, Jack. *The Age of Elizabeth in the Age of Johnson.* Cambridge: Cambridge UP, 2003.

Lyttleton, James, and Colin Rynne, eds. *Plantation Ireland: Settlement and Material Culture, c.1550–c.1700.* Dublin: Four Courts, 2009.

Macdonald, George. "General William Roy and His 'Military Antiquities of the Romans in North Britain.'" *Archaeologia* 68 (1917): 161–228.

MacPherson, C. B. *The Political Theory of Possessive Individualism: Hobbes to Locke.* Oxford: Clarendon, 1962.

Mahony, Robert. "The Irish Colonial Experience and Swift's Rhetorics of Perception in the 1720s." *Eighteenth-Century Life* 22.1 (1998): 63–75.

———. *Jonathan Swift: The Irish Identity.* New Haven, CT: Yale UP, 1995.

Manning, Susan. "Antiquarianism, the Scottish Science of Map, and the Emergence of Modern Disciplinarity." In *Scotland and the Borders of Romanticism,* edited by Leith David, Ian Duncan, and Janet Sorensen, 57–76. Cambridge: Cambridge UP, 2004.

Margey, Annaleigh. "Representing Plantation Landscapes: The Mapping of Ulster, c. 1560–1640." In Lyttleton and Rynne, *Plantation Ireland,* 140–64.

Martin, Catherine Gimelli. *The Ruins of Allegory: Paradise Lost and the Metamorphosis of Epic Convention.* Durham, NC: Duke UP, 1998.

Mayhew, Robert J. *Enlightenment Geography: The Political Languages of British Geography, 1650–1850*. New York: St. Martin's, 2000.

———. *Geography and Literature in Historical Context: Samuel Johnson and Eighteenth-Century English Conceptions of Geography*. Oxford: School of Geography, Oxford University, 1997.

———. *Landscape, Literature and English Religious Culture, 1660–1800*. New York: Palgrave Macmillan, 2004.

McGinn, Joseph. "A Weary Patriot: Swift and the Formation of an Anglo-Irish Identity." *Eighteenth-Century Ireland* 2 (1987): 103–13.

McKeon, Michael. *The Origins of the English Novel, 1600–1740*. Baltimore: Johns Hopkins UP, 1987.

———. *The Secret History of Domesticity: Public, Private, and the Division of Knowledges*. Baltimore: Johns Hopkins UP, 2005.

McLeod, Mary. "'Other' Spaces and 'Others.'" In *The Sex of Architecture,* edited by Diana Argret, Patricia Conway, and Leslie Kanes Weisman, 15–28. New York: Harry N. Abrams, 1996.

McRae, Andrew. *God Speed the Plough: The Representation of Agrarian England, 1500–1660*. Cambridge: Cambridge, UP. 2002.

Meier, Thomas Keith. *Defoe and the Defense of Commerce*. Victoria: Victoria UP, 1987.

Merritt, J. E. "The Triangular Trade." *Business History* 3 (1960): 1–7.

Meyers, Joanne. "Defoe and the Project of 'Neighbours Fare.'" *Restoration: Studies in English Literary Culture, 1660–1700* 35.2 (Fall 2011): 1–19.

Miller, Peter. "Accounting and Objectivity: The Invention of Calculating Selves and Calculable Spaces." *Annals of Scholarship* 9 (1992): 61–86.

Moir, D. G., and Harry Inglis. *The Early Maps of Scotland to 1850*. 2 vols. Edinburgh: Royal Scottish Geographical Society, 1973–83.

Montaño, John. *The Roots of English Colonialism in Ireland*. Cambridge: Cambridge UP, 2011.

Moore, John Robert. "The Geography of *Gulliver's Travels*." *Journal of English and Germanic Philology* 40.2 (1941): 214–28.

Moretti, Franco. *Atlas of the European Novel, 1800–1900*. London: Verso, 1998.

———. *Graphs, Maps, Trees: Abstract Models for a Literary History*. New York: Verso, 2005.

Neill, Anna. *British Discovery Literature and the Rise of Global Commerce*. New York: Palgrave Macmillan, 2002.

Netzloff, Mark. "Forgetting the Ulster Plantation: John Speed's *The Theatre of the Empire of Great Britain* (1611) and the Colonial Archive." *Journal of Medieval and Early Modern Studies* 31.2 (Spring 2001): 313–48.

O'Donoghue, Yolande. *William Roy, 1726–1790: Pioneer of the Ordnance Survey*. London: British Museum Publications, 1977.

Orlove, Benjamin. "Mapping Reeds and Reading Maps: The Politics of Representation in Lake Titicaca." *American Ethnologist* 18 (1991): 3–38.

Ostrander, Gilman M. "The Making of the Triangular Trade Myth." *William and Mary Quarterly* 30.4 (1973): 635–44.

Pacheco, Anita. "Royalism and Honor in Aphra Behn's *Oroonoko*." *Studies in English Literature 1500–1900* 34.3 (1994): 491–506.

Parkes, Christopher. "'A True Survey of the Ground': Defoe's *Tour* and the Rise of Thematic Cartography." *Philological Quarterly* 74.4 (1995): 395–415.

Paulston, Rolland G., ed. *Social Cartography: Mapping Ways of Seeing Social and Educational Change.* New York: Garland, 1996.

Pedley, Mary Sponberg. *The Commerce of Cartography: Making and Marketing Maps in Eighteenth-Century France and England.* Chicago: U of Chicago P, 2005.

Peluso, Nancy Lee. "Whose Woods Are These? Counter-Mapping Forest Territories in Kalimantan, Indonesia." *Antipode* 27.4 (1995): 383–406.

Petchenik, Barbara. *The Nature of Maps: Essays toward Understanding Maps and Meaning.* Chicago: U of Chicago P, 1976.

Peters, Jeffrey N. *Mapping Discord: Allegorical Cartography in Early Modern French Writing.* Newark: U of Delaware P, 2004.

Pickles, John. *A History of Spaces: Cartographic Reason, Mapping and the Geo-Coded World.* Abingdon: Routledge, 2003.

Pigg, Daniel. "Trying to Frame the Unframable: Oroonoko as Discourse in Aphra Behn's *Oroonoko.*" *Studies in Short Fiction* 34.1 (1997): 105–11.

Piggott, Stuart. *Ancient Britons and the Antiquarian Imagination: Ideas from the Renaissance to the Regency.* New York: Thames and Hudson, 1989.

———. *William Stukeley: An Eighteenth-Century Antiquary.* Oxford: Clarendon, 1950.

Pile, Steve, and Michael Keith, eds. *Geographies of Resistance.* New York: Routledge, 1997.

Poole, Steve. "Scarcity and the Civic Tradition: Market Management in Bristol, 1709–1815." In Randall and Charlesworth, *Markets, Market Culture and Popular Protest in Eighteenth-Century Britain and Ireland,* 91–114.

Poovey, Mary. *A History of the Modern Fact: Problems of Knowledge in the Sciences of Wealth and Society.* Chicago: U of Chicago P, 1998.

Price, Richard. *The Guiana Maroons: A Historical and Bibliographical Introduction.* Baltimore: Johns Hopkins UP, 1976.

Radner, John. "Constructing an Adventure and Negotiating for Narrative Control: Johnson and Boswell in the Hebrides." In *Literary Couplings: Writing Couples, Collaborators, and the Construction of Authorship,* edited by Marjorie Stone and Judith Thompson, 59–78. Madison: U of Wisconsin P, 2006.

Randall, Adrian, and Andrew Charlesworth, eds. *Markets, Market Culture and Popular Protest in Eighteenth-Century Britain and Ireland.* Liverpool: Liverpool UP, 1996.

Rawley, James. *The Transatlantic Slave Trade: A History.* New York: Norton, 1981.

Reinhartz, Dennis. *The Cartographer and the Literati: Herman Moll and His Intellectual Circle.* Ceredigion: Edwin Mellen, 1997.

Rogers, Pat. "Defoe's *Tour Thro' Great Britain*: Three Notes." *Notes and Queries* 51.1 (March 2004): 41–48.

———. "Defoe's Use of Maps of Wales." *English Language Notes* 42.2 (Dec. 2004): 30–35.

———. "Further Notes on Defoe's *Tour Thro' Great Britain.*" *Notes and Queries* 51.4 (Dec. 2004): 381–87.

———. *Johnson and Boswell: The Transit of Caledonia.* Oxford: Clarendon, 1995.

————. *The Text of Great Britain: Theme and Design in Defoe's Tour.* Newark: U of Delaware P, 1998.

Rundstrom, Robert. "Mapping, Postmodernism, Indigenous People and the Changing Direction of North American Cartography." *Cartographica* 28.2 (Summer 1991): 1–12.

Samuel, Raphael, ed. *Patriotism: The Making and Unmaking of British National Identity.* New York: Routledge, 1989.

Savage, George H. "'Roving among the Hebrides': The Odyssey of Samuel Johnson." *Studies in English Literature, 1500–1900* 17.3 (1977): 493–501.

Schellenberg, Betty A. "Imagining the Nation in Defoe's *A Tour Thro' the Whole Island of Great Britain.*" *ELH* 62.2 (1995): 295–311.

Scherwatzky, Steven. "Johnson, Rasselas, and the Politics of Empire." *Eighteenth-Century Life* 16 (1992): 103–13.

Schmiechen, James, and Kenneth Carls. *The British Market Hall: A Social and Architectural History.* New Haven, CT: Yale UP, 1999.

Scott, James. *Seeing like a State: How Certain Schemes to Improve the Human Condition Have Failed.* New Haven, CT: Yale UP, 1999.

Sen, Sudipta. *Empire of Free Trade: The East India Company and the Making of the Colonial Marketplace.* Philadelphia: U of Pennsylvania P, 1998.

Sharp, Joanne, Paul Routledge, Chris Philo, and Ronan Paddison, eds. *Entanglements of Power: Geographies of Domination/Resistance.* London: Routledge, 2000.

Sheridan, Richard. "The Commercial and Financial Organization of the British Slave Trade, 1750–1807." *Economic History Review* 11 (1958): 249–63.

————. *Sugar and Slavery: An Economic History of the British West Indies, 1623–1775.* Kingston: Canoe, 1974.

Sherman, Sandra. *Finance and Fictionality in the Early Eighteenth Century: Accounting for Defoe.* Cambridge: Cambridge UP, 1996.

————. "Servants and Semiotics: Reversible Signs, Capital Instability, and Defoe's Logic of the Market." *ELH* 62.3 (1995): 551–73.

Sills, Adam. "Eighteenth-Century Cartographic Studies: A Brief Survey." *Literature Compass* 4.4 (July 2007): 981–1002.

Slack, Paul. *The Invention of Improvement: Information and Material Progress in Seventeenth-Century England.* Oxford: Oxford UP, 2015.

Smith, Colin Stephen. "The Market Place and the Market's Place in London, c. 1660–1840." PhD diss. University College London, 1999.

Smyth, William. *Common Ground: Essays on the Historical Geography of Ireland.* Cork: Cork UP, 1988.

————. *Map-Making, Landscape and Memory: A Geography of Colonial and Early Modern Ireland c. 1530–1750.* Notre Dame, IN: Notre Dame UP, 2006.

Solow, Barbara, ed. *Slavery and the Rise of the Atlantic System.* Cambridge: Cambridge UP, 1991.

Solow, Barbara, and Stanley Engerman, eds. *British Capitalism and Caribbean Slavery: The Legacy of Eric Williams.* Cambridge: Cambridge UP, 1987.

Southern, Richard. *Changeable Scenery: Its Origin and Development in the British Theater.* London: Faber and Faber, 1951.

Steele, Ian K. *The English Atlantic, 1675–1740: An Exploration of Communication and Community.* Oxford: Oxford UP, 1986.

Sussman, Charlotte. "The Colonial Afterlife of Political Arithmetic: Swift, Demography and Mobile Populations." *Cultural Critique* 56 (Winter 2004): 96–126.

———. "The Other Problem with Women: Reproduction and Slave Culture in Aphra Behn's *Oroonoko*." In Hunter, *Rereading Aphra Behn*, 212–33.

Sweet, Rosemary. *Antiquaries: The Discovery of the Past in Eighteenth-Century Britain.* London: Hambledon and London, 2004.

Thompson, E. P. *The Making of the English Working Class.* New York: Vintage Books, 1963.

Todd, Janet, ed. *Aphra Behn Studies.* Cambridge: Cambridge UP, 1996.

Trotter, Eleanor. *Seventeenth Century Life in the Country Parish, with Special Reference to Local Government.* London: Cass, 1968.

Turner, James. "Bunyan's Sense of Place." In *The Pilgrim's Progress: Critical and Historical Views*, edited by Vincent Newey, 91–110. Liverpool: Liverpool UP, 1980.

Turnock, David. *The Historical Geography of Scotland since 1707: Geographical Aspects of Modernization.* Cambridge: Cambridge UP, 1982.

Vance, John. *Samuel Johnson and the Sense of History.* Athens: U of Georgia P, 1984.

Vincent, Andrew. *Nationalism and Particularity.* Cambridge: Cambridge UP, 2002.

Visconsi, Elliott. "The Degenerate Race: English Barbarism in Aphra Behn's *The Widow Ranter* and *Oroonoko*." *ELH* 69.3 (2002): 673–701.

Visser, Colin. "Scenery and Technical Design." In *The London Theatre World, 1660–1800*, edited by Robert D. Hume, 66–118. Carbondale: Southern Illinois UP, 1980.

Wagner, Peter. *Reading Iconotexts: From Swift to the French Revolution.* London: Reaktion Books, 1995.

Wall, Cynthia. "Grammars of Space: The Language of London from Stow's *Survey* to Defoe's *Tour*." *Philological Quarterly* 76 (1997): 387–412.

———. *The Literary and Cultural Spaces of Restoration London.* Cambridge: Cambridge UP, 1998.

———. *The Prose of Things: Transformations of Description in the Eighteenth Century.* Chicago: U of Chicago P, 2006.

Wallerstein, Immanuel. *The Modern World System: Capitalist Agriculture and the Origins of the European World Economy in the Sixteenth Century.* New York: Academic, 1974.

———. *The Modern World System II: Mercantilism and the Consolidation of the European World-Economy, 1600–1750.* New York: Academic, 1980.

Walton, Gary M. "New Evidence on Colonial Commerce." *Journal of Economic History* 28.3 (1968): 363–89.

Watts, Michael R. *The Dissenters.* Vol. 1, *From the Reformation to the French Revolution.* Oxford: Clarendon, 1978.

Webb, Sidney, and Beatrice Webb. *English Local Government from the Revolution to the Municipal Corporations Act: The Parish and the County.* London: Longmans, 1906.

Wechselblatt, Martin. "Finding Mr. Boswell: Rhetorical Authority and National Identity in Johnson's *A Journey to the Western Islands of Scotland*." *ELH* 60.1 (1993): 117–48.

Weinbrot, Howard D. "Samuel Johnson and the Domestic Metaphor." *Age of Johnson: A Scholarly Annual* 10 (1999): 127–63.

Whyte, Ian, and Kathleen Whyte. *The Changing Scottish Landscape, 1500–1800*. London: Routledge, 1991.

Williams, Eric. *Capitalism and Slavery*. New York: Russell and Russell, 1944.

Williams, Raymond. *The Country and the City*. Oxford: Oxford UP, 1975.

Withers, Charles. *Geography, Science and National Identity: Scotland since 1520*. Cambridge: Cambridge UP, 2001.

———. "How Scotland Came to Know Itself: Geography, National Identity and the Making of a Nation, 1680–1790." *Journal of Historical Geography* 21.4 (1995): 371–97.

———. "Reporting, Mapping, Trusting: Making Geographical Knowledge in the Late Seventeenth Century." *Isis* 90.3 (September 1999): 497–521.

Wittkowsky, George. "Swift's Modest Proposal: The Biography of an Early Georgian Pamphlet." *Journal of the History of Ideas* 4.1 (1943): 75–104.

Wood, Denis. *The Power of Maps*. New York: Guilford, 1992.

———. *Rethinking the Power of Maps*. New York: Guilford, 2010.

Wood, Ellen Meiksins. *The Origin of Capitalism*. New York: Monthly Review Press, 1999.

Woolf, Daniel. *The Social Circulation of the Past: English Historical Culture, 1500–1730*. Oxford: Oxford UP, 2003.

Young, Elizabeth V. "Aphra Behn, Gender and Pastoral." *Studies in English Literature, 1500–1900* 33.3 (1993): 523–34.

Zimbardo, Rose. "Aphra Behn: A Dramatist in Search of the Novel." In *Curtain Calls: British and American Women and the Theater, 1660–1820*, edited by Mary Anne Schofield and Cecilia Macheski, 371–82. Athens: Ohio UP, 1991.

# INDEX

*Account of an Attempt to Ascertain the Longitude, An* (Johnson), 260n62

*Account of Richard of Cirencester, Monk of Westminster, and of his Works, An* (Stukeley), 182

*Account of Roman Temple, and Other Antiquities, Near Graham's Dike in Scotland* (Stukeley), 181

*Account of the Present State of the Hebrides and Western Coasts of Scotland* (J. Anderson), 174–75

Acosta, Ana, 237n7

Act of Union (1707), 15, 117, 162, 166, 175, 177; advocates and critics of, 177; and definitions of Scotland, 15, 166, 175, 177; and formation of Great Britain, 117; and Whig topographies, 15, 175, 260n67

Adair, John, 167, 169, 171, 175, 180, 257nn9–10; and antiquarian interests, 180, 257n6; and Defoe's *Tour,* 167, 169; and geographic knowledge of Scotland, 169, 171; and Moll's *Maps of Scotland,* 169, 171, 257n10; *Queries,* 257n6; and rigorous approach to mapping, 167, 169; and Scotland's fishing industry, 169, 174–75; *Sea-Coasts and Islands of Scotland,* 257n9; Sibbald's ill-fated *Atlas Scotiae* and, 257n9; and surveys of Scotland, 167, 169, 257nn9–10

Adams, John, 141

Addison, Joseph, 111, 248n101

*Adulterous Alliances* (Helgerson), 247n87

"Advantages Proposed by Repealing the Sacramental Test, The" (Swift), 116

Africa, 43, 44, 48, 51–57, 101, 127, 128, 129, 141, 199; and the Americas, 43, 44, 46, 48, 51, 53, 57, 75, 127, 128; cartography and slavery and, 44–51; and colonialist expansion, 13, 44, 51; Congo, 43, 44; Guinea coast, 46–47, 53–55; Johnson and "discovery" of, 199; mapping of slave trade and, 50–57, 101, 240n8, 247n83; and *Oroonoko* (Behn), 13, 57–63, 72–73; Pratt's abolitionist "map of slavery" and, 43, 44, 57, 74; Royal Af-

rican Company and, 56, 58, 241n18; Swift on geographers and, 101, 247nn82–83; and triangular trade, 13–14, 43, 44, 57–60, 241n17, 241n20. *See also* Behn, Aphra; cartography; slave trade

*Africa Trade the great Pillar and Supporter of the British Plantation Trade in America, The* (Postlethwayt), 56

Agnew, Jean-Christophe, 131; on use and exchange value, 253n12

agriculture, 15, 132, 134, 165–66, 167, 208; agrarian and industrial capitalism, 83, 221–22; agrarian reform in Scotland, 15, 165–66, 191; agrarian revolution (Bunyan), 36–37; and colonial plantation system, 83; and economy, 15, 132, 134, 165–66; map and agrarian community ideal (Swift), 109–10; modernization of, 15, 166, 175; progressive theory of civilization and (Johnson), 208. *See also* plantation

allegory: baroque (Benjamin), 239n41; colonial violence and, 61, 240n58; domestic (Johnson), 216–17; and history, 196, 239n43; and marginalia, 94–95, 101; misread as literal, 30–31, 41; neighbor and, 28, 29, 32–33, 41; neighborhood and, 13, 23–24, 38, 41; of "the observer effect" (Swift), 106; in *Oroonoko* (Behn), 61, 74; and *Pilgrim's Progress* (Bunyan), 13, 23–24, 28, 29, 30–33, 40–41, 239n40; political allegory, 3, 74; of reading, 31–32, 239n40; of space, 31–33, 40–41, 136; as theography, 33–34. *See also* Bunyan, John; Swift, Jonathan

Americas, the, 48, 51, 52, 53, 57, 73, 75, 127, 128, 254n30; and Africa, 13, 43, 44, 46, 48, 51, 53, 57, 75, 128, 141; and Blaeu's *Atlas Major,* 46, 47, 141; and challenge to representations of triangular trade, 13–14, 43–44, 57–60; colonization of Africa and, 127; depictions of enslaved people and, 44, 45–46, 48–50, 56; and England, 13, 43; Europe and, 44; indigenous peoples